Philanthropy in America

A Comprehensive Historical Encyclopedia

About the Editor

Dwight F. Burlingame, Ph.D., is Associate Executive Director and Director of Academic Programs at the Indiana University Center on Philanthropy, and a Professor of Philanthropic Studies at IUPUI. At the Center on Philanthropy, Burlingame provides leadership for programs in philanthropy studies and nonprofit management as well as coordination with external agencies. He holds degrees from Moorhead State University, the University of Illinois, and Florida State University. He is an active member of the AFP Research Council, ARNOVA, and other professional organizations. As of July 2004, he is the coeditor of *Nonprofit and Voluntary Sector Quarterly.*

Dr. Burlingame has authored and coauthored eight books, more than forty articles, and more than one hundred book reviews. He is active in the nonprofit community and a frequent speaker, consultant, and author on topics relating to philanthropy, nonprofit organizations, libraries, and development.

Philanthropy in America

A Comprehensive Historical Encyclopedia

Volume 1: Entries A to H

Dwight F. Burlingame, Editor

A B C ⬥ C L I O

Santa Barbara, California • Denver, Colorado • Oxford, England

Library of Congress Cataloging-in-Publication Data
Philanthropy in America : a comprehensive historical encyclopedia / Dwight F.
Burlingame, editor.
     p.   cm.
   Includes bibliographical references and index.
   ISBN 1-57607-860-4 (hardcover : alk. paper)   ISBN 1-57607-861-2 (e-book)
   1. Charities—United States—History.   2. Endowments—United States—History.
3. Philanthropists—United States—History.   I. Burlingame, Dwight.

HV91.P58 2004
361.7'0973'03—dc22

                                                                                        2004013557

08 07 06 05 04   10 9 8 7 6 5 4 3 2 1

This book is also available on the World Wide Web as an eBook. Visit abc-clio.com for
details.

ABC-CLIO, Inc.
130 Cremona Drive, P.O. Box 1911
Santa Barbara, California 93116-1911
This book is printed on acid-free paper.

Manufactured in the United States of America

Contents

Contributors and Their Entries

Alan J. Abramson
Aspen Institute
Washington, D.C.
INFRASTRUCTURE ORGANIZATIONS FOR
NONPROFITS

Lesley Agard
Kamehameha Schools
Honolulu, HI
PAUAHI PAKI BISHOP, BERNICE (1831–1883)

Natalie Ammarell
Human Service Systems
Chapel Hill, NC
SETTLEMENT HOUSES

Alan R. Andreasen
Georgetown University
Washington, D.C.
SOCIAL MARKETING

Peter M. Ascoli
Spertus Institute of Jewish Studies
Chicago, IL
JULIUS ROSENWALD FUND

Jerome P. Baggett
Jesuit School of Theology
Berkeley, CA
HABITAT FOR HUMANITY INTERNATIONAL

Wolfgang Bielefeld
Indiana University–Purdue University Indianapolis
Indianapolis, IN
SOCIAL CAPITAL

Angela L. Bies
Texas A & M University
College Station, TX
PUBLIC PHILANTHROPY

Laura Carpenter Bingham
Peace College
Raleigh, NC
WOMEN, HIGHER EDUCATION, AND
PHILANTHROPY

Drew Blanchard
The Center on Philanthropy at Indiana University
Indianapolis, IN
BENEZET, ANTHONY (1713–1784)

Elizabeth T. Boris
Urban Institute
Washington, D.C.
NONPROFIT SECTOR

Thomasina Borkman
George Mason University
Arlington, VA
SELF-HELP GROUPS

Robert O. Bothwell
National Committee for Responsive Philanthropy
Washington, D.C.
ALTERNATIVE FUNDS
RESPONSIVE PHILANTHROPY

Eleanor L. Brilliant
Rutgers University
New Brunswick, NJ
FEDERATED FUNDRAISING
FILER COMMISSION
PETERSON COMMISSION
WALD, LILLIAN D. (1867–1940)

Robert G. Bringle
Indiana University–Purdue University Indianapolis
Indianapolis, IN
SERVICE LEARNING

Evelyn Brody
Kent College of Law
Chicago, IL
TAX DEDUCTION AND PHILANTHROPY

Lisa Browar
Indiana University
Bloomington, IN
FOUNDATION CENTER

Mary Jane Brukardt
The Center on Philanthropy at Indiana University
Indianapolis, IN
GATES, WILLIAM H., III (1955–), AND THE
BILL AND MELINDA GATES FOUNDATION

Robert J. Brulle
Drexel University
Philadelphia, PA
ENVIRONMENTAL MOVEMENT

A'Lelia Walker Bundles
Biographer
Alexandria, VA
WALKER, MADAM C. J. (1867–1919)

Dwight F. Burlingame
Indiana University–Purdue University Indianapolis
Indianapolis, IN
ALTRUISM
CARNEGIE, ANDREW (1835–1919)
CORPORATE GIVING

Sabina Calhoun
The Center on Philanthropy at Indiana University
Indianapolis, IN
THINK TANKS

Emmett D. Carson
Minneapolis Foundation
Minneapolis, MN
AFRICAN AMERICAN PHILANTHROPY

Alfred L. Castle
Samuel N. & Mary Castle Foundation
Honolulu, HI
CONTEMPORARY PHILANTHROPY

Jessica Chao
Consultant
New York City, NY
ASIAN AMERICAN PHILANTHROPY

Amelia E. Clark
The Center on Philanthropy at Indiana University
Indianapolis, IN
CHAVEZ, CESAR (1927–1993)
TRUTH, SOJOURNER (C. 1797–1883)

William W. Clohesy
University of Northern Iowa
Cedar Falls, IA
>MORAL PHILOSOPHY AND PHILANTHROPY

Ram A. Cnaan
University of Pennsylvania
Philadelphia, PA
>VOLUNTARISM

Michael Coatney†
Indiana University–Purdue University Indianapolis
Indianapolis, IN
>CAMPUS COMPACT

Robert S. Collier
Council of Michigan Foundations
Grand Haven, MI
>YOUTH AND PHILANTHROPY

Mike Cortés
University of San Francisco
San Francisco, CA
>HISPANIC PHILANTHROPY

Elizabeth R. Crabtree
The Center on Philanthropy at Indiana University
Indianapolis, IN
>COUNCIL FOR ADVANCEMENT AND SUPPORT OF
>   EDUCATION (CASE)
>UNRELATED BUSINESS INCOME TAX (UBIT)

David M. Craig
Indiana University–Purdue University Indianapolis
Indianapolis, IN
>COMMON GOOD

Donald T. Critchlow
Saint Louis University
Saint Louis, MO
>BROOKINGS, ROBERT SOMERS (1850–1932)

Douglas M. Czajkowski
The Center on Philanthropy at Indiana University
Indianapolis, IN
>HIGGINSON, HENRY LEE (1834–1919)

Hugh Davis
Southern Connecticut University
New Haven, CT
>BACON, LEONARD (1802–1881)

Laura Hansen Dean
Community Foundation of Southern Indiana
New Albany, IN
>PLANNED GIVING

Meredith Deneau
The Center on Philanthropy at Indiana University
Indianapolis, IN
>SALVATION ARMY

Jerome DeNuccio
Graceland University
Lamoni, IA
>KEAYNE, ROBERT (1595–1656)

Alan Divack
Ford Foundation
New York, NY
>FORD FOUNDATION

Aaron Dorfman
People Acting for Community Together, Inc.
Miami, FL
>COUNCIL ON FOUNDATIONS (COF)
>NATIONAL ASSOCIATION FOR THE
>   ADVANCEMENT OF COLORED PEOPLE
>   (NAACP)

H. Daniels Duncan
United Way of Tucson and Southern Arizona
Tucson, AZ
>ADVOCACY AND NONPROFIT ORGANIZATIONS
>COMMUNITY DEVELOPMENT AND
>   ORGANIZATIONS

Joellen El Bashir
Howard University
Washington, D.C.
>MOORLAND, REV. JESSE E. (1863–1940)

Mohamed A. Elsanousi
Islamic Society of North America
Plainfield, IN
    ISLAMIC SOCIETY OF NORTH AMERICA (ISNA)

Daniel Faber
Northeastern University
Boston, MA
    ENVIRONMENTAL MOVEMENT

Kyle Farmbry
San Diego State University
San Diego, CA
    SERVICE CLUBS
    UNDERGROUND RAILROAD

Julie Fisher
Kettering Foundation
Dayton, OH
    INTERNATIONAL NONGOVERNMENTAL
        ORGANIZATIONS (INGOs)

Kathryn K. Frey
The Center on Philanthropy at Indiana University
Indianapolis, IN
    WINTHROP, JOHN (1588–1649)

Siegrun Fox Freyss
California State University
Los Angeles, CA
    BENEVOLENT SOCIETIES
    FRIENDLY SOCIETIES
    POLITICAL PERSPECTIVES OF NONPROFIT
        ORGANIZATIONS

Lawrence J. Friedman
Indiana University
Bloomington, IN
    PUBLIC INTELLECTUALS ON PHILANTHROPY

Marybeth Gasman
The Center on Philanthropy at Indiana University
Indianapolis, IN
    BETHUNE, MARY MCLEOD (1875–1955)
    JOHNSON, CHARLES S. (1893–1956)
    MCCARTY, OSEOLA (1908–1999)
    PATTERSON, FREDERICK DOUGLASS
        (1901–1988)

Michael Gerrity
The Center on Philanthropy at Indiana University
Indianapolis, IN
    KRESGE, SEBASTIAN S. (1867–1966)

Roberta K. Gibboney
Indiana University–Purdue University Indianapolis
Indianapolis, IN
    BARTON, CLARA (1821–1912)

Teresa Gift
The Center on Philanthropy at Indiana University
Indianapolis, IN
    INSTITUTIONAL FOUNDATIONS
    MELLON, PAUL (1907–1999)

Steve Gilliland
Harrison County Community Foundation
Corydon, IN
    FORTEN, JAMES (1766–1842)

Susan L. Golden
The Golden Group
Cleveland, OH
    GRANTSEEKING

Robert I. Goler
American University
Washington, D.C.
    CULTURAL POLICY AND PHILANTHROPY

Nina Gondola
The Center on Philanthropy at Indiana University
Indianapolis, IN
    CUFFE, PAUL (1759–1817)
    TERRELL, MARY ELIZA CHURCH (1863–1954)

Gretchen C. Gordon

The Center on Philanthropy at Indiana University
Indianapolis, IN
> AMERICAN COUNCIL ON GIFT ANNUITIES
> (ACGA)
> ASSOCIATION OF FUNDRAISING PROFESSIONALS
> (AFP)

John Grabowski

Case Western Reserve University & Western Reserve
Historical Society
Cleveland, OH
> GOFF, FREDERICK HARRIS (1858–1923)

Janet Greenlee

University of Dayton
Dayton, OH
> ACCOUNTABILITY

Robert T. Grimm Jr.

The Center on Philanthropy at Indiana University
Indianapolis, IN
> ADDAMS, JANE (1860–1935)
> DAYTON FAMILY
> FRANKLIN, BENJAMIN (1706–1790)
> PEW FAMILY
> SMITHSON, JAMES (1765–1829)

Kirsten A. Grønbjerg

Indiana University
Bloomington, IN
> HUMAN SERVICES AND PHILANTHROPY

Michael P. Grzesiak

The Center on Philanthropy at Indiana University
Indianapolis, IN
> DAY, DOROTHY (1897–1980)

Susan Haber

The Center on Philanthropy at Indiana University
Indianapolis, IN
> GARCIA, HECTOR PEREZ (1914–1996)

Emily M. Hall

The Center on Philanthropy at Indiana University
Indianapolis, IN
> BRACE, CHARLES LORING (1826–1890)
> GALLAUDET, THOMAS HOPKINS (1787–1851)
> HOWE, SAMUEL GRIDLEY (1801–1876)
> KING, MARTIN LUTHER, JR. (1929–1968)
> TAPPAN, ARTHUR (1786–1865), AND TAPPAN,
> LEWIS (1788–1873)

Judy P. Hall

The Center on Philanthropy at Indiana University
Indianapolis, IN
> INDEPENDENT SECTOR (IS)
> LYON, MARY MASON (1797–1849)

Michael H. Hall

Canadian Centre for Philanthropy
Toronto, Ontario
> CANADIAN PHILANTHROPY

Peter Dobkin Hall

Harvard University
Cambridge, MA
> BEECHER, LYMAN (1775–1863)
> LOW, JULIETTE GORDON (1860–1927)
> LOWELL, JOHN, JR. (1799–1836)
> NONPROFIT GOVERNING BOARDS

David C. Hammack

Case Western Reserve University
Cleveland, OH
> COMMUNITY FOUNDATIONS

Femida Handy

York University
Toronto, Ontario
> ENVIRONMENTAL MOVEMENT

Joseph C. Harmon

The Center on Philanthropy at Indiana University
Indianapolis, IN
> DREXEL, ST. KATHARINE (1858–1955)

Ann Harris
The Center on Philanthropy at Indiana University
Indianapolis, IN
OLIN, JOHN MERRILL (1892–1982)

Ted Hart
ePhilanthropy Foundation & Hart Philanthropic
Services Group
Washington, D.C.
E-PHILANTHROPY

Kristine M. Haskett
The Center on Philanthropy at Indiana University
Indianapolis, IN
GRATZ, REBECCA (1781–1869)

Kerry Hepworth
The Center on Philanthropy at Indiana University
Indianapolis, IN
ASSOCIATION FOR HEALTHCARE
PHILANTHROPY (AHP)

Douglas R. Hess
Food Research and Action Center
Washington, D.C.
FOOD AND ANTIHUNGER CHARITIES

Virginia A. Hodgkinson
Georgetown University
Washington, D.C.
INDIVIDUAL GIVING BY HOUSEHOLD
VOLUNTEERING

Frances Huehls
Indiana University–Purdue University Indianapolis
Indianapolis, IN
CURTI, MERLE EUGENE (1897–1996)

Mamie L. Jackson
The Center on Philanthropy at Indiana University
Indianapolis, IN
GARVEY, MARCUS MOSIAH, JR. (1887–1940)

Thomas H. Jeavons
Philadelphia Yearly Meeting of the Religious Society of
Friends
RELIGION AND PHILANTHROPY

Mark C. Johnson
YMCA of the USA
Chicago, IL
YMCA

Tanya E. Johnson
The Center on Philanthropy at Indiana University
Indianapolis, IN
ASSOCIATION FOR RESEARCH ON NONPROFIT
ORGANIZATIONS AND VOLUNTARY ACTION
(ARNOVA)

Amy Jones
The Center on Philanthropy at Indiana University
Indianapolis, IN
CIVICUS: WORLD ALLIANCE FOR CITIZEN
PARTICIPATION

Grady Jones
The Center on Philanthropy at Indiana University
Indianapolis, IN
ASSOCIATION OF PROFESSIONAL RESEARCHERS
FOR ADVANCEMENT (APRA)
DONOR-ADVISED FUNDS

Andrea R. Kaminski
Women's Philanthropy Institute
Indianapolis, IN
WOMEN'S IMPACT ON PHILANTHROPY

Robert A. Katz
Indiana University–Purdue University Indianapolis
Indianapolis, IN
DONOR INTENT

Kathleen S. Kelly
University of Florida
Gainesville, FL
PUBLIC RELATIONS AND PHILANTHROPY FOR
NONPROFITS

Joseph C. Kiger
Croft Institute for International Studies
University of Mississippi
University, MS
    HISTORY OF AMERICAN FOUNDATIONS

Margaret J. Kimball
Stanford University
Stanford, CA
    STANFORD, LELAND (1824–1893), AND
        STANFORD, JANE LATHROP (1828–1905)

John Kloos
Benedictine University
Lisle, IL
    RUSH, BENJAMIN (1746–1813)

Roberta Knickerbocker
The Center on Philanthropy at Indiana University
Indianapolis, IN
    MATHER, COTTON (1663–1728)

Vicki W. Kramer
V. Kramer & Associates
Philadelphia, PA
    SOCIAL CHANGE FUNDS

Betsy Kranz
The Center on Philanthropy at Indiana University
Indianapolis, IN
    CENTER ON PHILANTHROPY

Linda M. Lampkin
National Center for Charitable Statistics at the Urban
    Institute
Washington, D.C.
    NATIONAL CENTER FOR CHARITABLE
    STATISTICS (NCCS)

W. David Lasater
Ball State University
Muncie, IN
    GOODRICH, PIERRE FRIST (1894–1973)

Mary Legan
The Center on Philanthropy at Indiana University
Indianapolis, IN
    ASSOCIATION FOR VOLUNTEER
        ADMINISTRATION (AVA)

Matthew Liao-Troth
Western Washington University
Bellingham, WA
    PROSOCIAL BEHAVIOR

David L. Lightner
University of Alberta
Edmonton, Alberta
    DIX, DOROTHEA LYNDE (1802–1887)

Roger A. Lohmann
West Virginia University
Morganton, WV
    CONFRATERNITY

Al Lyons
The Center on Philanthropy at Indiana University
Indianapolis, IN
    JACKSON, HELEN MARIA (FISKE) HUNT
        (1830–1885)
    U.S. SANITARY COMMISSION (USSC)

James H. Madison
Indiana University
Bloomington, IN
    LILLY, ELI (1885–1977)

Richard Magat
Yale University
New Haven, CT
    UNION MOVEMENT AND PHILANTHROPY

Ashley M. Magdovitz
The Center on Philanthropy at Indiana University
Indianapolis, IN
    EASTMAN, GEORGE (1854–1932)

Alexis Manheim
Corning Community College
Corning, NY
OWEN FAMILY

Rachel McCarthy
Aspen Institute
Washington, D.C.
INFRASTRUCTURE ORGANIZATIONS FOR
NONPROFITS

Robert D. McChesney
New York University
New York, NY
ISLAMIC PHILANTHROPY

Mark McGarvie
New York University
New York, NY
GIRARD, STEPHEN (1750–1831)
LAW OF CHARITY

Emily S. McQuade
The Center on Philanthropy at Indiana University
Indianapolis, IN
AMERICAN RED CROSS

Ruth B. Mills
The Center on Philanthropy at Indiana University
Indianapolis, IN
BOARDSOURCE

Michael Moody
Boston University
Boston, MA
RECIPROCITY
STEWARDSHIP

Asia M. Muhammad
The Center on Philanthropy at Indiana University
Indianapolis, IN
SAGE, MARGARET OLIVIA SLOCUM
(1828–1918)

Kym Mulhern
Nokomis Foundation
Grand Rapids, MI
FOUNDATION PAYOUT
KELLEY, FLORENCE (1859–1932)

Mark Neumeister
The Center on Philanthropy at Indiana University
Indianapolis, IN
HOGG, IMA (1882–1975)

Lynn O'Connell
Physician Assistant Foundation
Alexandria, VA
INTERNATIONAL SOCIETY FOR THIRD-SECTOR
RESEARCH (ISTR)
MCCORMICK, NETTIE FOWLER (1835–1923)

Michael O'Neill
University of San Francisco
San Francisco, CA
ETHICS AND PHILANTHROPY
MUTUAL BENEFIT ORGANIZATIONS

Mary J. Oates
Regis College
Weston, MA
CATHOLIC PHILANTHROPY

Teresa Jean Odendahl
National Network of Grantmakers
San Diego, CA
WOMEN AND NONPROFIT ORGANIZATIONS

Kathleen Odne
Dean & Margaret Lesher Foundation
Walnut Creek, CA
PACKARD, DAVID (1912–1996), AND PACKARD,
LUCILE (1914–1987)
VENTURE PHILANTHROPY

Joel J. Orosz
Grand Valley State University
Allendale, MI
    FORD, HENRY (1863–1947), AND FORD, EDSEL
        (1893–1943)
    GRANTMAKING
    KELLOGG, WILL KEITH (1860–1951)

Susan A. Ostrander
Tufts University
Medford, MA
    SOCIAL MOVEMENTS AND PHILANTHROPY

Andrea Pactor
The Center on Philanthropy at Indiana University
Indianapolis, IN
    AMERICAN INSTITUTE OF PHILANTHROPY
        (AIP)
    CHARITY WATCHDOGS

Betty J. Parker
Morgantown, WV
    PEABODY, GEORGE (1795–1869)

Franklin Parker
West Virginia University
Morgantown, WV
    PEABODY, GEORGE (1795–1869)

Aubrey Abbott Patterson
The Center on Philanthropy at Indiana University
Indianapolis, IN
    AMERICAN ASSOCIATION OF FUNDRAISING
        COUNSEL (AAFRC) AND AAFRC TRUST
        FOR PHILANTHROPY

Robert L. Payton
Indiana University–Purdue University Indianapolis
Indianapolis, IN
    PHILANTHROPY AND THE GOOD SAMARITAN
    STEWARDSHIP

Felice Davidson Perlmutter
Temple University
Philadelphia, PA
    SOCIAL CHANGE FUNDS

Juliann L. Peterson
The Center on Philanthropy at Indiana University
Indianapolis, IN
    NATIONAL ASSOCIATION OF STATE CHARITY
        OFFICIALS (NASCO)

Timothy J. Peterson
Messiah University
Philadelphia, PA
    CIVIL SOCIETY

Edward L. Queen
Indiana University–Purdue University Indianapolis
Indianapolis, IN
    CHARITABLE CHOICE
    CIVIL RIGHTS MOVEMENT

Brieanna Quinn
The Center on Philanthropy at Indiana University
Indianapolis, IN
    ASPEN INSTITUTE/NONPROFIT SECTOR
        RESEARCH FUND

James W. Reed
Rutgers University
New Brunswick, NJ
    SANGER, MARGARET (1879–1966)

D. Martin Reeser
Indiana University–Purdue University Indianapolis
Indianapolis, IN
    WASHINGTON, BOOKER T. (1856–1915)

David Renz
University of Missouri–Kansas City
Kansas City, MO
    GOVERNANCE OF NONPROFITS

Kevin C. Robbins
Indiana University–Purdue University Indianapolis
Indianapolis, IN
    HISTORY OF PHILANTHROPY

Kenneth W. Rose
Rockefeller Archive Center
Sleepy Hollow, NY
ROCKEFELLER FAMILY

Rebecca Roth
The Center on Philanthropy at Indiana University
Indianapolis, IN
GARRETT, MARY ELIZABETH (1853–1915)
WELLS-BARNETT, IDA B. (1862–1931)

Laura Rupkalvis
The Center on Philanthropy at Indiana University
Indianapolis, IN
SETON, SAINT ELIZABETH ANN (1774–1821)

Lester M. Salamon
The Johns Hopkins University
Baltimore, MD
GLOBAL NONPROFIT SECTOR

Alissa Saufley
The Center on Philanthropy at Indiana University
Indianapolis, IN
ALLIANCE FOR NONPROFIT MANAGEMENT
WILLARD, FRANCES E. (1839–1898)

Katie Schechter
The Center on Philanthropy at Indiana University
Indianapolis, IN
LILLY ENDOWMENT

Paul G. Schervish
Boston College
Boston, MA
WEALTH AND PHILANTHROPY

Joel Schwartz
National Endowment for the Humanities
Washington, D.C.
LOWELL, JOSEPHINE SHAW (1843–1905)
TUCKERMAN, JOSEPH (1778–1840)

Judith Sealander
Bowling Green State University
Bowling Green, OH
ROCKEFELLER, JOHN DAVIDSON, SR.
(1839–1937)
ROSENWALD, JULIUS (1862–1932)

Timothy L. Seiler
Indiana University–Purdue University Indianapolis
Indianapolis, IN
MISSION OF THE ORGANIZATION

David Horton Smith
Boston College
Boston, MA
GRASSROOTS ASSOCIATIONS

James Allen Smith
J. Paul Getty Trust
Los Angeles, CA
ANONYMOUS GIVING
EUROPEAN FOUNDATIONS

Michael B. Smith
Ithaca College
Ithaca, NY
MUIR, JOHN (1838–1914)

Steven Rathgeb Smith
University of Washington
Seattle, WA
GOVERNMENT–NONPROFIT SECTOR
RELATIONSHIP

Rusty Stahl
Ford Foundation
New York, NY
FORD FOUNDATION

Richard Steinberg
Indiana University–Purdue University Indianapolis
Indianapolis, IN
ECONOMIC THEORIES OF NONPROFITS

David L. Sternberg
Loring, Sternberg and Associates
Indianapolis, IN
    DIRECT MAIL FUNDRAISING

Nicole A. Streeter
The Center on Philanthropy at Indiana University
Indianapolis, IN
    UNITED NEGRO COLLEGE FUND (UNCF)

Martha A. Taylor
University of Wisconsin Foundation
Madison, WI
    WOMEN'S IMPACT ON PHILANTHROPY

Eugene R. Tempel
Indiana University–Purdue University Indianapolis
Indianapolis, IN
    FUNDRAISING AS A PROFESSION

Emanuel D. Thorne
Brooklyn College of the City University of New York
Brooklyn, NY
    BLOOD AND ORGAN DONATION

Karin E. Tice
Formative Evaluation Research Associates (FERA)
Ann Arbor, MI
    YOUTH AND PHILANTHROPY

Maggie Tittle
The Center on Philanthropy at Indiana University
Indianapolis, IN
    NATIONAL COMMITTEE ON PLANNED GIVING
        (NCPG)

Gary A. Tobin
Institute for Jewish and Community Research
San Francisco, CA
    JEWISH PHILANTHROPY IN AMERICAN SOCIETY

Richard W. Trollinger
Centre College
Danville, KY
    COOPER, PETER (1791–1883)

Mary Tschirhart
Syracuse University
Syracuse, NY
    MEMBERSHIP ASSOCIATIONS

Keight S. Tucker
The Center on Philanthropy at Indiana University
Indianapolis, IN
    HOOVER, HERBERT CLARK (1874–1964)

Richard C. Turner
Indiana University–Purdue University Indianapolis
Indianapolis, IN
    LITERATURE AND PHILANTHROPY

Craig Barton Upright
Princeton University
Princeton, NJ
    CONSUMER COOPERATIVES

Jon Van Til
Rutgers University
Camden, NJ
    CIVIL SOCIETY
    UTOPIAN THOUGHT, PHILANTHROPY IN

Lilya Wagner
Indiana University–Purdue University Indianapolis
Indianapolis, IN
    FUNDRAISING
    INTERNATIONAL FUNDRAISING
    NONPROFIT MANAGEMENT EDUCATION

Elizabeth Watkins
The Center on Philanthropy at Indiana University
Indianapolis, IN
    LOW, JULIETTE GORDON (1860–1927)

Ronald Austin Wells
Wells Associates, Inc.
Ridgeport, CT
    NATIVE AMERICAN PHILANTHROPY
    STOKES, CAROLINE PHELPS (1854–1909), AND
        STOKES, OLIVIA EGGLESTON PHELPS
        (1847–1927)

Fred Westcott
The Center on Philanthropy at Indiana University
Indianapolis, IN
> GUIDESTAR

Diane Winston
The Pew Charitable Trusts
Philadelphia, PA
> BOOTH, BALLINGTON (1857–1940), AND
> BOOTH, MAUD (1865–1948)
> BOOTH, EVANGELINE (1865–1950)

Martin Morse Wooster
The Philanthropy Roundtable
Washington, D.C.
> GUGGENHEIM FAMILY

Autumn Workman
Indiana University
Bloomington, IN
> HEALTH AND NONPROFITS

Walter W. Wymer Jr.
Christopher Newport University
Newport News, VA
> CAUSE-RELATED MARKETING AND
> SPONSORSHIPS

Dennis R. Young
Case Western Reserve University
Cleveland, OH
> COMMERCIALISM IN THE NONPROFIT SECTOR
> NONPROFIT MANAGEMENT

Alphabetical List of Entries

Preface

Some might consider the task of producing an encyclopedia for an emerging field of study a foolish, if not futile, undertaking. From time to time over the course of preparing this work, I did indeed feel this to be true. Time has won out, and this work represents a first of its kind in attempting to provide an overview of philanthropy as well as of the nonprofit, voluntary, independent, or third sector (terms all used interchangeably) in the United States.

Philanthropic and nonprofit studies have enjoyed a major growth spurt over the past twenty-five years in the United States, with recent increased attention around the globe. However, some still see the field as a marginal academic enterprise. With substantial contributions by many scholars in various disciplines and professional fields, philanthropic and nonprofit studies programs have given students and teachers alike a fresh perspective on critical issues in our society. Philanthropic studies instructors relate their material to broader cultural, historical, political, and economic themes. This integrative perspective is a defining element that encourages analytic skill and develops an intellectual, global view that emphasizes the complexity and thematic relationships of a civil society. The authors of the articles in this encyclopedia have made this objective central to their work in contributing to a liberal education.

In the mid-1990s, I had several conversations with my colleagues at Indiana University about the need for an encyclopedia of philanthropy. Those conversations usually ended with the conclusion that it would be an impossible task to get one's arms and mind around such a broad field. It wasn't until my friend and colleague in philanthropic studies at Indiana, David Smith, provided the sage advice that I should undertake this task as an opportunity to make a "significant" contribution to the field, that I decided to pursue the project. With support and encouragement from colleagues at the Center on Philanthropy and a former editor from ABC-CLIO, a contract was signed and work commenced.

Deciding what to include in this three-volume set was not an easy task, as philanthropic studies is a very broad field. To select the entries, I worked with an advisory committee composed of scholars, nonprofit practitioners, and educators. Final determination for what was included, however, was my responsibility. Volumes 1 and 2 include articles on notable people, events, and associations as well as on numerous other important topics in philanthropy. Volume 3 brings together original documents in the field.

More than 175 authors participated in the project. For the most part, the essays were written by well-known specialists in their chosen topical area. In a few cases, bright graduate students from the philanthropic studies or nonprofit management programs at Indiana University, Indianapolis, wrote entries.

Needless to say, thousands of significant individuals have contributed and are currently contributing to the history of giving, volunteering, and social action in the United States. Therefore, my inclusion of a historical figure is very selective and has been made on the basis of a representative type of those who have shaped the history of philanthropy, that is, the history of voluntary action (giving of time, treasure, and talent) intended for the public good. I was greatly assisted in this selection matter by a previous project, *Notable American Philanthropists: Biographies of Giving and Volunteering* (2002), which was directed by Robert T. Grimm Jr. and made possible by the Center on Philanthropy at Indiana University. Users may find more extensive philanthropic biographies of many of the people covered in this encyclopedia by consulting that work.

Organizations selected for inclusion are those most directly related to the philanthropic infrastructure of the field and its development over time. Needless to say, there is no attempt to include all philanthropic organizations or nonprofits. For profiles of current charitable nonprofits, readers are referred to GuideStar, available online at http://www.guidestar.org.

Contributors have attempted to introduce the reader to particular ideas and areas of study in philanthropy and have often included significant bibliographic references to allow the reader to further explore the topic under consideration.

In Volume 3, I endeavored to select the fundamental documents and excerpts that provided the foundation for the development of philanthropy and a nonprofit sector in America. Again, it is important to note that this needed to be a selective representation, and the final decision of what to include was dictated by availability of material and subjective judgment. In addition to historical documents, I sought some rep-

resentative works from literature that provided visions of what the state of philanthropy was or should have been within historical time frames. Even though the documents speak for themselves, I have included brief notes to provide a contextual guide for the reader.

Many historians have characterized the eleemosynary history of the United States as one of American exceptionalism and the individual quest for wealth. As my colleague Lawrence Friedman and his coauthors argued in their recent history of American philanthropy (*Philanthropy, Charity and Civility in American History,* 2003), the development of philanthropy in the United States is better understood as a missionary quest by givers (of time and/or money) to impose their view of what is good on society writ large. Taking this perspective, American history reads like an ongoing tension play between morals and money, or between obligations to others and those to self. One can make a reasonable case that the history of philanthropy in the United States seems to be informed by Adam Smith's ethical doctrines, a combination of Christian and Stoic virtues. For the student who wishes to pursue this idea, reviewing Smith's *The Theory of Moral Sentiments* (1759) is a good starting point.

During the course of compiling, writing, and editing, I have had the pleasure of reading my way back and forth in the history of philanthropy from the American colonial period to the present as a way to understand the relationship between self-interest and caring for others. I have come to believe that philanthropy in America is very much a story about the interests of others as well as self-interests.

Dwight F. Burlingame

Acknowledgments

Two colleagues in particular have encouraged me to embark on this project over the past eight years. Initially the topic was broached with me by Robert Payton, the first full-time executive director of the Center on Philanthropy at Indiana University. We both lamented the impossibility of deciding what would be included in a one- or two-volume work on such a broad topic as philanthropy in the United States. In 1998, my colleague and friend David R. Smith encouraged me to embark on this effort, as it was surely needed. To Bob and David I am especially grateful.

Subsequently, Marie Ellen Larcada from ABC-CLIO suggested that I submit a proposal for a three-volume work on the subject. In the spring of 2001, I signed a contract and work began in earnest. Marie Ellen went on to other endeavors, thus my special thanks to James Ciment, Martha Whitt, and their team for their assistance. During the three years it took to prepare the manuscript, the Center on Philanthropy at Indiana University, with support from the Lilly Endowment, has provided generous assistance, and Gene Tempel and other colleagues from the center have provided moral support. Four graduate assistants from the center have provided invaluable help, including Ben Imdicke, Sara Bosin, Aubrey Patterson, and most especially, Emily Hall. To these and others at the Center on Philanthropy I owe special thanks.

Of course, I am most indebted to all the authors who wrote and happily revised the entries herein. My gratitude and appreciation is heartfelt for their scholarly and philanthropic gifts. I have learned a great deal from their contributions as well as from our many hours of discourse—often electronic—which provided intellectual stimulation of the best kind. Particular thanks go to the advisory committee members Kathryn A. Agaard, Eleanor L. Brilliant, Peter Dobkin Hall, Robert L. Payton, Eugene R. Tempel, Cathlene Williams, and especially Lawrence J. Friedman, Robert T. Grimm Jr., David C. Hammack, and Paul G. Schervish, who gave most helpful criticism and suggestions for documents to be included. Thanks also to Fran Huehls, philanthropic studies librarian at IUPUI, and all the other librarians who provided assistance.

Finally, thanks to my wife, Audrey, for her encouragement and for understanding why so many books and articles, and the computer, needed to follow us on every vacation or trip during the past three years.

Dwight F. Burlingame

Philanthropy in America: A Timeline of Key Events

1600s — American Indians encounter Europeans and practice one of the oldest giving traditions in North America by giving the foreigners food and assistance.

1601 — The English Parliament enacts the Statute of Charitable Uses, a cornerstone of Anglo-American charity law and Elizabethan Poor Law and the basis of English and American public poor relief.

1630 — Puritan leader John Winthrop preaches his famous sermon "A Modell of Christian Charity" while en route to America. The sermon outlines the Puritan settlers' future society in American as well as his conception of charity.

1638 — John Harvard bequeaths his library and half of his estate to newly founded (1636) Harvard College at Cambridge, Massachusetts.

1656 — Puritan Robert Keayne dies and makes one of the earliest charitable bequests in America.

1657 — Scots' Charitable Society, the first American "friendly society," is created in Boston; it was reorganized in 1684 and is still in existence today.

1675 — The Massachusetts legislature provides relief for frontier settlers, an act that departs from the principle of exclusive local responsibility for relief.

1690s — Cotton Mather begins to promote voluntary associations in America.

1702 — Cotton Mather publishes *Magnalia Christi*, which celebrates philanthropy in America; in 1710, he publishes his practical work on public service, *Bonafacius: An Essay upon the Good*.

1715–1718 — Elihu Yale sends gifts to Collegiate School of Connecticut (chartered 1701); in 1718, the school changes its name to Yale College.

1727   Benjamin Franklin founds the Junto Club in Philadelphia. The club serves as a catalyst for numerous civic improvements.

1729   First orphan home in the United States is established at Ursuline Convent, New Orleans.

1750   Anthony Benezet begins teaching free African Americans in his home and devotes over thirty years to such educational endeavors, including the founding of the African School in 1770.

1751–1752   Dr. Thomas Bond, assisted by Benjamin Franklin and others who pioneered the matching-grant concept, establishes Pennsylvania Hospital.

1780   Pennsylvania becomes the first state to pass a law for the abolition of slavery.

1784   Benjamin Rush publishes *Inquiry into the Effects of Spirituous Liquors upon the Human Body, and Their Influence upon the Happiness of Society* and becomes known as the founder of the American temperance movement. In 1786, he sets up the Philadelphia Dispensary, one of the first free medical clinics in America.

1790   Upon Benjamin Franklin's death, his will establishes a fund for apprentices in Philadelphia and Boston.

1809–1813   Elizabeth Seton works to establish the Sisters of Charity of St. Joseph, the first American religious order, with a focus on education.

1810   Elizabeth Seton and the Sisters of St. Joseph create the first free Catholic school in the United States, which becomes the model for Catholic education.

1812   Returning to the United States from a trip to Africa, African American merchant Paul Cuffe encourages American blacks to assist their brothers and sisters in Africa. He enlists the support of black shipbuilder James Forten. Cuffe works in several American cities to spur the creation of black associations to develop transatlantic mutual aid initiatives.

1816   American Bible Society, the oldest national benevolent society, is established.

1817   Thomas Hopkins Gallaudet establishes in Connecticut America's first free school for the deaf, the American Asylum at Hartford for the Education and Instruction of the Deaf and Dumb (today known as the American School for the Deaf). Gallaudet's son continues to be active in the school until 1917.

1818   Economic depression spurs the establishment of the New York Society for the Prevention of Pauperism.

1819   After the state of New Hampshire passed a bill that took over the assets of Dartmouth College and replaced members of the board of trustees, the former Dartmouth College trustees take the case to the U.S. Supreme Court. In *Trustees of Dartmouth College v. Woodward,* the U.S. Supreme Court sided with the trustees and established protections from government interference to corporations (nonprofit or for-profit).

1825	The New York House of Refuge, the first reformatory for juveniles, is founded.
1825	Robert Owen opens communal experiment in New Harmony, Indiana.
1827	Despite the efforts of Robert Owen and Robert Dale Owen, the utopian community of New Harmony fails but it inspires others and other reforms in America.
1829	Matthew Carey attempts first federated fundraising in Philadelphia.
1831	Abolitionist William Lloyd Garrison begins to publish *The Liberator*, a paper significantly funded by black entrepreneur James Forten as well as white entrepreneurs Arthur Tappan and Lewis Tappan.
1832	Samuel Gridley Howe opens New England Asylum for instruction of the blind.
1833	Impressed by Samuel Gridley Howe's work, Thomas Perkins donates his mansion as well as $50,000 to aid Howe's efforts with the blind.
	Along with others, Arthur Tappan and Lewis Tappan establish the American Anti-Slavery Society. Arthur Tappan is named the first president of the society and Lewis Tappan provides leadership for the society's publication, the *Emancipator*.
1835	Evangelist Lyman Beecher delivers *A Plea for the West*, which details the role of religion's place in public life and promotes the value of voluntary associations.

	Alexis de Tocqueville publishes *Democracy in America,* which includes his observations on the disposition of Americans to organize and join voluntary associations.
	James Smithson's bequest to the United States stirs much debate about the role of government and philanthropy.
1837	Mary Lyon establishes Mount Holyoke Female Seminary (later named Mount Holyoke College), which pioneers higher education for women in the United States.
1838	Rebecca Gratz establishes the first Jewish Sunday school in the United States.
1841	The U.S. Supreme Court's decision in the *Amistad* case allows the Mendi Africans to return to their homeland. Lewis Tappan is the major benefactor of the *Amistad* cause.
	Dorothea L. Dix begins crusade for better treatment of insane.
1844	In *Vidal, Girard, et al. v. Philadelphia,* the U.S. Supreme Court sides with Stephen Girard's controversial will and ensures private individuals' right to have their bequests acted upon per their intent. In 1848, his orphanage opens.
1845	The Society of St. Vincent de Paul, a charitable organization of Roman Catholic laymen, is established in America.
1846	The U.S. Congress, after much debate, creates the Smithsonian Institution,

1846 cont.	which serves as the model for a pattern of public philanthropy.
1846–1847	Many Americans participate in providing help for Irish famine relief.
1847	Leonard Bacon's article "Responsibility in the Management of Societies," published in the *New Englander,* is possibly the first serious attempt to detail the responsibilities of charitable trusteeship.
1851	YMCA movement begins in the United States.
1853	Charles Loring Brace launches the Children's Aid Society in New York City.
1854	Dorothea Dix's bill that would provide acres of public lands to "several states" for building mental hospitals is passed by Congress but vetoed by President Franklin Pierce because he worries "that if Congress have the power to make provision for the indigent insane . . . it has the same power to provide for the indigent who are not insane, and thus to transfer to the federal government the charge of all the poor in all the states."
1859	Peter Cooper opens Cooper Union in New York City as center for free instruction in science and art. Cooper's school is later singled out by Andrew Carnegie as an example of the proper use of wealth.
1861–1865	During the Civil War, the Christian Commission and the U.S. Sanitary Commission—forerunner to the Red Cross—are established and work to improve the lives of soldiers.
1862	Freedmen's aid societies are established in the North to provide aid to former slaves. In 1865, the Freedmen's Bureau is founded and is active in relief and education in the South until the early 1870s.
1867	George Peabody establishes the Peabody Education Fund, which is often recognized as the first modern foundation in America.
1868	Hampton Institute School for Negroes opens in Virginia.
1879	Frances Willard is elected president of the Woman's Christian Temperance Union (WCTU). Her "Crusade Roundup" and her "Do Everything" approach and speaking engagements across the land made the WCTU the largest women's voluntary association in the world.
1881	Clara Barton establishes the American Association of the Red Cross.
	Booker T. Washington starts Tuskegee Institute for Negroes in Alabama.
	Andrew Carnegie supports his first public library project in his hometown in Dunfermline, Scotland.
	Henry Lee Higginson founds the Boston Symphony, the first permanent symphony in the United States.
	Helen Hunt Jackson publishes *A Century of Dishonor,* a work on the abuses inflicted upon Native Americans, which along with other works inspires many to support the rights of Indians.

1882	Josephine Shaw Lowell is instrumental in creating the Charity Organization Society of New York, the "flagship" of the charity organization movement. However, the first Charity Organization Society was created in Buffalo in 1877.		Leland and Jane Stanford found the Leland Stanford Junior University.

1882   Josephine Shaw Lowell is instrumental in creating the Charity Organization Society of New York, the "flagship" of the charity organization movement. However, the first Charity Organization Society was created in Buffalo in 1877.

1883   Bernice Pauahi Paki Bishop leaves the vast amount of her estate, including 9 percent of the landmass of Hawaii, for the establishment of the Kamehameha schools (which begin in 1887) and for native Hawaiians.

1884   Arguing for organized charity, Josephine Shaw Lowell publishes *Public Relief and Private Charity.*

1885   Because of a lack of college preparatory schools for women, Mary Elizabeth Garrett and four of her female friends start Bryn Mawr School for Girls.

1889   Andrew Carnegie publishes "Wealth" in *North American Review;* it becomes his most well known work under the title "Gospels of Wealth."

John D. Rockefeller gives $600,000 to help found the new University of Chicago.

Jane Addams and Ellen Gates Starr start Hull-House in Chicago, which becomes the model settlement house in America. It is patterned after Toynbee Hall in London, which was started in 1884.

1891   "Millionaire nun" Katharine Drexel starts the Sisters of the Blessed Sacrament for Indians and Colored People.

Leland and Jane Stanford found the Leland Stanford Junior University.

1892   John Muir starts the Sierra Club.

Ida B. Wells-Barnett organizes the first antilynching campaign in the United States.

The *New York Tribune* counts 4,047 millionaires in the United States.

1893   Pioneers of public-health nursing Lillian Wald and Mary Brewster provide nursing services for their neighbors, which leads to the creation of the Visiting Nurse Service of New York.

Mary Barrett's philanthropy makes possible the opening of the Johns Hopkins University Medical School. Her gift is conditioned upon equal admission for women and men.

1894   The first federal income tax law is enacted; it exempts organizations founded and conducted solely for charitable, religious, or educational purposes.

1895   Jane Addams, Florence Kelley, and other Hull-House colleagues publish *Hull-House Maps and Papers,* an early effort to make reforms based upon social science research.

1896   Ballington and Maud Booth form the Volunteers of America.

1900   The American National Red Cross obtains charter of incorporation from Congress.

1901   John D. Rockefeller Sr. founds the Rockefeller Institute for Medical

1901
cont.

Research based upon his advisor Frederick T. Gates's "wholesale philanthropy" (solving societal problems at their source) instead of "retail philanthropy" (alleviating individual suffering temporarily). This organization and subsequent Rockefeller philanthropies, such as the General Education Board, influence education and medicine significantly.

1902   Andrew Carnegie endows Carnegie Institution of Washington to encourage investigation, research, and discovery.

1903   Booker T. Washington secretly finances defense efforts in *Giles v. Harris* and *Giles v. Teasely* the following year; both cases challenge black disenfranchisement. Throughout his life, Washington secretly funded legal efforts in several racial discrimination cases and gave anonymous financial support to black newspapers.

1904   Mary McLeod Bethune starts and heads the Daytona Literary and Industrial School for Training Negro Girls.

Evangeline Booth becomes the head of the American Salvation Army. Building on the work of Ballington and Maud Booth as well as Emma and Frederick Booth-Tucker, Evangeline Booth transforms the Salvation Army into one of American's largest and most popular religious charities.

1905   The Carnegie Foundation for the Advancement of Teaching is founded.

1907   Using $10 million from her husband's estate, Margaret Olivia Sage establishes the Russell Sage Foundation,

important for the development of social work and social science research.

1909   The First White House Conference on the Care of Dependent Children recommends establishment of a federal Children's Bureau.

1910   Boy Scouts of America is founded. Girl Scouts of America is founded by Juliette Gordon Low in 1912.

Jane Addams publishes *Twenty Years at Hull-House.*

1911   Madam C. J. Walker amazes the city by pledging a gift ($1,000) equal to the amount pledged by wealthy white citizens for a Colored YMCA in Indianapolis.

Concerned that he would die rich and disgraced, Andrew Carnegie creates his largest foundation ($125 million), the Carnegie Corporation of New York.

1912   As the anonymous "Mr. Smith," George Eastman provides a new campus for the Massachusetts Institute of Technology. Preferring to give with little or no recognition, Eastman quietly gives his fortune to hometown charities in Rochester, New York, and to localities of Eastman Kodak Company.

Henrietta Szold establishes Hadassah, a national Zionist organization for women.

1913   The Revenue Act of 1913 exempts organizations operated exclusively for religious, charitable, scientific, or educational purposes; subsequent acts add "prevention of cruelty to children or animals" (1918), "literary" (1921), "community chest, fund or foundation" (1921), and "testing for public safety" (1954) to the list of exempt organizations.

1914   Frederick Goff sets up the Cleveland Foundation, the first community foundation.

Herbert Hoover establishes and leads the Commission for Relief in Belgium (CRB) during World War I.

Jesse Moorland donates his collection of books, artifacts, and other materials to Howard University to form the first African American research library.

1917   Roger Baldwin establishes the Civil Liberties Bureau, which becomes the American Civil Liberties Union (ACLU).

Julius Rosenwald creates the Rosenwald Fund to promote racial equality.

Income tax law permits individuals to deduct up to 15 percent of taxable income for charitable contributions.

Red Cross raises $100 million, the largest sum raised by any voluntary organization up to that time.

1918   George Draper Dayton creates the Dayton Foundation.

1919   Harvard uses professional fundraising counsel in $14 million endowment fund drive.

1920   Herbert Hoover's American Relief Administration European Children's Fund, a private charity, raises close to $30 million in the United States.

1921   The American Foundation for the Blind is founded; Helen Keller helps raise endowment.

Gertrude Vanderbilt Whitney founds the Whitney Museum of American Art.

1923   Mary McLeod Bethune's Daytona Literary and Industrial School merges with the Cookman Institute, forming the Bethune-Cookman College; Bethune becomes the president of this college for black women.

Margaret Sanger opens the Birth Control Clinical Research Bureau in New York City.

1924   Total annual charitable contributions reach $2 billion in United States.

Sebastian S. Kresge establishes the Kresge Foundation, which diverges from the activities of many earlier foundations by focusing on giving to existing organizations rather than new projects.

1925   Katharine Drexel and the Sisters of the Blessed Sacrament start Xavier University of Louisiana, which remains the only historically black Catholic university.

Simon Guggenheim creates the John Simon Guggenheim Memorial Foundation, which offers one-year fellowships to scholars aged twenty-five to thirty-five.

In *Pierce v. Society of the Sisters,* the U.S. Supreme Court strikes down Oregon antiparochial school law.

1926   Daniel Guggenheim establishes the Guggenheim Fund for the Promotion of Aeronautics.

1927   Robert Brookings creates the Brookings Institution by merging the Institute for Government Research and the Institute of Economics.

1929   Henry Ford dedicates what will become the Henry Ford Museum and Greenfield Village at Dearborn, Michigan.

Abby Aldrich Rockefeller cofounds the Museum of Modern Art.

1930   W. K. Kellogg starts the W. K. Kellogg Foundation with the goal of improving the lives of young people; major areas of interest included education and health, especially in rural areas.

1933   Dorothy Day and Peter Maurin start publishing *The Catholic Worker*, which leads to the Catholic Worker Movement.

Charitable giving during the years of the Depression reaches a low point.

1935   The Social Security Act is passed into legislation, beginning a permanent welfare program by the national government in part necessitated by the failure of the private voluntary sector to meet the social needs of the population.

The American Association of Fund-Raising Counsel is organized.

1936   Edsel Ford and Henry Ford establish the Ford Foundation. Although the founders had focused on Michigan philanthropy, upon their deaths in the

1940s, the focus of the foundation changes to be national and international.

1936 Tax Act allows corporations to deduct charitable gifts up to 5 percent of federal taxable income.

1937   Congress agrees to accept Andrew Mellon's offer to establish the National Gallery of Art in Washington, D.C.

Along with brother J. K. Lilly Jr. and father J. K. Lilly Sr., Eli Lilly establishes the Lilly Endowment in Indianapolis, a foundation that reflects Eli's preference for "personal philanthropy."

1939   Ima Hogg founds the Hogg Foundation for Mental Hygiene in her beloved Texas.

1944   Frederick Douglass Patterson leads in the creation of the United Negro College Fund.

1945   The Hill-Burton Hospital Construction Act makes the federal government a major player in health care.

1946   John D. Rockefeller Jr. donates seventeen acres in New York City for United Nations headquarters.

Five Dayton brothers institute an annual policy of giving 5 percent of Dayton's pretax profits to charity. Their company becomes a model of corporate giving.

1947   New York University alumni donate various businesses to their alma mater, including the C. F. Mueller Company, a gift that makes New York University the largest manufacturer of macaroni in the world and the recipient of harsh criticism from the U.S. Congress.

1948   Senator Charles Tobey investigates businesses' use of foundations for nonphilanthropic purposes.

Hector P. Garcia starts the American G.I. Forum, which advocates for the civil rights of all Latinos.

J. Howard Pew, J. N. Pew Jr., Mary Ethel Pew, and Mabel Pew Myrin establish the Pew Memorial Foundation, which becomes known as the Pew Charitable Trusts. During their lifetime, the four Pew siblings attempt to do all their giving anonymously.

Carrying out the stipulation of its founder, the Julius Rosenwald Fund folds.

1950   A revision of the Internal Revenue Code subjects foundations engaged in certain prohibited practices to loss of tax exemption.

1952   John D. Rockefeller Jr. assists his five sons in endowing the Rockefeller Brothers Fund.

Margaret Sanger serves as a founder as well as the first president of the International Planned Parenthood Federation.

The Select (Cox) committee of the House of Representatives investigates foundations.

1953   The decision of the New Jersey Supreme Court in *Barlow et al. v. A. P. Smith Manufacturing Co.* clarifies the

legal right of corporations to make contributions, even if the gifts do not offer a "direct benefit" to the corporation.

1954   John M. Olin founds the John M. Olin Foundation, which eventually becomes highly effective at shaping conservative public policy.

The Special (Reece) Committee investigates foundations.

In *Brown v. Board of Education*, the U.S. Supreme Court decides that enforced racial segregation in public schools is against the Fourteenth Amendment.

1955   Martin Luther King Jr. becomes the head of the newly formed Montgomery Improvement Association and leads bus boycott in Montgomery, Alabama, by promoting nonviolent voluntary action.

1957   Hector P. Garcia succeeds in ending the Texas public schools' segregation of Mexican Americans by leading the efforts of the American G. I. Forum and the League of United Latin American Citizens behind *Hernandez v. Consolidated ISD*.

1958   The National Foundation for Infantile Paralysis becomes the National Foundation with a change of mission after the Salk polio vaccine was developed in 1955.

James Herman Robinson forms Operation Crossroads Africa, which serves as the inspiration for the establishment of the Peace Corps.

1960	Pierre Frist Goodrich starts the Liberty Fund.	1970	Charitable giving in the United States reaches more than $21 billion.

1960   Pierre Frist Goodrich starts the Liberty Fund.

Philanthropic giving in the United States reaches an estimated $10.92 billion.

The Internal Revenue Service recognizes more than 45,000 tax-exempt organizations.

1961   President John F. Kennedy begins a federated fund drive among federal employees and military personnel that is later known as the Combined Federal Campaign (CFC).

1962   Cesar Chavez establishes the National Farm Workers Association, which becomes the United Farm Workers.

1964   David and Lucile Packard create their family foundation.

1965   The Johnson administration establishes Medicare and Medicaid to cover medical expenses of older and low-income persons.

The National Endowment for the Arts and the National Endowment for the Humanities are established.

1968   Lundberg's book *The Rich and Super Rich* discloses findings from Congressman Patman's (D-TX) investigation of foundations.

1969   President Nixon establishes the National Center for Voluntary Action, a nonprofit, to coordinate voluntary and government sectors.

Congress passes the Tax Reform Act of 1969, which approves many punitive actions affecting private foundations.

1970   Charitable giving in the United States reaches more than $21 billion.

1974   McDonald's restaurants team up with nonprofits to establish Ronald McDonald houses.

John D. Rockefeller III creates the Commission on Private Philanthropy and Public Needs (the Filer Commission). At the end of the following year, the commission reports its findings in an important work, *Giving in America: Toward a Stronger Voluntary Sector.*

1975   At Yale University, John D. Rockefeller III funds a feasibility study that leads to the establishment of the Program on Non-Profit Organizations (PONPO) in 1978; the first of many university-based academic research centers studying philanthropy and the nonprofit sector.

1976   A Tax Reform Act limits the amount charities may spend on lobbying.

1979   Robert Woodruff and George Woodruff give $105 million to Emory University, at the time the largest gift by living donors to an American college or university.

1980   In *Village of Schaumburg v. Citizens for Better Environment,* the U.S. Supreme Court rules that a city ordinance requiring fundraising groups to demonstrate that 75 percent or more of money raised goes for charitable purposes infringes freedoms protected by the First Amendment.

Charitable giving in the United States totals nearly $49 billion.

INDEPENDENT SECTOR is created.

1981 President Reagan appoints the Task Force on Private Initiatives.

1984 George Soros negotiates the creation of Soros Foundation–Hungary, the first private independent foundation within a Communist country.

1986 INDEPENDENT SECTOR launches an effort to double charitable giving and increase volunteer activity by 50 percent by 1991. The campaign is not successful and is discontinued by 1997.

1987 Due in part to its strong tradition of corporate philanthropy in Minnesota, the Dayton-Hudson Corporation is able to fend off a hostile takeover.

1988 Cesar Chavez fasts on water for thirty-six days to spotlight the dangers of pesticides.

1995 Mississippi washerwoman Oseola McCarty becomes a national figure by making a gift of $150,000 to the University of Southern Mississippi. Her action demonstrates the significance of philanthropy by "average" people.

1997 Kenneth Dayton and Joe Selvaggio found the One Percent Club, a group of individuals who commit to give away annually 1 percent of their net worth to charity.

1999 Bill and Melinda Gates form the Bill and Melinda Gates Foundation, which quickly becomes the largest charitable foundation in the world.

2000 Charitable giving in the United States exceeds $212 billion

Charitable nonprofits in the United States are estimated to number 1.7 million.

Part I
A to Z Entries

Accountability

Widely publicized revelations of financial improprieties, excessive compensation, and unethical behavior have highlighted the importance of accountability and oversight in both the business and nonprofit sectors. Examples in the business sector abound, but nonprofit organizations have not been exempt. Nonprofits as diverse as the American Cancer Society, the American Red Cross, New York City's Hale House, and the Amateur Athletic Union have faced public accusations of unethical or illegal behavior.

But what exactly is meant by the term "accountability" when it is applied to the nonprofit sector? Kevin Kearns described nonprofit accountability, in part, as that "wide spectrum of public expectations dealing with organizational performance [and the] responsiveness . . . of nonprofit organizations" (1996, 9). Thus, an organization is accountable when it is answerable *to* some other party *for* accomplishing some definite goal(s). In the United States, there are two types of accountability: legal and voluntary.

Legal Accountability

Accounting is "the process of identifying, measuring, and communicating economic information to various users" (American Accounting Association 1966, 1). James Greenfield and Richard Larkin held that "the whole purpose of accounting is to ensure that accountability happens" (2000, 55). In the nonprofit

sector, standards and practices set forth by the Internal Revenue Service (IRS), the Financial Accounting Standards Board (FASB), and the American Institute of Certified Public Accountants (AICPA) attempt to do just that. These entities determine what types of economic information are to be identified, measured, and communicated in the United States.

The Internal Revenue Service (IRS)

The Internal Revenue Service (IRS), as part of the U. S. Department of the Treasury, has as its primary responsibility the collection of taxes from individuals and businesses. According to IRS documents, "The Internal Revenue Service is the nation's tax collection agency and administers the Internal Revenue Code enacted by Congress. Its mission: to provide America's taxpayers with top quality service by helping them understand and meet their tax responsibilities and by applying the tax law with integrity and fairness to all" (U.S. Department of the Treasury, Internal Revenue Service, 2003).

The Tax Exempt and Government Entities Operating Division is responsible for tax-exempt organizations. This division has the authority to grant, withhold, or revoke tax-exempt status and to assess fines for noncompliance under certain conditions. Most tax-exempt organizations with gross receipts of more than $25,000 are required to file the IRS-designed Form 990, an annual document used to report information about finances and operations. Although the IRS's oversight authority is potentially quite powerful, it is rarely used. First, when an organization requests tax-exempt status, it is seldom denied: In 2002, less than 1 percent of the 87,342 applications for tax-exempt status were rejected. Then, once tax-exempt status is granted, it is rarely lost: Only twenty or thirty organizations per year lose their tax-exempt status (MacDonald and Schlesinger 1997). Finally, IRS employees rarely examine those returns that are filed. In 2002, less than 1 percent of the more than 775,000 Form 990s were examined (down from a 2.09 percent examination rate in 1994).

Until 1996, although Form 990s filed by nonprofit organizations were "public" information, one usually had to visit the organization in question or request a copy, in writing, from the IRS to obtain one. Since 1996, however, the document has been required to be "widely available" to anyone who requests it. As a result, Form 990 (which includes both financial and nonfinancial data) has become the primary source of information for a wide variety of users. GuideStar, a nonprofit organization with the goal of revolutionizing "philanthropy and nonprofit practice with information" (http://www.guidestar.org/about), has posted scanned Form 990s and other information about more than 850,000 nonprofit organizations on its Web site. The National Center for Charitable Statistics, as part of the Urban Institute, a Washington, D.C., think tank, has digitized the forms, making it fairly easy for scholars to conduct empirical research about the sector as a whole (http://www.nccs.urban. org). Several streams of research have resulted from the availability of Form 990 data.

One stream has focused on the quality of the information that nonprofits submit to the IRS. The results, which have been somewhat mixed, seem to suggest that although the quality of the data submitted may be reasonably accurate for the sector *taken as a whole* (Froelich and Knoepfle 1996; Froelich et al. 2000), *specific* Form 990s may be lacking (Gordon et al. 1999). For example, according to GuideStar, 20 percent of Form 990 filers in 2000 charged more than 50 percent of their expenses to "other." And some researchers have found that between 15 and 25 percent of nonprofits receiving funds from private (non-

governmental) sources reported zero fundraising costs (Lipman 2000; Greenlee and Gordon 1998).

A second area of research has focused on the impact of disclosures on the behavior of donors. Although this type of research is still in its early stages, several scholars have found that information presented on Form 990 does appear to have some impact on donor decisions (Baber et al. 2001; Pollack and Cordes 1999; Tinkelman 1999; Greenlee and Brown 1999).

A third area of research has looked at the usefulness of Form 990 data in assessing the financial condition of nonprofit organizations. Authors in the field have described ratios that nonprofit organizations could use in benchmarking with other, similar nonprofits and in conducting trend analysis over time (Greenlee and Bukovinsky 1998); adapted ratios (from Tuckman and Chang 1991) to develop models to predict the future financial health of a nonprofit organization (Greenlee and Trussel 2000; Trussel and Greenlee 2003); and, in an extension of these studies, found that the predictive value of the model does differ within different types of organizations within a subsector (Hager 2001).

The Financial Accounting Standards Board (FASB)
The Financial Accounting Standards Board (FASB) is a private-sector organization with the authority to determine the accounting standards, or rules, used in preparing the audited financial statements of both business and nonprofit organizations. Financial statements following FASB standards are said to have been prepared according to generally accepted accounting principles (GAAP). FASB standards, however, can and do differ significantly from IRS regulations. For example, the IRS permits nonprofits to use either the cash-basis or the accrual-basis method of accounting for revenue and expenses, but the FASB permits only the accrual-basis method. And, although Form 990 is public information, financial statements prepared according to GAAP are not required to be disclosed.[1] Since the data are not widely or easily available, little empirical research using audited financial statements has been conducted.[2] One study found that many nonprofits that reported fundraising costs on their (nonpublicly available) audited financial

statements disclosed zero fundraising costs on their (publicly available) Form 990 (Lipman 2000). Tremendous variation in what was included in operating income has also been found in the annual reports of private colleges and universities.

The American Institute of Certified Public Accountants (AICPA)

The American Institute of Certified Public Accountants (AICPA) is "the national professional organization for all Certified Public Accountants" (http://www.aicpa.org). Certified public accountants (CPAs) are licensed by the state to audit financial statements. In doing so, they examine not only the numbers in the statements but the records underlying those numbers. They then are empowered to express an opinion as to whether these statements were prepared according to GAAP. The rules that govern the audit are determined by the AICPA. The audit can be a powerful accountability tool for those both inside and outside of the organization. Unfortunately, however, the focus of accounting and auditing education has been on business entities. Many auditing firms are "firing" their nonprofit clients because they feel the benefits (profits) do not exceed the perceived risks.

In addition, many states require certain nonprofit organizations, usually charities, to register with a state agency and to file reports, usually some combination of Form 990, the audited financial statements, and a state-mandated form. Typically, the focus of these state regulations is to publicize excess fundraising costs.

Voluntary Accountability

Several independent organizations set standards that nonprofits (typically charitable organizations) must meet if they are to be "approved" by that organization. The standards can vary a great deal in what they include, in how they are designed, and in how they are implemented. Some are comprehensive; others are narrow in scope. Some of the organizations focus on the entire nonprofit sector; others focus on one type of organization within the sector. Moreover, some consult user groups when developing their standards, and others consult no one. Some of the standards are implemented by external review, some by a self-evaluation process, and some organizations use a rating system, while others use a compliance/noncompliance system. Each standard-setting organization is unique (INDEPENDENT SECTOR 2003). The following examples of standard-setting organizations illustrate some of the diversity that exists in the area of voluntary accountability. (For a more complete listing of organizations, see http://www.independentsector.org/issues/accountability/standards.html).

Better Business Bureau's Wise Giving Alliance

The Better Business Bureau's Wise Giving Alliance (http://www.give.org), the oldest of such standard setters and the most widely known, claims that it helps donors make informed giving decisions through charity evaluations, various "tips" publications, and the quarterly publication of its *Better Business Bureau Wise Giving Guide*. Its twenty standards[3] focus on full disclosure, ethical decisions, and sound management practices and are divided into four sections: governance and oversight, measuring effectiveness, finances, and fundraising and informational materials (see http://www.give.org/standards/newcbbbstds.asp for the specific standards and http://www.give.org/standards/implementation.asp for specifics on implementing these standards). The Wise Giving Alliance has evaluated several thousand, mostly national charitable organizations (see http://www.give.org/reports/index.asp for a list of charities evaluated and for access to their reports). It recently announced a program where charities meeting all standards would be given a "national charity seal" (Better Business Bureau 2003).

The American Institute of Philanthropy

The American Institute of Philanthropy rates approximately 500 national charities on a scale of A to F and publishes the results three times a year in its *Charity Rating Guide*. It uses only three financial performance measures in its ranking system: percent spent on charitable purpose, cost to raise $100, and years of available assets, that is, "how long a charity with large reserves of available assets could continue to operate at current levels without any additional fundraising" (http://www.charitywatch.org).

Charity Navigator

Charity Navigator uses a fairly complex rating system (see http://www.charitynavigator.org/index.cfm/bay/content.view/catid/2/cpid/35.htm) to rate more than 2,000 U.S. charities on a scale of four stars ("exceptional") to zero stars ("poor"). It focuses on the efficiency and the capacity of the organization.

Evangelical Council for Financial Accountability

The Evangelical Council for Financial Accountability (ECFA) is an example of a voluntary standard-setting organization that limits its scope to one type of nonprofit entity. Originally established as a response to some of the well-publicized improprieties that occurred in some television ministries in the 1980s and 1990s, its mission is to help "Christ-centered organizations earn the public's trust through developing and maintaining standards of accountability that convey God-honoring ethical practices" (http://www.ecfa.org/ECFA/ContentEngine.asp?Page=Mission). To receive the ECFA's "seal of approval," a ministry must adhere to fairly stringent standards focusing primarily on ethical and disclosure issues (see http://www.ecfa.org/ECFA/ContentEngine.asp?Page=7standards).

Conclusion

The present system of accountability for nonprofit organizations in the United States has resulted in a system where the accounting information that has been examined (audited) is *not* public information (and is rarely used) and the information that has *not* been audited *is* public information (and is used extensively). Voluntary standard-setting organizations attempt to overcome these limitations. Unfortunately, most of these organizations must rely, at least in part, on the public (and possibly suspect) information. Further, each voluntary standard setter has a unique (and usually not fully explained) method of evaluating an organization.

In order for the sector to grow and prosper, the public must have confidence and trust in the information that nonprofit organizations provide on their financial and fundraising activities. Although the IRS, the FASB, the AICPA, and voluntary standard-setting organizations have helped to make nonprofits more accountable, much is lacking in this regard. It is doubtful that the present system of accountability in the United States does enough to ensure reliable information and to foster the kind of public confidence in nonprofits that is needed for a vibrant nonprofit sector.

Janet Greenlee

See also American Institute of Philanthropy; Charity Watchdogs

Notes

1. Interestingly, in the business sector, the opposite is the case: Tax-return information is private and GAAP financial statements are public.

2. In this regard, too, the nonprofit sector contrasts significantly with the business sector: Audited financial statements for publicly traded companies are widely available on the Internet on a timely basis and are available in several easily searchable digitized formats.

3. New standards were effective beginning March 3, 2003. The twenty-three previous standards focused more on fundraising activities (see http://www.give.org/standards/cbbbstds.asp).

References and further reading

American Accounting Association. 1966. *A Statement of Basic Accounting Theory.* Evanston, IL: American Accounting Association.

Baber, W., A. Roberts, and G. Visvanathan. 2001. "Charitable Organizations Strategies and Program Spending Ratios." *Accounting Horizons* 15 (4): 329–343.

Better Business Bureau (BBB). 2003. "BBB Wise Giving Alliance to Brief Reporters on New Charity Accountability Standards and Announce National Charity Seal Program." Press Release, http://www.bbb.org/alerts/medadvisory.asp.

Froelich, K. A., and T. W. Knoepfle. 1996. "Internal Revenue Service 990 Data: Fact or Fiction?" *Nonprofit and Voluntary Sector Quarterly* 25 (1): 40–52.

Froelich, K. A., T. W. Knoepfle, and T. Pollak. 2000. "Financial Measures in Nonprofit Organization Research: Comparing IRS 990 Return and Audited Financial Statement Data." *Nonprofit and Voluntary Sector Quarterly* 29 (2): 232–254.

Gordon, T., J. Greenlee, and D. Nitterhouse. 1999. "Tax Exempt Organization Financial Data: Availability and Limitations." *Accounting Horizons* (June): 113–128.

Greenfield, J., and R. Larkin. 2000. "Public Accountability." In *Serving the Public Trust: Insights into Fundraising Research and Practice,* edited by Paul P. Pribbenow, vol. 2, 51–71. San Francisco: Jossey-Bass.

Greenlee, J., and K. Brown. 1999. "The Impact of Accounting Information on Contributions to Charitable Organizations." *Research in Accounting Regulation* 13: 111–125.

Greenlee, J., and T. Gordon. 1998. "The Impact of Professional Solicitors on Fund Raising in Charitable Organizations." *Nonprofit and Voluntary Sector Quarterly* (September): 277–299.

Greenlee, J., and D. Bukovinsky. 1998. "Financial Ratios for Use in the Analytical Review of Charitable Organizations." *Ohio CPA Journal* 57 (1): 32–38.

Greenlee, J., and J. Trussel. 2000. "Predicting the Financial Vulnerability of Charitable Organizations." *Nonprofit Management and Leadership* (Winter): 199–210.

Hager, M. 2001. "Financial Vulnerability among Arts Organizations: A Test of the Tuckman-Chang Measures." *Nonprofit and Voluntary Sector Quarterly* 30: 376–392.

INDEPENDENT SECTOR. 2003. *Compendium of Standards, Codes, and Principles of Nonprofit and Philanthropic Organizations,* http://www.independentsector.org/issues/accountability/standards.html.

Kearns, K. 1996. *Managing for Accountability.* San Francisco: Jossey-Bass.

Lipman, H. 2000. "Charities' Zero-Sum Filing Game." *The Chronicle of Philanthropy,* May 18: 1, 21–24.

MacDonald, E., and J. Schlesinger. 1997. "Group Targets Politically Active Churches for Audits." *Wall Street Journal,* March 20, A18.

Pollak, T., and J. Cordes. 1999. "Patterns, Trends and Determinants of Fund Raising and Administrative Cost Ratios Reported by Nonprofit Organizations." Paper at Arnova Conference, Arlington, VA, November 4–6.

Pristin, T., and N. Bernstein. 2002. "Ex-Head of Hale House and Husband Charged with Theft." *New York Times,* February 6, B1.

Schmadtke, A. 1999. "Factors Affecting the Relation between Donations to Not-for-Profit Organizations and an Efficiency Ratio." *Research in Government and Nonprofit Accounting* 10: 135–161.

Trussel, J., and J. S. Greenlee. 2003. "A Financial Rating System for Nonprofit Organizations." *Research in Governmental and Nonprofit Accounting.*

Tuckman, H. P., and C. F. Chang. 1991. "A Methodology for Measuring the Financial Vulnerability of Charitable Nonprofit Organizations." *Nonprofit and Voluntary Sector Quarterly* 20: 445–460.

U.S. Department of the Treasury, Internal Revenue Service (IRS). 2003. *Introduction and Mission.* Washington, DC: IRS.

Addams, Jane (1860–1935)

Jane Addams led the American social settlement movement, contrasted her philanthropic approach with contemporary Andrew Carnegie and others, and became a prominent pacifist. Through her social reform work and voluminous writings, she became one of the most famous American women of her time.

Born on September 6, 1860, to John Huy and Sarah Weber Addams, Jane Addams grew up in Cedarville, Illinois. In 1882, she graduated from Rockford Female Seminary (Rockford, Illinois) and began medical school in Philadelphia. After ill health forced her to leave medical school, Addams spent the next few years searching for her life's work. A member of the first generation of college-educated women, Addams had no interest in marriage and found most professions closed to females.

Ultimately, Addams—like many other college-educated women of the time—developed a lifelong career out of voluntary associations. After visiting Toynbee Hall, a London social settlement in which university men lived and worked among the poor, Addams decided to found a social settlement in the United States. In 1889, Addams and college friend Ellen Gates Starr started the Hull-House social settlement in a crumbling mansion located in an immigrant community on Chicago's South Side. Wishing to improve the lives of her immigrant neighbors and make privileged individuals (especially women) connected with the realities of the world, Addams believed that working and living with the poor would help her and others understand the best ways to combat poverty. At a time when the United States was undergoing rapid industrialization, urbanization, and immigration, Addams soon discovered a number of problems. In its first decade, Hull-House dramatically expanded—building- and service-wise—to meet the needs of the surrounding community. The settlement eventually offered a wide variety of classes (on topics such as carpentry and cooking) and included a gymnasium, a playground, a cooperative boardinghouse, a nursery, a music school, a theater, and an art gallery.

Primarily led and funded by women, Hull-House helped develop famous female reformers (such as Florence Kelley and Julia Lathrop) as well as the social work profession. In contrast to other philanthropists, such as Peter Cooper, who started Cooper Union, and Andrew Carnegie, famous for his funding of public libraries, Addams and her reform colleagues did not

Jane Addams (1860–1935) (Underwood & Underwood/Corbis)

believe that the poor could pull themselves out of poverty simply by taking the initiative and availing themselves of educational opportunities during their off-work hours. Instead, along with other social settlement reformers, she came to believe that environmental conditions—many beyond an individual's control—stopped people from rising out of poverty. In 1895, Addams and her reform colleges published *Hull-House Maps and Papers,* an early social science, systematic study that offered statistics ranging from housing conditions to child labor. Hull-House reformers subsequently fought for various reforms, including industrial safety and child labor legislation, limited working hours for women, and compulsory school attendance.

To promote these reforms, Addams gave numerous public speeches and produced a multitude of publications. In 1910, she penned her most famous work, the autobiographical *Twenty Years at Hull-House.* That year, Addams was the acknowledged leader of a movement that boasted 400 American settlements. She used her celebrity status to promote female suffrage and campaigned vigorously for Theodore Roosevelt's 1912 presidential bid because his Progressive Party represented many of the reforms she advocated.

When World War I began in Europe, Addams became a major figure in the U.S. pacifist movement. When the United States entered the war, her continued adherence to pacifism resulted in the public's condemnation. After the war, she spent much time in Europe working for the Women's International League for Peace and Freedom. Eventually, she earned the Nobel Peace Prize (1931) and returned to the status of an American icon. She died three days after an operation revealed she had cancer.

Robert T. Grimm Jr.

See also Kelley, Florence; Settlement Houses
References and further reading
Davis, Allen F. 1967. *Spearheads for Reform: The Social Settlements and the Progressive Movement, 1890–1914.* New York: Oxford University Press.
———. 1973. *American Heroine: The Life and Legend of Jane Addams.* New York: Oxford University Press.
Grimm, Robert T., Jr. 2002. "Jane Addams." In *Notable American Philanthropists: Biographies of Giving and Volunteering,* edited by Robert T. Grimm Jr., 1–5. Westport, CT: Oryx Press.

Advocacy and Nonprofit Organizations

Advocacy in the nonprofit world has a rich history and is often misunderstood by practitioners as well as by the general public and governmental officials. Nevertheless, nonprofit organizations must utilize advocacy skills almost constantly in carrying out their missions.

The history of advocacy in the United States has its roots with early humanitarian reform efforts and attempts to influence local, state, and federal political decisions. For example, cause advocates such as Dorothea Dix (1802–1887), who worked to improve the lives of those committed to prisons and insane asylums, and Reginald Heber Smith (1889–1996), who focused on improving legal representation for the poor, attempted to influence those in power during their day and alert them to the plight of certain ignored or exploited groups in society.

Various definitions have been developed to describe advocacy over the years. The essence of all of the definitions is that one group or individual is acting on behalf of another group or individual to help secure services or rights. Examples of advocacy range from a caseworker ensuring that clients receive all entitled services to an organization lobbying Congress to modify food stamp legislation to make it easier for individuals to apply for and receive assistance.

The activities of nonprofit organizations engaging in advocacy efforts may be categorized into six key arenas: (1) agency advocacy, which focuses on ensuring that individual clients or groups of clients receive the existing services to which they are entitled; (2) legislative advocacy, which attempts to persuade a legislature or governmental official to pass or not to pass a certain law or to amend or repeal an existing law; (3) legal advocacy, which aims to ensure the rights of individuals and groups through the legal system; (4) community advocacy, which educates citizens through the use of the media and through public demonstrations in support of or in opposition to an issue or policy; (5) issue advocacy, which utilizes research and education to identify social problems and potential solutions to them; and (6) political campaign advocacy, which supports the election or defeat of political candidates. Political campaign advocacy is the only

Dorothea Dix (1802–1887), a pioneer in the reform of the mental health industry (Bettmann/Corbis)

form of advocacy that is explicitly prohibited by federal rule for nonprofits that wish to retain tax-exempt status (U.S. Department of the Treasury).

Of the types of advocacy listed above, the most misunderstood is legislative advocacy and the role that nonprofits can play. The 1976 U.S. legislation governing lobbying and nonprofit organizations defines two types of lobbying: "direct lobbying," that is, any attempt to influence legislation through communication with a legislative body or government official who may participate in the formulation of legislation, and "grassroots lobbying," or communicating with the public to influence legislation by asking the public to act to support or reject certain legislation.

Nonprofit organizations are not prohibited from undertaking legislative lobbying. In fact, in some instances it is necessary for nonprofits to engage in such work to ensure their own survival. Nonprofit organizations can inform, educate, and persuade elected and administrative governmental employees, and unless they spend a considerable amount of time and money on lobbying, they will not endanger their tax-exempt status. Under the nonprofit tax-exempt regulations, public charities incorporated under Internal Revenue Code (IRC) 501(c)(3) are permitted to engage in lobbying activities but are not allowed to devote a "substantial" part of their activities to lobbying. Those violating this rule may lose their tax-exempt status or become subject to payment of taxes on their unallowable activities (ibid.).

Since 1976, nonprofit organizations have generally used two methods of determining whether their lobbying activities violate IRS regulations. The first has been to utilize the "nonsubstantial rule," that is, to rely on the commonsense approach of what would be viewed as "substantial," taking into account all of the circumstances of the situation and the organization. Neither the IRS nor Congress has precisely defined the term "substantial," however. Therefore, it is usually in a nonprofit organization's best interests to elect the second method, the "percentage rule," whenever possible (churches and private foundations may not make this election). The percentage rule, removing the ambiguity of the nonsubstantial rule, specifically quantifies a nonprofit organization's annual allowable lobbying activities based on the overall budget of the organization and the amount expended on specific lobbying activities. The limits established by Congress allow 20 percent of an organization's first $500,000, 15 percent of the next $500,000, 10 percent of the next $500,000, and 5 percent of an organization's remaining budget. The maximum amount allowable is $1 million (ibid.). Within these parameters, grassroots lobbying is limited to 25 percent of the allowable lobbying expenditures. For example, if an organization had a total exempt budget of $2 million, it would be permitted to spend a total of $250,000 on lobbying activities without jeopardizing its tax-exempt status. In addition, within the allowable $250,000, the organization's grassroots lobbying would be limited to $62,500.

According to current nonprofit legislation, lobbying does not include the following important advocacy tactics, which therefore are not included in the limitations prescribed in the 1976 legislation: making available the results of nonpartisan research; responding to a written request for technical assistance or advice from a governmental or legislative body; appearing before or communicating with any legislative body with respect to a possible decision of the body that might affect the existence of the organization, its powers, duties, or tax-exempt status, or the deductions of gifts; and communicating with bona fide members of the organization with respect to legislation or proposed legislation of direct interest to the organization.

Although public charities are currently provided great leeway in their lobbying activities, private foundations are, for the most part, constrained from any lobbying activities. The only exceptions are making available the results of nonpartisan research or studies and lobbying on their own behalf.

Finally, there are no clear rules to guide legislative advocacy and the use of the Internet, an emerging arena for advocacy for both direct and grassroots lobbying.

H. Daniels Duncan

See also Social Movements and Philanthropy
References and further reading

Alliance for Justice. "Nonprofit Advocacy," http://www. allianceforjustice.org/nonprofit/index.html (cited November 27, 2002).

Charity Lobbying in the Public Interest. "Educating Charities about the Important and Appropriate Role Lobbying Can Play in Achieving Their Missions," http://www.clpi.org/ (cited November 27, 2002).

Cohen, David. 2001. *Advocacy for Social Justice: A Global Action and Reflection Guide.* Bloomfield, CT: Kumarian Press.

Ezell, Mark. 2001. *Advocacy in the Human Services.* Toronto: Brooks/Cole.

Homan, Mark S. 1998. *Rules of the Game: Lessons from the Field of Community Change.* Pacific Grove, CA: Brooks/Cole.

Hopkins, Bruce R. 1993. *Charity, Advocacy, and the Law: How Nonprofit Organizations Can Use Charitable Dollars to Affect Public Policy—Lawfully.* New York: Wiley.

Jasson, Bruce S. 1999. *Becoming an Effective Policy Advocate: From Policy Practice to Social Justice.* Pacific Grove, CA: Brooks/Cole.

U.S. Department of the Treasury, Internal Revenue Service (IRS). "Lobbying Expenditures," http://www.irs.gov/ formspubs/page/0,id%3D12384,00.html (cited November 27, 2002).

African American Philanthropy

African American philanthropy—the giving of money, time, or goods by African Americans for various causes—has been shaped by the level of freedoms and rights afforded to African Americans at different points in history. As a result of the socioeconomic inequalities faced by African Americans, their philanthropy has supported both the charitable interests of individuals as well as African Americans' collective efforts to secure social equality.

There have been four distinct periods of African American philanthropy: slavery, reconstruction/Jim Crow, civil rights, and post–civil rights. In each period, the African American church has played a distinctive role because it was often the only institution with independent leadership that was financially supported and directed by the African American community. Because of this, the African American church has often operated like a community foundation, channeling individual donations to support collective community needs, a practice that continues today.

Slavery

African American philanthropy can be traced back to the first slaves arriving in the Americas. Recalling their African traditions of collective sharing and facing a common oppressor, African- and American-born slaves shared their limited resources to improve their common condition. Not all African Americans were slaves, and those who were not, most of them freedmen, formed self-help mutual aid organizations to provide for their immediate needs as well as to support the abolitionist movement.

One of the first mutual aid organizations was African Lodge No. 459, which was founded by Prince Hall in 1787 and received its charter from the Grand Lodge of England. As the number of African American freedmen grew, lodge members used their collective philanthropy to support numerous African American mutual aid societies and churches. The inability to fully participate in the larger society required African Americans to establish and support virtually all of their own institutions using their philanthropic capital. Many of the mutual aid organizations and churches were very active in educational efforts as well as in the abolitionist movement. Organizations such as the International Order of Twelve Knights, the Daughters of Tabor, and the Knights of Liberty, among others, were active in the Underground Railroad that helped more than 100,000 escaping slaves.

African American nonprofit organizations proved so successful that, by 1835, Maryland, Virginia, and North Carolina had laws prohibiting African Americans from creating lyceums, lodges, fire companies, or literary, dramatic, social, moral, or charitable societies. Such laws contributed to African Americans developing secret societies and clubs to continue their charitable self-help activities.

A number of African American freedmen who became wealthy were active philanthropists. Paul Cuffe (1759–1817), for example, a Massachusetts shipbuilder, established and financed a school for African American children and founded and supported the Friendly Society, which assisted free African Americans who wished to emigrate from the United States to Sierra Leone.

Reconstruction and Jim Crow

Although the Civil War brought an end to slavery, it did not bring equality for African Americans. As "separate but equal" became the country's standard, making possible a new onslaught of discriminatory "Jim Crow" laws and other racial inequalities, African American philanthropy was a cornerstone in helping to educate and train newly freed slaves. Many of the newly formed and existing mutual aid organizations focused on educating former slaves. These groups, along with churches, were active in numerous efforts to establish elementary schools, high schools, and colleges. The accumulated philanthropic capital of churches and mutual aid societies provided the necessary resources that led to the creation of the first African American banks and insurance companies. In addition, African American communities successfully matched their portion of the challenge grant sponsored by the Rosenwald Fund (a private foundation) that resulted in 5,000 new schools throughout the South.

As African Americans began to migrate to the industrial cities of the North in the early 1900s, new social justice organizations emerged with differing philosophies. For example, the National Association for the Advancement of Colored People (NAACP), the Urban League, and Marcus Garvey's Universal Negro Improvement Association were all supported, in whole or in part, by African American philanthropy. Many of the African American college fraternities and sororities were also established during this time, and they remain active in their philanthropy today. Wealthy African Americans continued to become active philanthropists during this era. For example, Madam C. J. Walker (1869–1919), who sold cosmetics, supported a wide range of causes, including a school for girls that she founded in West Africa. At her death, she left the school $100,000.

Civil Rights Period

African American philanthropy was the volunteer and financial fuel of the civil rights movement. Countless numbers of African Americans and their supporters made financial contributions, volunteered their time, opened their homes, and provided transportation and meals to demonstrators. The success of the civil rights movement not only improved the lives of African Americans but also led to increased equality for other racial and ethnic groups, women, and the disabled. All African Americans did not embrace the aims and tactics of the civil rights movement, however. The Nation of Islam, founded by Elijah Muhammad and endorsed, for a time, by Malcolm X, developed a wide array of schools and businesses relying on African American philanthropy to accomplish different objectives.

As the "separate and (un)equal" doctrine was slowly replaced by the concept of equal rights, African Americans developed new vehicles for their charitable giving. Maintaining that the United Way's monopoly access to federal workplace charitable campaigns was unfair, the National Black United Fund in the early 1980s successfully won two U.S. Supreme Court cases that allowed it access to the campaigns. These court victories allowed access to other campaigns that focused on women, Hispanics, and the environment.

Post–Civil Rights Period

The post–civil rights period has witnessed the sustained development of institutionalized African

A'Lelia Walker, daughter of Madam C. J. Walker, gets a manicure at one of her mother's beauty shops. Madam Walker's philanthropy supported a variety of causes, including a school for girls in West Africa. (Underwood & Underwood/Corbis)

American philanthropy. As greater numbers of African Americans enjoy economic success, they are establishing donor-advised funds through community foundations or commercial institutions as well as creating private foundations. Although churches, civil rights organizations, and charitable workplace campaigns continue to receive support, greater socioeconomic equality has meant a smaller proportion of collective African American philanthropy as individuals have had the freedom to pursue their personal charitable interests.

This period has produced a greater number of wealthy African Americans than any other. In particular, entertainers (such as Bill and Camille Cosby and Michael Jackson), athletes (such as Muhammad Ali), and business entrepreneurs (such as Oprah Winfrey), among others, have made significant charitable contributions. Oseola McCarty (1908–1999), who left school after sixth grade and spent her entire life cleaning and ironing other people's clothes, donated her life savings of $150,000 to create a scholarship fund for African Americans at the University of Southern Mississippi. She is a potent reminder that philanthropy has never been dependent upon wealth in the African American community.

Emmett D. Carson

See also Civil Rights Movement; National Association for the Advancement of Colored People; Walker, Madam C. J.

References and further reading

Carson, Emmett D. 1989. "The Evolution of Black Philanthropy: Patterns of Giving and Voluntarism." In *Philanthropic Giving: Studies in Varieties and Goals,* edited by Richard Magat, 92–102. New York: Oxford University Press.

———. 1991. "Contemporary Trends in Black Philanthropy: Challenging the Myths." In *Taking Fundraising Seriously: Advancing the Profession and Practice of Raising Money,* edited by Dwight F. Burlingame and Lamont J. Hulse, 219–238. San Francisco: Jossey-Bass.

———. 1993. *A Hand Up: Black Philanthropy and Self-Help in the United States.* Washington, DC: Joint Center for Political and Economic Studies Press.

———. 1996. "Philanthropy and Foundations." In *Encyclopedia of African-American Culture and History,* vol. 1, edited by Jack Salzman, David Lionel Smith, and Cornel West, 2137–2141. New York: Simon and Schuster.

organizations by strengthening support services. Members of the Alliance include management support organizations, independent consultants, foundations, academic centers, support associations, for-profit consulting firms, and others. Support organizations are strengthened through two primary services: membership networking on the Web and a skill-building, educational conference held each year. In addition to the conference, the Alliance offers its members a resource center, an online newsletter called *Pulse!,* and online services such as a provider search and career bank.

Alissa Saufley

References and further reading

Pocantico Conference Members. 1998. *Aspirations and Intentions, 1999–2003.* Washington, DC: Alliance for Nonprofit Management.

Pulse! 1997–1998. http://www.allianceonline.org

Alliance for Nonprofit Management

The Alliance for Nonprofit Management was created in 1997 in an effort to combine the resources of two previously existing organizations, the Support Centers of America (SCA) and the Nonprofit Management Association (NMA). Created in 1971, SCA provided a network of nonprofit management support organizations. These Support Centers are located in twelve communities across the nation and share training and expertise with nonprofit managers, staff, and board members. NMA, founded in 1975, represented an association of nonprofit management support professionals and promoted nonprofit management effectiveness through networking and collaboration.

In 1996, a strategic alliance committee discussed a merger between SCA and NMA, deciding that a new organization was needed in light of the similarities between the two groups and the growing need for services in the rapidly changing nonprofit world. In late 1997, the Alliance was created and an executive director was hired. On January 26, 1998, a ten-member SCA/NMA Merger Task Force became the founding board of the Alliance. In April, this group met with fifteen others to create the mission and goals.

Located in Washington, D.C., the Alliance is dedicated to improving the effectiveness of nonprofit

Alternative Funds

The creation and growth of "alternative funds" is a phenomenon of the latter half of the twentieth century. As private and community foundations and United Ways significantly expanded, a new category of private funding institution—alternative funds—originated and also greatly expanded. The first of these alternatives to mainline grantmaking foundations and United Ways was organized in 1958, and increasing numbers have come into existence every decade since. Approximately 340 existed in 2003.

There are two basic types of alternative funds: (1) funds that primarily solicit payroll deduction contributions in the workplace in competition with United Ways—numbering around 200 in 1997—and (2) funds that principally raise money from other sources and operate as grantmaking foundations. However, within these two basic types, there are numerous subtypes.

The workplace alternative funds include seven of these (listed in order of their initial entry into workplace fundraising campaigns): health funds, national federations, Black United Funds (BUFs), social action funds, united arts funds, environmental funds, and other local federations. These workplace alternative funds raised an estimated $179 million in 1997 (Bothwell and Delany 1998).

The foundation-like alternative funds array into six subtypes (listed in order of their creation): women's funds, Funding Exchange foundations, lesbian/gay foundations, Native American foundations/funds, Hispanic funds, and Asian Pacific American funds. These funds granted about $40 million in 1998. Figures on how much they raised, as opposed to granted, are not readily available, except for women's and lesbian/gay funds, which together raised $50 million in 1998 (Bothwell 2001).

These alternative funds are considered a group distinct from United Ways and mainline foundations for the following reasons:

1. Every type of alternative originated because of grave dissatisfaction with how United Ways were making allocations or how mainline foundations were conducting their grantmaking—hence, the identification of them as "alternatives."

2. These alternatives have organized themselves in structure and process in ways that are often contrary to the top-down approach of mainline foundations and United Ways.

3. The alternatives target their grants narrowly to benefit their special "communities" (for example, women, racial/ethnic groups, or gays and lesbians) or, in the case of the Funding Exchange foundations, to fund low-income, community-based organizations, and the alternative funds solicited at the workplace distribute their collections to their member organizations. Although some mainline foundations target their grants narrowly, they are few in number relative to the entire foundation universe.

4. Most of the alternatives are organized as public charities rather than as private foundations. Among the 60,000 grantmaking foundations tracked by the Foundation Center, the reverse is true, as private foundations far outnumber the 500–600 community foundations organized as public charities under IRS laws and regulations (Bothwell 2002).

Alternative Funds at the Workplace

Alternative funds primarily raising money from employees at the workplace are the most numerous group of alternatives. Of the approximately 200 funds in 1997, nineteen were national federations and the remainder were local- or state-based. Among the latter were fifty-five health funds, forty-four social action funds, thirty-four united arts funds, twenty-one Black United Funds, and nineteen environmental funds, and the remainder were other local federations (Bothwell and Delany 1998). Many originated because of dissatisfaction with United Way allocations.

The nineteen national alternative funds solicited around $109 million in 1997 from employee contributions at the workplace, 84 percent coming through the Combined Federal Campaign (CFC) of the federal government. The local and state funds raised an estimated $70 million from workplace contributions in 1997, only 20 percent from the CFC. Most of the $70 million derived from employee donations, but health funds received substantial corporate contributions (Bothwell and Delany 1998). Many local and state funds also raise small amounts from foundations and individual donors.

Workplace-focused alternative funds are primarily organized as federations of member charities. The number of member charities per fund ranges from about fifteen to ninety, though most local and state funds are at the low end of this spectrum. Their history can be traced as follows:

1. *Health funds*, the first workplace alternative funds to develop, started in Baltimore in 1958. The fifty-five health funds active in 1997 involved charities such as the Arthritis Foundation, the Leukemia Society, and the Sickle Cell Disease Association.

2. *National federations* were first organized in the early 1960s to participate in the CFC. From two national alternative funds initially, they grew to nineteen in 1997. They now include all types of charities, from international and human rights groups to environmental and conservation concerns and women's and children's organizations.

3. *Black United Funds,* originating in Los Angeles after the Watts neighborhood riot in the late 1960s, were the second type of local alternative fund to seek workplace donations. BUFs, unlike other workplace alternative funds, are not generally organized as federations of charities but set up instead as grantmaking foundations. BUFs were also the first of the identity-based funds. Women's funds, Native American foundations, Hispanic funds, Asian Pacific funds, and lesbian/gay funds all make up the total of twenty-one funds existing in 1997.

4. *Social action funds* first appeared in the early 1970s but only grew substantially in number in the 1980s. Sample member agencies of the forty-four funds active in 1997 were the American Civil Liberties Union (ACLU), the AIDS Task Force of the Deaf, the American Friends Service Committee, the Chinese Progressive Association, the Coalition for Consumer Justice, the Disabled Rights Action Committee, and Montanans for Choice.

5. *United arts funds* support artistic and cultural institutions in local communities. Of eighty in existence in 1996, thirty-four were involved in workplace fundraising campaigns. Some support large, mainstream arts and cultural institutions, others support small, emerging groups, and some support both types.

6. *Environmental funds* only appeared on the workplace scene in 1982 but have been the fastest growing type of workplace alternative fund. Only four in number in 1990, there were nineteen by 1997. Their revenues had grown 180 percent since 1991.

Alternative Funds as Grantmaking Foundations

The wide spectrum of alternative funds acting as grantmaking foundations began with women's funds, which, with more than seventy organizations, are the next most numerous of the alternatives after workplace alternative funds. The history of these foundations took the following path:

1. *Women's funds* are rooted in the nineteenth-century women's movement and the creation of the American Association of University Women's Educational Foundation. The forerunner of the current movement is the Ms. Foundation, set up in 1972. A first national conference of women's funds in 1985 led to the creation of the National Network of Women's Funds, now the Women's Funding Network. Women's funds began to grow in earnest after this turning point. The seventy members of the Women's Funding Network based in San Francisco raised more than $50 million and granted $25 million in 2000 (Women's Funding Network 2001).

2. *The Funding Exchange foundations (FEX)* were started by wealthy young heirs of famous fortunes, such as George Pillsbury, who started Haymarket People's Fund in Boston, beginning in the 1970s. A booklet entitled *Robin Hood Was Right!* provided inspiration and guidance for the movement. Now fifteen in number, these well-publicized alternatives and their national headquarters granted a total of $13 million in 1998 (Hanft 2000). The signature of FEX foundations is that, while seeking donors and their substantial gifts, they have also sought to divorce the donors from *control* of grantmaking by creating funding boards with low-income community residents as decision makers.

3. *Lesbian/gay foundations* and related foundations for bisexuals and transsexuals number seventeen. Fifteen are local or state based, and two are national. They raised a total of $4.7 million in 1998 and distributed $1.6 million "to organizations and programs that have the least access to philanthropic support," generating endowments totaling $4 million (Cunningham 2000).

4. *Native American foundations,* that is, those with American Indians composing half or more of the board and focusing on Native

American issues and causes, grew from three in 1973 to thirty-two in 1994. They are greater in number than any other racial/ethnic identity-based alternative. The grantmakers include twenty-two Native foundations and ten funds in nonfoundation organizations. Together, they granted $3.5 million in 1994 for Native causes and scholarships. In addition, the American Indian College Fund gave $5 million to the American Indian Higher Education Consortium for scholarships (Ewen and Wollock 1996).

5. The growth in Native grantmakers has occurred because Native leaders see an interrelationship between the loss of Native culture and the great poverty among Indian people. According to Alexander Ewen and Jeffrey Wollock, Native leaders "believe that the solutions are to be found in Native traditions, though often in combination with Western tools and concepts. For these grant-makers, Native people themselves must become involved in implementing the solutions needed to create lasting, functioning societies." Most Native foundations and funds "do not have endowments and every year must raise the money" for their grants. However, "much of the funds used by these foundations and [funds] come from other foundations and many Native organizations serve mainly as conduits for foundation funds" (ibid., 3).

6. *Hispanic funds* and funds for other identity-based groups are the newest of the alternatives. There are six Hispanic funds, which granted $0.9 million in 1997. Three of these raise money through the workplace, and three operate as field-of-interest funds within community foundations. Five work in concert with United Ways, while the other operates independently. All were created because traditional "philanthropy has largely ignored Latinos," as Henry Ramos and Gabriel Kasper explained. They wrote further that there was "a relative

dearth of institutional vehicles through which to capture and leverage available community giving resources in ways that are culturally acceptable" (Ramos and Kasper 1999, 167).

7. *Asian Pacific American funds*, like Hispanic funds, focus on an identity-based group. In 1997, there were three of these foundations granting a total of $285,000. All three raise money through workplace donations and were founded to fill a gap in Asian Pacific American funding options.

Alternative funds provide an important voice for minorities in American philanthropy. Although currently small in "dollar" sources, they are growing and are expected to become even more significant in the future.

Robert O. Bothwell

References and further reading

Bothwell, R. O. 2001. "Alternative Funding Institutions Have Become Serious Competitors with Mainline Foundations in Funding Progressive Social Change." Unpublished paper, Washington, DC: National Committee for Responsive Philanthropy.

———. 2002. "What Are the Alternatives?" *Foundation News and Commentary*, May/June, 43–45.

Bothwell, R. O., and D. Delany. 1998. *Charity at the Workplace, 1997*. Washington, DC: National Committee for Responsive Philanthropy.

Cunningham, N. 2000. Letter to Robert Bothwell from the Executive Director, The Working Group on Lesbian and Gay Issues, June 12.

Ewen, A., and J. Wollock. 1996. *Native Americans in Philanthropy: Survey of Grant Giving by American Indian Foundations and Organizations*. Lumberton, NC: Native Americans in Philanthropy.

Hanft, R. 2000. "Estimate of Grants to Groups and Issues Affecting Lesbians, Gay Men, Bisexual and Transgender Persons." Unpublished statistics. New York: Funding Exchange.

Ramos, H. A. J., and G. Kasper. 1999. "Latinos and Community Funds: A Comparative Overview and Assessment of Latino Philanthropic Self-Help Initiatives. In *Nuevos Senderos: Reflections on Hispanics and Philanthropy.*, edited by D. Campoamor, W. A. Diaz, and H. A. J. Ramos. Houston: Arte Publico Press, University of Houston.

Women's Funding Network. 2001. *Annual Report 2000*. San Francisco: Women's Funding Network.

Altruism

Altruism is often defined as unselfish action for the welfare of others without regard for oneself. It is often contrasted with "egoism," regard for one's own interest. Although Auguste Comte and his followers are usually credited with coining the French term *altruisme* in the nineteenth century, many scholars have traced helping behavior, more commonly referred to as altruistic behavior, to classical and even to prehistoric times.

Religious traditions have been active in promoting altruism. Most religious traditions also speak of the need for effective care of the self in order to be able to be of assistance to the larger good. In the Jewish Torah and the Christian Gospels, there are many references to loving our neighbors as we love ourselves. In addition, virtue theories, which dominated philosophy up to the Enlightenment, dwelled on the importance of being charitable and concerned about others. It is the utilitarian movement, however, that introduced new understandings of benevolence and beneficence that served as precedents for the modern term introduced by Comte. For humanists, relieving the suffering of others can provide meaning to the giver and contribute to the common good as well as to one's own happiness.

Psychologists Carl Rogers and Abraham Maslow have considered it to be part of human nature to act altruistically. Conversely, authors such as Thomas Hobbes and Sigmund Freud maintained that human nature is individualistic, selfish, and aggressive. During most of the twentieth century, arguments by behavioral psychologists who questioned whether individuals could really behave altruistically (since natural determination would cause one to act only in one's self-interest) dominated much of the scholarly debate. However, John Dewey (1976), Howard Margolis (1982), E. O. Wilson (1975), and Herbert Simon (1990), among others, have argued that both altruism and egoism are considerations in determining social choice and thus are bundled together in the human condition. Wilson and Simon also argued that altruism is rooted in the human trait of social receptivity and thus is in fact compatible with natural selection.

John Dovidio (1984) noted more than 1,000 empirical studies published on altruism between 1962 and 1982, and one could probably identify another 800 or so articles, books, and studies on the topic since then. Many of these studies have focused on the development of prosocial behavior as a form of altruistic behavior. Others have derived models of voluntary behavior and motivations for volunteering. Still other studies have focused on how such behavior is beneficial to one's physical and mental health.

Philanthropic behavior has come to be viewed as the result of a combination of altruism and egoism jointly at work. This is particularly true in contemporary giving in the United States. Karen Wright made a distinction between giving in the United States and in the United Kingdom, arguing that in Britain philanthropy still carries the disparaging notion of Victorian "do-gooderism and is often seen as elitist, patronizing, morally judgmental, and ineffective as well as old-fashioned" (Wright 2001, 400). Thus, in the United Kingdom people give to things that benefit others, she said, whereas Americans favor causes from which they will gain more personal benefit.

Acting altruistically does not always guarantee positive or philanthropic results. Likewise, acting in one's self-interest does not always produce bad or misanthropic results. Philanthropy is best understood as a combination of the two motivations, or perhaps as self-interest rightly understood.

Dwight F. Burlingame

See also Moral Philosophy and Philanthropy

References and further reading

Dewey, John. [1899–1924] 1976. "Altruism and Egoism." Reprinted in *John Dewey: The Middle Works, 1899–1924*, vol. 6, edited by Jo Ann Boydston, 368–369. Carbondale: Southern Illinois University Press.

Dovidio, John F. 1984. "Helping Behavior and Altruism: An Empirical and Conceptual Overview." In *Advances in Experimental Social Psychology*, edited by L. Berkowitz, 361–427. New York: Academic Press.

Margolis, Howard. 1982. *Selfishness, Altruism, and Rationality: A Theory of Social Choice*. Chicago: University of Chicago Press.

Simon, Herbert. 1990. "A Mechanism for Social Selection and Successful Altruism." *Science*, December 21, 1665–1668.

Wilson, Edward. 1975. *Sociobiology*. Cambridge: Harvard University Press.

Wright, K. 2001. "Generosity vs. Altruism: Philanthropy and Charity in the United States and United Kingdom."

Voluntas: International Journal of Voluntary and Nonprofit Organizations 12, no. 4 (December): 399–416.

American Association of Fundraising Counsel (AAFRC) and AAFRC Trust for Philanthropy

The American Association of Fundraising Counsel (AAFRC) was founded in 1935 to "advance professional and ethical standards in philanthropic fundraising consulting and to promote philanthropy in general" (AAFRC Trust for Philanthropy 2001, 5). In a field that was sometimes mistrusted and misunderstood, early leaders of the first fundraising consulting firms sought to ensure that their contributions to the field would be both positive and professional. Therefore, the AAFRC's first act of business as an association involved the creation of what is known today as the Standards of Practice and Professional Code of Ethics. In the 1980s, through collaboration with the Association for Healthcare Philanthropy (AHP), the Council for Advancement and Support of Education (CASE), and the Association of Fundraising Professionals (AFP), the association developed the Donor Bill of Rights. Both documents are widely accepted and used by professionals in the fundraising field and must be adhered to by member organizations.

AAFRC member firms, diverse both professionally and geographically, are held to strict practice standards and conduct extensive client reviews as part of a recredentialing process that occurs every three years. Membership standards include completing a letter of intent and formal application as well as obtaining high recommendations by peer organizations.

In order to "promote philanthropy in general," the association first published *Giving USA* in 1955 as a public service. Published annually, *Giving USA* provides an overview of giving trends, statistical analysis of the sources, recipients, and locations of charitable giving, and a list of AAFRC member firms. In 1985, association leaders Arthur D. Raybin, John Grenzebach, and Charles E. Lawson incorporated the AAFRC Trust for Philanthropy in order to fulfill the public service goals of the association and to commemorate the fiftieth anniversary of the creation of the AAFRC. That same year, the trust took over pub-

lishing *Giving USA,* and in 2001 the trust contracted with the Center on Philanthropy at Indiana University to research, write, and edit *Giving USA.*

AAFRC strives to offer its member firms the most current information and research on fundraising. From April 1955 until April 1973, *The Bulletin of the American Fund Raising Counsel, Inc.,* offered irregular reports on governmental legislation concerning charitable giving, ongoing fundraising campaigns, and personnel changes within the member firms. In May 1973, the publication name was changed to *Giving USA* and the irregular publication began to focus on broader trends in American philanthropy. In February 1982, the title became *Fund Raising Review* and there was added emphasis on major articles and speeches in the field in addition to the national trends. Since January 1988, the publication has been called *Giving USA Update.* Published four times a year, it highlights trends and practical information in the fundraising field.

Aubrey Abbott Patterson

References and further reading
American Association of Fundraising Counsel (AAFRC), http://www.aafrc.org (cited October 3, 2001).
American Association of Fundraising Counsel (AAFRC) Trust for Philanthropy. 2001. *Giving USA 2001: The Annual Report on Philanthropy for the Year 2000.* Indianapolis: AAFRC.

American Council on Gift Annuities (ACGA)

The American Council on Gift Annuities (ACGA) was formed in 1927 as the Committee on Gift Annuities for the purpose of providing educational and other support services to American charitable organizations engaging in planned giving techniques, specifically gift annuities. Formed as a voluntary association at a time when churches and other charitable institutions were utilizing the charitable gift annuity as a means to raise funds, it was incorporated under Internal Revenue Code (IRC) 501(c)(3) in 1993 and renamed in 1994.

The goal of the ACGA is to "promote philanthropy, primarily by means of the charitable gift annuity" (http://www.acga-web.org/faqs.html). A charitable gift annuity is a method of gift making, contractual in nature, in which the donor makes a large gift to a charitable organization in return for a life income. In this arrangement, the charitable organization agrees to pay a donor a fixed sum of money for life at a predetermined rate in return for a transfer of cash, stock, or other property, including real property. The donor is referred to as an "annuitant" or "beneficiary," and the donated or gifted property becomes part of the charity's assets. Payments to the annuitant from the charitable organization are backed by all of the charity's assets and not just by the property contributed.

Prior to the founding of ACGA, churches and other charitable organizations independently set their own gift annuity rates. This method soon became problematic as organizations began to compete with one another to offer more attractive payout rates, thus reducing the average gift to the organization at the end of the annuitant's life, known as the "residuum." Dr. George A. Huggins, a professional actuary and active Episcopalian, sought to address this problem and helped to found the ACGA under the auspices of the Federal Council of the Churches of Christ in America.

ACGA was formed for two purposes: first, to study and recommend the range of gift annuity payout rates that would be beneficial to both donors and charitable organizations, and second, to study the appropriate form for contracts, the amounts and types of reserve funds needed to fulfill a charitable organization's obligation to donors, and legislation affecting gift annuity programs. The first purpose was important to philanthropy because more standardized rates encouraged donors to give based on a charitable organization's mission rather than on competitive payout rates. The second served to educate charitable organizations about their obligations to donors and also gave a voice to charitable organizations regarding legislative policies affecting charitable giving and gift annuity programs.

ACGA is supported by approximately 1,200 charities that provide financial support as "sponsors." Most of these charities are involved in raising funds through charitable gift annuities and other planned giving methods. ACGA is governed by an eighteen-member volunteer board of directors that conducts an annual review of current payout rates using a formula with variables such as asset allocation of cash, stocks, and bonds; total returns of assets; an assumption of a 50 percent residual at the death of the annuitant(s); annual cost for issuing the agreements, making payments, and providing necessary reports to annuitants as well as to federal and state governments; and mortality rates (provided by an independent actuarial firm) to determine any changes that are advisable. Once approved, these new rates are published and become effective on July 1 of each year. In addition to publishing recommended gift annuity rates, ACGA provides information about state regulations for charitable gift annuities.

In 1991, the ACGA and the National Committee on Planned Giving (NCPG) adopted the *Model Standards of Practice for the Charitable Gift Planner*. Revised in 1999, these standards encourage responsible gift planning by all gift planners, including gift planning officers, nonprofit fundraising consultants, financial planners, accountants, attorneys, life insurance agents, and other financial consultants. The ten guiding principles include the following:

1. Primacy of philanthropic motivation
2. Explanation of tax implications
3. Full disclosure
4. Compensation
5. Competence and professionalism
6. Consultation with independent advisers
7. Consultation with charities
8. Description and representation of gift
9. Full compliance
10. Public trust

The goal of these principles is to also encourage professionals from various fields to work together to ensure that gifts are structured in such a way as to achieve a balance between the donor's interests and the organization's mission.

ACGA holds a biennial education conference with a focus in three areas: administration of gift annuity programs, introductory education for new planned giving officers, and continuing education for experienced planned giving officers. ACGA works closely with NCPG and shares expertise and office space with this organization in Indianapolis, Indiana.

Gretchen C. Gordon

References and further reading

American Council on Gift Annuities (ACGA), http://www.acga-web.org (cited July 28, 2002).

Baas, Charles A. 1991. *Committee on Gift Annuities: A History*. New York: self-published.

White, Douglas E. 1995. *The Art of Planned Giving: Understanding Donors and the Culture of Giving*. New York: Wiley.

American Institute of Certified Public Accountants

See Accountability

American Institute of Philanthropy (AIP)

The American Institute of Philanthropy (AIP), "a nonprofit charity watchdog and information service," was incorporated in 1992 and is currently headquartered in Bethesda, Maryland. Its mission "is to maximize the effectiveness of every dollar contributed to charity by providing donors with the information they need to make more informed giving decisions" (American Institute of Philanthropy).

Serving a national audience, AIP is a tax-exempt organization under Internal Revenue Code (IRC) 501(c)(3). Daniel Borochoff, founder of the organization and president of the five-member board of directors, has a master's degree in business administration from Indiana University and worked for five years at the National Charities Information Bureau prior to starting AIP. AIP also has two full-time and up to four part-time employees.

AIP's goals are the following: "to research and evaluate the efficiency, accountability, and governance of nonprofit organizations; to educate the public about the importance of wise giving; to inform the public of wasteful or unethical practices of nonprofits and give recognition to highly effective and ethical charities; to advise AIP members and conduct special investigations and evaluations of nonprofits; and to expand and redefine its programs periodically to meet the continuing challenge of keeping the contributor informed" (American Institute of Philanthropy).

The organization's main activity is publishing a quarterly newsletter, *AIP Charity Rating Guide &*

Watchdog Report. The guide lists information on the financial operations of more than 400 national charities. AIP rates these charities based on financial information gathered from annual reports, audited financial statements, and the Internal Revenue Service Form 990, with Schedule A, where applicable.

AIP considers three factors in determining its rating. First, it looks at the percentage of total expenses spent on the charity's purpose. For AIP, 60 percent or better is reasonable for most charities. Second, it calculates the cost to raise $100. For most organizations, this figure should be $35 or less. Finally, AIP examines the years of available assets. This factor considers how long a charity can continue to operate at current levels without additional fundraising. AIP views favorably an organization with available reserves of three years or less.

In addition to the quarterly guide, AIP operates a Web site, http://www.charitywatch.org, to teach donors about AIP and to provide articles and information to assist them in making informed giving decisions.

Andrea Pactor

References and further reading

American Institute of Philanthropy (AIP), http://www.charitywatch.org.

———. 2001. *AIP Charity Rating Guide and Watchdog Report*, May.

Goss, Kristen A. 1993. "New Charity Watchdog Vows to Tell Donors What They Really Want to Know." *The Chronicle of Philanthropy*, November 16, 31.

GuideStar, http://www.guidestar.org.

Roha, Ronaleen R. "Giving Back: A Friendlier Way to Check on Charities' Finances." *Exempt Organization Tax Review* 9 (3): 520–521.

American Prospect Research Association

See Association of Professional Researchers for Advancement (APRA)

American Red Cross

The American Red Cross, established on May 21, 1881, by Clara Barton in Washington, D.C., is a nonprofit organization devoted to disaster relief, biomedical services, health and safety, and community services. Its mission statement reads as follows: "The

Clara Barton, well known as a battlefield nurse during the American Civil War, dispensed nearly $2 million in humanitarian aid during her tenure as president of the American Red Cross. (National Archives)

American Red Cross, a humanitarian organization led by volunteers, guided by its Congressional Charter and the Fundamental Principles of the International Red Cross Movement, will provide relief to victims of disasters and help people prevent, prepare for, and respond to emergencies" (American Red Cross 2002). Barton brought the Red Cross movement to the United States after her travels in Europe during the Franco-Prussian War. From the efforts of Jean Henri Dunant, a future Nobel Peace Prize winner, "the International Red Cross and Red Crescent movement was founded in Geneva, Switzerland, in 1863, to provide nonpartisan care to the wounded and sick in times of war" (ibid.). The United States Congress granted the American Red Cross its first charter in 1900.

Two of the first disaster relief efforts of the American Red Cross were responses to the Michigan forest fires of 1881 and the flooding of the Mississippi River in 1882. In true grassroots fashion, the national headquarters appealed for assistance from local societies, who responded with donations of money and supplies.

Barton's role in the early stages of the American Red Cross was known to be its greatest strength as well as its greatest weakness. She directed the organization with all her energies but was reluctant to relinquish control. This inhibited the growth of the organization and created problems with public trust. Owing to the lack of uniformity of services and public pressure, Barton resigned from the American Red Cross in 1904.

It was during World War I that the American Red Cross experienced significant growth, increasing from just 562 chapters to 3,724 chapters nationwide and from 500,000 to more than 31 million members, including children and adults. Although the United States did not enter the war until 1917, the American Red Cross began its official wartime service by sending a mercy ship to provide soldier assistance in 1914. During the war, the American Red Cross provided "two out of every three navy nurses and four out of every five army nurses, including the first African-American nurses," (ibid.) who served as part of the Army and Navy Nurse Corps.

As well as responding to natural and manmade disasters, the American Red Cross serves the needs of the biomedical industry. "In 1948, the American Red Cross established a program to provide blood and its components to civilians without charge, and this program produces nearly half the blood collected in the United States" ("Red Cross, American," 1976). In fiscal year 2002, the American Red Cross "collected 6.3 million units of blood from over 4 million donors, making it the nation's single largest blood supplier" (GuideStar 2002). Today, the American Red Cross biomedical services include blood, plasma, and tissue services as well as research in "biomedical science, blood safety, plasma-derived therapeutics, and transfusion technology" (American Red Cross 2002).

The volunteer board of directors for the American Red Cross has fifty members, thirty of whom are elected by chapter delegates. It has more than 34,000 full-time staff members and some 1,175,000 total volunteers. For fiscal year 2001, the American Red Cross had total revenues of $2,711,606,718 and total expenditures of $2,702,061,488.

The American Red Cross has not existed without challenges. In the 1980s, the organization exposed millions of people to a blood supply contaminated by HIV, hepatitis, and other infectious and deadly diseases. New safeguards were instituted to protect the blood supply as more information became available.

The American Red Cross has also encountered a crisis in the management of its Liberty Fund, collected since September 11, 2001. Originally, it had planned to spend nearly half of the fund to build up blood supplies or prepare for possible future terrorist attacks. Due to public unrest, the organization changed its policy and agreed to spend the entire $543 million to benefit victims of the terrorist attacks.

Emily S. McQuade

See also Barton, Clara; U.S. Sanitary Commission
References and further reading

American Red Cross, http://www.redcross.org (cited October 24, 2002).

Barton, David H. 1995. *Clara Barton: In the Service of Humanity*. Westport, CT: Greenwood.

Bequette, Cathe. 1990. "Volunteers on Volunteering: A Narrative Analysis of Interviews with Red Cross Disaster Volunteers." Unpublished master's thesis, Regent University, Virginia Beach, VA.

"Clara Barton." 1997–1998. In *American Eras.* 8 vols. Farmington Hills, MI: Gale Group.

"Red Cross, American." 1976. In *Dictionary of American History.* 7 vols. Farmington Hills, MI: Gale Group.

GuideStar. "American National Red Cross," http://www.guidestar.org (cited October 24, 2002).

Reitman, Judith. 1996. *Bad Blood: Crisis in the American Red Cross.* New York: Kensington.

Sun, Lena H. 2001. "Red Cross to Give All Funds to Victims; Contrite Charity Changes Course on Sept. 11 Donations." *Washington Post*, November 15, A1.

Anonymous Giving

Anonymous giving is, literally, the concealment of the name or identity of a donor. It is one of the most ancient and esteemed philanthropic practices. By avoiding publicity and eschewing credit for the gift, the anonymous benefactor has long been celebrated as someone whose motives are more purely altruistic than those of the donor who makes gifts openly, expecting public acknowledgment or praise.

Yet anonymous giving is fraught with complexity. It can alter the fundamental nature of gift giving, which so often has been a means for creating a bond between giver and receiver and a way of solidifying social ties. Giving is considered a beneficial and praiseworthy act, and thus an individual's generosity ought to serve as an example to others. Contrary to this, anonymous giving dissolves the social connections inherent in the gift relationship and may conceal much more than the donor's name, perhaps hiding motives and sources of wealth or helping the donor to evade accountability for the gift and its consequences.

Despite its hazards, anonymous giving has a long history. For many ancient commentators, the value of anonymity lay in the simple fact that the gift did not have to be reciprocated. The recipient was not indebted to the donor in any way. Anonymity was thus a practical mechanism for easing some of the social discomfort intrinsic to the gift relationship, especially when the donor and recipient were not equals.

Writing in the first century C.E., the Stoic philosopher Seneca was among the ancient writers to weigh the advantages and disadvantages of anonymous giving. He knew that such gifts were likely to be infrequent and made only in the most exceptional circumstances. He reasoned that an anonymous gift was best used to keep the recipient from experiencing embarrassment or from feeling so indebted to the donor that resentment would arise. Moreover, for Seneca and his fellow Stoics, anonymity provided a means of avoiding the distractions of either praise or blame for one's actions. Acting anonymously, a donor could not be accused of merely cultivating the appearance of generosity or of currying political favor through gift giving.

Anonymity also holds a special place within the major religious traditions of the world. In a Talmudic story reputedly from the time of Herod, Rabbi Yannai reprimanded a wealthy man for publicly giving a large coin to a poor man, telling the donor that it is better not to give at all than to give in a way that puts a poor man to shame. Christians are reminded in Jesus' Sermon on the Mount that charitable actions should always be done in the proper spirit. Jesus asked his followers to give alms without making an ostentatious display of their giving and linked that duty to the humble acts of fasting and prayer (Matt. 6: 1–4). Anonymity is also praised in the Koran: "If you disclose your Zakat that is well, but if you conceal it, and give it to the poor, that is better for you. Allah will forgive you some of your sins" (Sura 2: 271).

In the twelfth century, Maimonides elaborated upon old and familiar Jewish practices, ranking eight levels of charity in the Mishneh Torah (10.1, 7–14). The highest form of almsgiving was a gift, loan, partnership, or assistance in finding work that would enable the poor person to escape the necessity of begging. Maimonides then carefully distinguished various forms of anonymous giving in the next highest tiers. In the second tier, he praised the person "who gives alms to the poor in such a way that he does not know to whom he has given, nor does the poor man know from whom he has received." This is the purest form of anonymity. Neither giver nor receiver knows the other. It was a form of anonymity institutionalized within temples, where an office, variously called the Chamber of Secret Gifts or Chamber of the Silent, was created for donors to give and for the poor to receive distributions discreetly. Maimonides then proceeded to distinguish and to rank third and fourth degrees of giving: alms given so that the recipient does not know his benefactor and alms given so that the recipient knows the benefactor but the donor does not know the recipient (Mishneh Torah 10.8–10).

For Christian commentators, anonymity was primarily a means of assuring that alms were given with the appropriate spiritual motivations. Early Christian charitable practices differed widely from place to place but tended to be centered on collections during the worship service and distributions to the poor by church officials rather than by the individual donors. This mechanism, like any method of aggregating and distributing resources through intermediaries, was conducive to anonymity, protecting the privacy of both donor and recipient.

From St. Augustine in the fourth and fifth centuries to St. Francis in the thirteenth, theologians and preachers offered continuing reminders that alms were to be given humbly and without seeking public credit. St. Augustine sought to disengage charity from a concern with social relationships and to redirect it toward the donor's relationship with God. St. Francis preached that charitable acts were undermined when the donor made a public display of

St. Augustine (Archivo Iconografico, S.A./Corbis)

virtue; he believed that the true charitable bond was the private relationship between the donor and God and had nothing to do with public recognition or earthly rewards for giving.

In the sixteenth century, Protestant reformers criticized the corruption of almsgiving in the late Middle Ages and reiterated earlier church teachings about avoiding ostentation and display. Martin Luther echoed the very words of the Sermon on the Mount, saying "sound no trumpet before you, as the hypocrites do in the synagogues and in the streets, that they may be praised by men. . . . (W)hen you give alms, do not let your left hand know what your right hand is doing, so that your alms may be in secret; and your Father who sees in secret will reward you." Anonymity was a means of assuring that charitable motivations were pure, since, according to Luther, "giving alms in secret means that the heart is not ostentatious, but is moved to contribute freely whether it makes an impression and gains the praise of the people or whether everyone despises or profanes it" (Luther 1956, 130, 136).

The mechanism of the Common Chest as the recipient of church income, the placement of alms boxes in the front of churches, and the renewed emphasis on passing a collection box or sack at weddings, funerals, and other religious services were Protestant practices that sought to return to the presumed habits of the early Christian church. They were the reformers' answer to the complicated and abusive system of indulgences and other spiritual rewards that had corrupted late medieval charitable activities. Protestant practice sought to prevent donors from seeking individual credit and reward for their donations, ensuring that alms were given in a spirit of piety rather than out of hypocritical calculation.

No modern or secularized concept of anonymity has emerged to replace these older religious doctrines. In the modern world, anonymity seems primarily to have become a practical decision, a matter of tactical choice more often than of deeply held spiritual conviction. Anonymous giving has not attracted a great deal of scholarly attention, and collecting data on it has proved difficult. Consequently, the extent of anonymous giving in the United States can only be crudely estimated and the motivations behind it only sketchily understood.

A survey of development officers conducted in the early 1990s found that 66 percent of the responding institutions received less than 1 percent of their contributed income anonymously and 17 percent received only 1–5 percent of their income anonymously (Cicerchi and Weskerna 1991). Most of the anonymous gifts were small. However, 20 percent of the 563 respondents to the survey said that at one time or another they had been involved with donors making anonymous gifts of $1 million or more. The report cited a separate analysis of publicly reported gifts in excess of $1 million that found that 1.3 percent of the large donations were made anonymously.

Total anonymity is rare in contemporary philanthropy. Of the largest gifts received by institutions, development officers reported that only 4 percent were completely anonymous, the donor unknown and untraceable. In the modern world, anonymity is usually only a relative matter, with a board chairman and chief executive typically aware of the donor's identity and perhaps other key board members, senior development staff, and fundraising consultants in the know as well. Sometimes contemporary anonymity is merely a matter of keeping the donor's name off public listings of supporters or withholding the donor's identity for a certain period of time. Often, a donor has given previously and publicly to an institution but prefers not to be associated with a particular donation at a particular moment. A board member and loyal donor, for example, might want to increase a gift to an institution and to do so as an anonymous challenge to fellow board members.

These varying degrees of anonymity hint at the diversity of motives among the donors who seek to remain anonymous. Their motivations are rarely singular; almost always they are mixed and complex. When development officers were surveyed about their perceptions of donor motives, they seldom focused on a single reason for the anonymous gift. Far and away the most frequently cited as the donor's primary desire was the hope of minimizing solicitations from other organizations, a reason mentioned about half the time by development staff. Other primary motivations were mentioned much less frequently. Religious convictions seemed to motivate only about 5 percent of the gifts. Approximately 5 percent were motivated by the desire to keep information about the gift from heirs or other family members. And the same percentage seemed to be motivated by a simple sense of modesty and a desire for privacy.

Conversations with donors themselves have provided elaboration on these motivations and suggested a complex mixture of both instrumental and personal reasons for remaining anonymous. Paul Schervish (1994) interviewed 130 donors and found that 35 had something to say about anonymity, whether they practiced it or not. Among the practical reasons for remaining anonymous was the desire to reduce what donors considered the most bothersome aspects of philanthropy, especially aggressive solicitations. Donors sometimes expressed the desire to conceal the fact of their wealth, to deflect embarrassment from particular gifts, to retain the simplicity of their modest lifestyle, to increase their philanthropic effectiveness, and to be able to observe the impact of their philanthropy more critically and accurately from behind the veil of anonymity.

Those who spoke of anonymity in ethical and moral terms expressed the hope that they could transcend the corrupting lures of their wealth, counter their feelings of superiority and decrease the status differential between donor and recipient, and prevent the recipient from feeling embarrassed. Some said that they wanted to pursue their philanthropy anonymously because it seemed psychologically healthier than to do so publicly.

The reasons donors give for remaining anonymous also reveal some of the arguments against the practice. In avoiding public scrutiny, the anonymous donor may also be avoiding public accountability. In providing anonymous financial help, the donor is setting no public example of generosity. In choosing to remain out of sight, the donor may also be limiting opportunities to volunteer and to provide institutional leadership. Nevertheless, this venerable practice survives as a modern philanthropic tactic even if it is no longer so widely celebrated as a charitable ideal.

James Allen Smith

References and further reading
Cicerchi, Eleanor T., and Amy Weskerna. 1991. "Survey on Anonymous Giving." Indianapolis: Center on Philanthropy, Indiana University.
Luther, Martin. 1956. *Works*, vol. 21. St. Louis: Concordia.
Schervish, Paul T. 1994. "The Sound of One Hand Clapping: The Case for and against Anonymous Giving." *Voluntas* 5 (1): 1–26.
Seneca. 1935. *De Beneficiis* (On Benefits). In *Moral Essays*, vol. 3. Cambridge: Harvard University Press (Loeb Classical Library).

Asian American Philanthropy

Asian Americans give to and volunteer for numerous nonprofit charitable vehicles. Myriad donor stories, most of which were obtained for this article as primary sources, result in a descriptive model of philanthropic behavior that starts with strategies for survival, moves through helping the less fortunate, and then develops into community investment as Asian Americans achieve financial stability, wealth, and a sense of permanence and identity with their communities in the United States.

What Is Asian America?

The experiences of Asian American communities in the United States influenced the way various subethnic groups created and used voluntary associations and pooled their funds to create community stability. Describing Asian America is challenging because it comprises many communities that defy generalization even among Asian Americans themselves, let alone by outsiders. It is dynamic and constantly changing. In addition to a variety of cultural, language, and religious backgrounds, increasingly diverse economic classifications and immigrant/citizenship status definitions influence the makeup of Asian America. In particular, the rapid increase in immigration that began when the Immigration Act of 1965 lifted restrictive Asian quotas, and other subsequent immigration regulations, increasingly favored specific, highly skilled professions and occupations. Increasing political and economic instability in many Asian countries also influenced immigration patterns. Compounding this complexity for mainstream America has been the economic growth of several Asian nations, with the resulting small, but significant presence of transnational Asians of wealth.

Asians' reasons for coming to America range from seeking political asylum or religious freedom to career advancement in the sciences, technology, and healthcare professions and from escaping war or poverty to building businesses or expanding family fortunes. Each immigrant wave and group also had different experiences with discrimination and acceptance by the majority U.S. population. Some groups, such as Japanese, Chinese, and Filipinos, some of whom immigrated as early as the mid-1800s as contract workers, migrant farmers, and laborers, as well as more recent Southeast Asians and South Asians, experienced abject discrimination and even repeated racist violence. Some elite groups have almost entirely escaped racial or cultural bias (until the campaign financing scandals of the 1990s broke) and often have difficulty identifying with those groups that have legitimate complaints. Others are perplexed by subtle "glass ceiling" experiences. No group or individual seems to fully avoid the "perpetual foreigner" syndrome.

Furthermore, the diversity of Asian America is growing with its size. Through each decade since the 1970s, the Asian American population almost doubled. By 1990, it reached 7 million, or 3 percent of the total U.S. population, and by 2000, figures close to 11 million. Projections estimate that Asian Americans will constitute as much as 10 percent of the total U.S. population by the year 2050. The Asian American population has surpassed the size of the Jewish population and is "catching up" to African Americans. The rate of population growth is faster than that of Latinos. Although Americans of Asian descent are truly a minority in this country, by comparison it is often said that half the world's population can trace its lineage to the continent of Asia. The growth of the Asian American population in this country, however, is primarily due to immigration.

Because of this diversity, even as the Asian American category has become commonly used, there are many Americans of Asian descent reluctant to use the all-encompassing multiethnic category, preferring cultural identification by their national origin or subethnic group rather than by racial categorization. They trace growing usage of this term to the convenience needs of "outsiders" (particularly government agencies, funders, academics, and the media) and to the political needs of "insiders" (primarily community activists and the politically oriented) to show greater solidarity with increased numbers. However, some scholars have observed that Asian Americans have multiple identities. Depending on the social, cultural, political, or economic situation or circumstance, even those who most often identify themselves as Chinese, Korean, or Vietnamese American may also self-identify as Asian American or simply American when appropriate. This is critical in understanding the patterns of voluntary associations and nonprofit groups that Asian Americans join, as they identify with multiple groups at various times for various reasons.

For all their differences, it is especially important to articulate those shared experiences that influence voluntary participatory activity, specifically charitable giving. For the most part, although there are growing numbers of American-born generations of Asian Americans (particularly among ethnic groups that began immigrating as early as the mid-1800s), Asian America is still largely an immigrant community. In 1990, approximately 68.2 percent of Asian Americans were foreign-born, with a high of 93.9 percent among Laotians and a low of 28.4 percent among the Japanese.

How these families and groups create home and community by creating, supporting, and utilizing nonprofit voluntary structures, both formal and informal, is illuminating. Need, identification, social access, and the options available to them at various stages of stability and acculturation influence the organizational structures that will aid them in creating community, regardless of how they define community.

The Descriptive Model: Strategies for Building Home and Community

The descriptive model that emerges from interviews with Asian Americans is one that follows a primarily immigrant population along a continuum of philanthropic motivations that moves from survival to help to investing. Specifically, the progression moves from survival of family and community and the need to share resources, to the impulse to help by giving to the less fortunate, and finally to a stage of building or strengthening community infrastructure by investing. Donors, nonprofit executives, and fundraisers used terms such as "surviving," "helping," and "investing" voluntarily in fairly similar contexts across ethnicity, economic background, and level of acculturation.

Although the suggested continuum of philanthropic motivations seems to be developmental, it should not be construed as a proposal of mutually exclusive, strictly sequenced stages. Several Asian Americans appeared to be in two different frames of mind regarding their philanthropy. However, they were consistent with the motivational terms used and the vehicles they employed under those circumstances. It was quite common to hear a donor speaking about relying on the social network and services of an ethnic voluntary association as well as "giving back" or "helping" the community through an ethnic-specific or Asian American nonprofit. It was also common to hear donors speaking about an obligation to "help" as well as an obligation to invest in the future of a given community. Donors did not, however, speak about surviving and investing during the same period of their lives, and they almost never described investing in major museums or universities at the same time they were talking about "sharing" resources with fellow voluntary association members. It also seems that Asian Americans do not refer to the financial and in-kind contributions shared during their "survival" stages as philanthropy. Although they refer to "helping" the community and other disadvantaged communities as "charity" or as "giving back," the somewhat lofty term of "philanthropy" is reserved for those major investments in the future of institutions—most often, but not exclusively, mainstream institutions and noncommunity causes. The term "obligation" was used throughout descriptions about mutual sharing, helping those less advantaged, or investing in permanent nonprofit structures.

To progress along this continuum of motivations, an Asian American must reach certain levels of confidence in his or her perception of stability and the stability of his or her family. Therefore, it appears from their stories that those donors who came to the United States with some family wealth, higher levels of education, and more social stability moved through this continuum much more rapidly than those who lacked these assets, sometimes skipping the "giving back" stage entirely.

Growing stability is often related to increasing age, with its related increases in disposable income and accumulation of assets (although because of the high presence of technology and communications entrepreneurs of Asian descent, many accumulate wealth at younger ages). For Asian Americans, a growing sense of stability is also related to increasing acculturation, which has several indicators. These indicators include birthplace, the ethnicity and culture of business and social circles, the community in which the Asian American grew up (that is, whether it was an Asian American ethnic enclave or the American majority culture), where he or she attended undergraduate college (in the United States or in Asia), language facility, and the more intangibles of personal ethnic and cultural identity.

Unlike European immigrant groups, which have been absorbed into the American character, some-

times seamlessly within a generation or two, Asian Americans are separated from the majority culture by additional stresses. The differences of race and the distance of "Far Eastern" cultures from Western sensibilities create greater obstacles to full assimilation, even when acculturation through education and profession have been successful. Therefore, many Asian Americans continue to have a strong need to find opportunities to socialize with co-ethnics and other Asian Americans even when they live and work with a high degree of cultural fluency in the mainstream community and economy.

Survival: Sharing Resources to Create a New Home

Whether the immigrant arrives with an empty pocket or with a family legacy of wealth back in Asia, and whether he or she comes with no English at all or from an English-speaking nation or colony, the early immigrant years are difficult. This first stage of the continuum is characterized by sharing resources—financial, emotional, informational, and skills-based—to survive. From interviews and casual "storytelling," it appears that most Asian immigrants consider life in the United States a "struggle" (even if better than the alternative of returning to the country of origin), and for many, if not for most, the struggle is for survival and some foothold on the economic ladder of opportunity. For some, it is a struggle to enter the elite of various professions. For a very few entrepreneurial individuals, it is a struggle for investment from elite business and banking circles.

In their isolation and struggle, Asian Americans create communities of shared need by sharing resources. For the working class, working poor, or most culturally isolated (by lack of facility with English, American customs, and occupational training), the mutual aid societies help remedy the loneliness and isolation. The myriad associations whose membership is defined not only by ethnicity but also by finer distinctions of village or province of origin, language dialect, surname or clan, or religion offer a way for social and economic peers to share information and financial, job-related, or in-kind resources. The giving and sharing is very personal and can be quite substantial relative to means. For some ethnic groups, particularly Koreans, Cambodians, and some South Asians, churches and temples serve dual purposes, providing a gathering place for socializing and a central point for sharing resources to improve the immediate conditions of those in need. The same was true for the early Japanese immigrants.

For Asian Americans who are in this "survival" frame of mind, the American notion of philanthropic generosity, which is to give to strangers, may seem somewhat odd, cold, and motivated by ego. One Asian American, for example, said, "Why is giving to those you don't know considered more generous than giving to those you know? How can I give to those I never met, when there are so many I know in need?" Indeed, what type of generosity places people you never met on a higher priority than your family, community, or neighbor? Some speculate, both inside and outside of Asian American circles, that Asian American informal philanthropy through numerous voluntary associations and faith-based organizations helps to account for the low levels of Asian American representation in American orphanages, jails, and public assistance rolls. It may also help account for the number of small businesses (such as groceries, shops, restaurants, manicure shops, and the like) and even large, high-tech companies that are started with relatively little access to mainstream forms of financing.

The Impulse to Help: Reaching Financial Stability

It would be simplistic and grossly misleading to say that Asian Americans share their good fortune only with their families, friends, and association members. Once they reach some personal critical level of financial stability, they frequently help others who are in greater need. The impulse to help, or "give back," is the second motivation on my proposed continuum. This stability, however, appears to be more a state of mind than an actual dollar amount. For Asians, it is not just measured in terms of one's own income but also in terms of the stability of the immediate and often the extended family. One cannot feel stable unless one's children, siblings, parents, cousins, aunts, uncles, nieces, and nephews are all stable. One does not have the luxury of following the impulse to help more distant causes when those within one's own cir-

cle of family and friends still need help. This "helping" motivation correlates with charitable giving from one with greater means and access to those in less fortunate circumstances. Because there is no realistic sense of return, it is more accurate to describe this type of philanthropy as "giving" rather than as "sharing."

The urge to help is motivated by highly emotional, deeply personal levels of compassion. One interviewee, when asked why she gives to charity, responded, "I give from the heart, not my brain. I even give to street people. It really slows me down on the way to work." This emotional trigger has its seeds in personal identification with either the type of person benefiting or the type of need. Why the hardship experiences of those transitioning from a survival state of mind to a more stable sense of well-being transforms into compassion in some and into bitterness in others is puzzling. But it appears that this transformation of hardship into compassion is a necessary antecedent for the "helping" impulse. It would be difficult to speculate on the reasons for those who do not give. Those who give, however, exhibit a high degree of empathy. The interviewees' levels of affluence, as well as their sense of stability, confidence, and self-possession, were striking. They truly were no longer in "need," which may have allowed them psychic space to identify with the plight of others.

For those who have more exposure and interaction with wider social and business circles, or those who do not come into direct contact with the less fortunate, the identification is more with the need and not necessarily the needy. The types of organizational structures used to facilitate this giving can again include family as conduits for more distant family members and indigenous voluntary associations. But the giving does not expect return, and it can be more structured because it is going to more distant circles of beneficiaries not always within the immediate social network.

The larger the cause, the larger the need for money, and therefore, within this "helping" state many Asian Americans become involved in more formally organized fundraising campaigns. Many of the indigenous alumni or professional associations are particularly active with organizing fundraising efforts not only on behalf of their alma maters in the country of origin but also for public works and other improvements.

Somewhere within the vast range of "helping" motivations, many Asian Americans begin utilizing more structured nonprofit vehicles. As the identification with the need becomes stronger than the relationships with specific beneficiaries, Asian Americans intuitively understand that the strategies for ameliorating the suffering require tools beyond the voluntary associations. The solutions do not just lie within the community but require effective interaction with government agencies, school systems, legal systems, and, most important, other communities beyond ethnic or racial boundaries.

Furthermore, for many American-born Asians, the mutual assistance associations are no longer an option because they no longer socialize with association members. Many second-generation Asian Americans, and most of the third generation and beyond, have little connection with the "old" country and no longer identify with the needs or with the people of concern to the mutual assistance groups.

For those who are no longer as concerned with human welfare issues of the community, but who now view themselves as members of viable American communities, interest in political empowerment and advocacy often leads to civic organizations and civil rights groups. These include the Japanese American Citizens League, Japanese American Associations, the Organization of Chinese Americans, and the many similar civic associations within the Filipino, Indian, Korean, Vietnamese, and other communities. Since the campus civil rights and identity movements of the 1970s, several Asian American social justice and legal aid organizations, such as the Asian American Legal Defense and Education Fund, the Asian Law Caucus, Asians for Equality, the Asian Pacific Legal Center of Southern California, have been created. Although the services of these organizations most often target social justice and legal rights issues of immigrant and indigent populations, the advocacy against racial and cultural stereotyping, "glass ceiling" issues, and anti-Asian violence cover all classes.

The Desire to Invest: Confidence, Permanence, and Philanthropy

The third motivation of the proposed descriptive model—to "invest" in charitable work—stems from a desire to build the ideal community. Instead of reacting to a need, the donor is creating his vision of the community within which he can imagine himself, his family, and his friends flourishing. Although several donors expressed this view in describing at least some of their voluntary and charitable giving activities, very few cited this category of motivating factors exclusively. It appears that the desire to invest requires a level of confidence in one's permanent residency in the United States as well as family financial stability. Those exhibiting these sentiments the most seemed to identify not so much with the sufferer or with the cause as with the facilitator of the remedy or solution.

"Investors" look for leadership and results in the charitable organizations they support, and although they did not explicitly articulate it, they seem to regard the nonprofit as a potential partner to their dream, not as a recipient of charity. They are looking for strong organizations to help them realize their visions for a better world. Two donors described their giving strategies in these contexts as "empowering."

It is no wonder, therefore, that the vehicles chosen within this realm of the continuum include not only the largest and most stable Asian American and ethnic nonprofits but also major mainstream institutions such as museums, universities, and research hospitals. The donors are not responding to crises and tragedies. Nor are they acting on personal sympathies with the downtrodden. Rather, they are either looking to obliterate the root causes of the problems or seeking ways to sustain the cultural and social values they wish to promote. They rarely choose indigenous religious organizations, voluntary associations, or grassroots nonprofits as vehicles for these philanthropic goals. They sometimes seek to promote their personal standing and social status within the ethnic, mainstream, or business communities. The community-based nonprofits and mutual aid associations have audiences that are too insular for their visions and too limited in their implementation tools to build investors' dreams.

"Investing" and "dreaming" donors were generally the most affluent and acculturated of those interviewed. More often than not, they were extremely successful entrepreneurs and self-made men and women. They were usually American by naturalization or by birth and had investments and significant assets that they were protecting for themselves and for their families. Their businesses generally dealt not only with Asian and Asian American communities but also with the wider community and, more important, depended on it for their continued success. Regardless of whether these investors felt comfortable within the elite settings of mainstream business and mega-philanthropies, they obviously had sufficient cultural fluency to work with these networks and systems to achieve their goals and personal satisfaction.

These donors also tended to be the oldest of those interviewed (sixties to early eighties). They had lived through a lot and survived, even though their backgrounds were quite different. A few were second-generation Japanese Americans who had fought for American democracy during World War II. They had lost their family savings and homes because of internment, but after more than thirty grueling years of toil, like a phoenix out of the ashes, they had slowly regained fortune and status. One investor, a Chinese American, came from an elite family that had taken refuge from war and political upheaval within the walls of top prep schools and universities and eventually built an investment firm. Another had escaped the poverty of the Philippines from a family of sixteen children and built a successful medical practice in Chicago, always including his family and others in his success.

If time of life, confidence with the outside community, and higher levels of wealth are predicting factors for reaching the "investment" period of philanthropy, it is no wonder that there were so few interviewees who exclusively fell into this part of the continuum of motivations. Asian America is still very young, in addition to being very "immigrant." Although Asian Americans on the whole have climbed several steps on the economic achievement scale, the major donor level of wealth is still relatively rare. In fact, among the Asian American donors interviewed, only a small handful had inherited their wealth. It will be fascinating to watch whether many more Asian Americans enter this stage of their giving and volunteering as their confidence and sense of permanence increase. Increasing rates of naturalization, voter registration, educational attainment, residency in mainstream neighborhoods, entrance into the professions, and the establishment of businesses suggest that more Asian Americans will soon be entering the investment stages of their lives in the United States.

Summary: Observations of the Descriptive Model

It would be simplistic to suggest that all Asian Americans begin at the survival stage and then progress smoothly to the helping and finally investing stages of philanthropic motivations. The community is much too complicated and diverse. Although most Asian Americans arrive in the United States in modest circumstances regardless of the family situation "back home," there are the many American-born and educated immigrants who do not necessarily start their philanthropic activity from a strong motivation for survival and mutual assistance. Supported by an education, professional skills, and language/cultural fluency, they have exposure and access to many more American systems. They may only use voluntary and religious organizations for social purposes and seek other opportunities to fulfill their charitable impulses. Whether one finds them in the "helping" mode or in the "investing" mode is most probably related to individual and family experience. For those whose families or close social networks experienced hardship and/or discrimination, it is likely that they developed strong feelings of identification with the disadvantaged and/or with the need. For the few who inherited wealth and whose family experience is more removed from the "hardship" stage, the "investment" motivation was more likely to be at work.

Upon reaching a level of financial, emotional, and social stability, many Asian Americans then have the capacity to reach out to "help" those still in need without any realistic expectation of commensurate return for themselves or their families. The individuals and groups they most often help and the level of help they give are probably related to the degree of identification with the social sphere and the particular need. The degree of identification is probably related to social access and exposure. Those with more access and exposure to outside communities are more likely to identify with the needs outside the family and community, particularly when they are similar, that is, immigrant rights, social justice, at-risk youth, and the like.

Finally, at the highest level of stability and confidence, when the individual perceives not only the self but the family as stable and flourishing, the Asian American has the luxury of attempting to realize his or her own vision of the ideal community. Although most of the Asian Americans interviewed who exhibited confidence in their American future were also quite affluent, it is most likely that the perception of wealth, not actual wealth, is key. They also tended to be older and more "Americanized." In other words, those reacting from the motivation to invest philanthropically are at a stage in life where they feel comfortable placing their own individual beliefs and dreams ahead of family and community. They not only can afford to do so, but it also seems that they feel it is socially and emotionally acceptable to do so.

The underlying social activities supporting the philanthropic interests are different throughout the continuum. Social contact is most active and intimate at the survival stage and most distant at the investment stage, although it is just as vitally important, just not as frequent or as informal. The relationships within the "surviving" category are more "obligatory" in the sense of being highly personal, close relationships among people one feels responsible for and accountable to. The sense of obligation that underlies the impulse to "help" is still at work, but the relationships with the recipients are not necessarily direct. Finally, the sense of "partnership" seems to be operative as Asian American donors move into investing strategies.

Implications for Increasing Philanthropic Activity among the Acculturated

There are several types of organizations that can help encourage more and increased participation from American-born and more acculturated Asians. These organizations and the more acculturated Asian Americans both fall under the "helping" mode of the motivational spectrum. These organizations include ethnic-specific and pan-Asian alumni, business, and professional associations; the many nonprofit Asian American and/or ethnic-specific human service, educational, and social justice agencies; and the smaller

number of noncommunity causes, such as social justice groups, scholarship funds, and at-risk youth programs that have attracted Asian Americans.

Moreover, there is a subset of these organizations that straddle or could straddle both the "helping" mode and the "investing" mode. Perhaps these organizations could act as conduits for encouraging Asian American donors in the "helping" state of mind as they transition into the "investing" state, where most major gifts, endowments, and sustainable approaches are made. These potential "transition conduits" include: Asian American and ethnic community centers, cultural centers, and museums; Asian American nonprofit educational and youth-serving programs; Asian American social justice, legal aid, and advocacy agencies; multiracial/ethnic social justice and legal aid organizations; and multiracial/ethnic educational and youth-serving programs.

The Asian American nonprofits are strategically positioned in that their social networks overlap with the existing networks in the community. However, they often do not have the capacity to structure and support the committees and social outreach needed to attract, cultivate, and maintain large numbers of members. The multiracial/ethnic agencies (that is, major youth-serving, social justice, and human rights agencies) tend to be large, institutionally mature organizations with the capacity to mount strategically targeted campaigns. These organizations, however, generally do not have access to the informal social networks within the Asian American community, nor do they appear to have a significant interest in creating them.

Philanthropic entities interested in increasing and strengthening the Asian American donor community have at least two main models to explore and support. First, to target the myriad informal social networks already existing in the Asian American communities, Asian American nonprofits need to build their institutional capacity. Most lack the staff time and training to maintain long-term, sustained, robust board and committee structures that can offer meaningful social and volunteer opportunities to large numbers of Asian Americans. Many also lack the fundraising sophistication to ascertain whether donor prospects are acting from a motivation to help or a motivation to invest so they can adjust their fundraising programs accordingly. Many of these nonprofits have access to these associations and various communities but do not have the institutional structures for supporting ongoing activities and communications with them.

Second, collaborations among mainstream or other noncommunity institutions or causes with Asian American nonprofits on specially targeted programs and campaigns might also be effective. Although mainstream and other large noncommunity organizations may have the structures and staff to maintain various "friends of" and special volunteer programs and committees, they do not necessarily know how to adapt these structures to the cultural and social interests of Asian Americans. For those mainstream and noncommunity organizations with strong mutual charitable interests (such as social justice organizations, human rights groups, disaster relief interests, and cultural or educational programs), collaborations with Asian American or ethnic nonprofits may be viable if they offer sufficient benefits to the Asian American nonprofit.

In any case, it is important to further develop and maintain the budding Asian American donor community for a variety of reasons important to both Asian Americans and the mainstream population. Perhaps most important is the connection between philanthropy, voluntarism, and civic participation. The voluntary nonprofit sector is a profound supporting structure of America's democracy and provides opportunities for participants to add their voice to the democratic process of community building. Therefore, Asian Americans need to tap into their philanthropic activities not just to grow greater charitable resources but also to strengthen their civic voice. They need to vote with their money, not just literally through the electoral system, but also figuratively through the nonprofit social structures that collectively define American culture. Both Asian American and mainstream nonprofits can serve their purposes under different circumstances. But whom Asian Americans choose to help, what causes they target, and where they invest their philanthropic dollars and energies will be of great importance as Asian America grows and matures.

Jessica Chao

References and further reading

Chao, Jessica. 1999. "Asian American Philanthropy: Expanding Circles of Participation." In *Cultures of Caring: Philanthropy in America's Diverse Communities,* 189–253. Washington, DC: Council on Foundations.

Espiratu, Yen Le. 1992. *Asian American Panethnicity: Bridging Institutions and Identities.* Philadelphia: Temple University Press.

Ilchman, Warren F., Stanley N. Katz, and Edward L. Queen II, eds. 1998. *Philanthropy in the World's Traditions.* Bloomington: Indiana University Press.

Joseph, James A. 1995. *Remaking America: How the Benevolent Traditions of Many Cultures Are Transforming Our National Life.* San Francisco: Jossey-Bass.

Shao, Stella. 1995. "Asian American Giving: Issues and Challenges." In *Cultures of Giving II: How Heritage, Gender, Wealth and Values Influence Philanthropy,* edited by Warren Ilchman and Charles Hamilton. San Francisco: Jossey-Bass.

Shinagawa, Larry Hajime. 1996. "The Impact of Immigration on the Demography of Asian Pacific Americans." In *The State of Asian Pacific America: Reframing the Immigration Debate,* edited by Bill Ong Hing and Ronald Lee, 59–126. Los Angeles: LEAP Public Policy Institute and UCLA Asian American Studies Center.

Smith, Bradford, Sylvia Shue, Jennifer Lisa Vest, and Joseph Villarreal. 1999. *Philanthropy in Communities of Color.* Bloomington: Indiana University Press.

Aspen Institute/Nonprofit Sector Research Fund

Founded in 1950 by Chicago businessman Walter Paepcke, the Aspen Institute was created to bring leaders from diverse organizations together to discuss important issues that society, organizations, and individuals face. The institute is a nonprofit organization with offices in Aspen, Colorado; Chicago; New York; Queenstown, Maryland; Santa Barbara, California; and Washington, D.C. It has international partners in Europe and Asia and publishes *Aspen Peaks,* a monthly online newsletter that highlights the people, activities, and publications of the organization.

The institute brings together leaders from the nonprofit, private, and public sectors as they strive to improve their leadership abilities to make an impact of lasting importance at the national and global level. Past U.S. presidents, statesmen, diplomats, and judges often attend various institute-sponsored events. The

A media conference at the Aspen Institute (Andanson James/Corbis Sygma)

isons, market-oriented activity of nonprofits and philanthropy, nonprofit advocacy and civic participation, and the performance and accountability of nonprofits and philanthropy.

Besides rewarding grants and conducting research, the fund also produces publications on the nonprofit sector, including its annual report. The fund produces a newsletter, *Snapshots,* which presents key findings from research studies supported by the fund. *Nonprofit Research News,* another publication, is easily accessible from the Internet and reports on current trends and news in the nonprofit sector as well as on research being conducted and funded by the fund. These publications offer the opportunity for leaders in the nonprofit and public sector to review the findings of the funded projects. Like its sister organization, the fund also hosts conferences to promote discussion and debate among national and world leaders on issues facing the world today.

Brieanna Quinn

References and further reading

Aspen Institute, http://www.aspeninstitute.org (cited October 12, 2001).

———. "Annual Report 2000," http://www.aspeninstitute. org (cited October 12, 2001).

Nonprofit Sector Research Fund, http://www. nonprofitresearch.org (cited October 12, 2001).

institute encourages informed dialogue among its members in the pursuit of wisdom and in the hope of improving the human condition. The mission of the institute, as a global forum, is "fostering enlightened responsible leadership through seminars, policy studies and fellowship programs" (http://www.aspen institute.org).

In 1991, the institute established the Nonprofit Sector Research Fund, which awards research grants and organizes meetings to assist in the expansion of knowledge regarding the nonprofit sector and philanthropy. The fund also helps improve nonprofit practices. Since its creation, it has supported more than 300 research projects with a total of $7 million in grants (http://www.nonprofitresearch.org). It has supported research, for example, on cross-sector compar-

Association for Healthcare Philanthropy (AHP)

The Association for Healthcare Philanthropy (AHP) is a not-for-profit international professional membership association dedicated to the advancement of healthcare institutions and organizations through philanthropy.

The AHP's work revolves around endeavors to enhance the effective performance and professionalism of its nearly 3,000 members and the institutions they represent. Comprehensive education and accreditation programs are offered and adherence to formally established professional standards for ethical conduct is encouraged. AHP assists members in earning the designation of Certified Fund Raising Executive (CFRE), the independent, industry-wide identification for practitioners who meet the specified standards for the fundraising profession. Several publications, including the newsletter *AHP Connect*, support networking between members and provide platforms from which to exchange professional expertise and share recognized fundraising and philanthropic principles. The organization promotes the value of philanthropy as well as the importance of not-for-profit healthcare institutions and organizations.

AHP is governed by a board of directors consisting of seven regional directors (Canada, New England, Mid-Atlantic, Midwest, Southeast, Rockies and Southwest, and Pacific) as well the officers of the association (elected from the membership), the chair of the AHP Board of Certification, and the president of the Health Systems Development Network. Together, these individuals form the chief policy-making body for the organization.

AHP traces its beginnings back to a Louisiana Hospital Association fundraising and financial development seminar held in New Orleans in 1964. After a successful conference the following year, an informal organization, Developartners, was created to enhance communication among hospital development professionals, to share pertinent information about successful fundraising techniques, and to strive to fill the lack of educational standards within the hospital fundraising field.

At the Developartners' 1967 conference, it was decided to formalize the organization. A committee chaired by William B. "Dub" Harris of Methodist Hospital of Lubbock, Texas, worked through the night to develop the structure and bylaws and nominate officers for the new organization, which was to be named the National Association for Hospital Development (NAHD). The following afternoon, members ratified the new name and bylaws and elected Dub Harris as their first president.

During the early years, the all-volunteer organization focused on membership building and education. At the same time, it began efforts to lobby for the interests of private philanthropy designated for hospitals. In 1970, when membership reached 200, the board approved the initiation of a professional journal *(AHP Journal)*, several achievement awards, and a system of professional accreditation. In the mid-1970s, the organization hired its first executive director and

moved its records and office from Kansas to Falls Church, Virginia, in the Washington, D.C., metropolitan area. In 1977, the first NAHD Hospital Philanthropy Institute was held at the University of Wisconsin in Madison, a week-long professional course that continues today.

In 1990, leadership advocated a new name for NAHD to better reflect the association's changing image—moving toward an international organization, including health organizations beyond the walls of hospitals, and emphasizing a purpose larger than development. A ballot at the end of the year led to the adoption of the new name, Association for Healthcare Philanthropy (AHP).

Kerry Hepworth

References and further reading
Association for Healthcare Philanthropy (AHP). 2001. *Membership Directory and Buyers' Guide.* Falls Church, VA: AHP.

Attal, Gene. 2001. "Everything You Ever Wanted to Know about AHP but Haven't Asked!" *AHP Connect* 1 (2): 2.

Roth, William S. 1992. "A Legacy of 25 Shining Years for Healthcare Philanthropy." *AHP Journal* (Spring): 5–16.

Association for Research on Nonprofit Organizations and Voluntary Action (ARNOVA)

The Association for Research on Nonprofit Organizations and Voluntary Action (ARNOVA), established in 1971 at Boston College as the Association for Voluntary Action Scholars (AVAS), is a nonprofit dedicated to creating and using research on nonprofit organizations and philanthropy.

To meet the changing needs of the burgeoning nonprofit sector, ARNOVA has changed over the years. Its primary goal is to strengthen the community of scholars by increasing diversity, increasing membership, creating research tools, and improving dissemination and collaboration among organizations. ARNOVA provides publications, annual conferences, electronic discussion groups, and an employment network. Publications include: *Nonprofit and Voluntary Sector Quarterly (NVSQ)*, a scholarly journal; *ARNOVA Abstracts; ARNOVA News,* a quarterly newsletter; and a series of *ARNOVA Occasional Papers,* the first of which was *Philanthropy in Communities of Color: Traditions and Challenges.*

The founding fathers, David Horton Smith and Bill Ready, had the vision of creating a forum for researchers and practitioners in this newly developing field to bring together ideas that would improve scholarship, research, and activities related to the nonprofit, voluntary action, and third-sector fields. AVAS held its first conference in 1974 in Denver, Colorado, in conjunction with two other organizations, the Association for Volunteer Administration and the Association of Volunteer Bureaus. In 1982, it held its first solo conference, in Lansing, Michigan. AVAS had several publications, including newsletters, abstracts, and *The Journal of Voluntary Action Research (JVAR)*, a scholarly journal for research in voluntary action. In 1972, it was replaced by the *Nonprofit and Voluntary Sector Quarterly*, which became more broadly focused and inclusive of the changing third sector.

AVAS eventually moved from its original home at Boston College to several different college campuses across the country, including Pennsylvania State University, Tufts University, and Washington State University. Owing to low membership and financial difficulties, a Strategic Planning Committee was formed in 1988 by Delwyn A. Dyer, which prompted the name change of the organization to the Association for Research on Nonprofit Organizations and Voluntary Action (ARNOVA) in 1990 (Smith 1991). The planning process furthered at two important retreats, one in Corpus Christi, Texas, in 1991 and one at the Mason Ranch Retreat in 1993. These retreats facilitated more organizational activities, membership growth, and collaborations with other organizations. Since 1994, ARNOVA has been quartered at the Indianapolis campus of Indiana University, where it is affiliated with the Center on Philanthropy.

In addition to its increased revenue from nongrant sources, ARNOVA's funders have included the Lilly Endowment, the W. K. Kellogg Foundation, the Rockefeller Brothers Fund, the Ford Foundation, the David and Lucile Packard Foundations, and the Charles Stewart Mott Foundation.

Tanya E. Johnson

References and further reading

Association for Research on Nonprofit Organizations and Voluntary Action (ARNOVA), http://www.arnova.org (cited October 27, 2001).

———. "The 2000 Annual Report."

———. 1972–1995. ARNOVA Records, Ruth Lilly Special Collections and Archives, University Library, Indiana University–Purdue University Indianapolis.

Smith, David H. 1991. *A History of ARNOVA*. Indianapolis: ARNOVA.

Association for Volunteer Administration (AVA)

The Association for Volunteer Administration (AVA) is a professional organization dedicated to building competent leaders of volunteers. Volunteers built the American nonprofit sector and are an essential dimension of the sector. Although the AVA is an international association, the future of philanthropy in the United States will continue to be closely linked with the volunteers who give of their time and those who lead them.

History

According to the AVA Web site, the organization was conceived in 1958 by American coordinators of volunteers from the mental health field. The AVA has steadily grown into an international entity. The organization adopted a charter in 1961 and a new name, American Association of Volunteer Services Coordinators (AAVSC), in 1961. The mid-1960s saw the advancement of educational goals and standards for the fledgling organization. Still closely linked to the mental health field, the early organization met prior to Mental Health Institute meetings.

The 1970s were a time a great growth for the organization, which again changed its name, to the Association for Administration of Volunteer Services (AAVS), in 1975. During this period, the AVA undertook collaborative efforts with other volunteer organizations and realigned itself as an organization for all volunteer administrators in human services, both paid and volunteer. An executive secretary was hired in 1976, and the office moved from Chicago to Boulder, Colorado. The name Association for Volunteer Administration (AVA) was adopted in 1979 at the annual meeting and staff was hired to provide for a firm financial base and to implement the certification program.

Through the 1980s, the certification program identified core competencies for volunteer administrators, whether paid or volunteer, and the first credential, Certified Volunteer Administrator (CVA), was granted. The AVA began publishing the quarterly *Journal of Volunteer Administration* in 1982.

In the 1990s, with financial help from major foundations, the international membership grew and greater efforts were put into recruiting. The AVA Web site was begun in 1997, and Richmond, Virginia, became AVA's new home. By 1999, there were 2,000 members of the AVA from sixteen different countries.

In 2001, the AVA leadership attended two international conferences and a new *Universal Declaration of Leading and Managing Volunteers* was collaboratively developed and adopted by the AVA board.

Mission and Goals

According to the AVA Web site, "The Association for Volunteer Administration, an international professional association, enhances the competence of its members and strengthens the profession of volunteer resources management" (http://www.avaintl.org). In 2002, the following goals were identified: to equip, support, and challenge AVA members; to develop and promote standards of excellence and competence for the profession; to define, interpret, and promote the profession of volunteer administration; to develop and strengthen local professional networks; to expand AVA's visibility, credibility, and membership in communities and countries worldwide; and to strengthen operational effectiveness.

Current Status

AVA members are given opportunities and information in a variety of ways. The CVA competency-based credential "assures . . . that the person has the knowledge base covering the essentials of coordinating a volunteer effort" (Ellis 1994, 14–16.) This assurance has helped to professionalize the volunteer administration position. *The Journal of Volunteer Administration,* written by and for professionals in the field, provides research, book reviews, and articles on

volunteer management. The bimonthly "AVA Member Briefing" newsletters include resources and affiliate news, keeping members updated on AVA issues. International networking is provided via a comprehensive Web site, through the journal, and through an annual, international conference that brings together professionals, researchers, and educators in the field of volunteering.

Mary Legan

References and further reading
Association for Volunteer Administration (AVA), http://www.avaintl.org (cited November 17, 2002).
———. *Journal of Volunteer Administration*. Various issues.
Ellis, Susan J. 1994. "Professional Standards: Should You Be Looking for a Certified Volunteer Administrator?" *NonProfit Times*, September, 14, 16.

Association of Fundraising Professionals (AFP)

The Association of Fundraising Professionals (AFP), formerly the National Society of Fund Raisers (NSFR) and then the National Society of Fund Raising Executives (NSFRE), is the largest professional association of "individuals responsible for generating philanthropic support for a wide variety of nonprofit, charitable organizations" (AFP 2001a).

The organization's purpose and mission, as outlined in its articles of incorporation, remain essentially the same today as in 1960 when they were first adopted. AFP was created to "unite those engaged in the profession of fund raising" and to serve as a conduit for educating, training, mentoring, and credentialing individuals in the field of fundraising (NSFRE 2000, 5). AFP seeks to advance philanthropy in order to promote stewardship and donor trust by setting ethical practice standards, promoting research in fundraising and philanthropy, advocating for public policy, and educating donors and the public.

The National Society of Fund Raisers (NSFR) was chartered on June 21, 1960, in New York City after discussions between Benjamin Sklar of Brandeis University, William R. Simms of the National Urban League, and Harry Rosen of the Federation of Jewish Philanthropies revealed the need for a code of ethics for fundraisers and an association to represent the fundraising profession. Sklar, Simms, and Rosen chose Dr. Abel Hanson, a professional fundraiser and instructor at Columbia University, as NSFR's first president.

At the end of its first year, NSFR had 197 members and began publishing a quarterly issue of *NSFR Newsletter*. In 1963, eighty-eight participants gathered to discuss "The Future of Philanthropy and the Full Development of Volunteerism" in Suffern, New York, at what would be the first NSFR convention. This meeting would become an annual event and later evolved into AFP's International Conference.

The already existing Association of Fund Raising Directors, an organization of fundraisers in New York City, became affiliated with and was established as NSFR's first chapter in July 1964. NSFR established its second chapter in May 1965 when the Fund Raisers Association of the National Capital became affiliated with the organization. By the end of 1965, membership approached 500 individuals from twenty-six states, including Hawaii.

During the 1970s, NSFR established the Institute of Continuing Education (now the AFP Foundation for Philanthropy) as a subsidiary and as its fundraising entity under Internal Revenue Code (IRC) 501(c)(3), moved the national headquarters to Washington, D.C., and changed its name to the National Society of Fund Raising Executives (NSFRE). The newsletter was reintroduced as the *NSFRE Journal*, and a certification program began to emerge.

In the 1980s, NSFRE began to evolve from a volunteer-driven to a staff-managed organization with volunteer input on policy and grassroots issues. NSFRE increased its involvement in national and state legislation and collaborated with "sister" organizations such as the Council for Advancement and Support of Education (CASE), the American Association of Fund Raising Counsel (AAFRC), INDEPENDENT SECTOR, and the Association for Healthcare Philanthropy (AHP). Through this collaboration, a Donor Bill of Rights developed. The first certification program (Certified Fund Raising Executive, CFRE) was instituted as a means of providing standards for the fundraising profession, and a course in fundraising was created and implemented. In 1985, the national headquarters moved to its current home in Alexandria, Virginia, and membership grew to 5,400 fundraisers across North America.

In the early 1990s, membership neared 14,000 members. Leaders testified before such groups as the House Ways and Means Committee, the Internal Revenue Service (IRS), and the Financial Accounting Standards Board (FASB). The *NSFRE Journal* was revised and published under its current name, *Advancing Philanthropy*. AHP and NSFRE consolidated their baseline certification programs, making CFRE the continuing credential for fundraising professionals, and a new accreditation program using continuing education units (CEUs) was established in 1996. By the end of the 1990s, membership surpassed 22,000 members. NSFRE officially changed its name to the Association of Fundraising Professionals (AFP) on January 1, 2001.

Gretchen C. Gordon

References and further reading
Association of Fundraising Professionals (AFP), http://www.afpnet.org.
———. 2001a. "AFP Fact Sheet." Alexandria, VA: AFP, http://www.afpnet.org/tier3_cd.cfm?content_item_id= 13026&folder_id=885.
———. 2001b. "History of the Association of Fundraising Professionals." In *AFP: Association of Fundraising Professionals*. Alexandria, VA: AFP.
National Society of Fund Raising Executives (NSFRE). 2000. "A Brief History of NSFRE, The Society." In *NSFRE Leadership Handbook*, 5–8. Alexandria, VA: NSFRE.

Association of Professional Researchers for Advancement (APRA)

The Association of Professional Researchers for Advancement (APRA) was founded in 1987 for the purpose of enhancing the expertise and status of its members. As the first national organization for researchers in advancement, APRA was dedicated to promoting educational and professional opportunities in fundraising research.

Those activities included teaching proactive research methods, ethics, prospect management systems, and marketing for the research department. APRA has more than 1,700 members and twenty-five chapters worldwide. Its goals are to promote professional growth and advancement; to advocate the highest standards of performance and ethical research; to facilitate interaction among researchers and other fundraising professionals; to advance the role of research in the philanthropic community; and to compile and disseminate data about the profession and its practitioners.

APRA was created by a group of professional researchers in Minneapolis who began meeting in 1981 under the name Minnesota Research in Fund Raising Association. Within two years, the group had expanded its membership and changed its name to Minnesota Prospect Research Association. Members were particularly interested in discussing the history of prospect research because no common source of information existed. They were also aware of the benefits derived from sharing information and networking with other professionals. By 1987, they had agreed to expand their membership and include chapters across the country.

The association's membership grew to more than 400 members within its first year. The rapid growth can be traced to factors present in the late 1980s. During that period, the number and dollar goals of capital campaigns significantly increased, creating a demand for information on major gift prospects that would support such major fundraising efforts. Additionally, the information and technology field experienced tremendous growth.

For the benefit of its members, the association conducts annual regional and international conferences and offers a mentoring program and a job quest line. APRA also produces two publications. *Connections,* a quarterly journal, focuses on new resources and methods. *The Bulletin,* published six times per year, details chapter activities and member news.

Grady Jones

References and further reading
Association of Professional Researchers for Advancement (APRA), http://www.aprahome.org.
———. 1997. "APRA History—1981–1997," http://www.aprahome.org/apralibrary/history.htm.

Audubon Society
See Environmental Movement

B

Bacon, Leonard (1802–1881)

Leonard Bacon was born in 1802 to Congregational missionaries who served on the frontier. He became an influential editor, reformer, Congregational clergyman, and benevolent activist who lived in New Haven, Connecticut, helped to establish and/or served as an officer or director of temperance, colonization, education, antislavery, missionary, Bible, and other reform and benevolent organizations. He was actively involved in developing their strategy and philosophy, disseminating information to the public, recruiting new members, and soliciting contributions. Although seldom able to contribute monetarily to the philanthropic associations that proliferated during his lifetime, he effectively employed the press, the lecture hall, and the pulpit to proclaim the virtues of philanthropic action. He frequently argued that it was incumbent upon Americans to donate their wealth to good causes.

One of Bacon's most important contributions to American philanthropy was an 1847 article in the *New Englander*, perhaps the first serious treatise on charitable trusteeship in the United States. In this article, he expressed concern that the executive committees of many voluntary organizations, such as the American Tract Society and the American Board of Commissioners for Foreign Missions (both of which he served on as a member of the board of managers), were not sufficiently accountable either to their members or to the churches. In order to guard against the perversion of their trust, he believed, executive committees must be responsible to a streamlined and truly representative board of managers. Such boards, he argued, should, in fact and not just in theory, play a significant role in these associations by appointing members of executive committees and engaging in a substantive review of committees' actions during the previous year. Such an arrangement, he concluded, would best serve to inspire public confidence and safeguard the interests of these organizations and the larger religious community.

Bacon was motivated by a number of considerations to write, speak, and organize on behalf of various voluntary associations. He believed, above all, that Christians were obligated to combat sin wherever it existed in the world and that the benevolent societies were the primary instruments for achieving this objective. These benevolent enterprises would, in turn, help to ensure the conversion of mankind to evangelical Protestantism in preparation for the return of Christ to earth for a thousand years. Evangelism, with its emphasis on the dangers to the soul and society posed by a rising tide of immorality and disorder, pointed, in some measure, to a conservative social philosophy. Bacon's involvement in the temperance, anti-Catholic, colonization, and missionary movements as well as the Bible and tract societies represented, in part, an effort to restore order, morality, and racial and religious homogeneity in a society experiencing rapid industrialization, urbanization, immigration, and westward migration. Yet his attachment to the concepts of immediate repentance for sin, free will, liberty, and social justice also moved him to champion public education, the abolition of slavery, temperance, fundamental rights for freedmen following the Civil War, and other causes. He served the last fifteen years of his life at Yale Divinity School, where he died in 1881.

Hugh Davis

References and further reading

Bacon, Leonard. Papers. Yale University Archives, New Haven, CT.

Bacon, Theodore Dwight. 1931. *Leonard Bacon: A Statesman in the Church.* Edited by Benjamin W. Bacon. New Haven, CT: Yale University Press.

Davis, Hugh. 1998. *Leonard Bacon: New England Reformer and Antislavery Moderate.* Baton Rouge: Louisiana State University Press.

Griffin, Clifford S. 1960. *Their Brothers' Keepers: Moral Stewardship in the United States, 1800–1865.* New Brunswick, NJ: Rutgers University Press.

Barton, Clara (1821–1912)

Clara Barton, born Clarissa Harlowe Barton in 1821, founded the American Red Cross in 1881 and devoted her life to humanitarian causes through direct service. During the Civil War, this "Angel of the Battlefield" organized and delivered care to Union soldiers, providing food, clothing, and medical supplies without regard for her own health and well-being. While under siege in Charleston, she also gave supplies to former slaves and taught some of them to read. After the war, she met Frederick Douglass and continued to support "Negro rights." However, Barton focused most of her energies in the early postwar period on organizing a letter-writing campaign to search for missing soldiers. She also spent two years lecturing throughout the North and worked closely with Dorrence Atwater, a prisoner of war at Andersonville Prison in Georgia, to mark the graves of Union soldiers who died there.

In 1869, with her health failing, Barton went to Europe to rest and recuperate. While in Geneva, Switzerland, she met founding members of the International Committee of the Red Cross and learned about the Geneva Convention (1864), an agreement regulating fair treatment of prisoners and of the sick or wounded in wartime. During the Franco-Prussian War (1870–1871), Barton helped the Red Cross distribute aid to European cities, including Strasbourg. There she assisted impoverished citizens not by giving them clothing, but by employing them to make garments from donated goods for two francs a day.

Barton returned to the States in 1873, still in poor health. In 1876 she entered a sanitarium in Dansville, New York, to recuperate. From there she moved to Washington, D.C., to lobby for her new cause: American accession to the Geneva Convention and establishment of a new Red Cross society. Success finally came in 1881, when she was named president of the newly chartered American Red Cross. A year later, the United States signed the Geneva treaty, and in 1884 signatories endorsed the "American Amendment" to the international treaty, so called because it grew out of Barton's realization that Red Cross societies could meet needs in times of peace as well as war by helping victims of famine, floods, earthquakes, and other natural disasters. As president of the Red Cross from 1881 to 1904, Barton worked in the field to bring aid to people in the United States, Russia, Turkey, and Cuba. Eventually, however, opponents forced her to resign, citing her advanced age, lack of careful financial records, and eccentric leadership style.

Barton's philanthropy and activism also supported several other causes. As a young adult, Barton taught for eighteen years in Massachusetts and New Jersey, where she promoted free public education. In 1854, she moved to Washington, D.C., and became one of the first women hired by the U.S. Patent Office. She also championed women's rights during her post–Civil War lecture tours. Later, she advocated prison reform, based on her experiences as superintendent of the Reformatory Prison for Women at Sherborn, Massachusetts, in 1883. Underlying all her efforts, from teaching to organizing aid, was her commitment to mutual respect and her desire to help others help themselves whenever possible.

Roberta K. Gibboney

See also American Red Cross
References and further reading
Barton, Clara. 1898. *The Red Cross in Peace and War.* Washington, DC: American Historical Press.
Burton, David. 1995. *Clara Barton: In the Service of Humanity.* Westport, CT: Greenwood.
Gibboney, Roberta. 2002. "Clara Barton." In *Notable American Philanthropists: Biographies of Giving and Volunteering,* edited by Robert T. Grimm, Jr. Westport, CT: Oryx Press.
Williams, Blanche. 1941. *Clara Barton: Daughter of Destiny.* Philadelphia: J. B. Lippincott.

Beecher, Lyman (1775–1863)

Lyman Beecher, an evangelist who promoted voluntary associations, was born in New Haven, Connecticut, in 1775. A descendant of the early settlers of the state, he received his primary education in country schools in New Haven and Guilford. In 1793, he entered Yale College, where he became a protégé of its president, Timothy Dwight, Congregationalist and Federalist leader.

After a decade of preaching in East Hampton, New York, Beecher accepted a call from the church in Litchfield, Connecticut. He arrived just as the political battle over religious establishment was reaching a fever pitch. Although Beecher defended establishment, he eventually became convinced that religious voluntarism would not only strengthen the church but also provide a basis for broader reforms of society.

An early organizer of the temperance movement, Beecher believed that people of faith should act as a moral force in society, working through inclusive secular voluntary associations to identify and address social problems. Seeking to "apply Christianity directly to man and to society," Beecher turned his attention to broader issues of social welfare, arguing that individual giving to support voluntary efforts to "educate, and stop the contagion of vice" was the ultimate solution to the problem of poverty (Beecher 1961, 1: 185–187).

In 1826, Beecher was called to the pulpit of the Hanover Street Church in Boston to lead the Congregationalists' struggle against Unitarian domination of the state. Organizing the young men of his congregation into a voluntary association, the group chal-

Portrait of Lyman Beecher (1775–1863), clergyman and father of several prominent Americans of the nineteenth century, including Henry Ward Beecher and Harriet Beecher Stowe (Corbis)

lenged Unitarian political candidates and took on the political corruption, intemperance, gambling, Sabbath breaking, and immoral entertainment that had flourished under the Unitarian regime. They also organized an assortment of voluntary associations—lyceums (public lectures), libraries, and mechanics, temperance, and missionary societies—intended to rescue young people from the temptations of the city. These became models for organizations throughout the nation.

Beecher accepted the presidency of Lane Seminary and the pulpit at Cincinnati's Second Presbyterian Church in 1832. When his antislavery views embroiled him in conflict with Lane's board, Beecher resigned the presidency, though he remained at the seminary as a professor of theology.

During his Ohio years, Beecher consolidated his reputation as a national religious leader and an eloquent proponent of voluntary associations. His most famous oration, *A Plea for the West* (1835), written for his campaign to persuade wealthy New Englanders to support schools and colleges in the western United States, offered a powerful vision of the public role of religion and the possibilities of associational action—and warned of the dangers posed by growing numbers of uneducated citizens and immigrants.

When Beecher's health broke down in 1850, he returned to the East. He died at the home of his son, famed evangelist Henry Ward Beecher, on January 10, 1863, and was buried in New Haven's Grove Street Cemetery.

Beecher's chief contribution to philanthropy was his role in changing public attitudes toward voluntary associations from the suspicion of factions and "self-created societies" expressed by the Founding Fathers to the view that they were indispensable to private action in the public interest. In doing so, he helped to change the public role of religion, transforming churches from direct political actors into institutions that empowered their members to act as moral agents in society, politics, and economic life.

Beecher is perhaps better known for the achievements of his remarkable children than for his own accomplishments. Of his sons, Henry Ward (1813–1887) succeeded his father as the nation's leading evangelical preacher; Edward (1803–1895) was a leading religious journalist and abolitionist; and Charles (1815–1900) was a religious writer, hymnodist, and education reformer. Of his daughters, Harriet Beecher Stowe (1811–1896) was the author of the hugely influential abolitionist novel *Uncle Tom's Cabin* (1852), and Catherine (1800–1878) was a leading abolitionist, domestic reformer, and advocate for women's education.

Peter Dobkin Hall

References and further reading
Beecher, Lyman. 1961. *The Autobiography of Lyman Beecher.* Edited by Barbara M. Cross. 2 vols. Cambridge: Harvard University Press.
Fraser, James W. 1985. *Pedagogue for God's Kingdom: Lyman Beecher and the Second Great Awakening.* Lanham, MD: University Press of America.
Smith, Timothy L. 1957. *Revivalism and Social Reform: American Protestantism on the Eve of the Civil War.* New York: Harper and Row.

Benevolent Societies

The tradition of people coming together to help others has a long history, and acts of group-sponsored benevolence can be documented for many of the great religions and world cultures. Accordingly, a substantial number of benevolent societies in the United States trace their origin to charitable activities in the countries from which immigrants arrived. The societies were formed as systematic, capacity-enhancing efforts when the sporadic efforts by individuals or by congregations to meet general human needs proved inadequate. On the one hand, charitable work was often inspired by religious teachings; on the other, ministry to the poor, ill, and elderly sometimes led to religious proselytizing. The organization of philanthropic work into stable benevolent societies made use of what nowadays are well-known ways to motivate volunteers and donors—group pressure and a higher calling.

Following the British model, "benevolent society" was a widely used term in the United States in the nineteenth century to denote institutionalized religious and charitable activities. Missionary work, help for a church's or synagogue's own congregants, the abolitionist movement, and African American self-help efforts, as well as support for newly arrived immigrants, all spawned benevolent societies. Robert Baird argued in 1844 that because of the separation of church and state in the United States, congregations could not rely on the state for financial support and had to mobilize their own volunteer spirit and resources to provide a physical home for their religious services and funds for their activities. Protestant, Catholic, and Jewish interpretations of their religious texts encouraged the faithful to help others by spreading God's word and doing good. Moral crusades against alcohol and prostitution led to the formation of new religious organizations, and widespread poverty spurred the growth of systematic charitable work. The Civil War, the Industrial Revolution, urbanization, and large-scale immigration created extensive misery that social entrepreneurs tried to alleviate through organized efforts.

Some individuals and families in the United States could respond to the call for benevolent work because improvements in their standard of living and the availability of servants made leisure time available that could be devoted to charitable activities. As the wealth of men in business, the professions, and manufacturing increased, their wives and daughters were released from necessary economic production and it became fashionable for women to join benevolent societies. Indeed, the number and types of benevolent societies increased so much that the term lost its significance in the American context, in contrast to its continued use in British nonprofit law.

In Britain, the Friendly Societies Act of 1974 defined benevolent societies as "societies established for benevolent or charitable purposes. In contrast to a Friendly Society, the benefits must not be restricted to members or their relatives. Activities range from the payment of cash benefits to the provision of services, such as medical assistance and accommodation for persons in need." The act allowed for the registration of incorporated societies in the Registry of Friendly Societies, which is located in Victory House in London and open to the public.

The equivalent terminology in the United States to the British distinction between benevolent societies and friendly societies is public-benefit versus mutual-benefit organizations, public-interest versus mutual-interest nonprofits, or public-serving versus member-serving entities. The former are usually incorporated under Internal Revenue Code (IRC) 501(c)(3) and enjoy two tax benefits: exemption from the corporate income tax and tax deduction of contributions for donors. Mutual benefit entities may seek tax-exemption, but payments are generally not tax deductible as charitable contributions.

The simple distinction between public interest and mutual interest commonly found in the academic and professional literature is not used by the Internal Revenue Service (IRS). Instead, the IRS states that organizations qualify for 501(c)(3) status when they operate exclusively for one or more of the following purposes:

- Charitable
- Religious
- Educational
- Scientific
- Literary
- Testing for public safety

- Fostering national or international amateur sports competition
- Prevention of cruelty to children or animals

In addition, two types of mutual benefit associations—fraternal beneficiary societies, incorporated under IRC 501(c)(8), and domestic fraternal societies, incorporated under IRC 501(c)(10)—enjoy a special tax status. Contributions are tax deductible as charitable contributions "if used exclusively for religious, charitable, scientific, literary, or educational purposes or for the prevention of cruelty to children or animals." The *Encyclopedia of Associations* shows that quite a few organizations that offer fraternal benefit life insurance and other member-serving programs also provide funds for charitable activities.

Furthermore, the distinction between public serving and member serving is not always clear to the casual observer because the IRS allows charitable organizations to create mutual benefit affiliates and permits member-serving entities to establish charitable funds to make optimal use of tax laws. However, the organizations themselves have to keep their funds in separate accounts, and persons considering a donation must make sure that their contribution falls into the categories for which a tax deduction can be claimed.

The National Center for Charitable Statistics developed the National Taxonomy of Exempt Entities (NTEE) in the 1980s to create a classification system that would facilitate the analysis of tax-exempt organizations. The core code, created to improve the fit with IRS classifications, has no category for "benevolent societies," and the term is not included in the index. The reason for this omission could be that the term was not considered useful to identify a class or group of tax-exempt organizations in the American context. Community service clubs such as Kiwanis, Lions, and Jaycees may come close to the traditional notion of benevolent societies.

A clearer picture emerges when one looks at organizations that have the term "benevolent society" in their names. The GuideStar database lists seventy-four such entities. Nearly half of them are private foundations, and the rest are public charities. A few got their start in nineteenth-century benevolent activities. About one-third were founded during and after World

War II, another third during the War on Poverty in the 1960s, and one-third are of relatively recent origin. The benevolent societies were established to help indigents in the local community, in congregations, or certain immigrant groups. Other missions include funding for scholarships and educational institutions or for the operation of retirement homes. The size in terms of assets varies substantially, from zero to several million dollars.

In general, in the United States the benevolent society may be defined as a group of philanthropic individuals, usually incorporated as a public charity or a private foundation, who pool their resources and make humanitarian donations or educational contributions on a regular basis.

Siegrun Fox Freyss

References and further reading
Baird, Robert. 1998 [1844]. "The Voluntary Principle in American Religion and American Life, 1844." In *Making the Nonprofit Sector in the United States,* edited by David C. Hammack, 163–173. Bloomington: Indiana University Press.
Guide to the Records of Religious and Benevolent Societies and Organizations. 1987. Compiled by Martha Lund Smalley. New Haven, CT: Yale University Library, Divinity Library Special Collections, http://webtext .library.yale.edu/diviflat/divinity.034.htm (cited September 17, 2002).
"GuideStar Pages," http://www.guidestar.org/search/report/ (cited September 17, 2002).
Hunt, Kimberly N. 2002. *Encyclopedia of Associations,* 38th ed. Vol. 1, *National Organizations of the U.S.* Farmington Hills, MI: Gale Group.
Lohmann, Roger A. 1992. *The Commons: New Perspectives on Nonprofit Organizations and Voluntary Action.* San Francisco: Jossey-Bass.
National Center for Charitable Statistics and the Foundation Center. 2001. *National Taxonomy of Exempt Entities—Core Codes.* Washington, DC, and New York: Urban Institute and Foundation Center.
Oates, Mary J. 1995. *The Catholic Philanthropic Tradition in America.* Bloomington: Indiana University Press.
"Registry of Friendly Societies," http://ws2. companieshouse.gov.uk/notes/friendly_socs.html (cited September 17, 2002).
Salamon, Lester M. 1999. *America's Nonprofit Sector: A Primer,* 2d ed. New York: Foundation Center.
Scott, Anne Firor. 1992. *Natural Allies: Women's Associations in American History.* Urbana and Chicago: University of Illinois Press.
Stanford, P. Thomas. 1897. *The Tragedy of the Negro in America.* Boston: Charles W. Wasto, http://docsouth .unc.edu/church/stanford/stanford.html (cited September 17, 2002).
U.S. Department of the Treasury, Internal Revenue Service. 2001. *Tax-Exempt Status for Your Organization,* Publication 557. Washington, DC: IRS, http://www.irs.gov/forms_pubs/ (cited September 17, 2002).

Benezet, Anthony (1713–1784)

Anthony Benezet, educator and abolitionist, was born in San Quentin, in Picardy, France, on January 31, 1713, to Jean Etienne and Judith Benezet. Fleeing religious persecution, the Benezet family migrated to London, England, in 1715, where they remained until 1731. There, Anthony Benezet received a formal liberal education. The Benezet family was associated with the London Quakers, and in France, Jean Etienne Benezet was involved with a French Protestant group called Inspires de la Vaunge, known for nonviolent protest philosophies. In 1731, the Benezet family moved to Philadelphia. Shortly after their move, Anthony Benezet joined the Society of Friends (Quakers). Anthony Benezet married Joyce Marriott in 1736. The couple had two children, who died during infancy.

Benezet studied at Germantown Academy and taught at the Friends' English Public School from 1742 until 1754. In 1754, he began a school for young women, the first in Pennsylvania to educate girls past the elementary level.

Appalled by the poor treatment of African Americans, Benezet also taught free African Americans in his home from 1750 until his death in 1784. In the 1750s, Benezet began to advocate the need for a school for African Americans. In 1770, the Society of Friends raised enough funds to do so. In its first five years of operation, the school, known as the African School, provided educational instruction to more than 250 African American children. Benezet was heavily involved in the coordination of the school and served as headmaster near the end of his life.

The Quakers began an antislavery campaign in the early 1770s in large part inspired by Benezet. In 1772, they required all members to emancipate their slaves

Illustration featuring reformer Anthony Benezet
(1713–1784) (Bettmann/Corbis)

or face expulsion. Benezet wrote numerous self-financed antislavery pamphlets, tracts, and books. He completed his first major abolitionist writing, *A Caution and Warning to Great Britain and Her Colonies,* in 1762. Benezet also founded one of the first antislavery organizations, the Society for the Relief of Free Negroes Unlawfully Held in Bondage, in 1775.

Benezet proclaimed equality across all ethnicities and extended his fight to include Native Americans. He induced the formation of the Friendly Association for Regaining and Preserving Peace with the Indians by Pacific Measures in an effort to eliminate enmity and warfare against Native Americans.

Benezet was a pacifist, an element of the Quaker philosophy that he extended beyond humanity. In his writings, he took a clear stance against disturbing nature and believed that harmony among people fol-

lowed pure and decent relationships with the environment. Accordingly, Benezet was also a conservationist. Later in life, he became a vegetarian, refusing to slay or eat animals. Benezet also strongly believed in living modestly and felt that the struggle for power and money was the root of slavery.

Anthony Benezet spent the months before his death in 1784 preparing the African School for a sustained future through effective fundraising and acquiring strong leadership to carry on the mission. He gave his entire estate to the school after the passing of his wife. Benezet spent his life giving to others and promoting equality. Although radical for his time, he made an impact on education and abolitionist movements worldwide.

Drew Blanchard

References and further reading

Armistead, Wilson. 1971 [1859]. *Anthony Benezet: From the Original Memoir.* New York: Books for Libraries Press.

Benezet, Anthony. Papers. Special Collections Division, Haverford College Library, Haverford, PA, and William L. Clements Library, Small Collections Division, University of Michigan Libraries.

Bruns, Roger. 1971 "Anthony Benezet's Assertion of Negro History." *Journal of Negro History* 56 (3): 230–238.

———. 1972. "Anthony Benezet and the Natural Rights of the Negro." *Pennsylvania Magazine of History and Biography* 96 (1): 104–113.

Hornick, Nancy Slocum. 1975. "Anthony Benezet and the Africans' School: Toward a Theory of Full Equality." *Pennsylvania Magazine of History and Biography* 99 (4): 399–421.

Jackson, Maurice. 1999. "The Social and Intellectual Origins of Anthony Benezet's Antislavery Radicalism." *Pennsylvania History* 66 (supplement): 86–112.

Kashatus, William C. 1989. "A Reappraisal of Anthony Benezet's Activities in Educational Reform, 1754–1784." *Quaker History* 78 (1): 24–36.

Kelley, Donald Brooks. 1982. "A Tender Regard to the Whole Creation: Anthony Benezet and the Emergence of an Eighteenth-Century Quaker Ecology." *Pennsylvania Magazine of History and Biography* 106 (1): 69–88.

Vaux, Robert. 1969 [1817]. *Memoirs of the Life of Anthony Benezet.* New York: Burt Franklin.

Bethune, Mary McLeod (1875–1955)

Mary McLeod Bethune was born to former slaves in Mayesville, South Carolina, in 1875. Her parents,

Mary McLeod Bethune (1875–1955), by Winold Reiss
(Bettmann/Corbis)

Samuel and Patsy McLeod, built a strict, religious home for their seventeen children. Upon the suggestion of her teacher, Mary's parents enrolled her in the Scotia Seminary in Concord, North Carolina, at age twelve. After graduating, she won a scholarship to study at the Moody Bible Institute in Chicago. There, she cultivated a deeper faith in God that provided the groundwork for all of her accomplishments. Her dreams of becoming a missionary were spoiled, however, when the institute told her that there was no need for black missionaries in Africa (Embree 1942).

After graduation, Mary McLeod secured a teaching position at the Haines Institute in Augusta, Georgia. It was in this predominantly female institution that she acquired the skills needed for leadership in education. From her mentor, Lucey Craft Laney, she learned much about educational philosophy as well as how to elicit community support. In 1897, she transferred to the Kendell Institute in Sumter, Georgia, where she met Albertus Bethune. The two were married in 1898 and had a child in 1899. When Albertus took a sales job, the couple moved to Savannah, Georgia. Shortly afterward, Mary began to observe the migration of large numbers of African Americans to Florida in search of jobs. Recognizing that this population would need educational opportunities, she moved south to Daytona Beach and opened the Literary and Industrial School for Training Negro Girls in 1904. Inspired and persuaded by Mary Bethune's efforts, James Gamble of Procter & Gamble supported the school during its early years. In 1923, the school merged with the Cookman Institute in nearby Jacksonville to become Bethune-Cookman College, which served young women rather than girls. Bethune's achievements in the area of education were recognized in 1935 when she received the National Association for the Advancement of Colored People's distinguished Spingarn Medal.

Encouraged by her success as an educational leader, Bethune branched out into the political arena. She advocated for antilynching laws, fair job and labor conditions, job training for women, and equality for all races. Bethune believed that women were the essential element in bringing about change in the United States (Love 1984). Her trust and belief in women was affirmed in 1924 when she was elected president of the National Association of Colored Women. Seeing the need for further work in the area of segregation and discrimination, Bethune founded the National Council of Negro Women in 1930 to combat these problems. Perhaps one of Bethune's greatest contributions came through her contacts with those in power. Her connections within the White House spanned three administrations but were strongest during Franklin D. Roosevelt's presidency (1933–1945). As a result of her leadership role in the women's movement during the 1920s and 1930s, Bethune caught the attention of Eleanor Roosevelt. Bethune's close relationships with the Roosevelt family were instrumental in her appointment to many government positions (Smith 1996). In addition to selecting Bethune to become director of Negro affairs for the National Youth Administration, Eleanor Roosevelt helped get Bethune involved in the National Counsel on

Negro Affairs—popularly referred to as the "Black Cabinet."

After a life of service to education and government, Mary McLeod Bethune died of a heart attack on May 18, 1955. She left a legacy of increased opportunities for African Americans and women and provided an example of how interracial cooperation can change society.

Marybeth Gasman

References and further reading
Egerton, John. 1994. *Speak Now against the Day: The Generation before the Civil Rights Movement in the South.* New York: Alfred E. Knopf.
Embree, Edwin. 1944. *13 against the Odds.* New York: Viking.
Howard-Pitney, David. 1990. *The Afro-American Jeremiad: Appeals for Justice in America.* Philadelphia: Temple University Press.
Love, Dorothy, ed. 1984. "Mary Jane McLeod Bethune." In *A Salute to Historic Black Women.* Chicago: Empack.
McClusky, Audrey, and Elaine M. Smith. 1999. *Mary McLeod Bethune.* Bloomington: Indiana University Press.
Smith, Elaine M. 1996. "Mary McLeod Bethune's 'Last Will and Testament': A Legacy for Race Vindication." *Journal of Negro History* 81 (Winter): 105–122.

Better Business Bureau's Wise Giving Alliance
See Accountability

Blood and Organ Donation

In North America, Europe, and Australia, approximately 42,000 organs were donated anonymously in 2000; an additional 8,000-plus kidneys were donated by living persons, generally to family members. Since there are, as yet, no substitutes for these life-giving organs, and payment for organs was outlawed in the United States in 1984 (and in Europe shortly thereafter), these gifts are an especially beneficent form of philanthropy.

The major intellectual and policy issues surrounding organ procurement center on the ban on markets in organs. The debate about organ markets is a manifestation of the larger debate concerning the appropriate domain of the market—a debate over the competing values of freedom, human rights and the commodification of human beings, economic justice, and, of course, efficiency in the alleviation of human suffering.

At a policy level, many of those opposed to an organ market fear that it would lead to exploitation of the poor—even, perhaps, to murder—in order to supply the organ market. This fear has not been borne out. However, despite the large number of organs procured from donation, many who need organ transplants are nonetheless unable to get them because the supply of donated organs is not sufficient. Indeed, in 2000, more than 95,000 people were on waiting lists for kidneys alone. In the United States, more than 6,000 Americans died waiting for an organ. The desperate need for lifesaving transplants has spurred worrisome developments. To illustrate:

- Increasingly, kidneys are being procured from living donors, putting those donors at significant health risks, even the risk of death.
- The practice of "organ swapping" is gaining adherents.
- Proposals to enlarge the definition of death are under consideration.
- Some fear that death might be hastened to make needed organs available.
- It has been alleged that in some countries prisoners have been executed for their organs.
- Black markets and organ trafficking have been documented.

The Debate over the Ban on an Organ Market
Economists have long debated the efficiency of relying on altruism, generally. In the context of human blood and organs, economists have articulated many angles in their debate regarding the market ban. Arguing from ethics and political philosophy, some economists have opposed restrictions on sales, citing reasons of personal liberty and efficiency. Others have justified some restrictions on markets on the nonconsequentialist ground that people have a "right not to act out of desperation."

Still others have tried to justify restrictions on market bans in cases of market failure, which has led to a

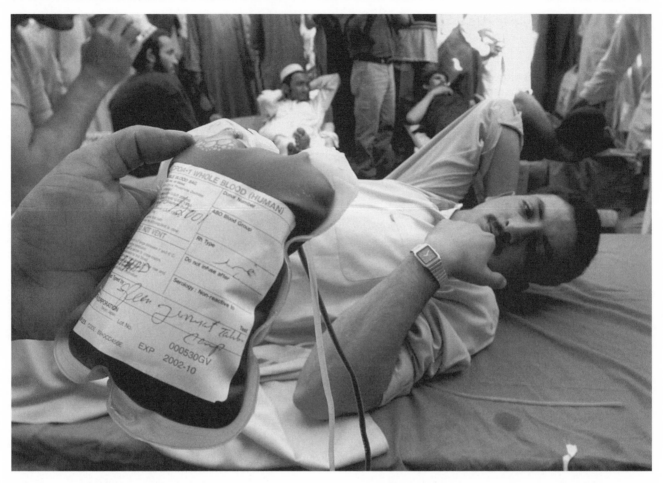

Pakistani Fahad Khan gives blood in Peshawar, October 2001, at a makeshift blood donation center set up to receive blood to assist Afghan civilians injured in the U.S.-led strikes on Afghanistan. (Reuters/Zainal Abd Halim; Reuters/Corbis)

hunt for efficiency-related reasons to ban a market in human organs. The modern debate over markets in human tissue began with Richard Titmuss, who argued that a blood procurement system relying on altruism was not only more ethical than a market but also more efficient. He found the basis for this claim of efficiency in comparisons of blood quality under the two systems: Titmuss presented evidence suggesting that a commercial system subjected both recipients and donors to unnecessary risks. He reported studies that showed that hepatitis rates from blood transfusions were much lower when the blood was donated rather than purchased. One might infer that, in the absence of effective tests for diseases such as hepatitis, donated blood is of better quality because donors who are not paid for their blood have no incentive to conceal their illnesses. An appeal to altru-

ism may also tend to attract people with healthier habits. Furthermore, offering financial incentives for blood could cause those in need of money to take unnecessary risks. They might, for example, supply too frequently, thereby endangering their own health.

Titmuss's book (1971) attracted the attention of many important social scientists, including future Nobel Prize–winning economist Kenneth Arrow. Arrow (1972) noted that the basic problem associated with procuring blood had parallels in the trade of other commodities and services in which the buyer is not in a position to know what he is buying, whereas the seller knows what he is selling, such as the market for used cars. Arrow and Titmuss disagreed fundamentally over how individuals respond when markets are introduced. Titmuss believed that the price incentives offered by markets would drive out altruism and

Professor Kenneth J. Arrow of Harvard, cowinner of the 1972 Nobel Prize for Economic Science (Bettmann/Corbis)

cause the donated supply to wither. In short, Titmuss believed that either a market *or* donation is possible, but not both, and that the introduction of a market would deny people "the right to give."

Arrow could find no evidence for the existence of such a phenomenon and could not understand why the creation of a market in blood would decrease the altruism expressed in giving blood. Arrow's analysis is consistent with the view that altruism is a limited resource, which must, therefore, be rationed. According to this view, altruistic and nonaltruistic individuals respond to different incentives. Altruistic individuals supply when sufficiently exhorted; nonaltruistic individuals supply when offered a satisfactory financial incentive. Neither responds to the other's incentives. Thus, for Arrow, the introduction of a market elicits new supply from nonaltruists, all the while leaving the donated supply from altruists undiminished. Equally, reducing effort to obtain donations does not increase market-generated supply.

Arrow's view on altruism reflects the general economist's view, captured nicely in Dennis Robertson's (1956, 147) answer to a question that he posed in the title to an article "What Do Economists Econo-mize?" Robertson's answer was "love," by which, Robert M. Solow explained, "[Robertson] meant that altruism is a scarce resource, and that society should seek to accomplish its purposes to the maximum extent possible without depending on disinterested kindness" (1971, 1706).

This discussion took place largely in the 1970s and early 1980s and in the context of blood procurement. Today, in the main, the issue appears largely settled for economists. Technological and scientific advances have allayed concerns about the quality issue among those who favor markets in human organs. Although a case can be made that a market would encourage murder (a major market failure that has not yet drawn the attention of those who favor markets), the search for more conventional types of market failure has, by and large, not succeeded.

Since 1984, when the United States banned the sale of human organs, the lines in the debate over commercialism have been more clearly drawn: On the one hand, those who favor a market in human organs argue primarily on efficiency grounds, contending that payments to suppliers would elicit greater supply, thereby reducing shortages; those who oppose a market, on the other hand, argue on grounds of ethical principle rather than efficiency.

Conclusion

Modern advances in biotechnology have made human beings—living and dead—useful to each other in radically new ways. Transplants of human hearts, livers, kidneys, blood, corneas, skin, and bones are now commonplace, and new uses for human body parts are proposed almost daily. If therapies based on transplants of fetal tissue or stem cells prove successful in treating such diseases as Parkinson's, diabetes, and Alzheimer's, then several million more could benefit. Beyond these developments in transplantation is the increasing use by biotechnology companies of human tissue to develop commercial products. In short, a large-scale production system involving physicians, hospitals, and pharmaceutical companies is emerging, and this industry relies on human tissue as a basic resource.

The question for the future is whether the objective of an efficient and ethical human-tissue industry, domestically and internationally, can be achieved by a policy of banning markets and by reliance on the nonprofit organizations that run the nonmarket in human tissue.

Emanuel D. Thorne

References and further reading

Arrow, Kenneth J. 1972. "Gifts and Exchanges." *Philosophy and Public Affairs* 1 (4): 343–362.

Robertson, D. H. 1956. "What Does the Economist Economize?" Reprinted in *Economic Commentaries*. London: Staples Press.

Solow, R. M. 1971. "Blood and Thunder." *Yale Law Journal* 80, no. 8 (July): 1696–1711.

Titmuss, Richard. 1971. *The Gift Relationship: From Human Blood to Social Policy*. New York: Pantheon.

Boards of Nonprofits

See Governance of Nonprofits

BoardSource

In the early 1980s, a survey conducted by the Association of Governing Boards of Universities and Colleges (AGB) and the INDEPENDENT SECTOR found that nearly 70 percent of respondents (nonprofit board members and other nonprofit executives) did not feel they were doing an effective job of board ed-

ucation and training. In addition, AGB received numerous requests for assistance in board training by nonprofits that desired the same services AGB already offered educational institutions.

Thus, in 1988 the W. K. Kellogg Foundation provided the lead grant to establish the National Center for Nonprofit Boards (NCNB), which was renamed BoardSource in January 2002. The mission of NCNB was to "increase the effectiveness of nonprofit boards." As a nonprofit organization with more than 13,000 members, NCNB provided programs and services designed to increase the effectiveness of nonprofit organizations by strengthening their boards of directors.

With the name change to BoardSource in 2002, this mission has not changed. In keeping with the perception that NCNB was a source of information and resources for nonprofit boards, BoardSource was designed to build on NCNB strengths in order to provide better service for nonprofit leaders throughout the world. Programs and services offered by BoardSource include publications, videos, workshops, training, help through consultants, and an annual conference. BoardSource addresses all areas of nonprofit governance issues through its publication series and provides a variety of opportunities for professional development for board members, nonprofit staff, and nonprofit consultants.

Although primarily a membership organization, nonmembers may request answers to board-related questions through the Web site, view the question of the week, and order through the online bookstore.

Ruth B. Mills

References and further reading

BoardSource, http://www.boardsource.org (cited October 22, 2002).

Booth, Ballington (1857–1940), and Booth, Maud (1865–1948)

Ballington Booth once said, "Our work is not all bread and shelter. The underprivileged, the weak, and the unfortunate need more. They need sympathy, the warmth of fellowship, and the instilling of courage" (Wisbey 1994, 110). Although he spoke these words at the end of the Great Depression, they capture the mix of spiritual solicitude and social pragmatism that characterized his philanthropic mission over six decades. Ballington and his wife, Maud, in their leadership of the Salvation Army (1887–1896) and the Volunteers of America (1896–1940), wed religion and humanitarianism at a time when social service delivery was becoming increasingly "scientific" and religion seemed less interested in this world than in the next.

The Booths, British evangelicals, believed that individual and social salvation were linked, and they expected followers to care for the material as well as the religious needs of the poor among whom they worked. Ballington Booth, by dint of his birth, was destined for a religious vocation. He was born in 1857 to William and Catherine Booth. His parents started the Salvation Army during his childhood, and they expected their children to lead it. Maud Charlesworth, Ballington's wife, was born in 1865, the daughter of an Anglican rector who left a comfortable country parish to work in a poor London church. Maud became acquainted with the Salvation Army when her mother took her to one of its religious revival meetings. There, the sixteen-year-old found her life's work, smitten as much by Ballington, who led the service, as by the Army's crusade.

In 1887, when the Ballington Booths assumed leadership of the Salvation Army's work in the United States, the movement was disliked because its hallmarks—female preaching, rowdy services, and military parades—seemed contrary to traditional Christianity. Although the Booths continued the Army's lively antics, they also reached out to the rich and powerful, whose good opinion could help the cause's reputation as well as finance its activities. After two years in New York, where the Army was headquartered, Maud decided its mission to the poor should include the type of direct ministry that Salvationists pioneered in London. This outreach, dubbed the Cellar, Gutter, and Garrett Brigade, sent young women to live in the slums, where they tended their neighbors, preparing food, cleaning homes, helping the sick, and caring for children. Linking social and spiritual salvation—meeting material needs was considered a prerequisite for saving souls—the Army expanded its social services and the Booths oversaw the nationwide creation of homeless shelters, slum posts, and rescue homes for "fallen women."

In 1896, Army headquarters in London informed the Ballington Booths that they were to be posted

elsewhere. Rather than leave the United States—where they had become citizens—the couple resigned from the Army and started a new religious organization, the Volunteers of America. Although the Volunteers shared many aspects in common with the Army (military titles, ranks, and uniforms), its differences were basic. The new movement was explicitly American and defined itself as a home missionary movement, an auxiliary to the churches rather than a Protestant denomination. Ballington devoted most of his time to administering the Volunteers and strengthening its spiritual foundation, and Maud pioneered its work in prison reform. In the early twentieth century, there were no advocacy groups lobbying for prisoners' rights or helping ex-convicts adjust to society. "Little Mother," as Maud Booth was called by prisoners, wanted to reform the worst aspects of prison life (such as the ball and chain, enforced idleness, and harsh discipline), assist the families of incarcerated men, and improve the ex-con's chances for rehabilitation.

In addition to prison work, the Booths also encouraged the Volunteers of America to become active in emergency relief, hospitals, shelters, and homes for unwed mothers. After World War I, the movement's focus increasingly shifted away from religion, and today it is a nonsectarian philanthropic organization. Known for its responsiveness to local needs, the Volunteers of America is among the nation's largest providers of affordable housing for the elderly, low-income families, and people with mental or physical disabilities. The Ballington Booths' love for their adopted homeland, their desire to find practical expression for religious commitment, and their affirmation of each individual's dignity are among the legacies that continue to shape the Volunteers' mission.

Diane Winston

See also Booth, Evangeline; Salvation Army
Note: See Booth family references and further reading on page 55, following entry for "Booth, Evangeline."

Booth, Evangeline (1865–1950)
Early Years and Education
Evangeline Booth, head of the American branch of the Salvation Army from 1904 to 1934, had a solid

grasp of her adopted countrymen's religious preferences. An American, she said, "needs a religion that does something for him and in him, and provides something for him to do in the way of helping others" (Winston 1999, 188). Booth followed her own counsel, establishing the Army as a preeminent religious philanthropy. Although she inherited an Army that most Americans viewed as a ragtag evangelical mission, she helped transform it into one of the nation's foremost charitable fundraisers. Booth's savvy leadership enabled the Army to institutionalize its mission, making its provision of social services a religious good that transcended sectarian differences.

Born in London on Christmas Day 1865 to William and Catherine Booth, founders of the Salvation Army in England, Evangeline Booth was viewed by her family as a special gift from God. The seventh of eight children, Evangeline grew up in a household where religion was paramount. At five, she was preaching to her dolls, and a few years later, William Booth found her exhorting the kitchen staff. Like her siblings, Evangeline was educated at home and began a ministry in her teens. Stationed in a slum brigade, at eighteen she won over skeptics by working as a flower girl and opening a toy hospital. In later years, she wove these memories into "The Commander in Rags," a dramatic monologue that served both as a religious witness and a fundraising appeal.

Career Highlights and Major Philanthropic Achievement

After rising through the ranks of the Salvation Army in London, Evangeline became territorial commissioner in Canada and Newfoundland. The Army prospered during her eight-year tenure, and in 1904 she was appointed head of the American branch. By then, the Army's street parades were a familiar sight and its social service network was expanding. Seeking to secure the movement's finances, Evangeline made institution-building a priority. When she arrived in New York, Army property was valued at $1.5 million; thirty years later, in 1934, that figure was $48 million plus a capital account of $35 million.

During the 1910s, Booth enlarged the Army's social programs and spotlighted its campaigns against the evils of the day, including cigarettes, alcohol, and white slavery. But the Army received its biggest boost when Booth received permission to provide social and welfare services to U.S. troops stationed in France during World War I. Intuiting the troops' needs for wholesome female companionship, Booth dispatched young women to "mother" American soldiers. Setting up "huts" near the front lines, Sallies, as Army women were called, sewed clothes, wrote letters, and prayed with the men. They also served coffee and doughnuts, frying thousands of crullers each day.

By the war's end, the Salvation Army's reputation was transformed from a street corner mission to a premier humanitarian philanthropy. Publicly downplaying their evangelical bent, Salvationists sought to provide nonsectarian social services, and Americans of all (or no) religious faiths came to support their charitable work. That work expanded rapidly during Evangeline's tenure. The Army turned rescue homes for "fallen women" into homes for unwed mothers and expanded its network of daycare services, salvage work, men's shelters, hospitals, and hotels for working women.

Evangeline's biggest challenge came with the Great Depression. As one of the few social service providers operating on a national scale, the Army was in a key position to offer assistance, especially in the years before the federal government was organized to do so. The Army helped millions while maintaining its core beliefs. For example, judging that the dole undermined an individual's self-respect, Salvationists often asked recipients to work for their bed and bread. They tried to treat clients with dignity and to keep families together. In 1934, Evangeline achieved her life's ambition when she was elected general of the Salvation Army. As head of the international movement, she returned to the London headquarters, but when her tenure ended in 1939, she went back to New York. Although she remained interested in the Army's welfare and enjoyed addressing Salvationist groups, she lived quietly in retirement. Evangeline Booth died in 1950.

In the years between 1904 and 1934, the Army's status changed from an outsider sect to a mainstream religious charity, and Evangeline Booth was at the center of that transformation. Her instinct for helping people in ways that directly addressed their needs—at the front lines or in breadlines—touched the public's imagination. That she did not foist religion on those whom the Army helped ensured the public's support and enabled the organization to become, by the end of the twentieth century, the nation's largest charitable fundraiser.

Diane Winston

See also Booth, Ballington, and Booth, Maude; Salvation Army

References and further reading

McKinley, Edward H. 1995. *Marching to Glory: The History of the Salvation Army in the United States, 1880–1992.* Grand Rapids, MI: William B. Eerdmans.

Taiz, Lillian. 2001. *Hallelujah Lads and Lassies: Remaking the Salvation Army in America.* Chapel Hill: University of North Carolina Press.

Welty, Susan F. 1961. *Look Up and Hope.* New York: Thomas Nelson.

Wilson, P. W. 1948. *General Evangeline Booth of the Salvation Army.* New York: Charles Scribner's Sons.

Winston, Diane. 1999. *Red Hot and Righteous: The Urban Religion of the Salvation Army.* Cambridge: Harvard University Press.

———. 2002. "Ballington (1857–1940) and Maud Booth (1865–1948), Founders of the Volunteers of America, and Evangeline Booth (1865–1950), Commander of the Salvation Army." In *Notable American Philanthropists: Biographies of Giving and Volunteering,* edited by Robert T. Grimm, Jr. Westport, CT: Oryx Press.

Wisbey, Herbert A., Jr. 1994. *Volunteers of America: 1896–1948.* Metairie, LA: Volunteers of America.

Brace, Charles Loring (1826–1890)

Born in Litchfield, Connecticut, on June 19, 1826, Charles Loring Brace pioneered foster care in the United States. His mother died when he was fourteen, leaving him in the care of his father, a history teacher who had read to Charles for two hours a day throughout his youth. The precocious Brace entered college at the age of sixteen, eventually graduating with degrees from Yale and Union Theological Seminary in New York City. He became a prolific letter writer; many of his letters survived and formed the basis for the account of his life later published by his daughter.

In February 1850, Brace's beloved sister Emma died and he subsequently embarked on a tour of Europe. As his letters attest, he returned two years later with a renewed sense of purpose. As an ordained Methodist minister living in New York City, Brace felt himself increasingly pulled away from the pulpit and toward social justice issues. He experimented with attempts to reform adult behavior on an orthodox Christian model. Lack of success in that area convinced Brace that his talents would be better directed at youth. He wished to counter the vices of the "big city" through old-fashioned preaching at "boys' meetings." These meetings gave way to organized schools for both boys and girls aimed at providing homeless children with job skills that would enable them to find work in the city. The schools, however, proved ineffective, as students often failed to attend regularly or to concentrate on their course work.

In 1853, Brace founded the Children's Aid Society. Still in operation today, the purpose of the society in the 1850s was to find suitable homes for orphans from New York City in the rural environment of "the West," which at that time consisted of such states as Indiana, Michigan, and Illinois. The potential families were screened by local committees and required to house, clothe, and educate the children in a pious environment. Ideally, each child was matched with a family prior to arriving from New York. A few hundred children would be sent at a time via railroad to their various destinations. Known as "Orphan Trains," the mass emigration of orphans from the city to the farm fulfilled Brace's dream of instituting Christian philanthropic work on a large scale.

Eventually, the program placed juvenile delinquents and those children whose families simply could not afford to raise them with rural families. Although many questioned Brace's methods, his success rate was high. A report issued in 1910 by the society claimed that 87 percent of the participants had "done well" ("Champion of Children," 2002). The Children's Aid Society initially tried to keep track of every child, but as that task became impossible, it used different methods to assess the efficacy of its placements. It was later determined that the Orphan Train program saved nearly 100,000 participants from almost certain death due to the violence and poverty they would have faced had they remained in New York City.

Brace served as executive secretary of the society until his death from Bright's disease in 1890. His son held the same position until 1928. One year later, the last Orphan Train transported children to Missouri; by that time, the society had expanded to include numerous charitable programs, including those designed to combat illiteracy and child labor abuses. Brace had remained steadfast in his belief in the role of religion in reform and was praised by his colleagues for his "Christ-like devotion" to the children of New York City (Brace 1894, 483).

Emily M. Hall

References and further reading
Brace, Charles Loring. 1972 [1872]. *The Dangerous Classes of New York, and Twenty Years' Work among Them.* New York: Wynkoop and Hallenbeck.
Brace, Emma, ed. 1894. *The Life of Charles Loring Brace.* New York: Charles Scribner's Sons.
"Champion of Children: Charles Loring Brace," http://www.childabuse.org/champions2.htm (cited December 13, 2002).
Children's Aid Society, http://www.childrensaidsociety.org.

Brookings, Robert Somers (1850–1932)

Philanthropist Robert Somers Brookings was born in 1850 in Cecil County, Maryland, the son of Richard Brookings, a physician, and Mary Carter Brookings. When Robert Brookings was three, his father died and his mother moved to Baltimore, where she later married Henry Reynolds, a carpenter. Brookings moved to St. Louis, Missouri, when he was seventeen to join his older brother, Harry. The brothers went to work for Cupples and Marston, a dry goods firm. Robert soon became a traveling salesperson for the company, and in 1872 he became a partner. By the time he retired in 1885, he had accumulated a fortune of more than $6 million.

Early on in his career, Brookings had aspirations of becoming a concert violinist, which led him to Europe for further training. Although skilled as a musician, Brookings realized he lacked the talent necessary to become a professional performer. He then turned to philanthropy. In 1886, Brookings was appointed president of Washington University, which at that time occupied a single building in downtown St. Louis. Brookings transformed the small college into a major university, in the process establishing Barnes Hospital and Children's Hospital as major medical research centers. During World War I, Brookings was appointed by Woodrow Wilson to serve as a commissioner of the War Industries Board.

Through his association with Andrew Carnegie, Brookings became a trustee of the Carnegie Peace Foundation in 1910 and a founding member of the Carnegie Corporation in 1911. In 1916, he became a founding trustee of the Institute for Government Research (IGR) in Washington, D.C., which was heavily funded by the Carnegie Foundation. As a trustee, Brookings played an instrumental role in creating a graduate program and an Institute of Economics associated with the IGR. In 1928, these programs were consolidated into the Brookings Institution. As the author of three books and a half-dozen pamphlets, Brookings called for economic reform, including free trade, agricultural cooperatives, federal unemployment insurance, and the establishment of a European trading union.

In 1927, Brookings married Isabel January, the daughter of a longtime St. Louis friend. Four years later, she donated a building on Lafayette Square to house the Brookings Institution. He remained chairman of the board there until his death in 1932. Although no longer housed on Lafayette Square, the Brookings Institution has developed into a highly respected center of research that still acknowledges the importance of Brookings's economic policies at the turn of the twentieth century.

Donald T. Critchlow

References and further reading
Brookings, Robert S. 1925. *Industrial Ownership: Its Economic and Social Significance.* New York: Ayer.
Brookings Institution, http://www.brookings.org.
Critchlow, Donald T. 2002. "Robert Somers Brookings." In *Notable American Philanthropists: Biographies of Giving and Volunteering,* edited by Robert T. Grimm, Jr. Westport, CT: Oryx Press.
Hagedorn, Hermann. 1937. *Brookings: A Biography.* New York: Macmillan.

C

Campus Compact

Campus Compact is a national coalition of college presidents committed to higher education's civic mission, including promoting student citizenship, campus/community partnerships, and faculty integration of public and community needs with teaching and research. It was created in 1985 by the presidents of Brown, Georgetown, and Stanford universities and the president of the Education Commission of the States, who thought the prevailing public image of college students as materialistic and self-absorbed was false. The presidents believed additional encouragement and a more conducive environment for students to engage in service could mold students into more committed, informed citizens and leaders.

Located in Providence, Rhode Island, with affiliate offices in more than twenty-five states, Campus Compact also runs the National Center for Community Colleges based at Mesa Community College in Arizona. These state-based offices link the national office to school systems, higher education, and community-based and government organizations, assisting member colleges and universities with information, resources, workshops, and conferences. In 2001, membership included 743 public and private colleges and universities spread over most states.

Member presidents commit their campuses to an educational mission, which inherently includes development of personal and social responsibility. In 1996,

they endorsed five central principles: advocating participation in public and community service, including individual student volunteerism and institutional efforts to improve communities' well-being; publicly articulating ideas contributing to the common good and influencing fair, impartial civic discourse; supporting cooperation between colleges and communities to renew civic life, improve opportunity, expand democratic participation, and apply college resources to community needs; supporting student, faculty, staff, and alumni in citizenship-building service activities; and supporting service learning by integrating academic study with service to include faculty and students in responsible and reflective involvement in communities (Campus Compact 2004).

Campus Compact's activities fall into several areas. Member campuses promote student involvement in community service, especially through service-learning course work, lending assistance and expertise to communities while students learn experientially. National Campus Compact advocates federal legislation promoting community service, has helped to pass legislation, including the National and Community Service Act in 1990, and provides leadership for national programs such as the America Reads initiative and the use of new Federal Work-Study funds for community service. It also forms education, government, business, and community partnerships to promote renewed civic, educational, and economic opportunities, democratic participation, and the application of higher education resources to community problems.

Campus Compact provides information, including statistics, analysis, and publications, on issues, findings, curricula, and innovative programs. Awarding grants to members and affiliates, it helps faculty to create curricula that combine service with academic achievement and helps state affiliates to build supporting infrastructures. It provides funding and awards for outstanding service by students and faculty in carrying out service initiatives, for programs integrating service into curricula, and for specific community needs. Finally, it provides conferences, workshops, forums, and meetings for exchanging ideas, expertise, and successful program models.

Michael Coatney

References and further reading

Bringle, Robert G., Richard Games, Catherine Ludlum Foos, Robert Osgood, and Randall Osborne. 2000. "Faculty Fellows Program." *American Behavioral Scientist* 43 (February): 882–895.

Brozan, Nadine. "Colleges Encourage Student Volunteers." 1987. *New York Times,* January 14, Late City Final Edition, C1.

Campus Compact. 2004. http://www.compact.org/about/about-content.html (cited October 20, 2001).

Gamson, Zelda, Elizabeth Hollander, et al. 1998. "The University in Engagement with Society." *Liberal Education* 84 (2): 20–26.

Canadian Philanthropy

Canada has a diverse and vibrant nonprofit and voluntary sector that is supported by the vast majority of Canadians through their contributions of time and money. It consists of a wide variety of organizations, including places of worship, social service organizations, shelters for the homeless, arts groups, food banks, foundations, self-help groups, health charities, recreation organizations, social clubs, and advocacy groups as well as hospitals and colleges and universities.

Nonprofit and voluntary organizations are privileged by Canadian governments in a number of ways. They are exempt from income taxes and certain other taxes, and donors to registered charities may claim tax credits for their donations. Registered charities are a distinct set of nonprofits registered by the Canada Customs and Revenue Agency (CCRA) to work in health care, poverty relief, education, religion, and other areas of a charitable nature beneficial to the community as a whole. Just over one-third of charities (36 percent) are places of worship, 14 percent are social service organizations, and about 10 percent are foundations (Hall and Macpherson 1997). In Canada, virtually all hospitals as well as colleges and universities are registered charities. However, hospitals and universities, although incorporated as nonprofit organizations and registered as charities, are so strongly influenced by government that they may be better considered as government institutions for some purposes (Hall and Banting 2000).

There are approximately 79,000 registered charities, according to the Canada Customs and Revenue Agency, and an estimated additional 100,000 other legally incorporated nonprofits (Quarter 1992). Although there is little information about their social impact, their economic contributions appear to be considerable. One study estimated that the nonprofit sector, at a minimum, accounts for 4 percent of gross domestic product (GDP) (Day and Devlin 1997), and another calculated that charities alone account for from 12 to 13 percent of GDP and employ about 9 percent of Canada's labor force (Sharpe 1994). Private giving is an important source of revenues for Canadian charities, providing 14 percent of all revenues (Hall and Macpherson 1997).

Virtually all Canadians contribute time or money to charitable and nonprofit organizations. According to a national survey, 91 percent of Canadians aged fifteen and older made either financial or in-kind donations to charitable and nonprofit organizations in 2000 and 27 percent volunteered their time (Hall et al. 2001).

In terms of financial contributions, 78 percent of Canadians made donations that totaled almost Can$5 billion. The likelihood of making a charitable donation and the amount donated are influenced by a variety of factors. Religiosity—or level of religious commitment—is associated with a heightened incidence of charitable giving and larger donations, both to religious organizations and to other types of charitable and nonprofit organizations. Giving also tends to increase with age, education, and income. Although donors with higher household incomes make larger donations, they tend to give a smaller percentage of their pretax household income to charity than do Canadians with the lowest levels of income. Women are more likely to make donations than are men (87 percent vs. 75 percent) but give approximately the same amounts.

Religious organizations receive the largest portion of the total value of donations in Canada. In 2000, they were given Can$2.4 billion, or 49 percent of the total value of donations. Health organizations received 20 percent of donation dollars, and social service organizations received 10 percent. The most common ways Canadians make donations is by giving to door-to-door canvassers (15 percent of all donations in 2000), responding to requests through the mail (15 percent), and sponsoring someone in an event such as a walkathon (15 percent).

Of course, the gift of time can be as important as the gift of money. According to one study, the approximately 6.5 million Canadians who volunteered in 2000 contributed a total of just over 1 billion hours in 2000, or the equivalent of 549,000 full-time jobs (Hall et al. 2001). Volunteers contributed 162 hours over the year, on average. However, 7 percent of all Canadians gave 73 percent of all volunteer hours.

Volunteering in Canada appears to be related to a variety of economic and social factors. For example, volunteer rates are lowest among seniors, yet seniors who do volunteer contribute substantially more time on average than the members of any other age group. In contrast, volunteer rates increase with income, but those with the lowest levels of household income give more time than the members of other income groups. Higher levels of education and religious activity are associated with higher rates of volunteering and with more volunteer hours than are low levels of education. Finally, women are somewhat more likely to volunteer than men (28 percent vs. 25 percent), but men contribute more volunteer hours per year (170 vs. 155 hours, respectively).

Arts, culture, and recreation organizations receive 26 percent of all volunteer hours, followed by social services organizations (20 percent) and religious orga-

nizations (16 percent). More than half of volunteers (57 percent) helped organize or supervise events for an organization, and about four in ten served on a board or committee or took part in canvassing, campaigning, or fundraising.

Most Canadians give money or time to nonprofit organizations to provide support to one another and their communities. However, the tendency to donate time and money are linked, and a small core group donates a significant portion of both (Hall et al. 2001). Forty-six percent of the total value of all donations and 40 percent of all volunteer hours are contributed by only 9 percent of Canadians. Canadian philanthropy, as a result, appears to have a remarkably broad yet vulnerably thin base.

Michael H. Hall

References and further reading
Day, K., and R. A. Devlin. 1997. *The Canadian Nonprofit Sector*. Ottawa: Canadian Policy Research Networks.
Hall, M., and K. G. Banting. 2000. "The Nonprofit in Canada: An Introduction." In *The Nonprofit Sector in Canada: Roles and Responsibilities*, edited by K. G. Banting. Kingston: Queen's University, School of Policy Studies.
Hall, M., L. McKeown, and K. Roberts. 2001. *Caring Canadians, Involved Canadians: Highlights from the 2000 National Survey of Giving, Volunteering and Participating*. Ottawa: Statistics Canada.
Hall, M. H., and. L. G. Macpherson. 1997. "A Provincial Portrait of Canada's Charities." *Research Bulletin* 4 (2, 3). Toronto: Canadian Centre for Philanthropy.
Quarter, J. 1992. *Canada's Social Economy*. Toronto: James Lorimer.
Sharpe, D. 1994. *A Portrait of Canada's Charities: The Size, Scope and Financing of Registered Charities*. Toronto: Canadian Centre for Philanthropy.

Carnegie, Andrew (1835–1919)

Andrew Carnegie was born on November 25, 1835, in Dunfermline, Scotland. At the age of twelve he immigrated with his parents to America and his formal education ended. They settled in the Pittsburgh area. Andrew, at the age of thirteen, found work as a bobbin boy in a cotton mill to help support his family. When his father died in 1855, Andrew took on the responsibility of supporting his mother and younger brother. While working in Pittsburgh, Carnegie educated himself by

Andrew Carnegie (1835–1919) (Library of Congress)

studying business practices and reading voraciously from the library of Colonel James Anderson, who opened his private library to young Andrew and other working boys in the area. Andrew would never forget the importance of the philanthropic action of Colonel Anderson as he developed his own view of how philanthropy should work.

From 1855 to 1865, Carnegie pursued a wide variety of business interests, but it was in the partnership he undertook in 1865 to form the Union Iron Mills that was the turning point in his career. By 1892, his Carnegie Steel Company dominated the U.S. steel industry. However, he was often portrayed as a ruthless businessman. His decisions during a strike among workers in 1892 at his plant in Homestead, Pennsylvania, were denounced, and the event became a symbol of the injustice owners did to workers. He sold Carnegie Steel Company to J. P. Morgan for almost $500 million in 1901, two years after he published his philosophy of wealth in a June 1889 essay in the *North American Review*. A second essay published in December of the same year discussed the best fields for philanthropy. The two were combined to form *The Gospel of Wealth*, an important work in philanthropy still today.

At the age of thirty-three, Carnegie was already a multimillionaire in today's terms. In a note to himself, he wrote, "The man who dies thus rich dies disgraced" (Wall 1992, 41). In this same memo, he told himself that he would retire in a couple of years to pursue good works and practice his belief that he should give his money away before he died. It wasn't until the turn of the century, however, that he actually began the task in earnest. He began his formal philanthropy in 1881 with a gift for a library in his hometown of Dunfermline, Scotland. By the end of his life, he had funded 1,681 public libraries in the United States and 828 in other parts of the English-speaking world. Because of his generosity in this area, he is often labeled "the patron saint of libraries." He did jump start the public library movement in this country by leveraging his gifts, requiring the communities to agree to provide public support through tax revenues into the future to operate and buy books for the buildings that he funded.

Carnegie is also often called "the father of scientific philanthropy" because of the philosophy that he presented in *The Gospel of Wealth*. He put forth three main arguments. First, he advised wealthy individuals not to spoil their heirs by leaving them large amounts of money. It is far better, he said, that each individual make it on his own in the capitalistic system. Second, he argued that it is best to give during one's lifetime to causes that assist in preventing the need for charity. In other words, donors should use their knowledge to engage in wise giving. Third, philanthropists should help those who are able and willing to help themselves within the system. "It were better for mankind that the millions of the rich were thrown into the sea than spent as to encourage the slothful, the drunken, the unworthy," he wrote (Burlingame 1992, 10). This belief led Carnegie to focus his giving on public libraries, educational institutions, and other public places that would benefit those who chose to participate in their own betterment.

In order to keep to his pledge of spending his fortune before he died, Carnegie set up several major philanthropic institutions. He founded the Carnegie Institution of Washington, a scientific research and educational organization, in 1902. In 1918 he set up the Carnegie Teachers Pension Fund, which was later changed to the Carnegie Foundation for the Advancement of Teaching and is now known as Teachers Insurance and Annuity Association–College Retirement Equities Fund (TIAA-CREF), the largest teachers pension fund in the United States. He also established the Carnegie Endowment for International Peace and the Hero Fund to support his pacifist roots. Finally, in 1911 he created the Carnegie Corporation of New York, which remains today as the most visible of his philanthropies, to receive the bulk of his remaining fortune of $125 million. Upon his death in 1919, editorial writers around the country declared an end of an era in American capitalism.

Dwight F. Burlingame

References and further reading
Burlingame, Dwight, ed. 1992. *The Responsibilities of Wealth.* Bloomington: Indiana University Press.
Carnegie, Andrew. 1920. *Autobiography of Andrew Carnegie.* Boston: Houghton Mifflin.
Hendrick, Burton J. 1932. *The Life of Andrew Carnegie, I and II.* New York: Doubleday, Doran.
Krass, Peter. 2002. *Carnegie.* New York: John Wiley.
Wall, Joseph Frazier. 1970. *Andrew Carnegie.* New York: Oxford University Press.
———, ed. 1992. *The Andrew Carnegie Reader.* Pittsburgh: University of Pittsburgh Press.

Catholic Philanthropy

The Roman Catholic presence in North America commenced in 1565 with Spain's first permanent settlement in Saint Augustine, Florida, and its later colonization of territories to the west and southwest. Colonization efforts by France, which began in the same era, focused on New Orleans and on northern and northwestern territories. During the extended colonization period, these European governments and the Catholic Church jointly financed the work of missionaries whom they commissioned to "civilize and Christianize" the numerous Native American tribes.

Catholicism was banned in most of the English colonies until 1776, although missionaries had served in a few small Catholic settlements in Maryland and Pennsylvania since the mid-seventeenth century. As a result, when John Carroll of Maryland was appointed the nation's first bishop in 1790, and the church was formally organized, his congregation numbered only about 30,000.

Since 1790, the Catholic Church in America has consistently called its members not only to support their local parishes and dioceses but also to unite as a church community to assist the needy. An emphasis on the spiritual merits of gifts of personal service as well as of money encouraged parishioners of every social class to participate actively in the church's charitable sector.

The first benevolent work undertaken by American Catholics was the education of girls. In 1805, Visitation nuns near Washington, D.C., established a small day school for poor girls and cared for a number of boarding orphans. Several years later, Mother Elizabeth Seton, who had just founded the Sisters of Charity, established a similar school in Baltimore. From these small beginnings evolved the vast and varied network of charitable and educational institutions that has come to exemplify Catholic philanthropy in North America.

The arrival of millions of impoverished immigrants, many of them Catholic, in the 1840s and 1850s posed an immense challenge for a scattered, working-class church. Benevolent laity, clergy, and members of religious orders joined forces to house and care for the destitute, especially orphans. Typically, local parishioners, with the approval of their pastor, would construct a small orphanage, engage an order of nuns to care for the children, and pledge ongoing financial support for the institution. Every parish orphanage had its own male board of trustees, female auxiliary, and benevolent society.

Catholic hospitals appeared in response to devastating typhoid, cholera, and smallpox epidemics that recurred regularly in the early nineteenth century. Founded by religious sisterhoods to serve the indigent, these small establishments were financed by free-will offerings and the sisters' contributed labor. In time, they became larger, broadened their services, and increased in number, from 18 in 1860 to about 140 by 1885.

Mainstream citizens distrusted the Catholic Church, not only because of its unpopular religious teachings, but also because its membership was predominantly poor and foreign-born. As a result, except in civic emergency, nineteenth-century Catholics rarely cooperated with other benevolent agencies in charity work. A separatist spirit also marked the church's own charities, since various ethnic groups preferred to concentrate their efforts on projects that aided their own nationalities.

Church leaders strongly encouraged generous young Catholics to join one of the many religious orders that were subsidizing church charities and schools through the contributed labor of their members. The response from women was especially enthusiastic, and by 1900, the nation's more than 40,000 sisters outnumbered clergy by a margin of nearly four to one. Religious sisterhoods continued to flourish until the mid-1960s, when their total membership peaked at approximately 180,000. Nuns were a ubiquitous and very important feature of the nineteenth-century Catholic charity system. In an era of narrow views about women's proper sphere of influence, they assumed leadership roles in hospitals, social agencies, schools, and child-caring institutions, a phenomenon remarked upon by Americans of every religious persuasion.

One aftermath of the Civil War was a sharp rise in the number of orphaned and abandoned children. In response to this critical problem, the Catholic community founded a number of urban orphanages with attached industrial schools. These huge enterprises appeared in most major cities, with seven opening in New York City alone between 1875 and 1885. The New York Catholic Protectory, accommodating nearly 3,300 children, was the largest child-caring institution in the United States in 1897.

Funding for the burgeoning charitable institutions, large and small, came from diverse sources. Contributions in occasional collections, although generous, were never sufficient. Most institutions relied for funding almost entirely on their own boards of trustees and benevolent societies. Society members raised money by sponsoring events that attracted the entire community, such as charity fairs, balls, and bazaars, as well as by selling subscriptions and lottery tickets. These various projects continued throughout the year and provided myriad ways for local parishioners to collaborate in charity as volunteers, financial donors, and event patrons.

By the early twentieth century, the church hierarchy generally agreed that, in comparison with mainstream charity organization, the Catholic philanthropic approach was disorganized and inefficient. Major reform was essential if the church was to collaborate meaningfully with other private charities and government service agencies. The bishops decided that the many charitable institutions in each diocese could no longer continue to operate autonomously in fundraising and in setting institutional policies. With the help of charity professionals, they devised the diocesan charitable bureau, a new structure that would allow them to bring all the charities under their direct control. By the 1930s, almost every diocese had a charitable bureau with the bishop at its head. He appointed its priest-director as well as the clergy and wealthy laymen who sat on its board. The bureau set common policies and all charitable institutions were required to observe them.

This comprehensive restructuring was accompanied by equally far-reaching reforms in the area of charity fundraising. Bishops banned all fundraising events for individual charitable institutions. Instead of a host of local charity fairs, lotteries, and bazaars, there would now be a single annual diocesan-wide charity collection. On "Charity Sunday," congregants in every parish in the diocese were asked to contribute in accord with their means for the support of all charities in the diocese. The funds collected were remitted to the central diocesan office, where the bishop and his advisers proceeded to distribute them among the various charitable institutions.

These radical changes in the church's charity sector disturbed grassroots parishioners. Of particular concern was the expanding involvement of bishops and clergy in the only area of church life where the laity had traditionally enjoyed considerable decision-making power. The ban on charity events to benefit specific institutions weakened the warm rapport between benevolent laity and the religious sisters, and it also reduced occasions for informal contact between donors and beneficiaries. Working- and middle-class parishioners who responded to the call to contribute generously in the annual diocesan charity collection no longer had the means to give much to their favorite charities. Realistically, only the wealthy could afford to designate their giving.

Since the 1960s, the proportion of household income that U.S. Catholics, on average, contribute annually to the church and its charities has declined appreciably, and membership in religious sisterhoods has experienced a dramatic downturn. These disquieting developments are linked, in part at least, to the far-reaching bureaucratization of the church's philanthropic sector in the first half of the twentieth century. Although the highly decentralized approach of nineteenth-century Catholic charity had its flaws, it fostered far more lay initiative and personal involvement than did the hierarchical model that succeeded it.

Several auspicious developments suggest that a revival of time-honored Catholic philanthropic values may be under way. Stewardship, sacrificial giving, and tithing programs are spreading in the nation's 19,000 parishes; parish communities are uniting to address the needs of the local poor; and laity, women as well as men, are again assuming leadership positions in church philanthropy at every level.

Mary J. Oates

References and further reading

Brown, Dorothy M., and Elizabeth McKeown. 1998. *"The Poor Belong to Us": Catholic Charities and American Welfare, 1870–1940.* Cambridge: Harvard University Press.

Greeley, Andrew, and William McManus. 1987. *Catholic Contributions: Sociology and Policy.* Chicago: Thomas More.

Oates, Mary J. 1995. *The Catholic Philanthropic Tradition in America.* Bloomington: Indiana University Press.

O'Brien, David, and Thomas Shannon, eds. 1995. *Catholic Social Thought: The Documentary Heritage.* Maryknoll, NY: Orbis.

Zech, Charles E., Francis J. Butler, and Mary Grant. 2000. *Why Catholics Don't Give . . . And What Can Be Done About It.* Huntington, IN: Our Sunday Visitor Press.

Cause-Related Marketing and Sponsorships

Cause-related marketing and sponsorships are important types of collaborative relationships between the business and nonprofit sectors. These relationships are growing in importance as businesses are coming to expect their involvement with the nonprofit sector to generate business benefits in addition to support for a worthy cause. Nonprofit organizations seek business-partner support to bolster their resource base in an era of declining government funding and stagnant corporate philanthropy.

Cause-Related Marketing

Cause-related marketing is a relationship between a business and a charity or other nonprofit organization in which the business agrees to contribute a proportion of the profits from sales of a product (usually up to a specified limit) to a specified cause. American Express led this trend in the business sector in the 1980s by demonstrating how cause-related marketing programs could increase sales and enhance the company's image. For example, in the last quarter of 1983, American Express heavily advertised that it would donate a penny to the Statue of Liberty restoration fund for every credit card transaction and a dollar for each new card member. The campaign resulted in $1.7 million in donations and a 28 percent increase in use of the American Express card. Other companies took notice.

In addition to supporting a worthy cause, businesses that become involved in cause-related marketing arrangements with nonprofit organizations usually view the campaign as a marketing tactic. Business managers seek increased sales of the targeted products. They also seek to enhance their reputation with customers. There has been sufficient research in the past decade to suggest that all cause-related marketing campaigns are not equally effective, however.

The public's perception of cause-related marketing campaigns is variable. Consumers can be roughly segmented into three groups in terms of their responses. There is a small group of consumers who are skeptics, believing that business always acts out of self-interest. This group is not influenced to purchase products that are targeted in cause-related marketing campaigns, nor is its image of the participating company enhanced. There is also a group of consumers who strongly support cause-related campaigns. These consumers will switch brands to purchase the products of companies engaging in such appeals and appreciate corporate support of a cause they care about. The majority of consumers, however, fall somewhere in the middle of these extremes. They believe businesses are doing well by supporting causes, but they will switch brands only if the targeted product is also a good value in terms of price and quality.

Other factors affect the potential success of cause-related marketing campaigns. Females, for reasons not fully understood, are more responsive to cause-related tactics than males. Also, consumers react more positively to companies that demonstrate long-term support for a nonprofit partner. Consumers' perceptions of company motivations are also important. Companies donating what consumers believe to be trivial amounts are perceived as exploitative.

To increase demand for their brands, corporate managers should look for well-known charities that appeal to the company's target market. Managers need to test different versions of the promotion prior to launching the campaign to ensure that consumers view the program in a positive manner.

Sponsorships

Sponsorships, another type of collaborative association between business and the nonprofit sector, involve agreements between a corporate sponsor and a nonprofit cause or other related event in which the business pays a sponsorship fee to support the cause or event and in return gets to have its name and logo associated with the cause and event.

A business participating in sponsorships is primarily interested in promoting its brand or company name, although sponsors may also want to fund and promote the event. Nonprofits are concerned about protecting their favorable public image and generally have the preponderance of control regarding how their sponsors advertise their association. Sponsors, however, have paid for the right to associate their name with the event and exercise some power in the relationship as well. There are several types of business-nonprofit sponsorships, including sponsorships for sports teams or events, book projects, exhibitions, education, expeditions, cultural activities, local events, and documentary films.

Sponsorships between businesses and nonprofits have experienced a sharp rise in corporate marketing budgets. Marketing dollars allocated to sponsorships in the United States increased from $2.1 billion in 1989 to nearly $7 billion in 2000. This amount covers the amount paid for sponsorship rights; the total sponsorship expenditures would be much higher.

Although businesses are motivated to enter into sponsorship agreements primarily by the opportunity to associate their brand and company names with a worthy cause in a way that will reach its target markets as well as the general public, nonprofits are motivated by the opportunity to generate funding. The desired funding may be used to support the event (for example, Special Olympics), or the sponsored event may be a fundraiser for the nonprofit (for example, Race for a Cure). Relationships with businesses will continue to be an important revenue source for many nonprofits as well as a way to gain further support for the mission of the business and nonprofit involved in sponsorship and cause-related partnerships.

Walter W. Wymer, Jr.

See also Commercialism in the Nonprofit Sector
References and further reading
Andreasen, Alan. 1996. "Profits for Nonprofits: Find a Corporate Partner." *Harvard Business Review,* November–December, 47–59.
Austin, James E. 2000. *The Collaborative Challenge: How Nonprofits and Businesses Succeed through Strategic Alliances.* San Francisco: Jossey-Bass.
Berger, Ida E., Peggy H. Cunningham, and Minette E. Drumwright. 1999. "Social Alliances: Company/ Nonprofit Collaboration." *Social Marketing Quarterly* 5 (3): 49–53.
Cornwell, T. Bettina, and Isabelle Maignan. 1998. "An International Review of Sponsorship Research." *Journal of Advertising* 27 (1): 1–22.
Nowak, Linda I., and Judith H. Washburn. 2000. "Marketing Alliances between Non-Profits and Businesses: Changing the Public's Attitudes and Intentions towards the Cause." *Journal of Nonprofit and Public Sector Marketing* 7 (4).
Sagawa, Shirley, and Eli Segal. 2000. *Common Interest, Common Good: Creating Value through Business and Social Sector Partnerships.* Boston: Harvard Business School Press.
Weeden, Curt. 1998. *Corporate Social Investing: The Breakthrough Strategy for Giving and Getting Corporate Contributions.* San Francisco: Berrett-Koehler.

Center on Philanthropy
History

The Center on Philanthropy was established in 1987 and has been a principal force in the movement to legitimize philanthropy as a field of study. Its activities have expanded over time to include academic programs that extend internationally, in-house research, and publications. According to its mission statement, the center "increases the understanding of philanthropy and improves its practice through programs in research, teaching, public service, and public affairs."

The center was conceived by a consortium of individuals, including Henry A. Rosso, fundraising consultant and the first director of The Fund Raising School; Robert L. Payton, professor emeritus in philanthropic studies at Indiana University–Purdue University Indianapolis (IUPUI); Charles A. Johnson, retired vice president for development, Lilly Endowment, Inc.; and Eugene R. Tempel, former vice president of the Indiana University Foundation and vice president of external affairs for IUPUI. Henry Schaller, a retiring dean of Indiana University, served as the first director of operations, followed by Payton as the first full-time executive director in 1987. Tempel succeeded Payton and is the center's current executive director. These individuals believed that the nonprofit sector and philanthropy was one of the "most misunderstood, understudied, under documented and least visible" areas of American life. To address this issue, the center was created with support from the Lilly Endowment to study and improve the understanding and practice of philanthropy. It is headquartered in Indianapolis, Indiana, on the IUPUI campus. Academic and research programs are based there and at the Indiana University–Bloomington campus and are conducted internationally. The university, as well as foundations and individuals, fund the center's programs and operations.

Major Activities

The Center on Philanthropy serves as a national clearinghouse for education, research, training, and public service programs pertaining to the nonprofit sector. Programs and services created to assist with the education and understanding of philanthropy, or "voluntary action for the public good," are the basis of activities. Areas of operation include academic programs, research, public services, and development and communications.

Regular, ongoing research activities include reports, such as the "Philanthropic Giving Index," which shares current trends and future expectations in philanthropic giving in the United States; "Indiana Gives" (a summary of Indiana giving and volunteering); assistance with *Giving USA,* a publication of the American Association of Fund Raising Counsel; and collaboration with the University of Michigan's Philanthropic Studies Institute. The only library devoted exclusively to philanthropic studies, the Robert and Matthew Payton Philanthropic Studies Library, is located on the IUPUI campus. It serves as a national and international resource for nonprofits and others on fundraising and charitable giving. In collaboration with Indiana University Press, the center edits a book series in Philanthropic and Non-Profit Studies. The library houses a collection of philanthropic archives that includes records from foundations, fundraising consultants, and other professionals in the field.

The Fund Raising School, the only university-based, national fundraising training program in the United States, is the cornerstone of the center's public services effort. Started in California and acquired by the university in 1987, the school conducts educational and training classes throughout the United States and internationally. Regular and customized courses for individuals and groups are offered; some include on-site training. The Fund Raising School was franchised in 1995 to include Procura, which offers Spanish training, in Mexico City, and CEDES (Centro de Estudios en Estado y Sociedad [Center for Studies in the State and Society]) in Argentina. A community foundations institute was added in 1999. The center's annual symposium, "Taking Fundraising Seriously," examines such topics as income sources, ethics, the role of trustees, the language and rhetoric of fundraising, the impact of technology, donor relations, youth and philanthropy, etc.

The first master's degree program in philanthropic studies was initiated by the center in 1993, and by 2001, the faculty numbered over sixty. The academic programs offered include the master of arts (M.A.) in philanthropic studies; the master of public affairs (M.P.A.) in nonprofit management; a dual M.A./M.P.A.; the executive master of arts; the Hearst Minority Fellowship; the Jane Addams–Andrew Carnegie Fellowship Program; the Certificate of Fund Raising Management (via The Fund Raising School);

an online certificate; and the Executive Leadership Institute, held annually in conjunction with the Association of Fundraising Professionals.

The Institute on Philanthropy and Voluntary Service was established for college undergraduates in 1997. Formed in partnership with the Fund for American Studies, the program, the first of its kind in the nation, offers intensive summer institutes that engage college students in an examination of philanthropy in economic concepts, political systems, and moral philosophy. This program moved to Washington, D.C., in 2004.

Books, essays, working papers, and multimedia materials are published by the center in an effort to further the understanding of philanthropy among students and practitioners. More than 200 titles are available. The center also publishes *Philanthropy Matters;* a quarterly newsletter; an annual report; and an occasional essay series.

Betsy Kranz

Reference and further reading
Center on Philanthropy, http://www.philanthropy.iupui.edu/.

Charitable Choice

The term "Charitable Choice" refers to a specific section (Section 104) of the Personal Responsibility and Work Opportunity Reconciliation Act of 1996, known popularly as the "Welfare Reform Bill." Although arousing little notice or controversy when adopted, Charitable Choice and the subsequent attempts to expand it eventually led to the creation of the Office of Faith-Based and Community Initiatives at the White House and became the subject of much political debate and public attention.

Most simply, the purpose of the Charitable Choice provision was to make it easier for faith-based organizations (FBOs) to bid for contracts to provide services funded by federal block grants to states under Temporary Assistance to Needy Families (TANF), the program that replaced Aid to Families with Dependent Children (AFDC). Many in Congress felt that such a law was needed to prevent discrimination against religious organizations in contracting. Many also felt that the wider use of FBOs would lead to greater success in moving individuals off of welfare and into employment.

The Charitable Choice Provision

The Charitable Choice provision has several major components. Although the legislation did not require states to contract with nonprofit organizations to deliver services paid for with TANF funds, it stipulated that states could not treat religious service providers differently from other contractors or demand changes in an organization's governance structure or religious character in order to receive such funds. Additionally, under the legislation, religious organizations need not remove religious objects, art, or iconography from the buildings or rooms in which the services are delivered. Finally, the law expressly exempts religious organizations from laws forbidding employment discrimination on the basis of religion.

The law also has provisions protecting the religious beliefs (or nonbeliefs) of beneficiaries and forbidding the use of governmental monies for religious purposes, including proselytization, worship, or instruction. Additionally, the service providers cannot discriminate against beneficiaries on the basis of religion or require that they attend religious services or engage in any religious practices. If a beneficiary does not wish to receive the service from a religious provider, the law requires that the state must ensure provision of an equivalent service by a secular provider.

Religious Providers before Charitable Choice

Although many viewed Charitable Choice as a new development, governmental use of religious organizations to provide services has a long tradition. FBOs were common in the international development field and quite prominent domestically before the adoption of Charitable Choice. Organizations such as Lutheran Social Services, Jewish Welfare and Family Services, and Catholic Charities received 50 percent or more of their operating budgets from public funds prior to 1996. The Charitable Choice provision, however, was the first legislation to explicitly address the ability of religious organizations to receive a particular type of governmental funding on an equal basis with other nonprofits and to do so without having to alter substantially their religious character. To a great extent, one could argue that the provision did little to change the prevailing landscape, at least on its face, although it did ensure a level of uniformity under existing law. What Charitable Choice will and will not do is, however, a question that will be answered as it is implemented. Six years after its adoption, the most visible result has been heightened interest in the role of religiously based service providers.

The Beliefs behind Charitable Choice

Charitable Choice elevated to the level of public policy a series of unexamined assumptions about the structural strengths of faith-based providers. These assumptions were that FBOs were more effective and more efficient than secular providers and capable of serving as major sources of services and funding to fill the gap brought about by decreases in government spending.

Such assumptions had almost no significant research data behind them. Indeed, research into the magnitude, scope, and potential of religiously motivated service providers was woefully inadequate at the time the legislation was adopted. As a result of the legislation, greater attention began to be paid to the role of religion and religious providers in the overall social service mix.

Despite the lack of knowledge about the "success" of Charitable Choice and the process of its implementation in the various states, there has been a marked push to adopt similar rules for other federally funded social service programs and to encourage greater use of religious providers. Part of this push resulted from a generalized feeling about the manner in which religious providers worked as well as from subjective assessments of the qualities of services they provided.

Much of the impetus behind welfare reform in the United States rested on the view that poverty—at least to some extent and for some individuals—resulted from bad values. If these values could be changed and those individuals removed from the welfare rolls, then more attention and funds could be provided to those who truly needed the monies. Since the end of poverty required a change in values, the best way to accomplish that change would be by increasing the places where recipients would come into contact with people modeling the necessary values. Moreover, it was believed that recipients would benefit more if they were viewed as people, not merely clients. Orga-

nizations driven by religious principles and motivations were assumed to satisfy these requirements. Even if the service provision had no religious content per se, the mere experience of being served by people in such a way would help to transform individuals.

Combined with this was a view shared by many across the political spectrum that local organizations familiar with local needs and already doing productive work had value and should be used more aggressively in service. Proponents of Charitable Choice pointed to the innumerable local organizations, many faith-based, that were doing wonderful work without governmental support. How much more work, they asked, could these organizations do if they could receive more funds? If the contracting system were made more welcoming, if religious organizations were not discriminated against or disfavored because they were religious, then they would be more willing to apply for funds and to submit bids. These very successful organizations would become even more successful, and the problems of poverty would soon begin to subside.

The Results

Such views drove the passage of Charitable Choice during the debate in 1996. A half-decade after its passage, questions about the validity of the assumptions that led to its adoption and the success of its implementation remained unanswered. Although some research has suggested an overall increase in the number of faith-based providers contracting with state governments, other studies have found significant problems in various states. Additionally, legal challenges to the manner in which the law was implemented in several states have suggested that despite the safeguards within the legislation itself, state officials have been lax in their oversight and enforcement of the bill.

Despite the problems, however, many have found the basic ideas driving Charitable Choice and the use of faith-based providers viscerally compelling. During the 2000 political campaign, both candidates spoke in favor of the idea. After his election, President Bush created the White House Office of Faith-Based and Community Initiatives and placed liaisons with FBOs in six of the cabinet departments. Although changes in the leadership of the White House office and the attack on the World Trade Center in September 2001 slowed the momentum somewhat, Charitable Choice remained a major part of the George W. Bush administration's domestic agenda.

Edward L. Queen

References and further reading

Cnaan, Ram. A, with Robert J. Wineburg and Stephanie C. Boddie. 1999. *The Newer Deal: Social Work and Religion in Partnership.* New York: Columbia University Press.

Olasky, Marvin. 1992. *The Tragedy of American Compassion.* Washington, DC: Regnery Gateway.

Wineburg, Bob. 2001. *A Limited Partnership: The Politics of Religion, Welfare, and Social Service.* New York: Columbia University Press.

Charitable Intent

See Donor Intent

Charitable Sector

See Nonprofit Sector

Charity Watchdogs

Charity watchdogs are independent agencies that monitor the management and financial activities of nonprofit organizations at the local, state, or national level. As the nonprofit sector has expanded, the desire for accountability and transparency in the sector has intensified.

Often, potential donors seek information about whether a nonprofit is a good organization to support. The rationale for charity watchdog organizations is to provide these potential donors with information about a charity's activities so they can make informed decisions about how to allocate charitable dollars. Generally, charity watchdog agencies use a set of standards as a benchmark for nonprofit effectiveness or publish via the Internet Form 990, the Internal Revenue Service's Information Return, for a variety of nonprofit organizations.

Nonprofit organizations are an increasing presence in the U.S. economy. From 1987 to 1998, organizations incorporated under Internal Revenue Code (IRC) 501(c)(3) grew by 74 percent. Nearly 30,000 new charities are created each year. In 2001, there were 1.2 million nonprofit organizations, and according to a 2001 INDEPENDENT SECTOR report, these organizations employed an estimated 10.9 million people and accounted for 6.1 percent of the national income. The dramatic expansion of the sector has created intense competition for funds. As more and more nonprofits use impersonal methods of fundraising, such as direct mail and telemarketing, donors, funders, and nonprofits seek accountability.

The desire for increased accountability stemmed also from scandals during the 1990s at notable nonprofits, including United Way, New Era, Covenant House, and Adelphi University and with televangelists Jim and Tammy Bakker. The scandals eroded trust in the nonprofit sector. Charity watchdogs, with their emphasis on standards and public disclosure of financial information, are one way the philanthropic sphere monitors itself.

Monitoring is conducted in a variety of ways. National organizations such as INDEPENDENT SECTOR and the Council on Foundations promulgate high standards for nonprofits to follow. The national associations of each subsector also promote standards and accreditation procedures. Government regulation at the state level is provided by the state attorney general and at the national level by the Internal Revenue Service (IRS). The Operation Missed Giving Web site of the Federal Trade Commission (FTC) is another resource to help donors make informed decisions. The site includes cases filed by the FTC, links to other charity watchdogs, and a charity checklist (http://www.ftc.gov/bcp/conline/edcams/giving). Historically, these government units are understaffed and unable to function proactively in this arena. One issue confronting the sector is whether monitoring should occur at the local, state, or federal level.

Some scholars have argued that nonprofit boards are the first level of regulation. Warren Ilchman and Dwight Burlingame estimated that 10 million individuals serve in board positions (Ilchman and Burlingame 1999, 200). When nonprofit boards meet their legal responsibilities of duty of care, duty of loyalty, and duty of obligation, the entire sector is enhanced. Ilchman and Burlingame cited three reasons why there has been minimal emphasis on public monitoring of nonprofit organizations. The first, trust, is

Jim and Tammy Bakker listen to the words of supporters during a rally in the driveway of the Bakkers' mountain home in Gatlinburg, Tennessee. (Bettmann/Corbis)

one of the defining characteristics of the nonprofit sector. Because society trusts nonprofits, the sector is seen to be less in need of attention than the for-profit sector. Second, the size and scope of the sector with its diverse organizations make it difficult for many to view it as a sector. Third, the sector is hard to regulate because it is dispersed and because its constituencies are small. The returns on the regulations are minimal (ibid., 204).

Joel Fleishman (1999), a lawyer and former president of the private foundation Atlantic Philanthropies, suggested three options for improved accountability. First, the sector should create one umbrella organization to self-monitor. A second option is a nonprofit/government partnership in which

the national Association of State Charities Officials creates a national clearinghouse of information on abuses by nonprofits. The option of last resort, according to Fleishman, is creation of a new federal agency, the U.S. Charities Regulatory Commission, structured much like the Securities Exchange Commission or the Federal Trade Commission.

Charity watchdog agencies have monitored the nonprofit sector at the state level for more than fifty years. The Charities Review Council, a nonprofit Minnesota organization, for example, has reviewed Minnesota charities since 1946. The council's mission states that donors have the right to choose how they will spend their charitable dollars and to expect that charities will conduct themselves in an accountable, ethical, and effective manner. Furthermore, the council states that the responsible actions of both donors and charities will sustain and enhance the climate for charitable giving. Nonprofit oversight agencies exist in several other states as well (Charities Review Council).

There are two nationally based charity watchdog agencies that directly monitor the activities of nonprofit organizations: the Better Business Bureau (BBB) Wise Giving Alliance and the American Institute of Philanthropy (AIP). Although their intent is the same, to provide potential donors with information to make informed decisions about what charities to support, the standards they apply to evaluate nonprofits differ. Another organization, the Evangelical Council for Financial Accountability (ECFA) serves as a Christian Better Business Bureau for its more than 1,000 members, overseeing financial practices and maintaining standards of accountability. Charitable, religious, missionary, social, and educational organizations are included in the ECFA directory.

The subjective nature of standards is problematic for charity watchdog agencies. At the BBB Wise Giving Alliance, standards are set by volunteers and are not substantiated by empirical data or research. Charities have no opportunity to refute or appeal a rating. The use of a one-size-fits-all set of standards may be detrimental to such a diverse and varied nonprofit sector. The biggest concern to nonprofits about the standards is the limitation of fundraising expense to no more than 35 percent of the operating budget. The new standards recommend that charities spend at least 65 percent of total expenses on program activities. Additionally, they stipulate that net assets available for use should be no more than twice the expenses budgeted for the current year.

Another valuable resource for potential donors is the Web site of the nonprofit philanthropic research organization GuideStar, which posts Form 990, the IRS informational return, for thousands of nonprofit organizations (http://www.guidestar.org). Nonprofit organizations are required to file the Form 990 when their annual income is greater than $25,000. (Faith-based organizations, however, are not required to file Form 990.) Web-based access to a charity's leadership and financial records heightens accountability and transparency in the nonprofit sector.

Form 990 has become a major tool for collecting and disseminating information about nonprofit operations. The federal government encourages donors to use it as an informational source to guide their giving. The form lists sources and amounts of income; program, management, and fundraising expenses; net assets; board members; and salaries of top staff.

Although charity watchdog agencies monitor nonprofit organizations, no comparable agencies monitor foundations. Foundation information returns, Form 990 PF, are not posted on the GuideStar site. Foundations initiated a variety of self-monitoring practices following the Tax Reform Act of 1969, however. At the national level, the National Committee for Responsive Philanthropy promotes effective philanthropy through public education campaigns.

An underlying premise of the charity watchdog movement is that as people learn more about nonprofit organizations and become better able to make informed decisions about their contributions, contributions to charities will increase.

Andrea Pactor

See also Accountability

References and further reading

American Institute of Philanthropy, http://www.charitywatch.org.
———. 2001. *AIP Charity Rating Guide and Watchdog Report* (May).
Association of Fundraising Professionals. "BBB Wise Giving Alliance Introduces New Charity Standards," http://www.afpnet.org (cited February 4, 2002).
Charities Review Council, http://www.crcmn.org (cited April 18, 2002).
Fleishman, Joel L. 1999. "Public Trust in Not-for-Profit Organizations and the Need for Regulatory Reform." In *Philanthropy and the Nonprofit Sector,* edited by Charles T. Clotfelter and Thomas Erlich, 172–197. Bloomington: Indiana University Press.
Goss, Kristen A. 1993. "New Charity Watchdog Vows to Tell Donors What They Really Want to Know." *The Chronicle of Philanthropy,* November 16, 31.
GuideStar, http://www.guidestar.org.
Hearts and Minds: Inspiration for Change, "Wise Giving to Charities," http://www.change.net/articles/wisegive.htm.
Ilchman, Warren F., and Dwight F. Burlingame. 1999." Pp. 198–211 in *Philanthropy and the Nonprofit Sector,* edited by Charles T. Clotfelter and Thomas Erlich, 198–211. Bloomington: Indiana University Press.
Roha, Ronaleen R. "Giving Back: A Friendlier Way to Check on Charities' Finances." *Exempt Organization Tax Review* 9 (3): 520–521.

Chavez, Cesar (1927–1993)

Throughout his life, Cesar Estrada Chavez fought a steadfast battle for the rights of farm workers in the United States. The plight of the farm worker was and continues to be a constant area for reform. Farm workers endured deplorable working conditions for meager wages. Further, the farm workers and their children were often exposed to harmful pesticides while working in the fields. Through the farm workers movement, Chavez fought for the rights of farm workers and the civil rights of all through nonviolent tactics.

Chavez, born March 31, 1927, encountered countless injustices as a child. For example, he and his classmates were punished for speaking Spanish at school. Because of the financial hardships endured by his family, he attended school only through the eighth grade, however, and then helped support his family by working in the fields as a migrant worker. As the Chavez family moved from field to field, Cesar witnessed the harsh conditions in which the field workers lived and worked.

As a young adult in 1944, Chavez enlisted in the U.S. Navy. After serving his country for two years at the end of World War II, he returned home and married Helen Fabela. The couple would have eight children.

United Farm Workers leader Cesar Chavez squeezes a bunch of grapes at a rally in New York City in 1986. (Ezio Petersen; Bettmann/Corbis)

In 1952, Chavez met Fred Ross, a community organizer with the Community Service Organization (CSO), a workers' rights group in Los Angeles. Chavez and Ross would become a great team, registering Latinos and Hispanics all over California to vote. Through the CSO, Chavez gained the knowl-

edge and confidence he needed to begin organizing farm workers.

Ten years later, in 1962, Chavez founded the National Farm Workers Association (NFWA). In 1966, the NFWA became the United Farm Workers (UFW), an affiliate of the AFL-CIO, a national labor federation. Before the name change, the NFWA negotiated a contract with Schenley Vineyards—the first ever between a grower and the farm workers. As Chavez organized the farm workers and continued to assert their right to unionize, he remained firm in the belief that reform could be accomplished through nonviolent means.

Chavez and the UFW organized countless boycotts, strikes, and marches against fruit and vegetable growers. Through Chavez's leadership, the farm workers were empowered to demand their rights. Chavez brought national attention to the UFW and the farm workers movement through fasting in 1968, 1972, and 1988. In 1968, Senator Robert Kennedy was with Cesar when he broke his fast. In 1988, Chavez fasted for thirty-six days and was visited by Ethel Kennedy and Jesse Jackson when he broke his fast.

Chavez remained active with the UFW until his death on April 23, 1993. Although Chavez is gone, he is certainly not forgotten. His legacy lives on through the UFW and through all battles for civil rights. In 1994, President Bill Clinton awarded the Medal of Freedom to Cesar E. Chavez posthumously.

Amelia E. Clark

References and further reading

Ferriss, Susan, and Ricardo Sandoval. 1997. *The Fight in the Fields: Cesar Chavez and the Farmworkers Movement.* Orlando, FL: Harcourt Brace.

Garcia, Richard, and Richard Griswold del Castillo. 1995. *Cesar Chavez: A Triumph of Spirit.* Oklahoma City: University of Oklahoma Press.

United Farm Workers, http://www.ufw.org (cited November 5, 2001).

CIVICUS: World Alliance for Citizen Participation

CIVICUS: World Alliance for Citizen Participation was created in 1994 to "promote a worldwide community of informed, inspired, committed citizens who are actively engaged in confronting the challenges facing humanity" (http://www.civicus.org). Founded in 1994 in Barcelona, Spain, after two years of planning, the organization grew during its first seven years from 171 to 604 members from 102 countries. The bulk of its membership consists of citizen organizations (84 percent), followed by individuals (10 percent) and donor organizations (6 percent).

The founders of the organization include Brian O'Connell from the United States, Miguel Darcy de Oliveira from Brazil, Carlos Monjardino from Portugal, and Eddah Gachukia from Kenya. CIVICUS headquarters is located in Washington, D.C., with regional offices in Germany, Hungary, Australia, South Africa, England, and Canada as well as additional regional staff in Europe, Latin America and the Caribbean, and Africa. Within a few years of its founding, CIVICUS also created "regional convener" positions for various world regions.

The most visible activity coordinated by CIVICUS is a biannual World Assembly focusing on specific topics within the general theme of civic society. The first assembly was held in 1995 in Mexico City, and subsequent assemblies were held in Budapest, Hungary, in 1997; Manila, Philippines, in 1999; Vancouver, Canada, in 2001; and Gaborone, Botswana, in 2004. In addition to the assembly, regional conveners coordinate conferences and workshops for members within their region. Through its assembly and regional activities, CIVICUS generates a variety of publications (including its newsletter *CIVICUS World* and its electronic resources) in each of its program areas.

CIVICUS has identified five specific program areas: Civil Society Watch, Civil Society Index, legitimacy and transparency, participatory governance, and the World Assembly. In 1997, CIVICUS developed *Legal Principles for Citizen Participation: Toward a Legal Framework for Civil Society Organizations.* CIVICUS also participates in advocacy programs to encourage governments and corporations to permit and develop citizen participation. It published *Building Civil Society Worldwide: Strategies for Successful Communications* in 1997. In resource mobilization, CIVICUS published *Sustaining Civil Society: Strategies for Resource Mobilization* and *Handbook on Resource Mobilization* in 1997. The Civil Society Index, a long-term project, attempts to assess and interpret the state of civil societies and their development over time. The first publication from the project was *The New Civic Atlas: Profiles of Civil Society in 60 Countries* (1997). CIVICUS also coordinates an international Gender Equality Initiative and promotes youth participation in their assembly. As part of their corporate engagement, it published *Promoting Corporate Citizenship: Opportunities for Business and Civil Engagement* in 1999.

In 1997, CIVICUS received "special consultative status" with the United Nations Economic and Social Council (ECOSOC).

Amy Jones

References and further reading
CIVICUS: World Alliance for Citizen Participation, http://www.civicus.org/main (cited December 29, 2003).
CIVICUS. "2002 Annual Report."

Civil Rights Movement

The civil rights movement, the struggle for the universal application of legal and social rights to all persons in the United States regardless of their religion, social background, race, color, gender, heritage, and other extraneous factors was (and remains) a milestone in American history. In its narrower meaning, the term "civil rights movement" defines the struggle for black political equality that leapt into public view in the 1950s and continued as a major political force through the late 1970s.

The civil rights movement of that era can reasonably be described as the first American social movement to be organized, managed, and often funded by formal nonprofit organizations. While most social and political reform movements in the United States historically have come from voluntary associations, the changes in legal and tax structures in the twentieth century led to a process whereby voluntary associations increasingly sought formal nonprofit status as a matter of course. Some of the impetus for this undoubtedly grew from concerns about legal liability; other factors, including foundation and (later) government funding, played a role as well. Perhaps more importantly, by the 1960s structural realities were such that individuals simply assumed the need for a formal nonprofit organization, either a 501(c)(3) or a 501(c)(4), before undertaking certain types of work.

The roots of the movement for black civil rights, however, are long and deep. It is not unreasonable to suggest that the movement began when the first African resisted the process of enslavement by fighting, running away, or committing suicide rather than submitting to captivity. Similar forms of resistance marked the entire slave period. From work slowdowns to poisonings, from feigned illness to rebellions, slaves resisted attempts to make them objects of slavery and worked to affirm their humanity and independence.

Such actions were not confined to the slaves alone. Freed blacks also resisted the social and legal constraints under which they labored and as groups often established their own voluntary associations to protect them from the racism of the surrounding culture. Racism in the churches led many into separate black churches and even denominations. Discrimination in social services and fraternal organizations convinced blacks to create organizations, voluntary associations that they controlled and ran.

Perhaps one of the most powerful movements in U.S. history, abolitionism—the struggle to end slavery—became, outside of the historically black denominations, the most institutionalized of the early attempts to recognize the dignity and equality of blacks. The abolitionist movement, one of a series of nineteenth-century reform movements, foreshadowed the civil rights movement in its form, its level of racial integration, and also in its internal conflicts and disagreements. Bursting on the scene with the first issue of William Lloyd Garrison's newspaper *The Liberator*, the abolitionist movement had been preceded by the so-called Negro conventions, organized by Bishop Richard Allen of the African Methodist Episcopal Church, which voiced black opposition to slavery and racial discrimination. Abolitionism brought blacks and whites into an integrated sociopolitical movement for the first time in U.S. history.

As the efforts of the abolitionists waxed and waned, the country divided and moved closer to the conflict that defined the nation for nearly a century. If the Civil War decided the question of slavery, Reconstruction attempted to settle the question of black political equality. The so-called Reconstruction amendments abolished slavery, defined citizenship, and forbade limitations on voting imposed solely because of color. But as Reconstruction faded due to political compromise, the promise of equality was replaced with the reality of white political and social domination known as Jim Crow. Enshrined in law by the Supreme Court's decision in *Plessy v. Ferguson,* establishing the legal acceptability of separate but allegedly equal facilities for blacks and whites, it also allowed an entire system of white domination and black subjection, white power and black degradation, a white world and a black one. It was this world that the civil rights movement challenged and changed.

The struggle for black civil rights in the twentieth century is an incomplete struggle in two parts. The first part encompasses the work of men like W. E. B. Du Bois, A. Philip Randolph, and Roy Wilkins and organizations like the National Association for the Advancement of Colored People (NAACP), Congress on Racial Equality (CORE), and the Fellowship of Reconciliation. The second part was the work of men like Martin Luther King Jr., Bob Moses, Ralph Abernathy, and newer organizations such as the Southern Christian Leadership Conference (SCLC) and the Student Nonviolent Coordinating Committee (SNCC). All of these organizations called the United States to its higher self, demanding that the country realize its values of freedom and equality, by ending racism and racial discrimination. Although much smaller in number, other groups such as the Nation of Islam under Elijah Muhammad rejected the American dream and worked for a complete separations between blacks and whites. They believed in a world in which blacks completely and totally controlled their own lives and destinies.

The first generation to struggle against racism and segregation in the twentieth century organized the National Association for the Advancement of Colored People in 1909 and used its journal *The Crisis* as its voice. Edited by W. E. B. Du Bois, *The Crisis* argued for a concerted legal attack on segregation and for the training of a black elite (the talented tenth) who could lead the black masses to social equality.

Under the direction of Walter White, who served the organization from 1918 until 1955, and his successor Roy Wilkins, the NAACP became the organizational center for black opposition to segregation. The NAACP remained, however, an elite organization centering its work on political and legal remedies.

More in touch with the masses of working-class blacks was A. Philip Randolph, longtime president of the Brotherhood of Sleeping Car Porters. Randolph was a working man and his concerns always extended beyond race to include issues of economic justice. Other leaders within the Pullman Porters Union, like E. D. Nixon in Montgomery, Alabama, provided much of the local organizational civil rights work prior to the 1950s.

The 1940s and 1950s saw growing successes in the area of civil rights. Franklin Roosevelt showed a greater interest in black concerns than any president since Theodore Roosevelt and had his own black "kitchen cabinet." His wife, Eleanor, took an even more active concern with civil rights issues, serving on the executive committee of the NAACP.

Black activists themselves also achieved marked success in this period. Randolph's threatened march on Washington in 1943 forced Roosevelt to issue an executive order integrating all war industries. The NAACP's legal attacks on segregationist laws during the 1940s and 1950s were increasingly successful and its lawyers won a series of cases striking down "whites-only" primaries and ending legal segregation in higher education. Their efforts culminated in the 1954 Supreme Court decision in *Brown v. Board of Education of Topeka, Kansas,* which declared public school segregation illegal.

To have the courts overturn legal segregation was not the same as ending it in fact. During the next two decades the civil rights movement tried to achieve in practice that which law and the courts had said were their rights. This struggle was long, savage, and bloody.

During the 1950s and 1960, the drive for civil rights became a mass movement, due primarily to the work of Martin Luther King Jr. When he and others formed the Montgomery Improvement Association in 1955 to end unfair treatment on the city's buses, the modern civil rights movement was born. Preaching a message of justice and nonviolence, King and his colleagues established the Southern Christian Leadership Conference and slowly began to unpeel the layers of racism and economic exploitation under which African Americans labored. The struggle was difficult, but dramatic successes in places like Birmingham and Selma, Alabama, where vicious attacks upon peaceful demonstrations showed the savageness of racism, led to the end of legal segregation and the passage of the Voting Rights Act of 1965.

One early attempt to silence King resulted in a major U.S. Supreme Court decision regarding the right of association. In this decision, *NAACP v. Patterson* (357 U.S. 449 [1958]), the Supreme Court expressly recognized that "the right of the members [of a voluntary association] to pursue their lawful private interests privately and to associate freely with others in so doing" comes "within the protection of the Fourteenth Amendment."

The SCLC taught that blacks could win their rights only through nonviolence. This message dominated the movement during the early 1960s. By the end of that decade, however, many began to question both nonviolence and white involvement in civil rights organizations.

Some of this opposition came from expected critics, primarily from the Nation of Islam's national spokesman, Malcolm X. The Nation of Islam began in Detroit in the 1930s with the teaching of W. D. Fard. Succeeded upon his death by Elijah Muhammad, the Nation of Islam emphasized black separatism, black empowerment, and black economic development.

Other critics of nonviolence included Roy Wilkins of the NAACP, who claimed blacks had a right to self-defense. A major change, however, was that of the Student Nonviolent Coordinating Committee. Organized as a younger, more active, and less clergy-driven counterpart to the SCLC, the SNCC achieved its greatest visibility in 1964 with the creation of the Mississippi Freedom Summer (partially funded by the Ford Foundation as part of a wider Voter Education Project) and the formation of the Mississippi Freedom Democratic Party, which nearly unseated the regular (all-white) Mississippi Democratic Party at the 1964 presidential convention.

The Freedom Summer brought students (primarily white northerners) into Mississippi to teach black children, participate in organizing, and to fight segregation. It led to the brutal murder of students James Chaney, Andrew Goodman, and Michael Schwerner in May 1964. This killing, accomplished with the participation of the local police, radicalized the SNCC.

King's assassination on April 4, 1968, and the resulting riots and violence also weakened the appeal of nonviolence. There were increasing calls for aggressive response to racism and injustice. These voices included the Black Panthers advocating armed rebellion on the one hand and the Conference of Black Churchmen demanding reparations on the other. As nonviolence gave way to Black Power, "We shall overcome" became "Burn, baby, burn." The refusal of entrenched white power structures to change and the violence with which they defended their bastions led to an increasing militancy among blacks. This militancy led to numerous violent confrontations with police and increasing violence in America's cities.

The election of Richard Nixon in November 1968 did little to ease the calls for increasing militancy. The Republican administration's apparent lack of concern for African Americans, the Vietnam War, and increasing social conflict moved attention away from civil rights. Although the movement was revived somewhat during the presidency of Jimmy Carter, Ronald Reagan's administration was particularly hostile to advances on the civil rights front.

Equally significant was the fact that after the ending of legal segregation and the guaranteeing of voting rights, the more complex and tedious issues of economic justice were less amenable to wide-spread public action and often even legal action. Economic decline during the last two decades of the twentieth century increasingly led to situations where economic justice for blacks was seen as an economic threat by poorer whites, thus exacerbating racial tensions and animosities.

By this time the scourge of drug abuse and the rise of what many perceived as a permanent underclass comprised primarily of people of color made many individuals question traditional approaches to questions of race. Opinion polls showed that blacks and whites in the United States had widely divergent views on the continuing power of racism and its affects on individuals' daily lives. Some commentators even claimed that the civil rights leadership intentionally favored policies designed to keep blacks subservient to the government in order to further their own ends. While such opinions remained minority views, their emergence suggested the seeming intractability that certain aspects of race had taken on. Additionally, questions surrounding police abuse and the disparity in the application of the death penalty continued to show the lingering vestiges of racial inequity in American society.

During these years many of the leading civil rights organizations went through periods of decline and difficulty. The SCLC lost much of its grassroots support following the end of legalized segregation. After King's assassination and the resignation of his successor, David Abernathy, as president, the SCLC experienced a leadership crisis and its importance dwindled. An attempt to revive and revitalize the organization under the leadership of Martin L. King III saw it increasingly adopt the language of the late-twentieth-century nonprofit world. Holding the title of president and CEO, Martin L. King III speaks of public/private partnerships and bridging the digital divide.

Similarly, the NAACP underwent a difficult organization period during the 1980s. Massive financial difficulties and conflicts with its 501(c)(4) partner the NAACP Legal Defense and Educational Fund, Inc., as well as leadership problems caused a decline its influence. Much of this was regained in 1996 when Representative Kweisi Mfume was chosen as the NAACP's president and CEO. A respected legislator who resigned his seat in Congress to take the helm of the NAACP, Mfume did a masterful job in reclaiming much of the organization's credibility and financial stability.

The civil rights movement remains a symbol of America's struggle to realize its most deeply held values. The religious dimension of King's vision and that of his colleagues stirred chords in the hearts of Americans everywhere and helped to bring an end to racial divisions enforced by law. The civil rights movement also exemplified the strength and power of America's voluntary spirit and the power of nonprofit organizations to work to transform society.

Edward L. Queen

See also King, Martin Luther, Jr.; National Association for the Advancement of Colored People

References and further reading

Branch, Taylor. 1988. *Parting the Waters: America in the King Years, 1954–1963.* New York: Simon and Schuster.

Du Bois, W. E. B. *The Souls of Black Folk.* New York: New American Library.

Franklin, John Hope. 1994. *From Slavery to Freedom: A History of African-Americans.* New York: McGraw Hill.

George, Carol V. R. 1973. *Segregated Sabbaths: Richard Allen and the Emergence of Independent Black Churches.* New York: Oxford University Press.

Harding, Vincent. 1990. *Hope and History: Why We Must Share the Story of the Movement.* Maryknoll: Orbis.

Lincoln, C. Eric. 1974. *The Black Experience in Religion.* Garden City, NY: Anchor Press.

Myers, Walter Dean. 1991. *Now Is Your Time: The African-American Struggle for Freedom.* New York: Harper Collins.

Paris, Peter. 1985. *The Social Teaching of the Black Churches.* Philadelphia: Fortress Press.

Taylor, Clarence and Jonathan Birnbaum, eds. 2000. *Civil Rights since 1787: A Reader.* New York: New York University Press.

Civil Society

The idea of civil society has become a central theme in contemporary thought about the third sector and philanthropy and yet is difficult to define, inherently complex, and resists being categorized or interpreted through a singular theoretical lens. The term is used to define conditions and characteristics that make the strength and expansion of the third sector possible within a sociopolitical context from community to international levels. An appealing aspect of this term is found in the linguistic root it shares with the behavioral concept of civility. Although it is increasingly used to describe how social life should function within and between societies and provides a fundamental way of describing public action and social responsibility, its meaning and implications remain difficult to grasp. In this globalized world of the twenty-first century, the defining and articulating of civil society carries both transnational and communitarian components that will condition and guide philanthropic activity.

Historical Background

Historically the term "civil society" has been used to describe the unique form of economic, political, and social relationships and structures in Western societies since the early eighteenth century. On the one hand, classical political economists such as John Stuart Mill and Adam Smith viewed civil society as a realm of virtuous freedom, both economic and personal, and contrasted it with the evils of the state. G. W. F. Hegel, on the other hand, used it to explain how government could find its niche in a market-driven society by nurturing cooperation in the face of economic and social conflict.

English philosopher and economist John Stuart Mill (1806–1873) (Library of Congress)

Karl Marx expanded Hegel's argument by delineating the terrain of civil society as resulting in social conditions of alienation, exploitation, and injustice. This theme was continued by neo-Marxist theorists who viewed civil society as the arena that economic and political actors used to maintain positions of power through the form and function of various social systems and institutions.

In more recent literature, the idea of civil society has moved beyond either a comparison of existing political conditions or an ideological characterization of dangers to avoid by being used to describe the response needed in emerging democracies of Eastern Europe following the evaporation of Communist structures in 1979 and thereafter. Attempts have been made in these changing societies to institutionalize specific aspects of Western economic and political systems with the expectation that the underlying civic

values and behavior will follow. But it is uncertain whether the "civil societies" that emerge in these and other non-Western systems will be similar to and compatible with their Western counterpart. In its current form, civil society goes beyond merely providing for open markets, free elections, and voluntary associations and means various things to a variety of people.

Contemporary Usage

To some, the concept of civil society is defined narrowly in reference to the initiatives and associations that occur at the community and grassroots level. To others, it is a broad term that works with and helps condition government and market forces. To people from both conservative and liberal perspectives, it is viewed as a primary characteristic of the independent sector and a replacement for much of what government has previously done by subsidizing charitable giving and legitimizing a variety of sociable behaviors and organizations. To still others, it represents the soul of democracy and gives social institutions moral cohesion and force rooted in and inspired by a venerable heritage of religious faith.

The social space of civil society has come to be viewed as commonly held principles of vernacular, local civic life expressed through "mediating structures" (Berger and Neuhaus 1977) and systems. It is used to initiate and maintain positive social change and to interface the shifting and changing conditions of an individual's private life with surrounding public circumstances. And these are changes for which the individual is in need of protection, assistance, and support from a "third" or "independent" party—those who do not have a vested interest in the dominant economic and political systems and who are not controlled by these forces.

Civil society appeals to people because of its many implications: It sounds better to be civil to each other than to be uncivil; things civil also seem rather less regimented than what is militarized or bureaucratic; and, of course, a civil society has a welcome ring to it in a time of uncertainty and social turbulence. But a wholesome sound goes only so far in social theory. The fact remains that the concept of civil society will have to be more solidly defined and constructed if it is to play a role in the reconstruction of

Characteristics of Civil Society

Principles of Civil Society	Systems of Civil Society		
	Economic Development	Political Governance	Social Institutions
Civic engagement	Commons	Office	Associations
Civic authority	Trusteeship	Sovereignty	Accountability
Civic responsibility	Equity	Justice	Reconciliation

modern society. Civil society is best understood as a very special space within and between the major institutions of society.

Characteristics of Civil Society

From this historical perspective, the concept of civil society can be viewed as highly interrelated with a market economy, democratic politics, and key social institutions serving as the framework for and encouragement of philanthropic activity. Nine indicators of civil society may be identified by linking the three systems of economic development, political governance, and social institutions to the three principles of civic engagement, civic authority, and civic responsibility.

Systems of Civil Society
Economic Development

The type of economic environment and activities conducive for civil society is characterized by the open availability and utilization of common resources necessary for constructing a satisfying and satisfactory life, the responsible care and management of those resources for current and future generations, and the equitable distribution of resources with a special concern for those who are impoverished. A symbiotic relationship exists between human social economies and the natural economy of ecosystems and bioregions upon which all life depends. Economic development and the improvement of human life cannot occur without preserving and enhancing environmental quality.

Political Governance

Political structures and activities found within civil societies are expected to seek, promote, and protect the welfare of the people. Political governance within this context includes full and active participation in

public decision-making by all members of society, allows for legitimatized control over civic space and resources, and maintains fairness in the political and judicial systems, with a special concern for those who are disenfranchised, through the protection of human rights. Participation in decision making and in the process of solving social problems challenges a number of current political attitudes and conditions: cynicism regarding motives for involvement in public life, incivility in public culture, and the futility of public action and community collaboration. Effective political involvement and control rests on a cultural basis of shared values and beliefs.

Social Institutions

The strength, vitality, and diversity of social institutions, especially those related to the independent sector, play a crucial role in the existence of civil society. Changes or shifts in the economy and in the organization of work, family, and neighborhood have occurred more quickly than the capacity of existing public, proprietary, and social institutions available to and used by individuals and communities to cope with and direct those changes. Communitarian institutions found in strong democratic settings are characterized by open groups and networks that form the context in which economic development and political governance occurs, holding community stakeholders accountable for the outcome of their actions and providing a context for resolving conflicts through nonviolent means with a special concern for those who are marginalized. Political theorist Benjamin Barber referred to this system of civil society as a voluntary realm "devoted to public goods," the "true domain" of "church, family, and voluntary association" (1998, 44).

Principles of Civil Society
Civic Engagement

The principle of civic engagement refers to involvement in and benefit from economic activities by having access to and use of resources held in common within this social context; by actively participating in civic action and political governance; and by taking the opportunity to join and be represented by social groups and associations that provide a sense of belonging on a community level. Public participation in civic action—that is, contributing to and benefiting from economic development and political governance within the context of public life through involvement in legitimate social institutions—is true civic engagement. The work of civic engagement extends from the basic level of helping someone in need to include empowering individuals and groups to effectively solve community (or national) problems.

Commons

Civic engagement and economic development form what is termed the "commons," referring to the context of public interaction and content of the public good. The context of commons suggests that there is a definable location where public resources are produced and exchanged. The content of commons refers to the open availability and utilization of those goods and resources. It also includes the right each community member has to participate in, contribute to, and benefit from the context and content of public commons. This right of participation carries with it responsibility for participants to act in ways that enhance and strengthen the commons.

Office

Civic engagement through political governance occurs within the framework of legitimatized positions and opportunities for participatory decision making in and through local leadership positions, that is, citizens recognizing their right and civic duty to take an active role in the governance of their community. To participate fully and equally requires knowledge of how systems work and what outcomes will result from decisions that are made. Increased participation through democratic structures necessitates an increased decentralization of power and authority. Elected officials have a responsibility to remember that they are first and foremost public servants who have been chosen to represent the interests, concerns, and needs of all members of society.

Associations

Effective civic engagement is especially aided by the strength and diversity of various social institutions operating within a social context. Social structures characterized by voluntary, free, open participation in and association with agencies, groups, and organizations provide individuals with active networks necessary for effective governance and social change. "Associations" refers to all of those social places where people gather and interact with others to exchange ideas, offer support, and receive a sense of belonging. These groups and affiliations occur within and through all three sectors of social life: public, proprietary, and independent. As Robert D. Putnam suggested, "Participation in civic organizations inculcates skills of cooperation as well as a sense of shared responsibility for collective endeavors" (2000, 90).

Civic Authority

The principle of civic authority is characterized by legitimate public authoritative rulership based on public control over the space and resources required to form and maintain community; the ability to place a high degree of trust that the needs of the community and its welfare (not self-interest) will serve as the basis for decisions made by community stakeholders; and the ability of local groups and associations to hold various actors accountable for the outcomes of policies and programs. There is a fundamental emphasis in this principle on the important role that independent sector organizations have in equipping (economically) and empowering (politically) its stakeholders (organizations and volunteer workers) with the resources (tools, knowledge, skills, and materials) required for bringing positive community change.

Trusteeship

"Trusteeship" refers to the civic authority all members of the community have for exercising sustainable, responsive stewardship of resources on behalf of the common good. Within market economies, community members need to be able to trust that those making economic decisions, especially corporate actors and business leaders, will act in ways that will strengthen and improve the local economy and its "capital" (human, social, material, and ecological). In civil society, trusteeship runs counter to forms of corruption that are evidenced by benefits going to the "haves" at the expense and exclusion of the "have-nots."

Sovereignty

Civic authority and political governance of "sovereignty" is expressed in the authority, right, and legitimacy actors have to make political decisions within a particular social setting and defined geographic location. In representative democracies, the sovereign rule of civil society is conditional and limited by various actors within the state and its bureaucracies. It is fundamentally important to the survival of civil society that political actors not be "captured" by special-interest groups or industries yet work to be responsive to and inclusive of the disenfranchised.

Accountability

Organizations within the independent sector play an important role in civil societies by providing community members with the ability to hold economic and political actors accountable for policies, programs, and distribution of resources. Accountability is based on transparency of rules and known expectations of public actors. The contestation of issues in the public setting is the best place for community members to assert themselves and monitor the actions of economic and political actors. The basic freedoms and rights associated with civil society (for example, free speech, a free press providing access to information, fair elections, and the freedom to organize in groups) are the mechanisms used to hold economic and political decision makers accountable.

Civic Responsibility

The principle of civic responsibility is characterized by mutual obligation and responsibility evidenced by a universally accepted and equally enforced "rule of law" that results in social order and stability. Strong and legitimate civic responsibility results in the practice of equity, justice, and nonviolent conflict resolution. In civil society, the rule of law is applied fairly and consistently to all members of society. No one is exempt from being held accountable to the law. No one is above or beyond the law. The globalization of the market economy, increased regionalization of political governance, and the expanding role of nongovernmental organizations indicates a universalization of the rule of law applied to all countries, especially in the context of international conflict. This universal application of the rule of law guarantees the protection of civil liberties and human rights and provides legitimate and effective avenues of appeal and response to cases of abuse and violations.

Equity

Civic responsibility is evidenced within the context of economic development when each member of the community has equitable access to resources for living a satisfying and satisficing life. The concept of civil society emphasizes allocative and procedural equity in terms of the impact of policy decisions on groups and classes of people, not just on individuals. An important question to be asked of all economic policy and program decisions is the following: How will this decision impact those already facing economic impoverishment and how will it affect the quality and availability of resources for future generations? Evidence indicates that a laissez-faire economy will not eliminate poverty and will continue to enrich the few while impoverishing the many. For this reason, civil society calls for a moral response of economic equity that permits, preserves, and maintains the resource conditions necessary for producing and sustaining a high quality of life for all people at the community level. Within the context of civil society, those in positions of power have an ethical responsibility to make decisions that will result in benefit for those suffering from economic impoverishment. A significant contribution of independent-sector actors is the preference and concern these organizations have for the poor.

Justice

In civil society, justice is defined as the overlapping obligations of exercising fairness and compassion. A law or policy is unjust if it is unconstitutional or contrary to the rule of law, but a law is also viewed as unjust if it is unfair and lacks compassion. In democratic governments, constitutions serve as the basis for forming and evaluating all civil laws. The forming and strengthening of social justice is characterized as a response to the needs of the disenfranchised and advocacy for those who are economically weak and politically vulnerable. Although social justice holds a strong moral claim within the context of civil society, often the ability to accomplish it is viewed as being politically and practically weak. People in positions of power are reluctant to follow through with policies and programs that will fully accomplish the goals of social justice because of the risk it entails to their political future. Independent-sector actors, by virtue of not being "captured" by these political interests, can work on behalf of those excluded from the political process and negatively affected by unjust laws.

Reconciliation

In civil society, social institutions and associations provide a context for divergent individuals and groups to come together to negotiate, mediate, and resolve conflict through peaceful, nonviolent means. Social institutions give groups and individuals access to the law and empower them to fairly enforce impersonal, equitable laws in socially transparent ways.

Conclusion

As we enter into the twenty-first century, the principles and systems of civil society will need to move from the nation-state level to include a global political economy of relations and groups. Every person is a neighbor to everyone else, and we are all mutually responsible for ensuring that the opportunity to experience a satisfying and satisficing life is available to all. Our global economy has brought us together and pushes us to the development of appropriate political and social systems whereby participation, authority, and responsibility are just, equitable, and nonviolent—responding with intentional concern for the disenfranchised, marginalized, and impoverished.

Timothy J. Peterson and Jon Van Til

See also Nonprofit Sector

References and further reading

Barber, Benjamin R. 1998. *A Place for Us: How to Make Society Civil and Democracy Strong.* New York: Hill and Wang.

Berger, Peter L., and Richard J. Neuhaus. 1977. *To Empower People: The Role of Mediating Structures in Public Policy.* Washington, DC: American Enterprise Institute for Public Policy Research.

Eberly, Don E. 1998. *America's Promise: Civil Society and the Renewal of American Culture.* Lanham, MD: University Press of America.

Lohmann, Roger A. 1992. *The Commons: New Perspectives on Nonprofit Organization and Voluntary Action.* San Francisco: Jossey-Bass.

Putnam, Robert D. 2000. *Bowling Alone: Civic Disengagement in America.* New York: Simon and Schuster.

Reisman, David, and Nathan Glazer. 1950. "Criteria for Political Apathy." In *Studies in Leadership: Leadership and Democratic Action,* edited by Alvin Gouldner, 505–559. New York: Harper.

Seligman, Adam. 1992. *The Idea of Civil Society.* New York: Free Press.

Shils, Edward. 1997. *The Virtue of Civility: Selected Essays on Liberalism, Tradition, and Civil Society.* Indianapolis: Liberty Fund.

Van Til, Jon. 2000. *Growing Civil Society: From Nonprofit Sector to Third Space.* Bloomington and Indianapolis: Indiana University Press.

Commercialism in the Nonprofit Sector

Commercialism in the nonprofit sector may be defined as a set of interrelated phenomena through which nonprofit organizations are acquiring some of the characteristics of for-profit businesses. Although commercial activities of nonprofit organizations have been recognized for many years (Crimmins and Keil 1983), awareness of this subject accelerated in the last decade of the twentieth century as they became more widespread. Commercialism in the nonprofit sector has been met with mixed reactions, promoted by some as the embodiment of new opportunities for nonprofit organizations and questioned by others as a cause for concern for the health and integrity of the nonprofit sector.

Manifestations of Nonprofit Commercialism

The ways in which nonprofit organizations are thought to be becoming more like for-profit businesses can be roughly divided into two interrelated categories: changes in the interface between nonprofit organizations and external markets, and changes in the internal operations and culture of these organizations.

Market Interfaces

In a variety of ways, nonprofit organizations are becoming more integrated into markets and, by implication, becoming less reliant on the "grants economy" of philanthropy and government. There are at least six overlapping ways in which this appears to be the case, including those described below.

Increasing Dependence on Fees and Other Forms of "Earned" Income

Several researchers have noted that fees, investments, and other forms of market-based income constitute the largest single source of revenue for nonprofit organizations in the United States. Estimates of this dependence and how it has changed over time vary depending on the definitions and assumptions associated with particular research efforts. For example, calculations in one study showed that overall, fees and charges represented 47 percent of the revenue of public-benefit nonprofits and that this figure had changed little since 1977 (Salamon 2002). The results of another study indicated that revenue from "program services" for all nonprofits increased from 69.1 percent to 73.5 percent from 1987 to 1992 (Weisbrod 1998). The difference between these findings derives not only from the different years of comparison and from the somewhat different groupings of nonprofits, but more importantly from the classification of income from government sources. In particular, the estimates in the second study showed that much of government-derived revenue is provided on a fee-for-service basis, much like other nonprofit earned income. Although most estimates show a declining share of nonprofit revenue from charitable contributions, they also confirm that the government share of nonprofit income has been growing. Hence, the classification of government income into payment for services versus grants influences whether dependence on earned income is thought to be growing or stable over time.

In any case, it is widely recognized that earned income, however derived, has certainly become the dominant source of nonprofit revenue overall. Researchers have also observed that dependence on earned income varies widely within the nonprofit sector, with health care and education organizations having the heaviest such dependence, arts and culture organizations having substantial dependence, social services nonprofits somewhat less dependence, and religious, civic, and international aid organizations less still. Moreover, it is not clear that dependence on fee income is growing in all subsectors. For example, research on museums suggests that such dependence did not increase in the 1980s and early 1990s (An-heier and Toepler 1998), although fee income became a notably greater part of the finance of zoos and aquariums from the mid-1970s through the 1980s (Cain and Meritt 1998). Finally, research on an international scale suggests that the nonprofit sector in some countries is much more fee-dependent than it is in others (Salamon and Associates 1999).

Undertaking Ventures with Profit-Making Objectives

As with fee-based income, the idea of undertaking ventures for the explicit purpose of generating net revenues for the organization has been a part of the culture and modus operandi of U.S. nonprofit organizations for many years. For example, in youth services, activities such as cookie or candy sales have long been common (Young 1998). What appears to have changed recently is the degree to which nonprofits are emphasizing this as a strategy for supporting themselves, the legitimacy they place on activities whose purpose is primarily income generation, and the variety of creative initiatives that are now undertaken, ranging from museum stores to travel services run by university alumni offices.

Some analysts have encouraged nonprofit organizations to embrace commercial ventures as a potentially lucrative and productive source of resource development (Skloot 1988), and researchers have recognized the place of profit-making ventures in the overall financing of nonprofit organizations. In particular, the prototypical nonprofit organization has been modeled as a "multi-product" firm in which some activities primarily address the organization's social mission while others are primarily intended to help finance that mission (James 1983; Schiff and Weisbrod 1991). A special insight has been to recognize that nonprofits can be expected to adjust their portfolio of revenue strategies as external conditions change (Weisbrod 1991). In particular, if public or charitable support declines, nonprofits can be expected to put more emphasis on commercial sources, even if they prefer to put their energies more directly into mission-focused services. This model also contains the reverse implication, that if sources of public support increase, nonprofits will de-emphasize commercial ventures, although such behavior has not been confirmed (James 1998).

Collaborating with Corporate Business

One particularly notable vein of nonprofit commercial activity in recent years has been to undertake collaborative ventures with profit-making corporations (Austin 2000). An early manifestation of this phenomenon was cause-related marketing, the promotion of a commercial product by associating it with a charitable cause. American Express launched this innovation in 1983 with a credit card that set aside a portion of the revenues from sales charged to the card for the restoration of the Statue of Liberty. This concept has caught on, and many charities now have credit cards in their name or similar arrangements with corporations that generate charitable revenues based on product sales. Moreover, a variety of new arrangements associate nonprofit missions with products ranging from orange juice to smoking patches. Museum shows may have commercial themes, and nonprofits may license their own products to commercial firms, taking advantage of the value of their intellectual property while exploiting the development and marketing capacities of business corporations. For example, *Sesame Street* characters are manufactured and sold as toys by commercial firms.

Finally, the nonprofit-corporate connection has strongly infiltrated traditional nonprofit fundraising efforts. Many charities, for example, host corporate-sponsored events such as marathon runs, walks, swims, and celebrity golf tournaments. Corporate volunteerism is another important part of this pattern. Increasingly, corporations have sought to engage their employees to work with nonprofits in various ways, as staff and board volunteers, to bring their skills to the management of nonprofits or their contributions to specific charitable projects. In return, businesses derive public relations, employee morale, and other benefits (Austin 2000).

Indeed, some corporations have more or less adopted certain charities in a holistic sense, and vice versa. City Year and Timberland, or Georgia Pacific and the Nature Conservancy, are two examples (Austin 2000). There is currently some debate surrounding the advisability of nonprofits forming exclusive arrangements with particular corporations (Young 2003). One school of thought is that the deeper the relationship with a corporation, the more trust is developed and the more creative and productive the opportunities that may be identified and undertaken together. Another school of thought recommends the diversification of corporate relationships to minimize the risk of dependence on any one corporate arrangement that might ultimately turn sour with serious financial or reputational consequences. The recent scandals at Enron, WorldCom, and other major corporations have increased the level of this concern.

Competing for Resources and Markets

Another way in which nonprofits are said to be becoming more like businesses is that they are more engaged in market competition along several fronts. First, as noted above, nonprofits are presumably more engaged in selling their services for fee income, often to make a profit. As such, they are engaged in competition for market share among themselves and in some instances with profit-making businesses. Hospitals compete with other hospitals, both for-profit and nonprofit. Nursing homes, home health services, day care, schools and colleges, arts and cultural organizations, community and recreation organizations, training and rehabilitation services, and mental health and social service organizations follow similar patterns of competition. Many industries in which nonprofits operate are so-called mixed industries in which both nonprofits and for-profits are substantially represented (Weisbrod 1988). Even outside these industries, nonprofits may compete with business if they undertake explicitly commercial ventures outside their traditional fields of activity. A social service organization that opens a restaurant or runs a bakery in order to employ clients and earn money competes with businesses in those industries. So does a museum that sells coffee mugs, a university that sells T-shirts, or an orchestra that sells compact discs. In some fields, such as zoos and aquariums, concession income has been the fastest rising source of revenue for nonprofits (Cain and Meritt 1998). In fact, sponsorship advertisements on nonprofit Web sites are becoming more popular as a source for more income.

Finally, nonprofits compete among themselves and sometimes with businesses and government for the critical (input) resources they need to operate. Charitable fundraising is the most obvious example.

Nonprofits have professionalized rapidly in this arena, using increasingly sophisticated marketing technology and competing more and more intensively for this highly valued yet slowly growing source of income, often employing for-profit telemarketing firms. For many decades, charitable contributions have remained static at approximately 2 percent of national income, while nonprofit expenditures have grown rapidly (Nonprofit Almanac 1997). As a result, charitable contributions are declining as a proportion of nonprofit revenues and competition for these revenues is becoming more intense.

Human resources is another area of increasing competition for nonprofits. Professionalization has meant entering the labor markets for employees in a variety of skill areas, many of which are sought by businesses as well as nonprofits. These include talent in generic areas such as management, information technology, marketing, communications, and accounting. Depending on their missions, nonprofits also compete for professional talent in their areas of service specialization. This competition is mostly within the nonprofit and public sectors for social workers, educators, and clergy but crosses strongly into the business sector for artists, scientists, and healthcare workers.

Although pressures vary over time, it is fair to say that competition is a growing fact of life for nonprofits, with some especially intensive competitive pressures experienced in recent years. During the late 1990s, for-profit corporations competed strongly for government contracts to administer welfare reform programs, a traditional area of nonprofit expertise. During this same period, one in which the economy was booming, nonprofits had difficulties competing in the labor markets for the talent they needed to adopt new information technology. The slower economy of the early twenty-first century has eased some of these competitive pressures. However, nonprofits have learned that they must think of themselves as market competitors if they are to survive and operate effectively over the long term.

Outsourcing
Nonprofits have tried to make themselves more competitive by paying closer attention to their compara-

tive advantages and by relying on the market for capacities for which they have no special edge (Ben-Ner 2003). This further market engagement is another way in which nonprofits are seen to have become more like businesses. Although there has been little systematic documentation of this trend, nonprofits are now known to outsource a wide variety of activities ranging from fundraising to accounting services and public relations. Outsourcing of fundraising has been the most controversial practice in this arena, as telemarketers and other firms and consultants have sometimes claimed for their compensation high proportions of gross contributed revenue, stirring resentment and controversy among donors and public officials.

Using the Market to Address the Mission
Perhaps the most intriguing way in which some nonprofits have become more "commercial" is in looking to the marketplace for strategies to address their social missions. This change in orientation is both external and internal in nature. Although it is difficult to say how pervasive this kind of thinking has become across the nonprofit sector to date, two things are clear. First, the core idea has long existed in the form of "protected workshops." Goodwill Industries, a national organization, and Vocational Guidance Services of Cleveland, Ohio, for example, both employ handicapped people to produce marketable goods and services.

But the notion that markets can be engaged to address social missions appears to have expanded significantly in recent years under the rubric of "social purpose enterprises" (Emerson and Twersky 1996). The basic concept is that people who are challenged in various physical, psychological, or social ways can have their needs best addressed by becoming more self-sufficient through the learning and application of marketable skills and employment experience. This notion has been applied to a wide variety of circumstances and projects, including a furniture factory employing low-income members of an Asian American neighborhood, a screen-printing business employing Hispanic youth, a gourmet bakery that hires and trains unemployable workers, a job-training service for inner-city residents, an aircraft parts manufacturing operation employing ex-offenders, and many others. Nor is the general concept of addressing the mission through the market limited to social services and employment. For example, environmental groups use the market in various ways, such as warehousing and reselling discarded materials or engaging in environmentally friendly projects, such as operating a bicycle valet service (Young and Salamon 2002).

Interestingly, there has also been convergence toward social enterprise from the for-profit side. Corporations such as the Body Shop, Newman's Own, and Ben and Jerry's have made their reputations by engaging in environmentally and socially progressive business practices and allocating profits for philanthropic causes. Ironically, this convergence of business and nonprofit practices around social enterprise is another factor that obfuscates differences between businesses and nonprofit organizations and may increase the perception that nonprofits have become more like commercial business (or vice versa).

Changes in Internal Operations and Culture

The growing interface with markets has been accompanied by changes in nonprofits' internal operations and culture. In addition to a newfound orientation to market-based solutions, these changes have been manifested in several other ways, including a new emphasis on professional management; the adoption of business language, methods, and practices; and a shift in emphasis from social to business goals.

Professional Management

In one sense, the trend toward employing professional managers is part of an overall professionalization trend in which paid staff have taken over work that once would have been carried out by volunteers and amateurs. The latter secular trend has several roots, including the increasing complexity and sophistication of work carried out by nonprofit organizations in social services, health care, education, environmental conservation, and other areas, as well as changes in labor markets that have opened up new opportunities for women and made them less available for volunteering. However, the move toward professional management is also unique in some ways. In particular, nonprofit administrators traditionally have been drawn largely from the ranks of direct service professionals who, over time, took on administrative responsibilities in the course of their careers. Thus, professors became deans, social workers became program and executive directors, doctors became hospital administrators, and so on.

Although this pattern is still common, a new stream of talent has begun to enter the ranks of nonprofit management—individuals with degrees in nonprofit management or another management-related discipline, and service professionals who have returned to school for professional management education. It is only within the past twenty years that professional education programs have existed for nonprofit managers (Young 2002). Within that time period, these programs have grown exponentially and are beginning to change the character of the management function within nonprofit organizations. In essence, through the engagement of professional management, nonprofits have in some ways come to operate more like business corporations and bureaucracies despite the fact that the new stream of nonprofit management education emphasizes the differences as well as the similarities between nonprofit management, business management, and public administration.

Changes in Methods and Language

Accompanying the shift to professional management, nonprofits now use words, concepts, and methods that were foreign to the sector just two decades ago. These include entrepreneurship, marketing, franchising, strategic planning, performance incentives, business plans, and other business concepts. Nonprofits are beginning to think about cost and profit centers and organizing their accounts so that they can determine the impact of their various units on both their social missions and their financial bottom lines. More than just language, these ideas and methods have been embraced by large segments of the nonprofit sector, mostly to good effect in helping nonprofits to pursue their social missions more effectively. At the same time, their adoption has clouded the differences between nonprofits and business organizations.

Goal Displacement

Several of the factors cited above raise the concern that some nonprofit organizations are beginning to give greater priority to organizational survival and financial well-being and less to the achievement of the social missions for which they have been established. Whether this has actually occurred to a substantial extent in practice remains unclear. However, the apprehension arises for several reasons. First, the changing mix of nonprofit personnel, with an increasing emphasis on paid professional and managerial workers, yields organizations in which the members have a greater economic stake in the organization's financial success. Second, the increasing competition that nonprofit organizations face in their service markets requires them to behave more like for-profit firms in order to survive. For example, a nonprofit hospital can afford only so much free charity care or may be reluctant to couple its care with unreimbursed teaching and research if its for-profit competitors avoid such work. Third, the increasing collaboration with business, including the engagement of business volunteers in nonprofit governance and operations and joint ventures with business, may influence nonprofit leaders to think more like business executives. Finally, engaging in profit-making ventures as sources of revenue and as means to achieving mission-related goals and engaging staff with entrepreneurial skills to develop such enterprises contain the potential to shift the organization's thinking. In effect, the confluence of these factors may have a profound impact on the goals and priorities that a nonprofit organization pursues over time, whatever its rhetoric may be.

Issues and Consequences

The cluster of phenomena grouped under the rubric of nonprofit commercialism raises important issues and concerns for the future of nonprofit organizations. Not all the potential consequences are negative by any means. Indeed, the pursuit of earned income opportunities, collaborations with business, and employment of business methods appear to hold great potential for increasing the efficiency with which nonprofit organizations utilize their resources, the effectiveness with which they pursue their social missions, and, indeed, the level of resources that they bring to bear in the pursuit of important social goals. Given contemporary limits to government support and the continued modest rates of growth of giving

and volunteering, market-based initiatives represent the most important source of growth of the nonprofit sector for the foreseeable future.

Still, the issues and concerns raised by nonprofit commercialism merit serious attention. As the discussion of goal displacement above suggests, nonprofit commercialism threatens to obfuscate the clear identity of nonprofit organizations by conflating their social character and goals with those of the business sector and even producing hybrid forms that are difficult to pigeonhole into one sector or another. Such loss of identity is threatening in a number of ways. It may have a chilling effect on donors and volunteers, inducing them to contribute less than they might otherwise because they may feel their contributions less necessary or because they lose trust in these organizations. Indeed, commercialism may also undermine the trust that clients and government officials place in nonprofit organizations, ultimately threatening the special tax exemption and other benefits that nonprofits currently enjoy.

Interestingly, the contemporary emphasis on accountability, performance measurement, and evaluation of nonprofit organizations reflects both sides of the nonprofit commercialism issue. On the one hand, a new emphasis on performance assessment follows logically from the deeper interactions of nonprofit organizations with the business sector. On the other, the need for performance assessment may have become more urgent because of growing skepticism about nonprofit organizations stemming from their growing commercialism.

Dennis R. Young

References and further reading

Anheier, Helmut K., and Stefan Toepler. 1998. "Commerce and the Muse: Are Art Museums Becoming Commercial?" In *To Profit or Not to Profit*, edited by Burton A. Weisbrod, 233–248. New York: Cambridge University Press.

Austin, James E. 2000. *The Collaboration Challenge.* San Francisco: Jossey-Bass.

Ben-Ner, Avner. 2003. "Outsourcing by Nonprofit Organizations." In *Effective Economic Decision Making by Nonprofit Organizations,* edited by Dennis R. Young, 67–82. New York: Foundation Center.

Cain, Louis, and Dennis Meritt Jr. 1998. "Zoos and Aquariums." In *To Profit or Not to Profit,* edited by Burton A. Weisbrod, 217–232. New York: Cambridge University Press.

Crimmins, James C., and Mary Keil. 1983. *Enterprise in the Nonprofit Sector.* New York: Rockefeller Brothers Fund.

Emerson, Jed, and Faye Twersky, eds. 1996. *New Social Entrepreneurs.* San Francisco: Roberts Foundation.

James, Estelle. 1983. "How Nonprofits Grow: A Model." *Journal of Policy Analysis and Management* 2 (Spring): 350–365.

———. 1998. "Commercialism among Nonprofits: Objectives, Opportunities and Constraints." In *To Profit or Not to Profit,* edited by Burton A. Weisbrod, 271–285. New York: Cambridge University Press.

Salamon, Lester M., Helmut K. Anheier, Regina List, Stefan Toepler, S. Wojciech Sokolowski and Associates. 1999. *Global Civil Society.* Baltimore: Johns Hopkins Center for Civil Society Studies.

———, ed. 2002. *The State of Nonprofit America.* Washington, DC: Brookings Institution Press.

Schiff, Jerald, and Burton A. Weisbrod. 1991. "Competition between For-Profit and Nonprofit Organizations in Commercial Markets." *Annals of Public and Cooperative Economics* 62(4): 619–639.

Skloot, Edward, ed. 1988. *The Nonprofit Entrepreneur.* New York: Foundation Center.

Weisbrod, Burton A. 1988. *The Nonprofit Economy.* Cambridge: Harvard University Press.

———, ed. 1998. *To Profit or Not to Profit.* New York: Cambridge University Press.

Young, Dennis R. 1998. "Commercialism in Nonprofit Social Service Associations: Its Character, Significance and Rationale." In *To Profit or Not to Profit,* edited by Burton A. Weisbrod, 195–216. New York: Cambridge University Press.

———. 2002. "The Evolution of University-Based Nonprofit Management Education in the U.S." *Nonprofit Review* 2(1): 1–10.

———, ed. 2003. *Effective Economic Decision Making by Nonprofit Organizations.* New York: Foundation Center.

Young, Dennis R., and Lester M. Salamon. 2002. "Commercialization, Social Ventures and For-Profit Competition." In *The State of Nonprofit America,* edited by Lester M. Salamon, 423–446. Washington, DC: Brookings Institution Press.

Committee on Gift Annuities

See American Council on Gift Annuities

Common Good

The idea of the common good presupposes that individual well-being depends on the existence of moral interdependence in some society, whether local, national, or global. In today's pluralistic societies, the common good consists largely in the recognition that every person requires certain social, civil, political, economic, and environmental conditions to flourish and that maintaining these conditions is a shared responsibility.

As a term in ethics, the "common good" can be distinguished from "private goods" and "public goods." Private goods are the ends that a person seeks for him or herself and for family members and other intimates. Public goods serve the interests of many—for example, good roads—but require state action to produce them. Although the common good may sustain private goods and may benefit from public efforts, it is located in what people hold in common as social beings.

That people are social shows first in the broader relationships that people develop in pursuit of shared goals. By working out agreements about these goals and cooperating to obtain them, individuals form bonds that shape their own sense of meaning and identity. In addition to these formative bonds, being social means that people depend on each other in meeting their basic needs. However loosely a society is structured, this material interdependence motivates a moral responsibility to ensure conditions conducive to everyone being able to realize these basic needs. Thus, the common good is reflected in the fabric of communal relationships and in the structures of interdependence that make people's lives meaningful and viable.

A brief review of the history of Western thought about the common good indicates why the concept is elusive today. For classical authors, the common good consisted in the collective ends pursued by the state's citizens (Aristotle) or by all of its people (Cicero). Christian thinkers, such as Augustine, identified the proper ends and ordering of people's lives with God's purposes, but he and Thomas Aquinas, more clearly still, argued that participation in a political community is instrumental to an ultimate fellowship with God.

These authors described the common good as a hierarchy of goods to which everyone should submit. Such a conception of the common good has met with considerable distrust in the history of the United States. In colonial times, appeals to a uniform vision

St. Thomas Aquinas (1225?–1274), Italian scholastic philosopher. Fresco by Fra Angelico. (Florence S. Marco Museum, undated. BPA 2 #4291; Bettmann/Corbis)

of the good legitimated the religious conformity of Puritan communities and mandatory taxes for established churches. White slave owners' control of African Americans and the imposition of restrictive roles on women were justified on similar grounds. Examples like these have caused some theorists to doubt whether the common good exists at all. The British utilitarian philosopher Jeremy Bentham argued that there is nothing beyond the "greatest happiness of the greatest number," understood as the best possible satisfaction of individuals' aggregated interests. Likewise, the long-held suspicion in the United States that the common good stands for the vision and privileges of an elite has contributed to this country's reliance on individualistic mechanisms of consumer choice and interest-group politics to grant priority to private

goods and to leave individuals free to pursue their own conception of the good life.

Advocates for the common good argue, however, that individualism cannot account for the forms of moral interdependence that people develop and require for personal well-being. Instead of detailing the one hierarchy of goods necessary to the one good life, recent theorists of the common good have investigated the conditions needed for a flourishing life lived with others, many of whom will disagree about the contents of such good lives. The French Roman Catholic thinker Jacques Maritain's "personalism" exemplifies this shift from uniform goals across the polity to enabling structures throughout society. He argued that certain liberal institutions are compatible with and necessary to the common good because the common good rightly serves people's dignity and well-being. That goal requires guaranteeing such conditions as political and civil rights, the freedom to participate in debates over public priorities, and the liberty to engage in initiatives by oneself and with others (1966 [1946]).

Defining the common good in terms of the conditions required for human flourishing does not remove the tensions addressed above. Even if it is agreed that the common good plays a critical role in people's lives, the fact of pluralism means that no clear conception of it will be held by everyone. That does not imply, though, that citizens cannot strive to imagine and extend the common good through action and debate aimed at fostering a mutually beneficial life for all. Engaged philanthropy offers one avenue for such contributions.

David M. Craig

References and further reading
Hollenbach, David. 1989. "The Common Good Revisited." *Theological Studies* 50 (1): 70–94.
———. 2002. *The Common Good and Christian Ethics.* Cambridge: Cambridge University Press.
Maritain, Jacques. 1966 [1946]. *The Person and the Common Good.* Translated by John J. Fitzgerald. Notre Dame: University of Notre Dame Press.
Mount, Eric, Jr. 1999. *Covenant, Community, and the Common Good.* Cleveland, OH: Pilgrim Press.
Nemetz, A. 1967. "Common Good." In *New Catholic Encyclopedia*, vol. 4, 15–19. New York: McGraw-Hill.
Wuthnow, Robert. 1998. *Loose Connections: Joining Together in America's Fragmented Communities.* Cambridge: Harvard University Press.

Community Development and Organizations

Community development is a comprehensive planned approach for addressing human care needs. Based on the assumption that the people impacted by an issue or condition should be involved in developing and implementing the solution, it incorporates the process of engaging residents and other stakeholders in sustained, collaborative efforts to strengthen and improve conditions in a defined geographic area. Effective community development is not a collection of agencies that provide separate programs for separate problems; rather, it is a process through which individuals, associations, and organizations assemble to exchange services and act together for the good of their community.

Community development starts by working with community or neighborhood residents and leaders to identify and mobilize assets—the skills, abilities, and resources of *all* residents, associations, and organizations—and, based on the collective agenda, leveraging community resources to complement, not replace, the existing assets. The long-term success and sustainability of community development depends on strong, active citizen involvement. Utilizing the community development approach, the work of organizations and institutions is to strategically leverage individual, neighborhood, and community resources to address community issues and to build strong communities through enhanced citizen involvement.

Many national foundations support community development efforts as a means to effectively address the issues of poverty and crime in low-income urban and rural neighborhoods. The Ford Foundation defines community development as "an approach to improve the quality of life and opportunities for positive change in urban and rural communities. Our goal is to develop community-based institutions that mobilize and leverage philanthropic capital, investment capital, knowledge, skills, and natural resources in a responsible and fair manner" (http://www.fordfound.org).

The Community Development Society, a professional society for community advocates, has developed the following community development principles to help guide organizations and professionals in carrying out their community development practice:

Promote active and representative participation toward enabling all community members to meaningfully influence the decisions that affects their lives; Engage community members in learning about and understanding community issues, and the economic, social, environmental, political, psychological and other impacts associated with alternative courses of action; Incorporate the diverse interests and cultures of the community in the community development process; and disengage from support of any effort that is likely to adversely affect the disadvantaged members of a community; Work actively to enhance the leadership capacity of community members, leaders, and groups within the community; and, Be open to using the full range of action strategies to work toward the long term sustainability and well being of the community. (http://www.comm-dev.org/principles.htm)

The two major types of organizations involved in community development are community development corporations (CDCs) and community development financial institutions (CDFIs). CDCs are community-based, nonprofit organizations created for the purpose of developing and improving low-income communities and neighborhoods through housing development, economic development, and other related activities. They are typically governed by a local board of directors comprised of residents from the CDC's geographic area and managed by a professional staff of community economic development professionals. The activities undertaken by a CDC usually include housing-related activities, including affordable housing development and home ownership, and economic development, including microenterprise development and small business training and incubation. Utilizing an asset-based approach, most CDCs address local issues by working to identify and build on existing neighborhood assets. The number of CDCs has grown steadily over the past twenty years, and CDCs are now located in most large and medium-sized cities in the country.

Community development financial institutions (CDFIs) are nonprofit organizations or financial intermediaries created to support community development activities by providing credit, capital, or support services to small businesses or home mortgage assistance to individuals. The primary mission of CDFIs is to promote economic development both in urban and rural areas that are underserved by traditional financial institutions. As in the case of the CDCs, CDFIs are typically governed by a citizen board of directors dedicated to representing and improving the quality of life in a targeted geographical area. CDFIs make loans and investments that are often considered inappropriate or "high-risk" for mainstream financial institutions. They provide access to capital for community development activities that normally would not have access to the capital needed. CDFIs serve as a bridge between the low- and moderate-income community and the normal credit markets. The services provided by most CDFIs include providing financial services, loans, and investments; offering training and technical assistance services; and promoting development efforts that enable individuals and communities to effectively use the credit and capital they offer.

The different types of CDFIs include community development banks, which provide financial loans and investments to support community development activities; community development credit unions, self-help credit unions that provide affordable credit and financial services to low-income individuals who do not have access to normal banking institutions; community development loan funds, which work to create below-market loan funds from socially responsible investors to support community development activities in low-income communities; community development venture capital funds, which provide start-up capital for real estate and new business development in economically distressed areas; and microenterprise loan funds, which provide microbusiness loans and technical assistance to low-income individuals interested in starting small businesses. In 2000, there were more than 500 CDFIs in the United States, with at least one in every state.

As the community development field has matured, more CDCs have become involved in what is termed comprehensive community initiatives (CCIs). In response to growing needs in the communities they serve, many CDCs have gone beyond their economic and housing development roots, expanding their programs and partnerships to provide an array of community-building activities, such as job training and career placement, child care, youth counseling and programming, cultural arts projects, and community advocacy and organizing. CDC participants have realized that to be effective in improving the quality of life in their communities they must go beyond their "bricks and mortar" approach to address a wide variety of needs through a comprehensive community development approach.

H. Daniels Duncan

See also Grassroots Associations
References and further reading
Annie E. Casey Foundation, http://www.aecf.org (cited January 20, 2003).

Asset-Based Community Development Institute (ABCDI), Community Development Program at Northwestern University's Institute for Policy Research, http://www. northwestern.edu/ipr/abcd.html (cited January 20, 2003).

Chapin Hall Center for Children, University of Chicago, http://www2-chc.spc.uchicago.edu/index.html (cited January 20, 2003).

Chaskin, Robert J. 2000. *Lessons Learned from the Implementation of the Neighborhood and Family Initiative: A Summary of Findings.* Chicago: University of Chicago, Chapin Hall Center for Children.

Community Development Society, http://www.comm-dev.org/ (cited January 20, 2003).

Ferguson, Ronald F., and William T. Dickens, eds. 1999. *Urban Problems and Community Development.* Washington, DC: Brookings Institution Press.

Ford Foundation, http://www.fordfound.org (cited January 20, 2003).

Homan, Mark S. 1998. *Rules of the Game: Lessons from the Field of Community Change.* Pacific Grove, CA. Brooks/Cole.

Housing and Community Development Knowledgeplex, http://www.knowledgeplex.org/ (cited January 20, 2003).

Kingsley, Thomas G., Joseph B. McNeely, and James O. Gibson. 1997. *Community Building Coming of Age.* Washington, DC: Urban Institute.

Kretzmann, John P., and John L. McKnight. 1993. *Building Communities from the Inside Out: A Path toward Finding and Mobilizing Community Assets.* Evanston, IL: Center for Urban Affairs and Policy Research, Northwestern University.

McKnight, John. 1995. *Careless Society: Community and Its Counterfeits.* New York. Basic Books.

National Community Building Network, http://www.ncbn.org (cited January 20, 2003).

Walker, Christopher, and Mark Weinheimer. 1998. *Community Development in the 1990s.* Washington, DC: Urban Institute.

Community Foundations

A community foundation is an unusual sort of philanthropic institution. Composed of a group (or "community") of funds, it serves a limited geographic region or occasionally an otherwise specified "community" of donors and potential beneficiaries. Community foundations offer donors the investment management and beneficiary selection services of a large foundation as well as a less expensive, more flexible means than the cy pres legal procedure to change beneficiaries when warranted. They enable like-minded donors to work together. A good number of community foundations also offer significant consensus-building and leadership services to the communities they serve.

In almost every case, community foundations are incorporated under the specific laws of their home state. At present, they operate under federal rules implementing the Tax Reform Act of 1969, which granted them exemption from new fees and regulations applying to private foundations so long as they remain "public charities" that not only spend (in operations and grants) 5 percent of the average value of their endowments over the previous three years, but also raise (from a number of different donors) the same 5 percent in new gifts to their endowments.

The first community foundations in the United States appeared in the World War I years. They flourished in three remarkable spurts, during the 1920s, the 1950s, and the 1990s, and recently they have grown more rapidly than other types of foundations. Until the 1980s, community foundations were concentrated in the states of the Midwest and the Northeast, and just six of the largest—in the Cleveland, New York City, Chicago, Boston, and San Francisco areas—held half of all community foundation assets. Since 1980, significant community foundations have appeared in almost every metropolitan region with a population of more than 1 million. Statewide community foundations have emerged in twenty states, including New Jersey, Arizona, Oregon, Rhode Island, and New Hampshire as well as most of the less populated states in the South, the Great Plains, and the Rocky Mountains. Extraordinary efforts led by the Mott, Lilly, and Kellogg foundations have greatly increased the numbers of community foundations in a few states, notably Indiana and Michigan. And growing community foundations have emerged across the South.

In 2001, community foundations held assets of about $31.6 billion, somewhat more than 6 percent of all foundation assets (see Table 1). The Council on Foundations and the Columbus Foundation, which annually survey the field, counted a total of 658 community foundations in 2001. Fewer than half of these had assets of more than $10 million, sufficient at 5

Table 1 U.S. Community Foundation Assets, 1921–2001

Year	Total Assets in 2001 Dollars (millions)	Average Annual Growth Rate in Period (%)	Assets of Six Largest Community Foundations as Share of All Assets (%)
1921	69		76
1931	431	52	58
1941	651	5	42
1951	749	1.5	45
1962	2,492	21	45
1973	4,787	8	48
1983	4,979	0.4	50
1987	7,357	12	44
2001	31,630	24	22

percent to support an annual budget of just $500,000 for all operations, including rent, office staff, and fundraising. These smaller community foundations must of necessity concentrate on fundraising; sometimes, they also distribute funds provided by other large donors. The sixty-four largest (including the statewide foundations of Oregon, Rhode Island, Hawaii, Arizona, New Hampshire, Delaware, and Maine) had assets of more than $100 million in 2001. Of 2001's twenty largest community foundations— the "peacocks"—eight were in the Midwest, four in the East, two in the South, and six in the West. (See Table 2 for the assets of community foundations in the largest metropolitan areas.)

Frederick Harris Goff, the architect of the first community foundation, the Cleveland Foundation, in 1914, emphasized two public purposes that have been widely influential: the accumulation of permanent charitable endowments (as distinct from the annual operating funds of the United Ways and the like), and efforts to implement locally, in private as well as public agencies, new policies for social welfare, health, and education that had been developed through the disciplined inquiry supported by such national foundations as Rockefeller and Carnegie. Because even the largest community foundations have never been able to make really large grants, however, they have emphasized services to donors and, in recent years, their roles as regional "conveners" for discussions of such complex matters as urban and rural economic development, the

concerns of women and racial minorities, the effectiveness of nonprofit organizations, and the response to emergencies such as those posed by AIDS and by the terrorist attacks of September 11, 2001.

The community foundation idea spread rapidly from its initial appearance in Cleveland because it constituted a key component of a new framework for philanthropic and nonprofit activity. This new framework distinguished religious from secular purposes; permitted more professional control of medical, educational, and social services; and developed funding and coordinating agencies that drew funds from the metropolitan community as a whole. In keeping with the new emphasis on interfaith cooperation that seemed essential as Cleveland's manufacturing plants attracted large new populations of Catholics, Eastern Orthodox Christians, and Jews to what had once been a predominantly Protestant region, the Cleveland foundation's funds were to be used for "mental, moral, and physical improvement . . . regardless of race, color or creed" (Magat 1989, 26).

During the 1920s, these broad purposes recommended community foundations to business leaders throughout the greater midwestern region that extends from Pittsburgh and Buffalo west to Denver and south to Dallas and Winston-Salem. The Trust Division of the American Bankers Association (ABA) established a Committee on Community Trusts in 1920, and midwestern chambers of commerce advanced community foundations and federated fundraising campaigns as devices to support healthcare and social agencies, to subordinate them to a central community chest, and to promote new professional standards in public health and social work.

Northeasterners saw the community foundation as a "mechanism" for the "conservation and distribution of charitable funds" (Magat 1989, 30). The New York Community Trust, established in 1920, early influenced the field by adopting from the start the "multiple trust plan" arrangement first employed in Indianapolis, whereby several banks served as trustees. The New York fund also emphasized service to donors: One of its first funds was established as early as 1925 to provide scholarships at the Hebrew University in Jerusalem; in 1931, it accepted its first "donor-advised fund." As they gathered large resources, however, many

Table 2 U.S. Community Foundations, Assets per Capita, Metropolitan Regions Greater than 1 Million, 2001

Metropolitan Region	Total Assets of Region's Community Foundations	Assets per Capita
Cleveland-Akron-Lorain-Elyria-Canton	$1,769,781,606	$527.82
Hartford	$572,952,397	$484.32
Columbus	$738,863,948	$479.78
San Francisco–Oakland–San Jose	$2,930,828,822	$416.37
Minneapolis-St. Paul	$1,188,174,679	$400.19
Kansas City	$636,106,000	$358.17
Oklahoma City	$363,174,929	$335.34
Providence–Fall River–Warwick	$366,300,103	$308.07
Pittsburgh	$561,925,137	$238.20
Indianapolis	$378,722,109	$235.67
Cincinnati-Hamilton	$450,911,304	$227.85
Greensboro–Winston–Salem–High Point	$270,152,971	$215.78
Portland, Oregon	$476,622,423	$210.43
Milwaukee-Racine	$312,875,374	$185.13
Charlotte–Gastonia–Rock Hill	$254,010,244	$169.45
Dallas–Fort Worth	$855,368,233	$163.80
Louisville	$160,137,429	$156.08
Rochester	$168,825,308	$153.76
Tulsa	$153,775,994	$149.88
Boston-Worcester-Lawrence-Manchester	$815,985,863	$140.23
Chicago-Gary-Kenosha	$1,175,149,684	$128.32
San Diego	$344,379,402	$122.38
Nashville	$143,581,345	$116.64
New York City	$2,206,170,504	$104.06
Seattle-Tacoma-Bremerton	$362,752,386	$102.04
Phoenix-Mesa	$323,381,648	$99.44
Buffalo–Niagara Falls	$113,327,275	$96.86
Detroit	$487,380,364	$89.33
Atlanta	$366,735,780	$89.19
Norfolk–Virginia Beach–Newport News	$137,398,667	$87.52
Denver-Boulder-Greeley	$447,572,172	$76.90
New Orleans	$100,400,000	$75.04
San Antonio	$100,047,697	$62.84
Jacksonville	$68,864,610	$62.60
Philadelphia–Wilmington–Atlantic City	$369,571,197	$59.72
Washington-Baltimore	$366,381,101	$48.16
Los Angeles–Riverside–Orange County	$717,468,861	$43.82
Austin–San Marcos	$53,066,977	$42.45
Tampa–St. Petersburg–Clearwater	$75,017,633	$31.31
Miami–Fort Lauderdale	$150,678,549	$30.09
St. Louis	$67,423,401	$25.89
Sacramento-Yolo	$36,226,140	$20.16
Houston-Galveston	$68,411,820	$14.65
Salt Lake City–Ogden	$3,573,773	$2.68

of the northeastern foundations began to assert themselves. By 1930, the Permanent Charity Fund of Boston reported to the American Bankers Association that it was requiring each of the 117 organizations that received its funds to "consider itself in relation to the whole work of the community, and to adopt a uniform accounting system" (Magat 1989, 30).

The Great Depression interrupted community foundation growth. The ABA Committee on Community Trusts ceased to function in 1933, and twenty-five of the ninety-one community foundations that had started by 1939 closed entirely. In 1949, just thirty-five earned the minimum $10,000 required to maintain the smallest office. A new group of leaders in community planning now took the lead, working through a new National Committee on Foundations and Trusts for Community Welfare. New community foundations often took the form of the self-perpetuating charitable corporation (already adopted, largely for tax purposes, in Boston and several other cities) to the bank trust agreement. They also preferred the multiple trustee plan, which gave all banks providing trust services a reason to encourage donors.

Definitions of community purpose continued to change and to attract controversy. Immediately after World War II, most postwar community foundation leaders insisted that their main purpose was to strengthen the community chest movement that had been devastated by the Depression. This was a serious matter at the time: In cities such as Cleveland, the community chest had been raising as much as half or more of the funds that supported local hospitals and social welfare agencies. Many established community foundations promoted the community chest; elsewhere, community chest leaders pushed community foundations. By the 1950s, more than half of community foundation grants seem to have gone for the operating expenses of social agencies.

But leaders of the San Francisco Foundation, founded in 1949, and other community foundations never embraced the community chest alliance. By the early 1950s, the civil rights and women's movements challenged the white Protestant men who had defined "community" for nearly all foundations. Paul Ylvisaker of the Ford Foundation, seeking ways "to move out of safe and sane hospital, university and similar do-nothing grants . . . to begin getting after the more gutsy urban problems" in the late 1950s, suggested that substantial Ford grants might "gain the large-scale leverage necessary for getting this country to wake up to social change" (Magat 1989, 37). Such Ford initiatives with community foundations in Kansas City and Cleveland launched important community organizing and voter registration efforts; the relatively large community foundations in Chicago, San Francisco, and Boston followed with similar initiatives.

Wright Patman of Texas and other congressional critics cited these Ford Foundation and community foundation efforts, in part, in their drive for the 1969 revisions of foundation regulations. It was not surprising that donations to community foundations lagged while this legislation was debated, a period of nearly ten years. To respond more effectively to Patman's criticisms, the National Committee on Foundations and Trusts for Community Welfare reinvented itself as the comprehensive Council on Foundations, with permanent offices in Washington, D.C. Ultimately, the new regulations approved in the late 1970s gave community foundations, with their accountable boards and more adequate professional staffs, advantages over small family foundations. Most community foundations continued to value unrestricted endowments, but in the 1980s and 1990s nearly all also moved aggressively to attract money that might previously have gone into family foundations by emphasizing "special-interest" and "donor-advised" funds through which donors (and sometimes their heirs) might control and continue to influence the use of their money.

The extraordinary expansion of federal support for health and social welfare, together with the equally extraordinary increase in the ability and willingness of Americans to pay for secondary and higher education, presented an even greater challenge than the new rules imposed by the Tax Reform Act of 1969. In 1960, private gifts accounted for a third or more of the income of schools, hospitals, and private welfare agencies; by 2000, they counted for only about a sixth—or less. Lacking sufficient resources to influence these nonprofit organizations, many community foundations—especially those that were small or new—simply emphasized their ability to serve as agents for their donors. In this field, they faced increasing competition from other charities, including United Ways and Catholic and Jewish federations. They also faced strong competition from some of the nation's largest mutual fund companies—and found new ways to cooperate with such financial institutions as Merrill Lynch to provide increased services to donors. In the context of the international conflict with terrorism, all of these philanthropic intermediaries faced the challenge of ensuring that their beneficiary-evaluation services reliably directed funds to legitimate charities. Community foundations and competing funds also faced the challenge of making sure that donors met federal and state "hands off" requirements for receiving a charitable tax deduction when the donation went to a "donor-advised" fund.

Across the United States, community foundations responded to these challenges with campaigns that attracted many new donors during the 1990s. Long-established foundations in Buffalo, Atlanta, and other cities expanded their focus to encompass their entire metropolitan regions; many of the larger foundations set up affiliates in nearby areas. Leaders in almost every large city that lacked a community foundation got together to create one. In Indiana, Michigan, and other states, philanthropic leaders built central offices to provide investment and grantmaking assistance to many small community foundations.

The larger community foundations continue to seek to play catalytic roles, at least among substantial groups of donors in their communities. Many provide critical support for the arts and for public radio and television. Several manage special funds for women's concerns, for African Americans and other minorities, and for those concerned about the environment. Several community foundations seek to advance the cause of local economic development—in rural counties, in urban neighborhoods, and in downtown areas. Some work to create and sustain new networks of community development or housing organizations. A few have joined with chambers of commerce, think tanks, and universities to find and begin to implement comprehensive regional economic development plans. Overall, as community foundations became more and more diverse, it became more and more difficult to characterize them in a single, coherent way.

David C. Hammack

See also Goff, Frederick Harris
References and further reading
Hammack, David C. 1996. "Philanthropy." In *The Encyclopedia of Cleveland History*, edited by David D. Van Tassel and John Grabowski, 764–768. Bloomington: Indiana University Press.
Loomis, Frank Denman. 1962. *The Chicago Community Trust: A History of Its Development, 1915–62*. Chicago: Chicago Community Trust.
Magat, Richard, ed. 1989. *An Agile Servant*. New York: Foundation Center.
Newman, Diana S. 2002. *Opening Doors: Pathways to Diverse Donors*. San Francisco: Jossey-Bass.
Tittle, Diana. 2000. *Rebuilding Cleveland: The Cleveland Foundation and Its Evolving Urban Strategy*. Columbus: Ohio State University Press.

Confraternity

Broadly, "confraternity" is an English-language term derived from the Latin *frater* (brother) and referring to any Roman Catholic membership association operating under the authority of a bishop and canon law. Although the usual references are to male-membership and lay associations of a nonoccupational type, this is not always the case. Catholic membership associations whose members are predominantly or exclusively women, however, may be designated as "sodalities."

The *Oxford English Dictionary* defines confraternity as "a brotherhood; an association of men united for some purpose or in some common profession; esp, a brotherhood devoted to some particular religious or charitable service." *The Catholic Encyclopedia* uses confraternity and sodality interchangeably as "voluntary associations of the faithful." In general, it is possible to think of confraternities as philanthropic organizations devoted to practical tasks or instrumental missions, so long as one gives rather wide latitude to what may be deemed practical at different times in church history. Confraternities are distinguishable from such other forms of Catholic social organization as dioceses, parishes, and orders in part by this shared purpose or mission.

Confraternities, which were especially prominent in the social order of medieval Europe, where they were often distinguished primarily from guilds (or "gilds") formed by groups of merchants or craftsmen, are comparable in many respects to the American concept of voluntary associations. Participation in any association sanctioned by episcopal authority, ecclesiastical obligation, and divine sanction may hardly be designated "voluntary" in the ordinary sense, however. The importance of explicit grants of authority, obligation, and sanction are evident when one contemplates the line between confraternal actions and heretical movements (including the Protestant Reformation) in the history of Catholicism.

Philanthropy organized through confraternities reaches deep into the history of Christianity and other world religions. Christianity produced a wealth of philanthropic institutions associated with monastic establishments, cathedrals, parishes, chantries, and local dioceses. As early as the fourth century, bishops such as John Chrysostom of Antioch laid down rules for the foundation and operation of local associations within the broader penumbra of the organized church (Wilkin 1983). Lay confraternities such as the well-known Knights of Columbus (KoC) represent one of the most interesting and least studied modern survivals of medieval Christendom within the organizational network of the contemporary Roman Catholic Church (http://www.kofc.org/; http://www.new advent.org/cathen/08670c.htm). As of this writing, the Library of Congress catalog lists only twelve entries on the KoC, none of which appears to be a critical or scholarly work.

One of the most distinctive periods in the history of confraternities was the late nineteenth century, which saw a rapid rise of fraternalism in the United States. Equally remarkable is the European upsurge that occurred in the wake of St. Francis of Assisi within the indigenous local political dynamics of the Italian city-states. The movement quickly spread to other localities, including Spain (Henderson 1997; Trexler 1991).

The activities of confraternal organizations in medieval Europe were sometimes rather different from the activities engaged in today. One rather dramatic example is the confraternity from the thirteenth to fifteenth centuries in Florence that specialized in the creation and use of "images of shame" (tavolettas), paintings on religious subjects held in front of the eyes of condemned prisoners on their way to the gallows by a confrater walking backward, who would pray with the condemned (Edgerton 1985).

There is little doubt that life in medieval urban social worlds struggling with plague, warfare, famine, and the many other ills was well characterized by the English political philosopher Thomas Hobbes in *Leviathan* as "mean, nasty, brutish and short." In such contexts, preoccupation with death was a suitably

practical task of much interest to various confraternities. James R. Banker (1988) examined the evolving commemoration of death over two centuries, from 1250 to the coming of Florentine rule in 1440, in the small Tuscan town of San Sepolcro in the Upper Tiber Valley.

Confraternities were not always concerned just with the harsh realities of life. The tie between confraternities and the arts—notably painting, music, architecture, and sculpture—is an important one and has been a strong interest of humanist scholars. Recent studies have examined the architecture produced by a Venetian confraternity between 1437 and 1550 (Sohm 1982); the music in Venetian confraternities (Glixon 2003); the role of confraternities in patronizing the visual arts (Wisch 2000); and the role of confraternities in Seville, where patrons sponsored the creation of wooden sculptures used in processions during Holy Week (Webster 1998).

Piety was an important dimension of medieval confraternities and deeply intertwined with art, charity, and politics (Barnes 1994; Crouch 2000; Eisenbickler 1991; Henderson 1997). An important subclass of medieval and modern confraternities are known as "confraternities of penitents." In the thirteenth century, their numbers increased to such an extent that there were eventually more than 100 organizations in Rome alone. Each was distinguishable by the colors of its processional robes—white, black, blue, gray, red, violet, or green. Typically, members would combine penitential acts such as fasting, discipline, or wearing of hair shirts with activities somewhat similar to contemporary social care services. Taking care of the sick, burying the dead, bringing medical aid to the indigent, and providing dowries for poor girls were considered penitential acts for white penitents. Black penitents consoled criminals, accompanied them to the gallows, and buried them along with the poor and unidentified bodies found within the Roman Campagna.

The confraternity movement was not limited to medieval Italy, however. In addition to the Knights of Columbus, an interesting and controversial modern form of penitential confraternity in the contemporary United States are the *penitentes* of New Mexico (Ahlborn 1986; Carroll 2002; De Aragon 1997; Steele and Rivera 1984). Likewise, throughout the former territories of New Spain, New France, and predominantly Catholic cities and neighborhoods of the United States today, confraternities continue to be important forms of religious association for Catholics.

In addition to the authority of the bishops, most confraternities had (and have) one or more patron saints, as well as patrons in a more earthly political and economic philanthropic sense. Thus, for example, St. Bonaventure, inquisitor-general of the Holy Office during the thirteenth century, prescribed the rules, as well as the white habit, of the most important of the white pentitents, the Archconfraternity of the Gonfalone, established in 1264 at Rome.

Confraternities may be distinguished from other forms of Catholic voluntary association by at least three important variables: gender, occupation, and status. Most medieval and modern references to confraternities, in accordance with the Latin root of the term, refer to male associations that might be considered symbolic rather than genetic brotherhoods. Ronald F. Weissman captured precisely this connotation in the title of his 1981 book, *Ritual Brotherhood in Renaissance Florence*. The role of confraternities in preserving and maintaining the fundamentally patrimonial authority structure of Catholicism is evident but little studied in the women's literature. Women's sodalities were not unknown in late medieval Florence, according to Richard C. Trexler (1991, 14). One might question his conclusion, however, that "they played no perceptible civic or neighborhood role" (ibid., 14). At any rate, Florentine women, as well as adolescents, youths, and adult salaried workers, were generally excluded from occupational associations (gilds) and from religious groups until the late fifteenth century (ibid., 14).

Although confraternities are usually not occupationally based, there have been notable exceptions to this rule. In Renaissance Florence, for example, foreign artisans (who may not have been Catholic, but whom the Florentines nevertheless wished to keep in the city) were in some cases allowed to organize into confraternities (ibid., 14). Trexler also noted that Florentine gilds and confraternities both maintained constitutional distinctions between major and minor members along status lines. Confraternities were organized primarily by and for taxpaying nongildsmen,

although the leadership often came from important gilds (ibid., 15).

The political and status dynamics of confraternities in Renaissance Florence were intimately tied up in traditional connotations of philanthropy going back to the Greeks. No less an authority than Niccolo Machiavelli noted, in his *History*, that the nobility had brought the city both necessary military virtue and a certain "generosity of feeling," which were obliterated by the subsequent rise of the *popolo*, or common people, in the early sixteenth century (Machiavelli 1901 [1525], Book 3, ch. 1).

Catholicism poses a host of special problems for contemporary philanthropic and religious studies: Is the Roman Catholic Church a single organization, a collaborative network of hundreds of distinct organizations, or even an international subculture? Is it an entire hierarchical social order ("Christendom," "the church universal") as rhetoric perfected in the High Middle Ages still proclaims today? Is the "communion of saints" an association of currently living persons or, as is claimed theologically, an association of the presently living and dead and all those unborn? In what sense are associations formed as an expression of religious obligation "voluntary" associations? These are questions much easier to pose than to answer.

There is a rich literature on confraternities, only a small portion of which is available to the English-reading audience. The Library of Congress catalog, for example, lists almost 200 books on the subject in English, French, Spanish, German, Latin, and other languages dating from the 1500s.

Easy entry points into the literature of confraternities include an essay by Andrew Barnes (1991) that reviews several books on Italian and Spanish confraternities in the fifteenth to eighteenth centuries, and entries on the subject in *The Catholic Encyclopedia*. The rich literature, some of which is cited here, on confraternities in Florence, Venice, and the other Italian city-states has many strong ties to contemporary civil society and social capital discussions (Putnam 1995). For those with a more intense interest in the subject, the Society for Confraternity Studies, based in Toronto, produces a regular online newsletter (http://www.library.utoronto.ca/crrs/Confraternitas/scs.htm).

Roger A. Lohmann

References and further reading

Ahlborn, Richard E. 1986. *The Penitente Moradas of Abiquiâu.* Washington, DC: Smithsonian Institution Press.

Banker, James R. 1988. *Death in the Community: Memorialization and Confraternities in the Italian Commune in the Late Middle Ages.* Athens: University of Georgia Press.

Barnes, Andrew. 1991. "Poor Relief and Brotherhood." *Journal of Social History* 24 (3): 603–611.

Carroll, Michael P. 2002. *The Penitente Brotherhood: Patriarchy and Hispano-Catholicism in New Mexico.* Baltimore: Johns Hopkins University Press.

Crouch, David J. F. 2000. *Piety, Fraternity, and Power: Religious Gilds in Late Medieval Yorkshire, 1389–1547.* Woodbridge, Suffolk, UK, and Rochester, New York: York Medieval Press.

De Aragon, Ray John. 1997. *Hermanos de la Luz: Living Tradition of the Penitente Faith.* Santa Fe, NM: Clear Light.

Edgerton, Samuel Y. 1985. *Pictures and Punishment: Art and Criminal Prosecution during the Florentine Renaissance.* Ithaca, NY: Cornell University Press.

Eisenbichler, Konrad. 1991. *Crossing the Boundaries: Christian Piety and the Arts in Italian Medieval and Renaissance Confraternities.* Early Drama, Art, and Music Monograph Series, 15. Kalamazoo, MI: Medieval Institute Publications, Western Michigan University.

Glixon, Jonathan Emmanuel. 2003. *Honoring God and the City: Music at the Venetian Confraternities, 1260–1807.* Oxford and New York: Oxford University Press.

Henderson, John. 1997. *Piety and Charity in Late Medieval Florence.* New York: Oxford University Press.

Knights of Columbus, http://www.kofc.org/.

"Knights of Columbus," http://www.newadvent.org/cathen/08670c.htm.

Machiavelli, Niccolo. 1901 [1525]. *History of Florence and of the Affairs of Italy from the Earliest Times to the Death of Lorenzo the Magnificent.* New York: W. Walter Dunne.

Putnam, Robert D. 1995. *Making Democracy Work: Civic Traditions in Modern Italy.* Princeton: Princeton University Press.

Society for Confraternity Studies, http://www.library.utoronto.ca/crrs/Confraternitas/scs.htm.

Sohm, Philip L. 1982. *The Scuola Grande Di San Marco, 1437–1550: The Architecture of a Venetian Lay Confraternity.* Outstanding Dissertations in the Fine Arts. New York: Garland.

Steele, Thomas J., and Rowena A. Rivera. 1985. *Penitente Self-Government: Brotherhoods and Councils, 1797–1947.* Santa Fe, NM: Ancient City Press.

Trexler, Richard C. 1991. *Public Life in Renaissance Florence.* Ithaca, NY: Cornell University Press.

Webster, Susan V. 1998. *Art and Ritual in Golden Age Spain: Sevillan Confraternities and the Processional Sculpture of Holy Week.* Princeton: Princeton University Press.

Weissman, Ronald F. E. 1981. *Ritual Brotherhood in Renaissance Florence.* Population and Social Structure. Advances in Historical Demography. New York: Academic Press.

Wilkin, Robert L. 1983. *John Chrysostom and the Jews: Rhetoric and Reality in the Late Fourth Century.* Berkeley: University of California Press.

Wisch, Barbara, and Diane Cohl Ahl, eds. 2000. *Confraternities and the Visual Arts in Renaissance Italy: Ritual, Spectacle, Image.* Cambridge: Cambridge University Press.

Consumer Cooperatives

A cooperative is a form of economic organization in which a business is owned and governed by a group of voluntary members for the benefit of these members, rather than being established for the profit of its investors. This organization may range from a loose association of individuals who come together for a single purpose and then disband to a formal, self-sustaining legal entity with an ongoing mission. The members of a cooperative might be individuals, families, households, or more formal organizations such as businesses or other cooperatives. The main difference between an incorporated cooperative and a stock-issuing corporation is that ownership is distributed equally amongst all members and it is not possible for one member to acquire the ownership stakes, privileges, and responsibilities of other owners.

Membership implies not only a commitment to the organization and the ability to receive benefits, but partial ownership of the organization and a voice in governance issues. The resources contributed by the individual members may include financial support, labor, legal expertise, and a physical space in which business can be conducted. Both membership criteria and distributed benefits may vary widely from one cooperative to the next. Although each member/owner has a potential voice in the operation of the cooperative, the members may delegate some decision-making authority to any person or body within or outside the organization. Managers, for example, might be hired to oversee day-to-day operations, or accounting firms might be hired to handle financial transactions.

Workers at Fruit Growers Packing Co-op (James L. Amos/Corbis)

A consumer cooperative is a special type of cooperative in which individuals pool resources in order to purchase goods as a single collective body and then distribute these goods through various mechanisms. In general, a consumer cooperative is at least a semi-formal business organization that seeks to provide benefits on an ongoing basis. When the organization is a legal entity, it may acquire assets, hire employees, register as a nonprofit corporation, receive charitable donations, and protect its members from some forms of financial liability.

A consumer cooperative is inherently philanthropic in that in order to attract and retain membership it must provide some selective incentive that cannot be more easily obtained through individual consumer actions or from other organizations. This incentive might take the form of lower prices for goods purchased by members, forms of personal interaction made possible when conducting actions of collective

behavior, or the personal satisfaction obtained when the organization provides benefits and services to those beyond its membership. By channeling the money that would be spent on these goods through a single organization, the cooperative can offer the benefits of collective action in areas beyond the direct market transaction. The degree and kind of philanthropy supported by the cooperative depends on both type of benefits extended as well as the scope of intended recipients, which are generally outlined in the organization's bylaws or mission statements.

Many consumer cooperatives focus on providing benefits to members within a specific geographic location. Others might concentrate on specific goods that are purchased with some degree of frequency, such as food products, clothing, or electricity. These products might be purchased for individual use and consumption, but they could also be used in the manufacture of other products or sold as retail items in noncooperative venues. In rural areas, for example, farmers might form a consumer cooperative in order to secure better pricing and distribution of seed or fertilizer, and then form a producer cooperative for the collection, storage, and selling of harvested grains. Many regional grocery stores are members of consumer cooperatives, competing with each other for customers but working together to obtain lower wholesale and distribution costs overall.

The Rochdale Equitable Pioneers Society formed in England in 1844 is generally recognized as the first successful "modern" cooperative in the Western hemisphere. With an initial membership of twenty-eight individuals, the cooperative was established "to form arrangements for the pecuniary benefit, and the improvement of the social and domestic condition of its members" (Brown 1944, 23). Other consumer cooperatives, such as the Co-operative Wholesale Society in England and Wales (1863) and Scotland (1867), established wide-ranging distribution networks, providing imported food products at reasonable prices for the rising and increasingly prosperous working class. By 1900, consumer cooperatives in England had an estimated 1.7 million members.

In the United States, many cooperative movements associated with agricultural or labor groups began in the nineteenth century, such as the National Grange movement and the Knights of Labor. Most of the cooperatives created by these organizations, however, failed owing to insolvency. The most successful consumer cooperatives were primarily in rural areas with a limited consumer base that could not support competitive markets. The economic disarray created during World War I provided the strongest foothold for the cooperative movement. Consumer cooperatives were later actively supported by the U.S. government during the Great Depression and World War II as an economic tool to help ensure the delivery of products to financially distressed Americans. The town of Greenbelt, Maryland, was one of three planned communities created by the federal government during the 1930s in which the majority of services were provided by cooperative organizations.

The term "new-wave cooperative" describes consumer cooperatives formed primarily during and after the 1960s in mostly urban areas. It is generally used by consumer cooperatives that support liberal or progressive political agendas concerned with participatory democracy, consumer health, and environmental protection. Most new-wave cooperatives directly associate themselves with the original principles of the Rochdale Pioneers, including (1) open voluntary membership; (2) democratic control; (3) limited return, if any, on equity capital; (4) net surplus belonging to member/owners; (5) education; and (6) cooperation among cooperatives. These co-ops focus on benefits beyond providing lower costs to their members, such as offering products not available elsewhere (especially organic food), supporting local producers and economies, and actively engaging in political movements sympathetic to the membership's ideologies.

Craig Barton Upright

References and further reading
Brown, William Henry. 1944. *The Rochdale Pioneers: A Century of Cooperation.* Manchester: Co-operative Union Limited.

Merret, Christopher D., and Norman Walzer. 1999. *Bibliography of Cooperatives and Cooperative Development.* Macomb, IL: Illinois Institute for Rural Affairs.

Neptune, Robert. 1977. *California's Uncommon Markets: The Story of the Consumers Cooperatives, 1935–1977.* Richmond, CA: Associated Cooperatives.

Reddy, T. Subbi, and M. Hampanna. 1990. *Essays on Consumer Co-operatives.* New Dehli: Deep and Deep Publications.

Sekerak, Emil, and Art Danforth. 1980. *Consumer Cooperation: The Heritage and the Dream.* Santa Clara, CA: Consumers Cooperative Publishing Association.

Contemporary Philanthropy

Philanthropy has been the subject of more study in the past twenty-five years than at any other time in U.S. history. This popular and scholarly attention, reflected in a spate of books, articles, and university courses on the subject, have enriched our understanding of an important national characteristic.

One hotly debated issue for scholars studying the role of charity in national institutions is whether philanthropy preserves economic inequalities in a capitalist society. Critics of Western democratic capitalism see private philanthropy as one of the many ideological means by which the capitalist class maintains its privileged status. In Western societies of the past, religion supplied the dominant ideology by which the lower classes were reconciled to their fate on earth with the promise of heavenly rewards. In contemporary U.S. society, such principles as equality of opportunity, economic growth, individual initiative, and the absolute value of private property integrate citizens into a belief system that makes the financial success of some and the failure of others appear natural, even inevitable or just. From this critical viewpoint, a commitment to philanthropy—as opposed, for example, to efforts to achieve a more equal distribution of wealth—serves the interests of the capitalist class.

Defenders of philanthropy, however, argue that the right to associate freely and to support formally such associations is a key to safeguarding American liberties. Conservatives may also find philanthropy, with its frequent progressive agenda, suspect, but they argue that volunteer associations provide a critically needed layer between citizens and government. The right of people to "vote their values" through charitable giving is viewed as essential in a pluralistic democracy. Another major issue is the public's lack of understanding of the important historical role philanthropy has played in shaping U.S. history. Since the 1980s, more universities, however, began studying charitable giving in order to understand its effect on the nation's past and present. Excellent programs in nonprofit management and philanthropy exist at Harvard University, the University of Southern California, Indiana University, and the University of San Francisco, among others.

The range, extent, and growth of giving in the United States is astonishing. Donors gave an estimated $212 billion to charity in 2001, and donations outpaced inflation despite a weak economy from 1970 to the mid-1990s (AAFRC Trust for Philanthropy 2002). Giving by the nation's 50,000 active grantmaking foundations ($25.9 billion in 2002) has increased more than other sources of contributions since 1990. The continuing importance of foundation giving lies in the ability to concentrate funds on selected projects, call attention to trends in special needs, and provide capital for unproven solutions to social problems. The formation of new foundations, as well as more openness and accountability among grantors and grantees, is a trend that should continue. Corporate giving continues to raise controversy. In an era of downsizing, corporate officers have reduced charitable budgets, putting emphasis on gifts that enhance the marketability of their products and advance their business agenda. Short of cash, many corporations emphasize cause-related marketing partnerships with prestigious nonprofits, from major universities to human services groups such as Red Cross. The connection between giving and corporate interest has increased scrutiny of this sector. Should corporations engage in philanthropy with the funds of stockholders? Is corporate philanthropy just another marketing tool? These are avidly discussed questions in the early years of the twenty-first century.

Biennial national surveys by the INDEPENDENT SECTOR reveal important trends in charitable behavior. There are 1.23 million nonprofits that benefit substantially from people giving their time and talent. In 2000, 44 percent of adults over age twenty-one volunteered this way; of these, 63 percent reported that they volunteered on a regular basis at least once monthly. An estimated 83.9 million adults volunteered some 15.5 billion hours. This labor force represented the equivalent of more than 9 million full-time employees at a value of $239 billion. Rates of volunteering continue to positively correlate with certain factors, including being asked to volunteer, gender (women are more likely to volunteer than men), and membership in religious organizations (Toppe 2002).

Much scholarly attention on the part of INDEPENDENT SECTOR and other research organizations has focused on the diverse sources and recipients of giving. In 2001, $212 billion was given to charities. Approximately 84 percent of this came from individuals and bequests; the rest came from foundations (12 percent) and corporations (4 percent). The relative prosperity of the economy in the 1990s accounts for the use of foundation giving and the number of foundations of all types being started. Of the $212 billion, religious causes received 38 percent, education 15 percent, human services 10 percent, health 9 percent, arts and culture projects 6 percent, and environmental projects 3 percent of the total. These percentages have been relatively stable over the past decade (AAFRC Trust for Philanthropy 2002).

In 2000, 89 percent of households made charitable donations. The average contributing household gave $1,620, or 3.1 percent of household income. Contributions included gifts of money, property, stocks, and other items of value. Households in which the respondents also volunteered typically gave substantially more than nonvolunteers. For donor households, the average contributions were $2,295 from volunteers and $1,009 from nonvolunteers. Moreover, higher rates of giving typically correlate positively with religious faith, childhood experiences where parents volunteered and made financial contributions, optimistic perceptions about the state of the economy, and being asked to give (only 57 percent of households were asked to give to one or more nonprofit organizations in 2000).

In the early years of the twenty-first century, the age of electronic information and Internet access have created new opportunities for volunteers and donors. In 2000, about 10 percent of those with Internet access used it to search for volunteer opportunities, learn about nonprofits, or engage in research. Three percent of those with Internet access reported volunteering over the Internet, doing such things as tutoring, Web site development, or monitoring. Moreover, 3 percent of Internet users actually made a cash donation via the Web, and 17 percent of contributing households reported that online methods of contributing had replaced older forms of contributions. This trend is likely to expand as more Americans become comfortable with computer use and information (Toppe 2002).

Motives for giving are complex. Surveys agree that giving correlates with identifiable attitudes and feelings. Citizens who believe that those possessing wealth are responsible for the less fortunate, people with well-defined personal philanthropic goals or who are concerned about reinforcing traditional moral values, and those giving for religious reasons tend to give more than others. Tax considerations can affect the timing and amount of gifts but are not more important than a host of other donor motives, including having a sense of personal satisfaction; furthering activities of institutions from which the donor benefited in the past; responding to the request of a friend, influential business associate, or employer; and creating a memorial to a family member. Americans continued to support charities in record numbers and record amounts despite changes stipulated by the 1986 Tax Reform Act that disallowed tax deductions to certain donors.

The changing culture of philanthropy helps to define the ethos of the country as a whole as well as its regions. Historians, philosophers, economists, and sociologists are interested in what attitudes, beliefs, values, and expectations shape the giving and receiving of gifts. Scholars such as Lester Salamon and Michael O'Neill have provided perspectives on how, why, and where ethnic and racial groups define need and support for communities. Solid information about trends among groups other than traditional Catholic, Protestant, and Jewish donors was still sketchy in the mid-1990s, but scholarly attention began focusing on African American, Hispanic, Asian American, Native American, and other groups heretofore underexamined. Clearly, traditional philanthropy, which tends to dictate solutions from the top of society down, is unsatisfactory. Complex social problems require sensitivity to multiculturalism, grassroots community planning, and multisector (private, government, and nonprofit) funding.

With the return of Republican control of Congress in the 1994 elections and fewer public resources for a host of familiar programs in support of the arts, education, health, and welfare, the 1990s witnessed a renewed debate about philanthropy's role. Many conservatives argued that reduced government spending would be adequately replaced by private giving. With a slow-growth economy and lingering recession in key states, such as California, there was little likelihood that giving rates could keep pace with human needs. Indeed, the traditional debate about the proper mix of public- and private-sector responsibility for the welfare of the country was revived. Many, particularly in the charitable foundations sector, continued to feel that organized philanthropy is best limited to social research, advocacy, and innovation, with government remaining responsible for primary social services. The outcome of the debate promised to help shape policy in important ways as the twentieth century drew to a close.

Philanthropy in the United States helps to characterize society. It is not likely that voters will ever allow government to restrict free association of the right of donors to help shape their communities by expressing values through giving. For all its imperfections and occasional waste, philanthropy will continue to help define the United States as a culturally distinct part of the world.

Alfred L. Castle

References and further reading
AAFRC Trust for Philanthropy. 2002. *Giving USA 2002: The Annual Report on Philanthropy for the Year 2001, 47th Annual Issue.* Indianapolis: AAFRC Trust for Philanthropy.

Bremner, Robert H. 1988. *American Philanthropy.* Chicago: University of Chicago Press.

Nisbet, Robert A. 1986. *The Making of Modern Society.* New York: New York University Press.

O'Neill, Michael. 1989. *The Third America.* San Francisco: Jossey-Bass.

Salamon, Lester. 1999. *America's Nonprofit Sector: A Primer.* New York: Foundation Center.

Toppe, Christopher M., Arthur D. Kirsch, and Jacobel Michel. 2002. *Giving and Volunteering in the United States: Findings from a National Survey.* Washington, DC: INDEPENDENT SECTOR.

Peter Cooper (1791–1883) (Corbis)

Cooper, Peter (1791–1883)

Despite his success as an inventor and industrialist, Peter Cooper was haunted throughout his life by a lack of formal education. His response was to use his considerable wealth to build and endow a free school in New York City, the Cooper Union, where working youth could attend night classes. The philosophy of life that animated such thoughtful generosity is captured in Cooper's comment that "while I have always recognized that the object of business is to make money in an honorable manner, I have endeavored to remember that the object of life is to do good" (Curti and Nash 1965, 76).

Born in New York City in 1791, Cooper grew up mostly around Peekskill, New York. Like many working-class children of his day, he had little formal education and attended school for less than a year. At the age of seventeen, he returned to the city of his birth and was apprenticed to a leading coachbuilder.

It was during this apprenticeship that Cooper's talent for invention emerged. Among his inventions were a device for mortising the hubs of carriages, a cloth-shearing machine, and the first commercial glue in America that could compete with European imports. The latter became the foundation upon which Cooper would build his fortune. As an inventor, however, he is best remembered as the creator of the first steam locomotive in America, an engine he nicknamed the "Tom Thumb" because of its small size.

As a philanthropist, Cooper made his most lasting mark in the field of education. For three decades, as he worked to establish himself as a leader in business and industry, he nurtured a dream of what he would do with the wealth he was accumulating. The dream came to fruition in 1859 with the opening of the Cooper Union—a school inspired by a friend's account of the free education offered to young Frenchmen at the Ecole Polytechnique in Paris. Recalling his own experience, Cooper reflected: "How glad I would have been, if I could have found such an institution in my youth in [New York City], with its doors open to give instruction at night, the only time that I could command for study" (Curti and Nash 1965, 76).

Built at an initial cost of more than $600,000 in downtown New York City, the Cooper Union offered all of its services free and made itself accessible to the working class by offering night classes, public lectures and concerts, and an excellent library. Moreover, there were no distinctions of class, creed, race, or sex among its beneficiaries. Today, the Cooper Union for the Advancement of Science and Art is the only private college in the United States dedicated exclusively to preparing students for careers in architecture, art, and engineering and providing full-tuition scholarships for its students.

Cooper dedicated nearly thirty years of life to Cooper Union but never gave up his interest in technological innovations. During the late 1850s, he was the original president and a principal investor of New York, Newfoundland & London Telegraph Company, the first firm to lay a transatlantic cable. Cooper and his wife, Sarah, also invented instant gelatin at this time. An inventor, industrialist, and civic leader, Peter Cooper used the rewards of his business success to create for generations of youth the opportunity for an education that had not been available to him.

Richard W. Trollinger

References and further reading

"About the Cooper Union: History." Cooper Union for the Advancement of Science and Art, http://www.cooper.edu/administration/about/history.html.

Cooper, Peter. Papers. Special Collections Division, Cooper Union Library, New York.

Curti, Merle, and Roderick Nash. 1965. *Philanthropy in the Shaping of American Higher Education.* New Brunswick, NJ: Rutgers University Press.

Lach, E. L. 1999. "Peter Cooper." In *American National Biography,* edited by J. A. Garraty and M. C. Carnes, 454–455. New York: Oxford University Press.

Nevins, Allan. 1967 [1935]. *Abram S. Hewitt: With Some Account of Peter Cooper.* New York: Octagon Books.

"Peter Cooper and His Legacy," http://www.cooper.edu/engineering/chemechem/general/cooper.html.

Rossiter, W. Raymond. 1972. *Peter Cooper.* Freeport, NY: Books for Libraries Press.

Corporate Giving

American business interacts with the nonprofit sector primarily through what has been referred to as corporate social responsibility (CSR), or those actions through which businesses meet the expectations of society in any particular time (Sethi 1979). Other terms that have been used to express this concept include "corporate philanthropy," "corporate community investment," "corporate community involvement," and more recently "corporate citizenship." Corporate citizenship is usually meant to convey "a multi-faceted concept which brings together the self-interest of business and its stakeholders with the interest of society more generally" (Logan, Roy, and Regelbrugge 1997, iii).

"Corporate giving" and "corporate philanthropy" are understood to be narrower terms restricted to the charitable giving and volunteering that a company does that meets part of its felt citizenship responsibilities. Cause-related marketing and sponsorship fall outside the scope of this article.

In the United States, corporate giving has developed along the lines of the legal history of the corporation. In the early twentieth century, the issue was how much of the company profits could be used for community benefit without having a shareholder revolt. Examples of early donations were to YMCAs that provided housing for company workers. From 1921 to 1953, companies could only give to causes that benefited the company. In 1953, the *Smith v. Barlow* case in the New Jersey Supreme Court cleared the way for A. P. Smith Manufacturing Company to donate $1,500 to Princeton University without violating shareholder interest. In essence, the principle of direct corporate benefit was overturned, and a rationale for public responsibility of business was established in the United States.

According to *Giving USA 2003,* giving by corporations in 2002 was approximately $12.19 billion—an increase from the previous year. This represented 5.1 percent of all contributions. Over the last twenty-five years, corporate giving as a percent of profits has declined from 2.3 to 1.3 percent in 2001, and back up to 1.8 percent in 2002. The major reasons for this decline have been the changing philosophy of the role of corporate giving, the role of the CEO, a changing corporate culture, and an increase in global competitiveness.

After examining research in this field, Young and Burlingame (1996) identified four models that categorized why companies engaged in volunteering and giving. The four paradigms are the stakeholder model, the neoclassical or productivity model, the ethical or altruistic model, and the political model.

The stakeholder model posits that a company is a complex entity with various constituents—shareholders, customers, suppliers, managers, community groups, and the like—that hold different claims on the company. How the various groups interact to determine corporate policy is unclear. For a review of the empirical research on corporate social performance, see Wood and Jones (1995).

The neoclassical/corporate productivity model operates from the frame of reference that the business of business is to make money, and giving to community groups will enhance the bottom line. In other words, enlightened self-interest, which is focused on the long-run profitability of the corporation, is the order of the day.

The political model takes as its external reference corporate power and autonomy by building relationships with nonprofits as an alternative to government growth. Internal to the company, this model suggests that the corporate giving officer is a larger player within the company, in which departments attempt to build allies among each other to succeed in their respective missions.

The ethical model is based upon the premise that companies are given the right to exist by society and thus have a social obligation to do what is right for the greater good. It encourages management to make gifts that will maintain the business as a partner in addressing societal needs.

These models suggest that there is no one motive for corporate giving. Therefore, can the corporate contributions function be empowered in the twenty-first century by using the expression of global corporate citizenship, which suggests that companies have an interest in strategic social investment because it is necessary for a successful business environment? If one agrees that the main purpose of businesses is to provide efficient means for capital for stakeholders as well as shareholders, then it would appear that corporations can benefit themselves as they benefit society.

Dwight F. Burlingame

See also Cause-Related Marketing and Sponsorships

References and further reading
Giving USA 2003. 2002. Indianapolis: AAFRC Trust for Philanthropy.
Logan, David, Delwin Roy, and Laurie Regelbrugge. 1997. *Global Corporate Citizenship: Rationale and Strategies.* Washington, DC: Hitachi Foundation.
Muirhead, Sophia. 1999. *Corporate Contributions: The Views—from Fifty Years.* New York: Conference Board.
Sethi, S. Prakash. 1979. "A Conceptual Framework for Environmental Analysis of Social Issues and Evaluation of Business Response Patterns." *Academy of Management Review* 4 (1): 63–74.
Wood, Donna J., and Raymond E. Jones. 1995. "Stakeholder Mismatching: A Theoretical Problem in Empirical Research on Corporate Social Performance." *International Journal of Organizational Analysis* 3 (3): 229–267.
Young, Dennis R., and Dwight F. Burlingame. 1996. "Paradigm Lost." In *Corporate Philanthropy at the Crossroads,* edited by Dwight F. Burlingame and Dennis R. Young, 158–176. Bloomington: Indiana University Press.

Council for Advancement and Support of Education (CASE)

The largest education-related association in the world and leading professional membership organization for all areas of institutional advancement, the Council for Advancement and Support of Education (CASE) has a membership comprising more than 3,000 colleges, universities, and independent elementary and secondary schools in the United States, Canada, Mexico, and forty-two other countries. Within these member institutions, more than 38,000 advancement professionals, working at all levels in alumni relations, communications, and development, are represented.

CASE was established in 1974 as the result of a merger between the American Alumni Council and the American College Public Relations Association. In 1994, the organization expanded beyond the North American continent and officially opened a European office located in London to better serve the needs of its growing international membership.

The primary purpose of CASE is to assist its membership in promoting and advancing the merits of the educational institutions that they represent. In support of this mission, CASE promotes a variety of mentoring and networking activities that help members strengthen their institutions' advancement operations as well as enhance their own professional development. Activities include the annual sponsorship of nearly 100 regional, national, and international professional conferences, workshops, and educational institutes; publication of *CURRENTS*, a member magazine; development of topic-oriented research and benchmarking studies; and promotion of various advancement-related products, services, books, and publications. Another important activity of CASE is its government-relations efforts. By monitoring legislative and policy debates and communicating the interests, views, and needs of its members to policy makers, CASE provides its members with timely, critical information and advocates on their behalf.

Headquartered in Washington, D.C., CASE is classified as a nonprofit 501(c)(3) organization under the Internal Revenue Code (IRC) and is governed by a board of trustees who are elected by the member institutions. The board elects and hires the organization's president, who also serves as the chief executive officer. CASE's North American member institutions are grouped into eight geographic districts, with each district providing additional support to members through regional programs and services.

CASE's strong encouragement of professional ethics and standards, leadership, and service to education is demonstrated through a number of distinguished recognition and award programs. The Circle of Excellence Awards Program acknowledges best practices in advancement operations and research. The Chief Executive Leadership Award recognizes effective and outstanding institutional leadership. Other programs include scholarships and fellowships to promote diversity in the advancement profession and awards for exceptional service to the field of education, teaching, scholarly research, volunteer involvement, and government relations.

Elizabeth R. Crabtree

References and further reading
Council for Advancement and Support of Education, http://www.case.org.

Council on Foundations (COF)

The Council on Foundations (COF), founded in 1949 as the National Committee on Foundations and Trusts for Community Welfare, was created to promote responsible and effective philanthropy. It is the largest association of grantmakers in the United States, assisting staff and trustees of foundations with their grantmaking activities. COF provides one-on-one technical assistance to its members and other services of benefit to foundations, such as conducting research, producing publications, convening conferences and workshops, and providing legal services. It also plays a major advocacy role, lobbying the U.S. Congress on issues that affect foundations, philanthropy, and the nonprofit sector. Commonly, the Council on Foundations is viewed as a centrist voice for foundations, positioning itself between the more conservative Philanthropy Roundtable and the more liberal National Committee for Responsive Philanthropy.

COF adopted its current name in 1964 after two previous name changes. The organization's offices were in Chicago from 1949 to 1954 and in New York City from 1954 to 1979. They have been in Washington, D.C., since 1979.

A thirty-five-member board of directors, consisting primarily of high-level foundation executives and corporate philanthropy officers, governs the organization. Dues paid by member foundations produce a majority of operating revenues for COF. The organization also includes thirty-six affinity groups—small or large groups of foundations that share similar funding interests, such as education, religion, Hispanics, neighborhoods, or the environment. Some of the affinity groups maintain their own staff and have separate budgets from COF.

Since the watershed Tax Reform Act of 1969, which established a 4 percent excise tax on foundation assets and a 6 percent minimum annual payout, the Council on Foundations has played an increasingly important role in representing the interests of foundations to members of Congress. The Tax Reform Act of 1969 came in response to public concern about scandals involving private foundations and marked the first instance in which private foundations were defined and regulated by law. The passage of this act, which was generally viewed by the Council on Foundations as hostile to foundations, led to the organization's recognition of the need to maintain better relationships with congressional representatives. Through its involvement with the Filer Commission (the Commission on Private Philanthropy and Public Needs) in the 1970s, COF helped reduce the excise tax on foundation assets to its current 2 percent level and the minimum foundation payout to its current 5 percent level. Efforts by COF to completely eliminate the excise tax have been unsuccessful.

The excise tax is meant to cover costs incurred by the Internal Revenue Service (IRS) in regulating private foundations, but in reality the tax generates far more revenue for the IRS than is needed to oversee foundations. COF maintains that nonprofit groups will benefit most if the excise tax is eliminated because foundations currently count the 2 percent excise tax as a portion of the mandatory 5 percent payout. If the tax is reduced or eliminated, COF argues, foundation grants to nonprofit organizations will increase dramatically.

Aaron Dorfman

References and further reading
Council on Foundations, http://www.cof.org.
Edie, John A. 1987. *Congress and Private Foundations: An Historical Analysis.* Washington, DC: Council on Foundations.

Cuffe, Paul (1759–1817)

Upon returning from a visit to Sierra Leone in the early 1800s, Paul Cuffe wrote, "As I am of the African race I feel myself interested for them and if I am favored with a talent I think I am willing that they should be benefited thereby" (Thomas 1986, 40). Upon examination of his life, one can readily see that Paul Cuffe's statement embraced not only Africans on the continent but also those across the diaspora. At a time when blacks were considered not more than property and less than human beings, Paul Cuffe, an abolitionist and pan-Africanist, succeeded at becoming an entrepreneur, a sea captain and merchant, and a community benefactor and philanthropist. He was most probably the wealthiest African American of his time and used his talents to benefit his African brethren on both sides of the Atlantic.

Early Years and Education
Born on Cuttyhunk Island, Massachusetts (near Martha's Vineyard), on January 17, 1759, Cuffe was the seventh of ten children born to Kofi Slocum and Ruth Moses. Kofi (whose name means "born on Friday") was an Ashanti slave of Akan ancestry who had been brought to the North American colonies when he was about ten. By 1728, he had reached Newport, Rhode Island, where he was acquired by Ebenezer Slocum, a Quaker. On February 16, 1742, Ebenezer sold Kofi to John Slocum, his nephew. Due to the growth of antislavery sentiments among Friends (Quakers), Kofi was emancipated, quite unexpectedly, in 1745. That same year, he became engaged to Ruth Moses, a Native American of the Wampanoag group. Kofi took his master's last name, and he and Ruth were married in 1746.

After living in Dartmouth for a time, the couple moved to Cuttyhunk, in the Elizabeth Islands. They had ten children, who were reared along the Quaker principles the couple espoused, though they were not accepted as members of the Society of Friends. In 1766, Coffe (he had changed the spelling of his name) Slocum bought a 116-acre farm in Dartmouth. The following year, the entire family moved there, and at the age of eight Paul began helping with the work and farming. After his father died in 1772, Paul became interested in sea life. At the age of thirteen, Paul could barely read and write, but he persisted in his studies, occasionally with the help of a private tutor.

He was very interested in navigation, which he found very difficult at first but finally grasped. Cuffe once told a Professor Griscom: "There were always three things that I paid attention to—latitude, lead, and lookout" (Sherwood 1923, 156). Around the age of sixteen, he became a seaman and joined the crews of whaling merchants such as Joseph Rotch and Joseph Russell. On his third voyage, the British captured the ship he was on and he was imprisoned in New York. After three months, Cuffe returned to Dartmouth and wrestled with his identity. The white Slocums did not want Paul's family to use their name. About 1778, Paul decided to take his father's African name as a surname, but continued to acknowledge his mother's Native American ancestry. All of the other children followed suit, with the exception of his youngest sister, Freelove.

The family farm weathered heavy tax increases from 1777 to 1780, when Paul and his brother John, along with five other Dartmouth blacks who had been recently freed, petitioned the state of Massachusetts, noting that they were being unfairly taxed without representation. The petition failed; however, these efforts led the way to African and Native Americans getting voting rights and privileges in 1783. On February 25, 1783, Paul married Alice Pequit (a Native American), and to this union seven children were born.

Career Highlights and Major Philanthropic Accomplishments

Paul Cuffe began his quest for economic independence in his early twenties. Though he had basic seafaring skills and plenty of drive, his entrepreneurial skills were still wanting. He learned the subtleties of entrepreneurial success by observing the family enterprises of successful Quakers such as the Rotches (Thomas 1986, 13). At age twenty, Cuffe built a boat with the help of his brother David in order to engage in trade with people of Connecticut. Life at sea was very dangerous, however, with its natural hazards and pirates always in pursuit. Thus, David decided to return to farm work, leaving Paul to cope for himself. With the Revolutionary War ensuing, Paul also thought it best to work in agriculture until it was safer to go back to sea. He returned to the farm for a time, but it wasn't long before his desire to become a sea merchant surfaced once again.

As Paul had spoken with David repeatedly about his desires, David agreed to build Paul a boat if he would supply the materials. With borrowed money, Paul purchased some goods. After narrow escapes with pirates, the undaunted Paul finally managed to reach Nantucket with his cargo, though the voyage was not financially profitable (Sherwood 1923, 156). On a second voyage, he was robbed by pirates and injured, but the third voyage was successful. With the war over, the sea became safer and his business began to prosper. Around this time, Cuffe's brother-in-law, Michael Wainer (a Native American), entered into business with him.

Three vessels were registered by the Cuffe-Wainer family between the years 1785 and 1795: the *Sunfish* (a 25-foot schooner), the *Mary* (a 42-foot schooner), and the *Ranger* (a 62-foot square-sterned schooner).

Cuffe had sold the *Sunfish* and the *Mary* in order to pay for the *Ranger*, "thus displaying in finance the same daring that had earned him respect at sea, for one disaster would have wiped out his maritime investment" (Thomas 1986, 16). He determined that the family would always own his vessel, and whenever possible, her captains and crew would be from the family as well. It was on the *Ranger* that Wainer's sons gained their seafaring knowledge and expertise. Cuffe would eventually own several ships, including schooners, brigs, and barks.

On the *Ranger*, Cuffe sailed the Chesapeake to Norfolk and Vienna in Virginia to purchase corn. Upon his arrival, the townspeople were amazed and alarmed to witness a vessel commanded by a black man with an all-black crew. At first, these whites were very concerned about the influence Cuffe and his crew might have on their slaves. This spectacle, they feared, could incite an uprising. Cuffe and his crew, however, conducted themselves prudently and with "conciliating propriety" (Sherwood 1923, 158). The venture was so successful that Cuffe made another trip.

Cuffe knew about the African refuge of Sierra Leone through Quakers in and around Westport. Granville Sharp, a British philanthropist, had sent three shiploads of free blacks (former American slaves living in London) to West Africa and hoped to establish a "Province of Freedom" there. When Quakers around New England began seeking a haven for their slaves, Cuffe began receiving proposals for black emigration.

Cuffe resisted the idea because he believed that black survival, as well as independence, depended upon assimilation with whites (Thomas 1986, 19–20). This belief was manifested in his life through his service to the community. As a result of the very profitable ventures he had experienced in purchasing Vienna corn, Captain Cuffe was able to purchase a $3,500 farm along the Westport River. Since there were no educational facilities in his new neighborhood, Cuffe called his neighbors together to discuss building a schoolhouse. Unfortunately, this meeting was unsuccessful because there was such a difference of opinion. Cuffe, however, eventually used his own funds to build a schoolhouse on his property and made it available to the public. The school he established there was racially integrated.

By 1804, Cuffe had learned of profitable whaling exploits around southeast Africa. Though entering waters where slavers lurked was certainly a risky proposition, Cuffe successfully met the challenge. In 1807, British abolitionists were forming the African Institution, an organization that promoted black emigration as well as African "civilization and happiness" (Thomas 1986, 32). British Quakers corresponded with their American counterparts, who soon joined in this enterprise. Cuffe was sought to assist in this effort since he was considered an exemplary man of color.

Cuffe, along with his family, still held Quaker beliefs. Though his parents had not been allowed membership, Cuffe became a member of the Westport Society of Friends in 1808 after much deliberation on the part of the Society. The Westport Friends built a new meetinghouse in 1813, with Cuffe contributing at least half of the material and "overseeing the business end of the matter" (Sherwood 1923, 160–161).

When the slave trade ended in 1808, Cuffe began to think more seriously of pursuing trade in Africa (particularly whaling) and promoting African civilization through trade and ethical principles. He sailed to Sierra Leone with an all-black crew on December 27, 1810. There, the company met an array of people in the vicinity of Freetown, Sierra Leone, the overwhelming majority of whom were people of color. Yet three-fifths of all property was controlled by twenty-eight Europeans. Tensions often rode high, but the settlers were determined to succeed. Cuffe, along with John Kizell (another respected black merchant), formed the Friendly Society of Sierra Leone, a mutual aid society concerned with commerce (Thomas 1986, 51, 54).

Observing that Africans were being exploited by British trade monopolies and that blacks were still in bondage in the United States, Cuffe reluctantly believed that blacks might become a people in Africa. He had come to the sad conclusion that they could never do so in America. The founders of the American Colonization Society (ACS), an organization established in 1816 with the supposedly goodwill intentions of transporting free blacks to Africa of their own consent, hoped that Cuffe would align himself with their organization. Cuffe soon realized that this organization was simply a vehicle for racist white Americans, as evidenced by the words of Henry Clay, Speaker of the House of Representatives and a member of ACS, who asserted that he wanted "to rid our country of a useless and pernicious, if not dangerous portion of our population" (Thomas 1986, 111). Francis Scott Key, the composer of the U.S. national anthem and a member of ACS as well, felt that the ACS must protect slavery as an institution.

Cuffe, who felt that free blacks should emigrate to Africa only if it was their choice, thought it best that blacks withdraw from the organization. After his death in 1817, the country of Liberia was founded with the help of the ACS. Despite his differences with the society, there is little doubt that Cuffe would have been pleased that the African nation he had long hoped for had been formed.

Nina Gondola

References and further reading
Cuffe, Paul. Papers. Free Public Library, New Bedford, MA.
Johns, Robert C. 1999. "Paul Cuffe." In *Notable Black American Men,* edited by Jessie Carney Smith, 241–243. Detroit: Gale.
Sherwood, Henry Noble. 1923. "Paul Cuffe." *Journal of Negro History* 8, no. 2 (January): 153–229.
Thomas, Lamont D. 1986. *Paul Cuffe: Black Entrepreneur and Pan-Africanist.* Urbana and Chicago: University of Illinois Press.
Wiggins, Rosalind Cobb. 1996. *Captain Paul Cuffe's Logs and Letters, 1808–1817: A Black Quaker's "Voice from within the Veil."* Washington, DC: Howard University Press.
Woodson, Carter G. 1920. "The Relations of Negroes and Indians in Massachusetts." *Journal of Negro History* 5, no. 1 (January): 45–57.

Cultural Policy and Philanthropy

Direct, sustained governmental support for cultural activities in the United States began in the 1960s. Few formal policies on cultural matters have been established, however, and the level of support has been limited in comparison with that of other developed nations. Of the $15 billion that was given by the private sector to support arts and culture organizations in the United States in 2000 *(Giving USA 2001; Americans for the Arts),* $2 billion came from the federal government,

$447.5 million from state governments, and roughly $1 billion from local governments. The vast majority of funding for the arts, however, was donated by individuals, with foundations and corporations combined contributing about 10 percent of the total. The relatively low government funding levels are mirrored by the lack of a cabinet-level political position such as the ministries of culture that exist in other countries, as well as by the fact that the vast majority of the cultural organizations in the United States are privately governed. Efforts to stimulate additional support and to develop a coherent statement of policy have been primarily generated by private foundations.

The single most consistent form of governmental funding for cultural endeavors remains the indirect support granted to nonprofit organizations. Under the relevant tax provisions, individuals and corporations are able to deduct charitable contributions to organizations with 501(c)(3) status under the Internal Revenue Code (IRC). These benefits have occasionally been extended to cover specific cultural activities, indirectly constituting a national policy. For example, the revisions to the 1976 tax code provided significant credits for the preservation and restoration of historic structures (these provisions were expanded in 1981). Similarly, periodic tax allowances for items of appreciated value have contributed significantly to high-value gifts of art to museums. The Business Committee for the Arts, formed in 1967 largely through the efforts of David Rockefeller, has helped to increase awareness of the value of such tax deductions to cultural organizations.

During the 1930s and again in the 1970s, the federal government provided short-term, direct support to culture workers. The Works Progress Administration (WPA), established under President Franklin D. Roosevelt, helped to establish a nationwide investment in artistic endeavors, from theater and writing to music and the visual arts. The WPA, however, was eliminated in the face of the rising wartime economy of World War II. The Comprehensive Education and Training Act (CETA) of 1973 offered employment and job training in the arts for thousands until it was discontinued by the Ronald Reagan administration in 1981.

The watershed event for the formation of cultural policies and the establishment of continuing direct government support to the nation's cultural life came with the adoption of the National Endowment for Arts and Humanities Act in 1965. This legislation created two agencies, the National Endowment for the Arts (NEA) and the National Endowment for the Humanities (NEH), which have provided a combination of operating, capital, and special project support for nonprofit cultural organizations in the United States. At various times, these agencies also have provided support to individuals engaged in cultural work—including artists, writers, poets, and filmmakers—although some of these award programs have been revised or eliminated in the face of public concerns about the creation of pornographic or sacrilegious work.

Despite the creation of federal agencies to support cultural programs, federal policy remains a weak link in the American system. Struggles between the state and local agencies have exacerbated controversies over federal funding of the arts and have made it difficult to provide anything other than minimal support for cultural activities. To date, no formal federal policy has been created, nor has there been any significant public debate over what that policy should be.

The creation of the NEA and the NEH in 1965 reflected many years of behind-the-scenes efforts by those in the private sector, an effort that continues to the present. A Rockefeller Brothers Fund report issued in 1965, *The Performing Arts: Problems and Prospects*, outlined the dire economic straits of many private arts groups and called for a major investment in America's nonprofit professional arts community. The research findings of William Baumol and William Bowen, *Performing Arts: The Economic Dilemma* (1966), complemented the Rockefeller report by demonstrating the ongoing need for unearned income by arts organizations. Policy makers within the John F. Kennedy administration had advocated increased support for the arts, but action was postponed when Lyndon B. Johnson assumed the presidency. Nevertheless, these voices helped make a strong case for governmental support of the arts and efforts to reach economically diverse audiences.

America's Museums: The Belmont Report (1969), written under the auspices of the American Association of Museums for the Federal Council on Arts and

Humanities, focused attention on the financial needs of the nation's museums. In response, the Institute of Museum Services (IMS) was created in 1976 at the federal level with the intent of providing general operating support to private-sector museums. In subsequent years, IMS expanded its programs to include support for conservation and management services, and in 1996, it absorbed the library activities of the U.S. Department of Education to create the Institute of Museum and Library Services (IMLS).

The few policy discussions that have addressed arts and culture have focused primarily on the economics of arts organizations. In the pre-1965 era, perhaps the largest impact on cultural development came through the decision of the Ford Foundation, beginning in 1957, to provide major support to nonprofit arts groups. Staff of the Rockefeller Foundation, together with Ford Foundation staff, frequently met cultural leaders and convened private roundtable discussions on the proper role of foundation and government support. Private foundations also funded the preparation of numerous studies on the economics of the arts, such as a 1974 Ford Foundation study *(The Finances of the Performing Arts)* and a 2001 Pew Charitable Trusts study *(The Performing Arts in a New Era).* Under the auspices of the American Assembly, W. McNeil Lowry of the Ford Foundation organized national conferences on the arts in 1977 and 1984, each of which generated publications that underscored the need for continued government support. A third American Assembly, held in 1990, called for increased advocacy efforts.

Although additional governmental bodies have been established over the years to advance issues associated with cultural policy, none has provided significant leadership in this area. The Filer Commission report of 1977 discussed the need for public funding to supplement the largesse of private philanthropy in the arts but had little effect. The President's Committee on the Arts and Humanities (PCAH), created in 1982 by executive order to bring together the heads of twelve federal agencies that support the arts along with twenty-four citizens appointed by the president, has commissioned a number of reports on private support of the arts, but these have rarely gotten a wide readership. Disappointingly, PCAH's most public ac-

tivity has been the annual National Medal on the Arts and Humanities awards. Congressional efforts to examine cultural funding have intermittently coalesced into the Congressional Arts Caucus with occasional involvement of private-sector representatives. These efforts have been aided by long-standing advocacy efforts of discipline-based support associations.

State and local government support, however, has proven to be an important element of financial stability for many arts organizations. Some municipalities have long underwritten the costs of city museums and symphonies, and beginning with New York State's Council on the Arts in 1963, states also began to provide operating support for cultural activities. Spurred by the availability of "block grant" funds from NEA and NEH, every state in the union had arts and humanities councils by the early 1970s. These state agencies have become significant sponsors of arts activities, often working together through the National Assembly of State Arts Agencies. Local agencies have also been active in conducting studies of the economic impact of the arts that have introduced a new perspective into policy discussions. Despite such active sponsorship, little has been done to develop comprehensive cultural policies.

Attacks on federal spending for the arts—particularly by Reagan in 1981 and by conservatives during the "Culture Wars" of 1989–1995—underscored the fact that there is no national cultural policy. Initiatives in the private sector have sought to fill this need. Since 1982, Americans for the Arts (first established as the American Council for the Arts in 1960) has held annual Arts Advocacy Days in Washington and, beginning in 1988, has tried to spotlight cultural issues in the annual Nancy Hanks Lectures on Arts and Public Policy. These efforts are likely to be enhanced by the receipt of a $120 million endowment from the estate of a Lilly heiress in 2002. Similar efforts have been adopted by many state arts groups across the nation.

Beginning in the 1990s, some foundations have pursued more tightly focused goals relating to cultural activities with the intent, sometimes implicit and sometimes explicit, of leveraging additional support for the cultural sector from the government. Among the most influential of these have been efforts by the

Lila Wallace Fund to develop minority audiences for arts organizations, by the Andrew W. Mellon Foundation to support regional theaters, and by the Pew Charitable Trusts to encourage the training of journalists in cultural issues. The last is of particular interest as critics of American cultural policy have consistently cited the paucity of reliable and consistent data as a primary flaw in the development of a coherent discourse. The Creativity and Culture Division of the Rockefeller Foundation, long interested in international affairs, has chosen to focus its resources on multiculturalism and globalization.

During the "Republican Revolution" of 1995–1996, funding for the NEH dropped from $177 million to $110 million and that for the NEA fell from $167 million to $99.5 million. In response, a number of private foundations helped to establish the Center for Arts and Culture in Washington, D.C. (This approach parallels the efforts of private foundations to create the Foundation Center following the Cox and Reece commissions of the 1950s.) This nonprofit research institute is developing a coherent database on arts issues in order to help promote effective advocacy efforts for increased support of the arts and to foster dialogue for a comprehensive cultural policy at the federal level. A related effort is the Pew Charitable Trusts–funded development of an informational infrastructure for research on performing arts audiences through the Cultural Policy and the Arts National Data Archive at Princeton University. Both efforts build on earlier attempts of the NEA to encourage policy research on the cultural sector, culminating with *The Arts in America* report to Congress in 1988. Americans for the Arts also maintains a National Arts Policy Database with materials dating from 1960.

The rise of governmental support for arts and cultural endeavors in the past generation has brought with it an increasing obligation for arts organizations to provide public accountability. In addition, a number of foundations and donors have begun to ask nonprofits to explore ways of generating income for long-term sustainability. One tangible response to this impulse has been the creation of a national online database of financial reports on nonprofit organizations, spearheaded by GuideStar and the Urban Institute in collaboration with the Internal Revenue Service and with funding from a variety of national foundations. This push toward social enterprise is likely to continue in future years.

American cultural policy, then, has taken the form of an ungainly amalgam in which private and local groups push for funding and policy statements from government rather than a system in which government takes the lead in developing and implementing a national policy. In this setting, private foundations and professional associations have the opportunity to continue having crucial but limited influence on the formation of a comprehensive cultural agenda.

Robert I. Goler

References and further reading

Baumol, William, and William Bowen. 1966. *The Performing Arts: The Economic Dilemma.* Cambridge, MA: The MIT Press.

Benedict, Stephen, ed. 1991. *Public Money and the Muse.* New York: W. W. Norton & Company.

[Fleming, John R.] 1969. *America's Museums: The Belmont Report.* Washington: American Association of Museums.

Lowry, W. McNeil, ed. 1978. *The Performing Arts and American Society.* Englewood Cliffs, NJ: Prentice-Hall.

———. 1984. *The Arts and Public Policy in the United States.* Englewood Cliffs, NJ: Prentice-Hall.

McCarthy, Kevin F., Arthur Brooks, Julia Lowell, and Laura Zakaras. 2001. *The Performing Arts in a New Era.* Santa Monica, CA: Rand.

[Rockefeller Brothers Fund]. 1965. *The Performing Arts: Problems and Prospects.* New York: McGraw-Hill.

Wyszomirski, Margaret. 1999. "Philanthropy and Culture: Patterns, Context, and Change." Pp. 461–480 in *Philanthropy and the Nonprofit Sector in a Changing America.* Edited by Charles T. Clotfelter and Thomas Ehrlich. Bloomington, IN: University of Indiana Press.

Curti, Merle Eugene (1897–1996)

Merle Eugene Curti was born in 1897 in rural Nebraska. Curti studied with Frederick Jackson Turner at Harvard, where he earned a Ph.D. in 1927. An eminent social and intellectual historian, he directed the History of American Philanthropy Project of the University of Wisconsin from 1957 to 1961.

Curti's interest in research on philanthropy was spurred by criticisms of the Rockefeller, Carnegie, and Ford foundations by the congressional commission headed by B. Carroll Reece in 1954. The commission suggested that the foundations were forcing socialism on the American public. Following a meeting of scholars and foundation representatives at Princeton in 1956, the Ford Foundation agreed to provide $100,000 for historical research on philanthropy, headed up by Curti, who was on the faculty at the University of Wisconsin from 1942 to 1968. Although the project was not able to accomplish as much as Curti might have wanted, the report to the Ford Foundation included an impressive listing of published articles, books, master's theses, and doctoral dissertations on philanthropy. A major impediment to the project was the unwillingness of foundations to open their records for research. Curti and his codirector, Irvin G. Wyllie, encouraged other historians to undertake research on philanthropy and its role in American life, but project funds were primarily used to provide stipends to graduate students who were interested in doing research on the field.

In his 1958 essay "American Philanthropy and the National Character," Curti traced the history of philanthropy as an idea in American culture, showing how definitions and social meaning have changed over time. He set forth the notion of philanthropy as an "index and agent" of American national character and suggested that philanthropy historically may have been the "American equivalent for socialism." Curti recognized that the breadth of American philanthropy could only be revealed through an interdisciplinary approach to history. He suggested research on all areas of the history of philanthropy, including religion, humanitarianism, economics, social welfare, corporations, and law, as well as studies of individual charitable institutions and organizations, fundraising, changes in the definitions and social meaning of philanthropy, and biographies of individual philanthropists. He died in Madison, Wisconsin, in 1996 at the age of ninety-eight.

Frances Huehls

References and further reading
Curti, Merle E. 1957. "The History of American Philanthropy As a Field of Research." *American Historical Review* 62: 352–363.
———. 1958. "American Philanthropy and the National Character." *American Quarterly* 10: 420–437.
———. 1961. "Tradition and Innovation in American Philanthropy." *Proceedings of the American Philosophical Society* 105: 146–156.
———. 1963. *American Philanthropy Abroad.* New Brunswick, NJ: Rutgers University Press.
Curti, Merle Eugene, Judith Green, and Roderick Nash. 1963. "Anatomy of Giving: Millionaires in the Late Nineteenth Century." *American Quarterly* 15: 416–435.
Curti, Merle Eugene, and Roderick Nash. 1965. *Philanthropy in the Shaping of American Higher Education.* New Brunswick, NJ: Rutgers University Press.

Cy Pres
See Donor Intent

D

Dartmouth College v. Wooster

See Law of Charity

Day, Dorothy (1897–1980)

Because of her strong commitment to the dignity of the poor, Dorothy Day founded the Catholic Worker movement in the United States and personally embraced a life of voluntary poverty. Her outspoken dedication to pacifism and to equal treatment and justice for all people provide a strong example of philanthropy that has earned her consideration for sainthood in the Catholic Church.

Dorothy Day was born in 1897 in Brooklyn, New York, the daughter of a newspaper-journalist father who frequently moved his family to follow writing opportunities. One such stop was San Francisco in 1906, where the family survived the well-chronicled earthquake of that year. Day observed firsthand as her family and others gave of their own belongings to help those who had lost everything.

Day later attended the University of Illinois and pursued general studies. As a student, her political awareness blossomed, and she began to identify with the plight of the working masses. Day was deeply affected by the chasm she perceived between the wealthy and the poor, and she subsequently joined the Socialist Party. After leaving the university, she moved east and, for a short time, wrote for a New York City–based party newspaper, the *Masses*, which was closed down by the government.

A common-law marriage to Forster Battingham yielded a daughter, Tamar Teresa, but the marriage ultimately ended because of Day's conversion to Catholicism. While Socialism and Catholicism may seem at odds, Day saw commonalities with the dedication each voiced for those of the working class.

Day continued to write, and as her reputation grew, Peter Maurin, a French immigrant with his own dedication to the poor, noticed her work. Maurin sought out Day in 1933, and the two began to copublish a newspaper, the *Catholic Worker*, charging a penny a copy (the price of which remains the same today). The newspaper became an outlet written for the poor and covered such subject matter as the support of labor unions, reports of civil unrest, and commentary on the inequities of a capitalist system.

As the economic depression continued, Day and Maurin observed the dramatic increase in the number of homeless and hungry individuals. Later in 1933, they opened the first of many houses of hospitality (providing food and shelter) in New York City, where they also assumed lives of poverty and lived in the houses themselves. Day and Maurin viewed their own poverty as an essential tenet of the Catholic Worker movement—to give all they had to the poor was the only way they could credibly serve the poor and God.

The Catholic Worker movement relied almost exclusively on the work of volunteers, many of whom were university students. As the students graduated from their respective schools, they took the Catholic Worker concept to their hometowns. Soon, Catholic Worker houses began to form around the country and the world, many publishing their own newspapers.

Pacifism was another crucial ideal for Day, and she did not let the threat of arrest stop her from protesting wars and nuclear armaments. First apprehended as a young writer for picketing with suffragists, she continued to participate in protests and was arrested when she was well into her seventies.

Day died in 1980 at the age of eighty-three. The Catholic Worker movement thrives today through the continued publication of the *Catholic Worker* newspaper and the proliferation of settlement houses serving the poor. While some still publish their own newspapers, many others have turned to the Internet to continue the teachings of Dorothy Day. Her selfless commitment to the poor and constant striving for peace have made her a candidate for canonization for sainthood in the Catholic Church.

Michael P. Grzesiak

References and further reading

The Catholic Worker Movement, http://www.catholic worker.org

Coles, Robert. 1987. *Dorothy Day: A Radical Devotion.* Reading, MA: Addison-Wesley.

Day, Dorothy. 1952. *The Long Loneliness.* New York: Harper and Row.

———. 1963. *Loaves and Fishes.* New York: Harper and Row.

Ellsberg, Robert, ed. 1992. *Dorothy Day: Selected Writings.* Maryknoll, NY: Orbis Books.

Dayton Family

Through the course of the twentieth century, George Draper Dayton, his children, and his grandchildren built a retail empire known initially as Dayton's, then as the Dayton-Hudson Corporation, and now as the Target Corporation. Through their long-standing policy of annually giving 5 percent of their pretax profits to charity, the Dayton family also became regarded as leading corporate philanthropists. In 1987, this corporate giving tradition even helped them fight off a hostile takeover.

David Day Dayton and Caroline Wesley Draper Dayton bore George Draper Dayton in Clifton Springs, New York, on March 6, 1857. While growing up, George Dayton considered a career in the ministry—due to his parents' strong religious beliefs—but began a career in business instead. He married Emma Willard Chadwick in 1878 and they had four children: David Draper, Caroline Ward, George Nelson, and Josephine. At the age of twenty-four, Dayton traveled to Minnesota to investigate some central New York businessmen's investments and ultimately moved to that state. In 1902, he became a silent partner in a retail enterprise in Minneapolis that he and son Draper Dayton soon ran as Dayton's and transformed into a large department store. Son George Nelson Dayton joined the enterprise in 1911, and the Dayton Company continued to reap sizeable profits. When George Nelson Dayton retired in the 1940s, his five sons (Donald Chadwick, Bruce Bliss, Wallace Corliss, Kenneth Nelson, and Douglas James) took over the company. In the next few decades, Dayton's expanded dramatically: starting the first Target store in 1962, going public in 1967, merging with retailer Hudson's in 1969, and buying Mervyn's California in 1978.

All through this growth, the company maintained a strong corporate giving program. In 1946, the Dayton brothers instituted the policy of giving 5 percent of the corporation's pretax profits to charities. The decision to give a certain percentage of their profits honored and mirrored their family's philanthropic tradition. Grandfather George Draper Dayton tithed at a young age, gave away 40 percent of his income by midlife, and became a strong tithing advocate later in life. As the second corporation to have such a generous giving program, Dayton's implemented this policy while the legality and appropriateness of corporate philanthropy remained highly questionable. Even after the *Smith v. Barlow* case of 1953, corporations slowly, if ever, chose to develop a substantial giving program. The Commission on Private Philanthropy and Public Needs (1974) found that corporations with a giving program gave 0.85 percent of their pretax profits on average.

Bucking this trend, the Daytons believed their giving represented a long-term investment in their profitability (making their communities stronger), a social responsibility, and a way to separate themselves from other companies. Even when the company went public, the Daytons made it clear that their 5 percent program would continue. Starting in the 1960s, the Dayton-Hudson Foundation particularly focused on social action and the arts and encouraged many Minnesota corporations to make a similar giving commitment by creating 2 percent and 5 percent giving clubs. In 1987, the Dart Group attempted a hostile takeover of Dayton-Hudson, but the company's philanthropic commitment paid valuable dividends: numerous charities and citizens immediately lobbied against the takeover, and the state's governor called a special session. A week after Dayton-Hudson announced the possibility of a takeover, the Minnesota legislature responded by passing antitakeover legislation. Although the Dart Group made a second takeover attempt, the 1987 stock market crash foiled that effort.

The Dayton brothers' commitment to philanthropy did not stop with the family business. Each brother also gave substantial amounts individually. In particular, Bruce Dayton became recognized as the major art patron of Minneapolis, and Kenneth Dayton wrote about his philosophy of giving (*The Stages of Giving*) and urged other wealthy Americans—following in his grandfather's footsteps—to be more generous with and thoughtful about their philanthropy.

Robert T. Grimm Jr.

Further reading

Dayton, Kenneth N. 1999. *The Stages of Giving.* Washington, DC: INDEPENDENT SECTOR.

Grimm, Robert T., Jr. 2002. "Dayton Family." In *Notable American Philanthropists: Biographies of Giving and Volunteering,* edited by Robert T. Grimm, Jr., 72–80. Westport, CT: Oryx Press.

Mathews, John B., Kenneth E. Goodpaster, and Laura L. Nash. 1991. "Dayton Hudson Corporation: Conscience and Control." In *Policies and Persons: A Casebook in Business Ethics,* 256–284. New York: McGraw-Hill.

Direct Mail Fundraising

Excellent fundraising is the result of a blending of strategies that advance the case for support of an organization. Direct mail fundraising is one of those strategies. It is the systematic process of mailing a gift request to individuals who are likely to make a contribution to a given organization. The method often produces consistent revenue and can be an effective communication tool for the constituents of any organization.

The earliest printed fundraising appeals can be traced to efforts on behalf of Harvard College in the 1640s (Cutlip 1965, 4). As the philanthropic sector and its traditions grew in the United States over the next 350 years, so, too, did the use of direct mail fundraising.

Creating a direct mail program requires an understanding of expectations. The early phases of a mail program, typically referred to as "acquisition," require multiple mailings, and it may be a number of years before the program becomes profitable. Response rates will be low and gifts may be smaller than anticipated. In contrast, mature direct mail programs achieve higher response rates to mailings and higher average gifts and may become effective enough to cost as little as eight or ten cents to raise one dollar.

An effective direct mail program starts with determining who will be receiving the fundraising letter and developing letter copy and package design that will appeal to that audience. For example, lapsed donors might be reminded when they last gave and at what level and informed of how their last gift made a difference. Non-donors should be informed about the organization's mission and how their gift can have an impact. Direct mail audiences include the following: nondonors, donors, lapsed donors, alumni, friends, parents, members, clients, and prospects. Each different audience can then be broken down into "segments," a term that refers to a smaller group within an audience—for example, alumni who graduated between 1950 and 1955. Audience segmentation improves the response to direct mail appeals since the message can be tailored more specifically for a focused group of people.

Many organizations have a database comprised of the many audience types solicited using direct mail. For many other organizations, building a database requires renting or purchasing a list of prospects. Many fundraising publications, such as the *Chronicle of Philanthropy* and the *Nonprofit Times,* have helpful resources.

Illustrator's rendering of direct mail transforming into money (Images.com/Corbis)

Direct mail pieces should be designed to appeal to specific audience segments. The artwork chosen for envelopes, stationery, and reply devices often influences response rates. Recipients take only a few moments to decide whether to open a direct mail piece. The whole process, from first seeing a solicitation to opening it and scanning its contents, takes only five to eight seconds (Warwick 1994, 47).

Many direct mail packages are comprised of the carrier (outer) envelope, the letter, a reply device (envelope), and some type of insert, such as a brochure. Inserting these parts into the carrier envelope may be time consuming, and an organization must determine whether to use volunteers, staff, or a professional mailing house to complete the assembly. Each of these options has costs associated with it and will ultimately increase or decrease the overall expenses.

Direct mail letter copy should make an effective case for support by focusing on the needs served by an organization. It should also create a sense of urgency. The text should be conversational in tone, reflecting what might be said in a personal visit. Each paragraph should express only one thought, typically in five lines or less. Readers are more likely to read pieces that have sufficient white space; thus, it is important to indent paragraphs, leave a line of space between paragraphs, and format the document with appropriate margins. In repeated focus groups, it has been observed that the P.S. is the most often read part of a fundraising letter. Including a P.S. can strengthen the overall letter and help boost response rates. Finally, those receiving a direct mail appeal expect a request for a specific amount of money. Recipients must understand what the expectation of the gift request is as they consider whether or not to respond. There has been much debate about the proper length of a fundraising letter. After years of testing direct mail packages, researchers have concluded that the length of a letter should be dictated by the space needed to make an effective case for support.

In addition to the letter itself, a direct mail package often includes inserts that enhance the case for support, such as a small lift letter on distinct stationery that demonstrates how someone was impacted by a particular program or a thank-you note from a grateful recipient. Organizations may also choose to include premiums such as mailing labels or pocket calendars that the recipient may keep even if a gift is not sent in reply. These free items may remind the recipient many times of the organization and its cause, increasing his or her chances of responding at a future time.

The postage to be used in mailing appeals varies and may be researched at any post office branch or on the Internet at http://www.usps.com. The most expensive postal rate is first class. The least expensive is third class bulk rate, which is usually about a third of the first class rate. Each postal rate has requirements that determine whether an organization is eligible for specific discounts.

It is important to be able to evaluate the effectiveness of a direct mail letter. This not only provides a measuring tool as a mailing program grows but also helps organizations improve their direct mail campaigns as they learn from experience. There are various formulas commonly used in evaluating mailings. The response rate, for example, is equal to the number of gifts made divided by the number of pieces mailed. The average gift can be determined by dividing the total income by the number of gifts made. The total expenses divided by the income equals the cost per dollar raised. Finally, the net income is derived by subtracting the total expenses from the income. Successful and mature direct mail programs have a low cost to raise a dollar, produce high net income, and achieve high rates of response.

Direct mail fundraising—like any fundraising effort—requires much forethought and planning. A well-run direct mail program is successful because there is a systematic way to move a solicitation from a concept to the mailbox. If the letter copy and package contents reflect a convincing case for support, create a sense of urgency, and are tailored to the desires and interests of an organization's audience in a precise manner, the direct mail appeal letter may reap great benefits.

David L. Sternberg

References and further reading

The Chronicle of Philanthropy, http://philanthropy.com (cited September 10, 2002).

Cutlip, Scott. 1965. *Fund Raising in the United States: Its Role in America's Philanthropy.* New Brunswick, NJ: Rutgers University Press.

Dove, Kent. 2001. *Conducting a Successful Annual Giving Program.* San Francisco: Jossey-Bass.

Huntsinger, Jerry. 1989. *Fund Raising Letters: A Comprehensive Study Guide to Raising More Money by Direct Response Marketing.* Richmond, VA: Emerson.

Johnston, Michael. 2000. *Direct Response Fundraising.* San Francisco: Jossey-Bass.

Lister, Gwyneth. 2001. *Building Your Direct Mail Program.* San Francisco: Jossey-Bass.

Nonprofit Times, http://www.nptimes.com (cited August 15, 2002).

U.S. Postal Service, http://www.usps.com (cited August 15, 2002).

Warwick, Mal. 1994. *How to Write Successful Fundraising Letters.* Berkeley, CA: Strathmoor Press.

Dix, Dorothea Lynde (1802–1887)

By dedicating four decades of her life to the cause of the mentally ill, Dorothea Dix became one of the most famous and admired women of nineteenth-century America. Born in Hampden, Maine, on April 4, 1802, Dix had an unhappy childhood until, as a teenager, she went to live with her well-to-do grandmother in Boston. There, she joined the Unitarian Church and achieved success both as a schoolteacher and as an author of religious and instructional works. In 1836–1837, she visited England and became acquainted with British reform activities, including parliamentary inquiries into the care of the insane.

In 1842, Dix decided to investigate the plight of the indigent mentally ill in Massachusetts. After an exhaustive tour of local facilities throughout the state, she submitted to the legislature a memorial containing shocking descriptions of insane men and women enduring cold, filth, and abuse as inmates of jails and poorhouses. The legislature responded by appropriating funds to enlarge the state asylum at Worcester. Elated at that modest result, Dix took her crusade far afield. In state after state, she compiled evidence, wrote memorials, and lobbied legislatures either to create a new mental hospital or to enlarge an existing one. By 1848, she had traveled more than 60,000 miles and had carried her campaign to most parts of the United States and also to Canada.

Dix now turned her attention to the federal government, lobbying Congress to transfer 10 million acres of public lands to the states in order to provide them with a perpetual source of support for their asylums. Her bill passed both houses of Congress in 1854 but was vetoed by President Franklin Pierce. Dix then went to Europe, visited hospitals from France to Turkey, and won improved facilities for the insane in Scotland, Jersey, and the Vatican. During the Civil War, she volunteered her unpaid services as superintendent of women nurses. After the war, she resumed her work in the states until old age and ill health at last ended her travels. On a visit to the New Jersey State Lunatic Asylum in 1881, she became too weak to move on. The asylum set aside a small suite of rooms for her use, and she resided there until her death on July 17, 1887.

Dorothea Dix did not single-handedly deliver America's mentally ill from their suffering and chains. Almost everywhere she went, she did not begin a new movement but instead came to the aid of local reformers already working for the cause. Some dozen public hospitals for the insane already existed in the United States before she began her crusade. Moreover, even in her own lifetime, many hospitals became hopelessly overcrowded and failed to deliver the prompt cures that she had expected. Yet her impact was enormous. Local activists constantly pleaded for her to come and often declared that only her personal intervention had secured the passage of bills or the donation of funds. For thousands of mentally ill men and women, hospital care was better than any alternative existing at the time, and no one did more than Dorothea Dix to make it available to those in need.

David L. Lightner

References and further reading

Brown, Thomas J. 1998. *Dorothea Dix: New England Reformer.* Cambridge: Harvard University Press.

Gollaher, David. 1995. *Voice for the Mad: The Life of Dorothea Dix.* New York: Free Press.

Lightner, David L. 1999. *Asylum, Prison, and Poorhouse: The Writings and Reform Work of Dorothea Dix in Illinois.* Carbondale: Southern Illinois University Press.

Tiffany, Francis. 1890. *Life of Dorothea Lynde Dix.* Boston: Houghton, Mifflin.

Donor Intent

When a person donates property to a charitable organization ("charity" or "donee"), she invariably hopes and expects the recipient to use it in certain ways: to pursue some purposes but not others, to benefit some classes of persons but not others, and to employ some means but not others. In ordinary usage, "donor intent" denotes the donor's subjective preferences regarding the charity's use of her gift as these preferences were actually formulated in her mind. In law, "donor intent" refers to the restrictions, if any, that the donor expressed an intention to impose upon the charity's use of her gift at the time she donated the property. By accepting a gift with restrictions attached, a charity thereby creates a "trust" or a trustlike arrangement. (A charitable trust is a type of trust, an arrangement for managing property in which one party [the trustee] holds property at the request of another [the settlor] for the benefit of a third party [the beneficiary]. In a charitable trust, the property must be used to advance a legally charitable purpose [e.g., relief of poverty, education, religion] and to benefit the entire community or a significant portion thereof. The terms "trust" and "restricted

gift" are used interchangeably.) In using a restricted gift, a charity's primary legal duty is to ascertain and execute the donor's charitable intentions as expressed in the gift's terms. For a variety of reasons, the donor's subjective wishes may diverge, sometimes significantly, from the "intent" imputed to her for legal purposes and from the ways that the law permits her gift to be used. This is demonstrated most vividly when the charity cannot comply with the gift's terms as originally formulated. At that point, courts claim to use the gift's balance based on what the donor actually wanted or would likely have wanted to happen under the circumstances.

Charities and courts lack direct access to a donor's actual, subjective will. Instead, they must look to external expressions of such intent. The donor's first obstacle is thus language in general and legal language in particular: she must express her wishes in ways that the donee is legally obliged to heed and that provide it with meaningful guidance. The former task may be accomplished by using written or spoken words to dictate mandatory terms for the gift's use, as opposed to mere requests or recommendations. Alternatively, an individual can give in response to a fundraising appeal; the gift's terms will then consist of the charity's representations as to how contributions will be used.

A donor can "speak her mind" with varying degrees of specificity. A gift "to create a summer camp for Israeli and Palestinian teenagers" will steer and constrain the donee more than a gift "to promote the peaceful resolution of the Israeli-Palestinian conflict." Even with very detailed instructions, however, questions will inevitably arise as to how to follow a gift's terms that the terms do not definitively answer—even if the background conditions remain constant and the donor's assumptions valid. Because she is not omniscient, moreover, the donor cannot foresee every contingency that might impair the charity's ability to realize her intentions. Because the donor has better things to do, she does not try. For all these reasons, the donor must delegate to others the task of filling in gaps in her expressed intent, and responding to unanticipated obstacles to their realization.

To whom are such decisions delegated, and by what standards are they decided? As a matter of black letter law, a charity's managers have authority only to *interpret* a gift's terms in the ordinary course of events. Courts, by contrast, have authority to *change* terms themselves in some cases. The legal standard for effecting such change depends on how the court categorizes the contested term: does it specify a means by which the gift's ends must be pursued (also known as an "administrative term") or does it identify the ends themselves (also known as "purposes")? All these distinctions can of course be manipulated at the margins: common law courts, for example, have been making law through "interpretation" for centuries, and one donor's means can be another donor's end-in-itself. Even so, these distinctions work in a large number of cases.

Consider a donor who contributes 100 shares of Corporation X's stock to Charity A with two restrictions: (1) Never sell this stock; and (2) Use the dividends to build a sanatorium for treating tuberculosis patients. Here, the charity's managers have discretion to select where to build the sanatorium, its design, the number of beds, and so forth. If accounting and self-dealing scandals at Corporation X cause the value of the stock to plunge, however, the charity's managers may petition a court for permission to sell the stock, notwithstanding the first term. If the court determines that this restriction is merely an administrative term, it will approve the petition where (1) complying with the restriction (i.e., holding on to this stock) will undermine the charity's ability to achieve the gift's purpose (i.e., to build the sanatorium); and (2) this unhappy prospect is due to circumstances that the donor neither knew nor anticipated (Rest 2d Trusts § 381). This is known as the doctrine of deviation. In this way, the court mimics what it believes the donor would have done in this situation had she anticipated it.

Implementing a donor's intent is much harder where a gift's primary purpose has failed, has already been accomplished, or has otherwise been overtaken or undermined by events. In our hypothetical situation, for example, tuberculosis has been largely eradicated in the United States, and sanatoriums are no longer used to treat the few patients so afflicted. What happens then to the unused portion of the gift? Under the traditional default rule (which applies whenever the donor does not provide explicit instructions for

this contingency), the balance reverts to the donor or those claiming under her (*Holmes v. Welch* 1943, 463–464). When a donor restricts her gift's use to a single charitable purpose, the law has traditionally presumed that she intended to aid that charitable purpose and none other, unless she affirmatively "manifested a more general intention to devote the property to charitable purposes" (Rest 2d Trust § 399). If it becomes "impossible," "impracticable," or illegal to carry out that single purpose or if that purpose has already been accomplished, then the gift is withdrawn from charitable channels and reverts to the donor et al. (Rest 2d Trusts §§ 399, 400). Courts are more willing to jettison an administrative term that thwarts a gift's charitable purpose than to replace the donor's thwarted charitable purpose with one of the court's choosing.

This presumption—that a charitable gift whose purpose has failed or been fulfilled reverts to the donor—may be overcome if the donor manifested a "general charitable intent." (ibid.) This means that if the donor had been presented with the current situation and two options—(1) let the court apply the gift's balance to another charitable purpose; or (2) let the balance revert to the donor et al.—she would have preferred the former. In that case, the court will reapply the balance to a related charitable purpose that falls within the general scope of the donor's intent. This is known as the doctrine of "cy pres," which is Norman French for "as near as." When courts apply this doctrine, the correlation between a particular donor's actual intentions and those that the law imputes to her can become especially attenuated.

Cy pres entails three inquiries: (1) Has it become impossible, impracticable, or illegal to carry out the gift's purpose, and/or has that purpose already been accomplished? (2) If yes, did the donor have a "general charitable intention"? (3) If yes, what new purpose should be substituted for the original one? The first inquiry asks how low or high to set the threshold for setting aside the gift's original purpose and hence the donor's expressed intent. Some commentators have criticized the current prerequisites (impossibility, impracticality, illegality) as too deferential to donor intent at society's expense: cy pres should be available, they argue, "to the extent it is or becomes wasteful to apply all of the [gifted] property to the designated purpose" (Rest 3d Trusts § 67). If adopted, this principle would give courts more latitude to modify a donor's wishes to advance efficiency goals. At least one court, however, has considered and roundly rejected this idea. The case involved the Buck Trust, which was created to benefit the poor and to advance other charitable purposes in Marin County, California (also known as the "hot tub capital of the poor"), and which was producing relatively large sums per capita for a population that was generally very well-off. The trust's administrator, the San Francisco Foundation, petitioned the California Superior Court of Marin County for permission to use some trust income to benefit the other four Bay Area counties it served. The court rejected the request, holding that "ineffective philanthropy, inefficiency and relative inefficiency, that is, inefficiency of trust expenditures in one location given greater relative needs or benefits elsewhere, do not constitute impracticability" or impossibility within the meaning of cy pres (In the Matter the Estate of Beryl H. Buck, 1987).

The second inquiry—"Did the donor have a general charitable intent?"—is somewhat peculiar. It asks what the donor would have thought about something she did not actually think about, or at least did not express an opinion about, that is, how to dispose of the gift balance if it were to become impossible, impracticable, or illegal to execute its purpose, or if the purpose were already accomplished. For example, was this donor's sole charitable aim to help persons with tuberculosis, such that her next best use of the gift would have been retaining it for herself or those claiming under her? Or did she care more generally about, say, people suffering from respiratory and thoracic diseases, so much so that she would have preferred any balance to benefit members of that class rather than her or her estate? In most cases, the court lacks enough information about any given donor to make an intelligent or insightful prediction as to how that individual would answer the question (Laird 1988 at 979). In the absence of such information, courts must use a default rule.

There are at least two approaches to formulating a default rule for this situation: (1) One could try to predict and then mimic what the average or reasonable donor would want to happen in this situation; or (2) One could try to produce a socially or normatively desirable outcome. It is unclear which approach underlies the traditional rule, wherein the donor is presumed to have wanted the gift to revert to her unless she affirmatively expressed a general charitable intent. Perhaps it reflects the normative view that family members should be the natural objects of one's bounty and that departure from that norm should be narrowly construed. The modern trend reverses the presumption: the donor is deemed to have a general charitable intention unless she expressly dictates another disposition for the balance (Rest 3d Trusts § 67 and comment b). This approach is grounded firmly in policy: where the evidence regarding the donor's intent is equivocal, speculative, or nonexistent, charity law favors an interpretation that keeps the gift's assets flowing in charitable channels, where they will presumably generate more public benefit than if returned to the donor or her estate. Any invocations of donor intent are rhetorical, anecdotal, or wishful thinking. Of course, survey research might reveal that most contemporary donors do in fact give with what the law calls a "general charitable intent." That would provide an even more solid grounding for the modern trend.

Once the first two conditions for cy pres have been established (i.e., the original gift's purpose has failed or been fulfilled, and the donor had general charitable intent), what principles guide the court's selection of a substitute purpose? The doctrine's name is suggestive: "cy pres" is shorthand for *cy pres comme possible*—Norman French for "as near as possible." In practice, however, many modern courts do not feel obliged to substitute a purpose as near as possible to the donor's original one (Rest 2d Trusts § 399 comment b; Rest 3d Trusts § 67 comment d). The proper analogy is not a bull's eye, with the donor's purpose at the center and the substitute purpose the shortest possible distance away. Rather, the donor's purpose is (or was) simply one means to a larger charitable end or one species in a genus of charitable purposes. In selecting a substitute purpose, a court may prefer to look for the most effective means to the same larger end (Rest 2d Trusts § 399 comment b) or for the species within the same genus that generates the greatest public benefit (Rest

3d Trusts § 67 comment d). Here too the selection criteria are grounded on social policy. Even so, one might hope or suppose "that among similar purposes charitably inclined [donors] would tend to prefer those most beneficial to their communities" (ibid.) Yet these speculations about the hypothetical, charitably inclined donor are a far cry from what we ordinarily mean by "donor intent."

Although this article has discussed cy pres at some length, these situations are really the exception, not the rule. Most of the time, charities do not find it impossible or impracticable to comply with the terms of a donor's gift. The issue is generally not whether they *can* do so, but whether they *will*. How can the legal system make charities honor donor-imposed restrictions, and to what extent does it do so? Federal tax law is generally unhelpful in this regard. Section 501(c)(3) of the Internal Revenue Code requires nonprofit organizations seeking tax exemption to pursue some charitable purpose or purposes and not to bestow excessive benefits on private parties. When a charity uses a restricted gift for a charitable purpose *other* than the one designated by the donor, the charity is still using the gift for a charitable purpose and without benefiting a private party. State law provides some mechanisms for enforcing the terms of restricted gifts, but many regard these as inadequate. Donors generally cannot sue to enforce these terms unless they expressly reserved the right to do so (*Carl J. Herzog Foundation, Inc. v. University of Bridgeport* 1997). Nor can other private parties bring suit, generally speaking, absent either a specific statutory grant (Fishman and Schwarz 2000, 273, 277) or an ad hoc judicial determination that they have a "special interest" in the matter (Blasko, Crossley, and Lloyd 1993). Apart from a charity's own trustees or directors, usually only the state attorney general can sue to enforce the terms of a gift. Yet these officials have more responsibilities than resources and deem many responsibilities more weighty and urgent than enforcing the terms of charitable gifts. This situation results in chronic under-enforcement of such terms, punctuated by occasional involvement in the most high profile and/or egregious cases.

Fortunately for donors, the legal system is not the only inducement for charities to honor donor-imposed restrictions on gifts. One instrument is the ability of disgruntled donors to generate bad publicity for a charity, thereby harming its ability to compete in the market for charitable dollars (Fishman and Schwarz 2000, 271). This works best with charities that rely on an ongoing stream of contributions and whose managers' performance is measured in terms of their fundraising ability. This approach clearly does not affect fully endowed private foundations—because they do not seek additional contributions, there are no potential donors to punish them for disobeying the wishes of past donors. This helps explain why some commentators (mostly conservatives) allege that the clearest violations of donor intent have occurred in such entities—at least in the sense of disappointing their founders' hopes and expectations for their activities (Wooster 1994; Halcombe 2000, 135–152).

Another force that leads charities to comply with gift terms is their managers' desire to cultivate and maintain personal reputations for honesty and scrupulousness (Macey 1988, 320). Such managers will likely take some care to avoid misusing donor funds out of fear of losing "reputational capital" among the relevant group, be it fellow philanthropic professionals or other pillars of the local community (ibid.). Managers who (also) view their stewardship of restricted gifts as a serious moral responsibility will behave the same way, but for a different (though mutually reinforcing) reason.

Robert A. Katz

References and further reading
Blasko, Mary Grace, Curt S. Crossley, and David Lloyd. 1993. "Standing to Sue in the Charitable Sector." 28 U.S.F.L. Rev. 37.

Bork, Robert H., and Waldemar Nielsen. 1993. *Donor Intent.* Indianapolis: Philanthropy Roundtable.

Carl J. Herzog Foundation, Inc. v. University of Bridgeport, 699 A.2d 995 (Conn. 1997).

Fishman, James J., and Steven Schwarz. 2000. *Nonprofit Organizations: Cases and Materials.* New York: Foundation Press.

Holcombe, Randall G. 2000. *Writing Off Ideas: Taxation, Foundations, and Philanthropy in America.* New Brunswick, NJ: Transaction.

Holmes v. Welch, 49 N.E.2d 461 (Mass. 1943).

In the Matter of the Estate of Beryl H. Buck, No. 23259 (Cal. Super. Ct., Marin County August 15, 1986), reprinted in 21 U.S.F.L. Rev. 691 (1987).

Laird, Vanessa. 1988. "Phantom Selves: The Search for a General Charitable Intent in the Application of the Cy Pres Doctrine." 40 Stan. L. Rev. 973.

Macey, Jonathan R. 1988. "Private Trusts for the Provision of Private Goods." 37 Emory L.J. 295.

Restatement (Second) of Trusts (1959).

Restatement (Third) of Trusts (Tentative Draft No. 3, March 5, 2001).

Smith, David H. 1995. *Entrusted: The Moral Responsibilities of Trusteeship.* Bloomington: Indiana University Press.

Turner, Richard C., ed. 1995. *Taking Trusteeship Seriously: Essays on the History, Dynamics, and Practice of Trusteeship.* Indianapolis: Indiana University Center on Philanthropy.

Wooster, Martin Morse. 1994. *The Great Philanthropists and the Problem of "Donor Intent."* Washington, DC: Capital Research Center.

Donor-Advised Funds

A donor-advised fund is a legal instrument through which an individual establishes a fund for the purpose of making tax-deductible contributions to organizations recognized by the Internal Revenue Service (IRS) as qualified charities under Internal Revenue Code (IRC) 501(c). Such funds are usually established through community foundations or through commercial financial institutions such as banks and brokerage firms. Donors choose them because they allow the donor to suggest or advise the fund's administrator about his or her preference of qualified recipients, may provide a significant tax advantage, and offer a vehicle of sustained giving that may lead to a permanent endowment.

There are several factors of which the donor should be aware. First, money that is donated to the fund is irrevocable. Second, the fund administrators are not obligated to accept the recommendations of the donor. It is customary for administrators to attempt to accommodate donors' wishes, however. Third, community foundations do not have a standardized method of managing donor-advised funds. Areas in which the administration of funds might differ are the time periods for processing grant applications, the minimum balance required to maintain the fund, rules that stipulate whether an annual allocation of assets is mandatory, and administration practices regarding accepting advice from the donor.

The process of establishing a donor-advised fund is designed to be accessible to a wide range of donors. Community foundations may require an initial donation of as little as $200, whereas many major brokerage firms require a minimum of $10,000. It is customary for the organization administering the fund to charge an annual administration fee.

Donors receive many benefits from the arrangement with an administrative agency. In addition to the possibility of remaining active in the grantmaking process, donors are allowed to name the fund and determine whether the fund will be temporary or permanent (endowed). In some cases, the donor decides that a fund should be spent during his or her lifetime. But it is possible to make the fund an endowment. In this case, the donor names another person to continue advising the administrator after his or her death. Donors often use this option to involve family members in a philanthropic tradition. By establishing the fund through an organization already involved in philanthropy, the donor gains the expertise of professionals and reduces the investment of time in administrative duties.

Donor-advised funds may be funded by a one-time contribution of cash or by periodic contributions of stocks, bonds, mutual funds, and other marketable financial assets. Under current tax laws, donors can receive a significant benefit from contributing appreciated stock. The donor benefits by avoiding the capital gains tax, and the fund does not pay taxes on the fund's earnings. The consequence of these savings is reflected in the amount the fund can provide to charities.

Donor-advised funds have been in existence since the 1930s and have grown rapidly in recent years. Individuals should consult a tax adviser or an attorney before entering into an agreement to establish a donor-advised fund in order to determine changes in tax laws and to assess how the fund might affect their individual financial situation.

Grady Jones

References and further reading

Columbus Foundation. 2002. "A Flexible and Growing Service to Donors: Donor-Advised Fund in Community Foundations," brochure. Columbus, OH: Luck, J., & Feurt, S.

Community Foundation. 2002. "About Donor-Advised Funds," http://www.givingcapital.com/ (cited September 2, 2002).

———. 2002. "What Are Donor Advised Funds?" http://www.communityfund.org/advisedf.htm (cited September 6, 2002).

National Philanthropic Trust. 2002. "What Is a Donor Advised Fund?" http://www.nptrust.org/03_about_DAFs/3_00_about_daf.htm (cited September 2, 2002).

Rotary International. 2002. "Donor Advised Funds," http://www.rotary.org/foundation/development/advisedfunds (cited September 2, 2002).

Tides Foundation. 2002. "Become a Tides Donor Advisor," http://www.tidesfoundation.org/donor_advised_funds.cfm. (cited September 6, 2002).

Drexel, St. Katharine (1858–1955)

In 1858, Katharine Drexel was born into a prominent Philadelphia family. Her father, Francis Anthony Drexel, was a banker and business partner of J. P. Morgan. The Drexels were a devout and pious Catholic family and conscious of their philanthropic obligations. The Drexel children watched and learned as their elders prayed, received the sacraments of the church, and gave generously to churches, hospitals, schools, missions, and asylums. Katharine developed a particular concern for the welfare of Native and African American children. She is now considered the patron saint of Catholic schools and missions to Native Americans and African Americans.

Francis Drexel died in 1858, leaving for his three daughters a trust worth $15 million (about $250 million in today's dollars). Katharine shocked her friends by indicating a desire to leave her life of privilege to live as a nun. In 1891, she founded the Sisters of the Blessed Sacrament for Indians and Colored People (SBS).

One of the the order's first missions, St. Catherine's Boarding School for Pueblo Indians in Santa Fe, New Mexico, was founded in 1894. The following year, St. Emma Military Academy, a vocational school for African American boys, was opened at Rock Castle, Virginia, and the nearby St. Francis de Sales school for girls opened in 1899. By 1903, additional schools had opened in Arizona and Tennessee. Xavier, a coeducational secondary school for black children, was founded in New Orleans, Louisiana, in 1915. It became Xavier University of Louisiana in

The Reverend Mother Mary Katharine Drexel (1858–1955) (Bettmann/Corbis)

1925, with an initial enrollment of forty-seven students. By 1936, the enrollment had jumped to 829. It remains the country's only predominantly Catholic black university.

In these early years, SBS schools stressed both religious formation and practical skills. Boys were taught agricultural skills such as farming, equipment maintenance, cannery management, and accounting as well as blacksmithing, iron working, printing, carpentry, and masonry. Girls were taught such skills as homemaking, needlecraft, sewing, and nursing.

By the time of Katharine's death in 1955, SBS had established some sixty schools in the West, Midwest, and South and had provided generous support to missions in Alaska, Canada, and Africa. Vowed to poverty and simplicity in her own life, this "millionaire nun," as she was sometimes called, distributed some $20 million to feed, clothe, educate, and save the souls of Native American and African American children.

One can hardly overstate the impact of Katharine Drexel's work. At a time when most white Americans were indifferent, or even hostile, toward minorities, Katharine, the SBS, and the Catholic Church were determined to tear down the barriers of racism and civil inequality that were so much a part of American society during the first half of the twentieth century. Some communities were so hostile to the education of minorities that the order was forced to resort to third parties, also known as "straw buyers," to purchase land and materials for the schools. Yet, in spite of such opposition, tens of thousands of black and Native American children were given the tools with which to lift themselves out of poverty and become contributing members of their communities.

In 1939, Katharine was awarded an honorary doctorate by Catholic University. By then it was obvious to all that her health was failing. Having suffered a heart attack in 1935, she was forced to give up the day-to-day running of the SBS but remained its inspiration and soul. She continued to receive many visitors, including bishops of dioceses in which the order had founded schools, papal representatives, friends, and family. Katharine Drexel died on March 3, 1955. She was beatified on November 20, 1988, and canonized on October 1, 2000.

Joseph C. Harmon

References and further reading

Baldwin, Lou. 2002. "Giving It All: Mother Katharine Drexel's Habit of Charity." *Philanthropy* 13 (March–April): 13–15.

Burton, Katharine. 1957. *The Golden Door: The Life of Katharine Drexel.* New York: P. J. Kenedy and Sons.

Duffy, Consuela Maria. 1966. *Katharine Drexel: A Biography.* Philadelphia: Reilly.

Sisters of the Blessed Sacrament, http://www.katharinedrexel.org/.

Tarry, Ellen. 1990. *Katharine Drexel: Friend of the Oppressed.* Nashville, TN: Winston-Derek.

E

Eastman, George (1854–1932)

Through the lens of a camera, George Eastman became one of the largest, most enigmatic philanthropists in the United States during the first quarter of the twentieth century. Eastman's importance in the history of philanthropy lies in his decision to give away his amassed fortune during his own lifetime. As the founder of the Eastman Kodak Company, Eastman became one of the wealthiest individuals of the Industrial Revolution. He donated approximately $125 million to institutions of higher education, medical and dental health, the arts, and the city of Rochester, New York.

Born on July 12, 1854, in Waterville, New York, George Eastman was the youngest child and only son of George Washington and Maria Kilbourn Eastman. He learned the meaning of philanthropy at an early age through the influence of his abolitionist parents, who were active in the Underground Railroad, and the entrepreneurial spirit of his father, who started a small business college in Rochester, New York. In 1862, two years after moving the family to Rochester, his father died, leaving the family with little money. George Eastman the younger worked diligently throughout his adolescence and eventually made enough money to relieve his mother of the financial responsibilities for their home.

From an inherent sense of adventure and curiosity, Eastman became intrigued with photography, quickly acquired the necessary equipment, and began to enjoy his new hobby. The 50 pounds of photographic equipment required to take pictures soon inspired him to develop a simpler method for capturing pictures. Eastman's inventions and his company's products made photography affordable for millions. Compared to his philanthropy and personal life, Eastman's business accomplishments are well known.

Aside from the city of Rochester, the Massachusetts Institute of Technology (MIT) was the largest recipient of Eastman's wealth. Because Eastman wanted to support the school where many of his chemists received their training, he provided MIT with an initial gift of $2.5 million to build a new chemistry building. The gift was given on the condition that the donor would remain anonymous. Ultimately, the mysterious "Mr. Smith," as the MIT president called him, gave $11 million in total to the school. The three other educational institutions benefiting from his generosity were Tuskegee Institute, Hampton Institute, and the University of Rochester, where his donations made possible the School of Music.

Eastman never married or had any children. Throughout his very private life, his time was primarily divided between his business, his musical interests, and his philanthropic projects; he approached each project with intense scrutiny. By the early 1930s, Eastman's physical health had declined. Not wanting to

Inventor and industrialist George Eastman (1854–1932) (Corbis)

live in such a debilitating state, Eastman took his life at age seventy-eight in 1932. His estate was valued at $25 million and was designated for immediate distribution to charities that he had supported in the past.

Ashley M. Magdovitz

References and further reading
Ackerman, Carl W. 1930. *George Eastman.* Boston and New York: Houghton Mifflin.
American Council of Learned Societies. 2002 [1944–1958]. "George Eastman." In *Dictionary of American Biography, Supplements 1–2: To 1940.* Farmington Hills, MI: Gale Group.
Brayer, Elizabeth. 1996. *George Eastman: A Biography.* Baltimore: Johns Hopkins University Press.
Collins, Douglas. 1990. *The Story of Kodak.* New York: Harry N. Abrams.
DeVinney, James A. 2000. *The Wizard of Photography.* WGBH Educational Foundation, Green Light Productions. Distributed by PBS Home Video.
Public Broadcasting Service. "People and Events: George Eastman," http://www.pbs.org/wgbh/amex/eastman/peopleevents/pande02.html (cited November 6, 2002).

Traub, Carol G. 1997. *Profiles: Philanthropists and Their Legacies.* Minneapolis: Oliver Press.

Economic Theories of Nonprofits

Most philanthropy flows through private nonprofit organizations, defined as organizations that can make profits but cannot distribute them to the board of directors or others in control of the organization. As such, they stand between the philanthropist and the ultimate beneficiaries of his or her largesse. Why are organizations necessary to mediate these transactions? And why is the nonprofit form selected for these organizations? These questions lie at the core of economic theories of nonprofits, which elaborate on the supply and demand of alternative institutional forms, the effects of institutional form on organizational behavior, and the effects of government policies on institutional choice and behavior.

Why Organizations Are Needed

Organizations are formed to economize on "transactions costs"—the costs of arranging production and distribution. Consider the transaction costs faced by a lone philanthropist seeking to help a group of people. First, the philanthropist must identify potential beneficiaries and determine their worthiness. Second, the philanthropist must develop a plan to help these beneficiaries. Can beneficiaries be trusted to use cash gifts effectively, or should they be provided with specific services and counseling? What is the most efficient and effective way to provide those services? Third, the philanthropist must coordinate his or her plans with others who care about the same beneficiaries. Will gifts by one philanthropist add to the pot, or will they simply lead other philanthropists to make corresponding reductions in their gifts? Will some potential beneficiaries receive more help than they need while others go unserved?

Organizations economize on these transaction costs. One organization serves many philanthropists, eliminating duplication of effort by collectively identifying the beneficiaries, providing them with effective and efficient services, and coordinating the allocation of total donations across beneficiaries. Instead of each donor developing expertise in each of these subjects, donors need only learn about the quality of the mediating organization. If that quality is found lacking, the philanthropist can seek to improve it, search for a better one, found a new organization, or resign themselves to individual action. Transaction costs govern this choice as well. In order to found a new organization, the philanthropist must identify and assemble a collection of other philanthropists who care about the same beneficiaries, determine whether their collective desire to help is sufficient to cover the costs of helping, and establish a governance mechanism that ensures that the stakeholders will trust the organization with their donations.

Consequences of Nondistribution

What defines an organization as nonprofit, and why do philanthropists employ them? Nonprofit organizations can and do retain financial surpluses as reserve funds or endowments, so the definition does not lie in a prohibition on profit making. Instead, a nonprofit is defined as an organization that is constrained by laws, regulations, or internal structure from distributing its financial surplus to those who control the organization. This definition is implicit in most legal codes, practices, and common understandings of the term and serves as the foundation of most subsequent analysis by economists. Nonprofit organizations cannot pay dividend checks to board members or stockholders; suppliers of at-risk capital must instead take their rewards in other forms, such as the warm glow of knowing that they have helped others or as nonfinancial perks and other private benefits.

Suppose a philanthropist is dissatisfied with existing opportunities to help and decides to form a new organization. This organization could be created as either a for-profit or a nonprofit, in accord with the wishes of the founding entrepreneur. It seems puzzling that founders ever select the nonprofit form, because this choice means that they will never receive a dividend check no matter how popular the venture proves to be. However, by selecting the nonprofit form, the founder makes it more likely that other philanthropists will contribute toward the cause. Other philanthropists do not have to worry that their gifts will benefit owners rather than the intended beneficiaries, because profit distributions are prohibited. If ex-

pected profits are modest and potential gifts by others are large, the founder will rationally choose the nonprofit form.

Nondistribution of profits implies that nonprofits are different from for-profit firms in four important ways. First, nonprofits receive a far greater volume of donations and volunteer labor for the reason explained above. Second, they cannot raise capital by selling shares of stock that return dividends to the owners. Instead, they rely, at least initially, upon donations. This difference in the market for ownership leads to the third distinction: Nonprofits are not subject to takeover bids by financially motivated stockholders. With no fear of takeover bids, nonprofit organizations are free to pursue goals other than profit maximization, although they may still seek to maximize profits from some activities in order to finance unprofitable mission-related activities. Fourth, the kinds of people who choose to found, run, and contribute to nonprofit organizations, on average, will be different from the kinds that start and manage for-profit firms. Nonprofit stakeholders presumably care more about nonfinancial performance than do for-profit stakeholders.

This combination of financial structure, freedom from takeovers, and stakeholder sorting allows nonprofits to differ from for-profits in both good and bad ways. On the plus side, nonprofits may provide "collective goods," defined by economists as goods or services that benefit a group of people regardless of whether each member of the group pays for that service. For example, charity care for the indigent benefits all potential philanthropists who care about that group, regardless of whether each of those philanthropists donates to the charity or directly pays for services for the poor. Art museums preserve aesthetic experiences for future generations who cannot pay for that option today. Those aesthetic experiences are preserved regardless of whether future generations choose to pay museum admission fees.

Another advantage of the nonprofit form is that surpluses generated from one activity or group of customers may be used to finance lower prices or free provision of mission-related services. We see this when colleges offer financial aid (in effect, reducing the price), when day-care centers offer sliding-scale fees based on ability to pay, or when medical clinics offer free vaccinations.

The last advantage of the nonprofit form is that these organizations can act less opportunistically in situations where for-profit firms would exploit consumer ignorance. For example, for-profit nursing homes might skimp on the invisible aspects of quality in order to reduce costs and enhance profit distribution. The problem is worse when philanthropists pay a for-profit firm to feed starving residents of a foreign country. It would be difficult enough for philanthropists to confirm that the paid-for food is provided, but nearly impossible to confirm that more food is provided when one's own donation is added to the pool of donations by others. For-profits would rather use the philanthropists' money to increase the size of their dividend checks, and could safely do so.

Contracts protect consumers, but only when the consumers can confirm whether the terms of the contract have been met. Thus, the cases cited above are examples of "contract failure." Nonprofits help remedy contract failure because they cannot pay dividend checks and because they attract workers who are less motivated by financial payoffs. Consumers and donors know this, so nonprofits are both more trustworthy and more trusted (although there is dispute about how important and widespread this advantage is in practice).

Unfortunately, nonprofits sometimes depart from profit-maximizing behavior in three ways that are less desirable. First, scarce resources might be wasted or improperly used, resulting in higher costs and lower levels of service. Managers and employees may not work as hard as they would in the for-profit sector, may not keep their training up to date, and may spend too much money on enhancing their working environment. Second, cross-subsidies and price discrimination are sometimes used to accomplish what is arguably a wrong-way redistribution from the poor to the rich. All students (including those who are less well-off), for example, may be charged a higher tuition in order to finance athletic scholarships or to provide financial aid to the sons and daughters of well-off alumni. Third, nonprofits may be less nimble, because of both their differing objectives and their inability to issue shares of stock to finance expansion.

They may react to increases in demand by becoming more selective rather than by increasing capacity. Nonprofits may also be slow to cut back when the need for their services diminishes.

Comparing the Behavior of Nonprofit and For-Profit Firms

Although nonprofits differ from for-profit firms, there are many similarities. For-profit firms rely chiefly on revenues from sales of goods and services. This is also true for nonprofit organizations, although the share of revenues coming from sales is low in some charitable subsectors. When the charitable mission requires the nonprofit to provide particular services, financial or programmatic considerations may require that they charge a fee. Job training, psychological counseling, and substance-abuse services provide illustrations of mission-related services. Under the U.S. tax code, such "related income" is tax-exempt. Sometimes, the organization sells one service just to generate profits that can be devoted to its charitable mission. Museum shops and health spas are examples, and the income generated from them is taxed by an "Unrelated Business Income Tax."

Nonprofits behave just like for-profits when they seek unrelated business income. In contrast, when organizations seek related income, the charitable mission may war with the need to remain solvent. The organization may wish to provide low-cost services to those who cannot afford them at market prices or to expose the largest possible audience to symphonic music. In these cases, nonprofits use market prices and donations to obtain the revenues needed to offer sliding-scale fees or other need-based discounts, special days when admission is not charged, and free care for selected clients. Mission also wars with solvency when the organization selects its location. Nonprofits may locate where the need is greatest, rather than where the profit potential is greatest, selecting inner-city and rural sites that for-profit health clinics would avoid. Thus, nonprofits behave very differently from for-profits when they seek related income.

Like for-profits, nonprofits must engage in advertising and other forms of marketing. However, nonprofits do so in a distinctive way. In addition to marketing sales of items that generate unrelated business income, nonprofits market the importance of their cause when seeking gifts, grants, and volunteers. Sometimes, the charitable mission requires "social marketing" as well—communications designed to change detrimental behaviors—as in public service announcements designed to reduce drunk driving, smoking, or unsafe sexual practices. Finally, organizations that provide public education or advocacy turn to their own brand of marketing.

Like for-profits, nonprofits must consider the strategic interactions among their activities. For-profits must consider whether a new product line will prosper at the expense of competitors' products or their own existing product lines. Nonprofits must consider sales interactions, but must also consider interactions between sales and donations. There are many reasons to suspect that individual donations would change when the organization starts a new commercial venture, either related or unrelated to its mission, or when it receives a foundation grant or a government contract.

Government money has both positive and negative effects on donations. On the plus side, donors are assured that their gifts will be well spent by organizations that have received the government's seal of approval in the form of a major contract or grant. The government's pregrant review process and ongoing grant monitoring are designed to insure that funded organizations are professionally run, well managed, accountable, and efficient. In addition, government may fund services that are complementary to donor wishes. For example, government may pay for the symphony hall, making it more sensible for donors who want to improve the quality of the orchestra to give generously. Finally, government money may allow the organization to realize economies of scale so that donations may be used more efficiently. On the minus side, government grants and contracts often require the recipient to compromise their charitable mission. For example, faith-based organizations may have to limit their proselytization of clients when they accept contracts to provide social services, and organizations that provide shelter for the homeless may be required to curtail their client and program advocacy efforts in the legislature and the courtroom in return for government money. Such compromises would

generally discourage donors who supported the original mission. Even when government money supports a charity's mission, it may cause donors to believe that other charities, those without a governmental patron, need their contributions more. In this sense, government money crowds out private donations.

There are also positive and negative effects of commercial activity. Donors, especially foundation grant-makers, may view it as a positive sign that the programs they support with seed money will eventually be self-sustaining through cross-subsidization. However, donors may also worry that managers will devote too much attention to unrelated business income generation at the expense of accomplishing the organization's core mission. Similarly, they may fear "mission creep" as the organization hires managers with commercial expertise but less understanding and devotion to nonfinancial objectives. Finally, commercial activity may cause donors to feel that their help is no longer needed.

Private or Public Nonprofits?

Governments are also constrained against the distribution of profits. What distinguishes them from private, nonprofit organizations, and what determines the public/private division of responsibilities? The answer is that government finances collective goods at a level supported by political consensus. People who want more of the collective good than government provides will support and contribute to nonprofit organizations to supplement public finance and provision. In societies where there is a reasonable consensus about the amount to spend on collective goods, the privately financed part of the nonprofit sector is relatively small. In more diverse societies, those who object to low levels of government finance will look for opportunities to supplement public provision, and nonprofit organizations provide an ideal outlet for that desire. Note that societal diversity does not explain whether services are provided by government or private nonprofits, only whether they are financed by the two sectors. Political consensus may support government grants to or contracts with nonprofit organizations, so that publicly financed private nonprofits play a prominent role in more harmonious societies.

Diverse demands for collective goods are necessary but do not suffice to explain a large nonprofit role in the financing of collective goods. For one thing, the government must be willing to tolerate private action for the public good. Some extremely diverse communities find private action threatening to the legitimacy of government and so suppress the nonprofit sector. Another problem arises when no one is willing to take on the entrepreneurial role of founding and running nonprofit organizations. This problem is less severe if existing nonprofits provide seed money and leadership for new organizations. New ventures are an important strategy when nonprofits compete for members and legitimacy. In particular, religious denominations compete for converts and increase the commitment of their members by founding faith-based social-service agencies, hospitals, and educational institutions. Thus, societal diversity, religious competition, and tolerance for private action explain much of the public/private division across societies and time.

Richard Steinberg

See also Commercialism in the Nonprofit Sector; Federated Fundraising; Nonprofit Management; Public Philanthropy; Social Marketing

References and further reading
Ben-Ner, Avner, and Theresa Van Hoomissen. 1991. "Nonprofits in the Mixed Economy: A Demand and Supply Analysis." *Annals of Public and Cooperative Economics* 62: 519–550.
Bilodeau, Marc, and Al Slivinski. 1996. "Volunteering Nonprofit Entrepreneurial Services." *Journal of Economic Behavior and Organization* 31: 117–127.
———. 1997. "Rival Charities." *Journal of Public Economics* 66: 449–467.
———. 1998. "Rational Nonprofit Entrepreneurship." *Journal of Economics and Management Strategy* 7: 551–571.
Frech, H. E., III. 1980. "Health Insurance: Private, Mutuals, or Government." In *The Economics of Nonproprietary Organizations,* edited by Kenneth W. Clarkson and Donald L. Martin, 61–73. Greenwich, CT: JAI Press.
Hansmann, Henry. 1980. "The Role of Nonprofit Enterprise." *Yale Law Journal* 89: 835–901.
———. 1987. "Economic Theories of Nonprofit Organization." In *The Nonprofit Sector: A Research Handbook,* edited by Walter W. Powell Jr., 27–42. New Haven, CT: Yale University Press.
James, Estelle. 1983. "How Nonprofits Grow: A Model." *Journal of Policy Analysis and Management* 2: 350–366.
———. 1993. "Why Do Different Countries Choose a Different Public-Private Mix of Educational Services?" *Journal of Human Resources* 28: 571–592.
James, Estelle, and Susan Rose-Ackerman. 1986. *The Nonprofit Enterprise in Market Economics.* Chur, Switzerland: Harwood Academic.
Ortmann, Andreas, and Mark Schlesinger. 2003. "Trust, Repute, and the Role of Nonprofit Enterprise." In *The Study of the Nonprofit Enterprise: Theories and Approaches,* edited by Helmut K. Anheier and Avner Ben-Ner, 77–114. Dordrecht: Kluwer/Plenum.
Rose-Ackerman, Susan, ed. 1986. *The Economics of Nonprofit Institutions.* New York: Oxford University Press.
Steinberg, Richard. 1993. "Public Policy and the Performance of Nonprofit Organizations: A General Framework." *Nonprofit and Voluntary Sector Quarterly* 22: 13–32.
Steinberg, Richard, and Bradford Gray. 1993. "'The Role of Nonprofit Enterprise' in 1992: Hansmann Revisited." *Nonprofit and Voluntary Sector Quarterly* 22: 297–316.
Steinberg, Richard, and Burton A. Weisbrod. 1998. "Pricing and Rationing by Nonprofit Organizations with Distributional Objectives." In *To Profit or Not to Profit: The Commercial Transformation of the Nonprofit Sector,* edited by Burton A. Weisbrod, 65–82. New York: Cambridge University Press.
Wedig, Gerard. 1994. "Risk, Leverage, Donations and Dividends-in-Kind: A Theory of Nonprofit Financial Behavior." *International Review of Economics and Finance* 3: 257–278.
Weisbrod, Burton A. 1975. "Toward a Theory of the Voluntary Nonprofit Sector in a Three-Sector Economy." In *Altruism, Morality, and Economic Theory,* edited by Edmund S. Phelps, 171–195. New York: Russell Sage Foundation.
———. 1988. *The Nonprofit Economy.* Cambridge: Harvard University Press.
Young, Dennis R. 1983. *If Not for Profit, for What?* Lexington, MA: D. C. Heath.

Environmental Movement

Philanthropy is not new and neither is our concern for nature, clean air, and water. However, the term "environment" is relatively recent. Although "environ" has meant "surroundings" since the fourteenth century, and "environment" assumed a similar meaning in the nineteenth, it wasn't until the 1960s that the latter came into general usage as a term for ecosystems and natural habitats.

American naturalist George Bird Grinnell (1849–1938) helped found the Audubon Society. (Corbis)

Precursors to today's environmental groups, organized as hiking clubs, such as the Williamstown Club, established in 1863, and the Appalachian Mountain Club, founded in 1876, were influenced by Henry David Thoreau's book *Walden* (1854). New groups rose throughout the country in the late nineteenth century to combat the destruction of wilderness and pristine natural areas brought about by the growth and expansion of the Industrial Revolution. Among the organizations involved in the study, exploration, and advocacy for the protection of nature were the Audubon Society and the Sierra Club.

The Audubon Society was formed in 1886 when George Bird Grinnell, editor of *Forest and Stream,* encouraged his readers to join him in forming the country's first bird preservation organization. In only three months, more than 38,000 people joined the society. The Sierra Club was founded in 1892 by John Muir and in the early years relied on membership support for its activities, though sometimes personal contributions were made to make up deficits. Club members explored the Sierra, opening new routes and leading outings, and advocated for the protection of the wilderness.

After World War II, the traditional conservation and preservation movement became more broad-based among the middle class. Efforts to protect America's threatened species and natural wonders, to increase national park and wilderness protection systems, and to promote local greenbelts and residential zoning expanded and increased. New conservationists spearheaded efforts to protect national treasures from development. David Brower, for example, led the Sierra Club in a successful effort to stop the U.S. Bureau of Reclamation from flooding part of the Grand Canyon in the 1960s.

Beginning in the 1970s, the so-called "environmental decade," a newly emerging wing of the ecology movement began organizing around issues of environmental quality, industrial pollution, toxic waste sites, nuclear power, pesticides, and environmental health. Inspired by the dire warnings by Rachel Carson in *Silent Spring* (1962) and the struggle led by Lois Gibbs and the residents of Love Canal against the contamination of their community, the environmental health movement initiated new organizing efforts—often linking the occupational health and safety and public health movements into ad hoc coalitions—that included working-class Americans. Environmentalists also joined consumer health and safety organizations led by advocates such as Ralph Nader that were concerned with the proliferation of dangerous household products, unsafe automobiles, drugs, foods, pesticides, and other commodities. Traditional conservation organizations such as the Audubon Society, the Sierra Club, the Wilderness Society, and the National Wildlife Federation increased in popularity and a host of new, nationally based environmental organizations sprang forth, including the Environmental Defense Fund, the Environmental Policy Institute and Friends of the Earth (now merged), Greenpeace, the Natural Resources Defense Council, and Environmental Action (Faber and O'Connor 1993, 14).

By 1975, 5.5 million people contributed financially to nineteen leading national environmental organizations and perhaps another 20 million donated to more

The Greenpeace ship MV *Greenpeace,* shown at the Esmark Glacier in Spitsbergen in the north Arctic Sea in August 1999, protests the spread of polluntants to the most remote and pristine regions of the planet. (jre/Greenpeace/Photo by John Cunningham, Reuters; Reuters/Corbis)

than 40,000 local groups (Sandbach 1980, 13). Environmentalism had arrived as a mass-based movement. Today, the environmental movement remains one of the largest and more influential social movements in American society. There are currently more than 10,000 environmental advocacy organizations operating in the United States. These organizations have a combined membership of between 19 million and 41 million members, employ approximately 28,000 staff, have an income of $2.6 billion a year, and possess assets of $5.8 billion (Brulle 2000, 114).

The Environmental Movement and Philanthropy

Americans are a generous people when it comes to supporting the environment. According to *Giving USA 2003,* of the estimated $241 billion donated to charity in 2002, environmental causes of all kinds, including wildlife and habitat conservation, garnered nearly $6.59 billion (or 2.7 percent). The total dollar amounts donated to such causes have steadily grown in recent years. In fact, contributions to the environment increased by 68 percent from 1996 ($3.81 billion) to 2001 ($6.41 billion). Individuals account for nearly 75.8 percent of the contributions, with the rest coming from foundations (12.2 percent), corporations (4.3 percent), and bequests (7.7 percent). Out of this total, approximately two-thirds goes to environmental advocacy organizations that make up the environmental movement. The remainder goes to wildlife preserves, zoos, aquariums, and natural history museums. Giving to environmental advocacy organizations, such as the Sierra Club, Greenpeace, or the Natural Resources Defense Council, totaled approximately $2.7 billion in 1995 (Brulle 2000, 103).

Foundation support plays a particularly important role in sustaining the environmental movement (Walker 1983, 1991; Cockburn and St. Clair 1994). It is estimated that 5.4 percent, or $1.23 billion, of total foundation giving ($22.8 billion) went to the environment in 1999 (Faber and McCarthy 2001a). In a 1992 national survey of environmental organization leaders, these leaders rated foundation funding as second in importance to membership contributions (Snow 1992, 64). Foundation support made up 21 percent of environmental organization funding, whereas membership dues provided 24 percent of environmental group income (ibid., 63). Another study also found that foundation grants were the second largest source of income, making up between 22 and 29 percent of total organizational income (Brulle 2000, 251–253). By providing approximately 20 percent of the total funding of the environmental movement, foundations play a key role in the maintenance of these organizations (ibid., 255–256).

However, this funding is not uniform. Although the total pool of environmental funding has grown rapidly, by almost fivefold per decade since the 1970s, it has been concentrated on a relatively small number of large movement organizations involved in political advocacy work (Brulle and Jenkins forthcoming). For example, both the Audubon Society and the Sierra Club Foundation remain membership organizations and receive the majority of their funds from gifts and bequests. In 2001, the Audubon Society reported that nearly 67 percent of its annual operating revenues of $68 million were received as contributions and bequests, and only 11 percent in membership dues. The Sierra Club Foundation in 2001 received over 90 percent of its operating revenues of over $73 million from contributions and bequests (ibid.). These two examples illustrate the role of philanthropy in supporting environmental organizations.

The bulk of foundation funding goes to a handful of politically moderate national environmental organizations. Most are professional movement organizations with at most a "paper" membership of direct mail contributors who lack participatory mechanisms. A comprehensive analysis of environmental movement funding between 1970 and 2000 showed that over 80 percent of foundation funding goes to staff-dominated professional movement organizations that lack a grassroots base, and over 90 percent to organizations that rely exclusively on institutional tactics rather than base building and community organizing (ibid.).

Foundation funding thus bypasses some of the most vital and innovative sectors of the environmental movement. Instead of investing in the environmental justice, deep ecology, eco-feminist and eco-theological wings of the movement, foundations have focused their efforts on the environmental mainstream, making them more prominent and visible in the movement. A small group of alternative foundations, representing less than 1 percent of total foundation funding for the environment, are the only significant supporters of more innovative and politically informed environmental discourses. These alternative foundations also fund more participatory environmental organizations.

Potential Impacts of Foundation Support

Critics charge that the impact of such a heavy reliance on foundation support has been to channel the environmental movement into moderate discourses and conventional forms of action. Although there are notable cases of foundations attempting to directly control movement activities, the general pattern is a more indirect process of creating incentives for specific discourses, styles of organization, and tactics that draw the movement into the institutional system. Because so little environmental funding goes to participatory membership associations, rather than being governed by citizens, the environmental movement has become increasingly controlled by foundations that represent large corporate wealth and rationalized power in the U.S. political economy. This serves to systematically limit the range of viewpoints represented in the public arena and restricts the participation of citizens in environmental governance.

Foundation funding thus significantly influences the priorities and institutional structures of the U.S. environmental movement. It promotes organizational competition by selecting organizations that fit foundation priorities and, in the process, significantly shifts the agenda of the movement. By funding movement organizations with particular discourses, foundations in effect promote particular environmental viewpoints and hinder others. In addition, foundation funding strongly encourages the growth of professional organizational forms. Taken together, these effects have blunted the movement's impact. At the same time, foundation funding is not monolithic. Some foundations have funded the more radical environmental discourses and membership organizations.

Environmental Grantmakers Association

In 1987, a number of foundations banded together to form the Environmental Grantmakers Association (EGA). This organization has grown to a membership of several hundred foundation and corporate givers that provide a large majority of foundation grants to ecological causes (Cockburn and St. Clair 1994, 761). To realize these purposes, the EGA schedules annual retreats for its members at which representatives of the various foundations are given briefings on selected environmental issues by leading government officials, congressmen, scholars, and representatives of different environmental movement organizations. The EGA also helps coordinate funding for environmental organizations through the formation of working groups on specific issue areas.

The Evolution of the Environmental Justice Movement

The environmental justice movement represents a new wave of grassroots environmentalism in the United States. In poor African American and Latino neighborhoods, on Native American reservations, and in Chicano and Asian American communities across the country, populations traditionally relegated to the periphery of the mainstream environmental movement have created autonomous organizations committed to reversing past decision-making practices that place disproportionately large ecological and economic burdens onto people of color. Although mainstream environmentalism tends to focus on single issues without addressing the larger social context of environmental problems, the environmental justice movement aims to address both by focusing on the connections between ecological abuse, poverty and economic inequality, racism, the lack of democracy, and the consolidation of corporate power. The environmental justice movement also charges mainstream environmentalism with adopting corporate-like advocacy models that inhibit broad-based citizen empowerment and participation by people of color (Bullard 1994; Faber 1998). In essence, the base-building goals

and grassroots organizing efforts of the movement aim to fortify the mobilization of community residents to fight through the systemic barriers that bar poor people of color from directly participating in the identification of environmental and health-related problems and solutions—so that they may *speak and act for themselves* (Alston 1990).

The contemporary environmental justice movement is grounded in the convergence of six formerly independent social movements: (1) the civil rights movement, in that it focuses on issues of environmental racism and the disproportionate impacts of pollution in communities of color, the racial biases in government regulatory practices, and the glaring absence of affirmative action and sensitivity to racial issues in the established environmental advocacy organizations; (2) the occupational health and safety movement, because it promotes labor rights and opposes job hazards faced by nonunion immigrants and undocumented workers; (3) the indigenous lands movement, as it joins struggles by Native Americans and other marginalized, indigenous communities to retain and protect their traditional lands; (4) the environmental health movement, which largely developed out of the mainstream environmental movement in general, and the antitoxics movement in particular; (5) community-based movements for social and economic justice, which have expanded their political horizons to incorporate issues such as lead poisoning, abandoned toxic waste dumps, the lack of parks and green spaces, poor air quality, and other issues of environmental justice into their agenda for community empowerment; and (6) the human rights, peace, and solidarity movements, particularly those campaigns that first emerged in the 1980s around apartheid in South Africa and U.S. intervention in Nicaragua and Central America (Faber and McCarthy 2001b).

The environmental justice movement first emerged over the course of the 1980s as hundreds of community-based organizations began to address the disparate social and ecological hardships borne by communities of color. These organizations, however, were largely isolated or loosely connected to one another and focused on local issues. With the First National People of Color Environmental Leadership Summit in 1991, a recognition developed of the need to build stronger institutional linkages between these local community-based groups. As a result, a number of strategic, regionally based networks, as well as national constituency-based and issue-based networks for environmental justice, were created and consolidated during the 1990s. The regionally based environmental justice networks include the Southern Organizing Committee (SOC), Southwest Network for Economic and Environmental Justice (SNEEJ), and the Northeast Environmental Justice Network (NEJN). The Asian Pacific Environmental Network (APEN), the Indigenous Environmental Network (IEN), and the Farmworker Network for Economic and Environmental Justice (FWNEEJ) constitute the national constituency-based networks.

In the new century, the movement is entering a third stage of development as a new infrastructure for building intergroup collaboration and coordinated programmatic initiatives emerges. This shift was evident at the 2002 National People of Color Environmental Leadership Summit II. New organizational entities, such as the Environmental Justice Fund and the National Environmental Justice Advisory Council (NEJAC) to the Environmental Protection Agency (EPA), and consolidation of the regional and national constituency-based networks are leading initiatives that are taking the movement beyond the local level to have a broader policy impact at the state, national, and international levels (Faber and McCarthy 2001b).

The Environmental Justice Movement and Philanthropy

In contrast to mainstream environmentalism, the foundation community largely neglects environmental justice. Given the high number of organizations and the large size of the constituencies being served, the environmental justice movement is currently one of the most underfunded major social movements in the country. It is estimated that only $27.498 million in grants came to the environmental justice movement in 1996, and that this number rose to just over $49 million in 1999 (Faber and McCarthy 2001a).

The lack of resources for organizations serving people of color and low-income communities is particularly noticeable given the funding of the traditional environmental organizations. In comparison,

just eight mainstream environmental organizations, including the Leadership for Environment and Development, the Nature Conservancy, the World Wildlife Fund/Conservation Foundation, the Golden Gate National Parks Association, the Environmental Defense Fund, the National Audubon Society, the Population Council, and the Natural Resources Defense Council, received 212 foundation grants totaling over $48 million in the year 2000—an amount equivalent to all 200-plus grassroots environmental justice organizations in the country. In 2001, foundations provided 22 percent, or $8.93 million, of the $40.598 million in income received by the Natural Resources Defense Council. To provide another, more extreme example, the Nature Conservancy alone received approximately $97 million in foundation grants in 1994, a figure significantly higher than the amount received by any other environmental organization in the country.

Although funding for environmental justice has increased recently at Ford, Liberty Hill, Hewlett, San Francisco, and other foundations, grantmaker support for the movement remains insufficient. It is estimated that only 0.2 percent of all foundation grant dollars are dedicated to the environmental justice movement. Well over four-fifths of the actual grant dollars offered to environmental organizations are provided by Environmental Grantmakers Association members, and the grants are concentrated in a handful of (mostly) EGA foundations. In fact, estimates are that out of 47,000-plus foundations in the United States, just twelve foundations alone—Beldon, Bullitt, Charles Stewart Mott, Jessie Smith Noyes, Needmor, New World, Norman, Public Welfare, Solidago, Tides, Turner, and the Unitarian Universalist Veatch Program at Shelter Rock (Veatch)—provided $34.858 million (20.5 percent) out of the estimated total of $169.923 million in funding for the environmental justice movement between 1996 and 1999. With a couple of exceptions, most of the current foundation backers are providing maximum levels of funding and cannot be expected to increase support.

The ability of the environmental justice movement to grow and prosper depends on the future grantmaking of the entire philanthropic community. The resource disparities plaguing the movement relative to mainstream environmentalism has resulted in growing resentment by organizations led by people of color toward the foundation community. The June 10, 2002, protests at Stone Mountain, Georgia, reflected this disillusionment. Activists are calling for the overall funding base of the environmental justice movement to be enhanced through the creation of a broader base of EGA and non-EGA member supporters. One of the primary obstacles to this goal is the lack of racial diversity in the philanthropic community in general, and in the EGA membership in particular.

In response, the foundation community is beginning to develop policies for promoting greater diversity and inclusiveness in philanthropic circles. In the early 1990s, several environmental grantmakers organized a group called Funders Concerned about Minorities and the Environment, which sponsored briefings, workshops, and meetings at foundation events and published a newsletter with the intended goal of raising the profile of environmental justice organizations led by people of color. More recently, the EGA management and program committees have consciously placed people of color in leadership roles at the EGA annual fall retreats and have promoted greater inclusion of environmental justice leaders and environmental professionals of color as plenary speakers, facilitators, and workshop participants.

Robert J. Brulle, Daniel Faber, and Femida Handy

See also Muir, John

References and further reading

Alston, D. 1990. "We Speak for Ourselves." In *We Speak for Ourselves: Social Justice, Race, and Environment,* edited by R. Bullard and D. Alston, 3. Washington, DC: The Panos Institute.

Bastian, A., and D. Alston. 1993. "An Open Letter to Funding Colleagues: New Developments in the Environmental Justice Movement." New York: New World Foundation.

Brulle, R. 2000. *Agency, Democracy, and Nature: The U.S. Environmental Movement from a Critical Theory Perspective.* Cambridge: MIT Press.

Brulle, R., and C. Jenkins. Forthcoming. "Foundations and the Environmental Movement: Priorities, Strategies, and Impact." In *Foundations for Social Change: Critical Perspectives on Philanthropy and Popular Movements,* edited by D. Faber and D. McCarthy. Philadelphia: Temple University Press.

Bullard, R., ed. 1994. *Unequal Protection: Environmental Justice and Communities of Color.* San Francisco: Sierra Club Books.

Cockburn, A., and J. St. Clair. 1994. "After Armageddon: Death and Life for America's Greens." *The Nation,* December 19, 760–765.

Faber, D., ed. 1998. *The Struggle for Ecological Democracy: Environmental Justice Movements in the United States.* New York: Guilford Press.

Faber, D., and D. McCarthy. 2001a. *Green of Another Color: Building Effective Partnerships between Foundations and the Environmental Justice Movement.* Boston: Philanthropy and Environmental Justice Research Project, Northeastern University.

———. 2001b. "The Evolution of the Environmental Justice Movement in the United States: New Models for Democratic Decision-Making." Special issue of *Social Justice Research: Applying Social Justice Research to Environmental Decision-Making* 14 (4): 405–421.

Faber, D., and J. O'Connor. 1993. "Capitalism and the Crisis of Environmentalism." In *Toxic Struggles: The Theory and Practice of Environmental Justice,* edited by R. Hofrichter, 12–24. Philadelphia: New Society.

May, Elizabeth. 2002. "Environmental Movement: The Rise of Non-Government Organizations (NGOs)." In *Encyclopedia of Global Environmental Change,* edited by P. Timmerman. West Sussex, UK: Wiley.

Sandbach, F. 1980. *Environment, Ideology, and Policy.* Montclair, NJ: Allanheld, Osmun.

Snow, Donald. 1992. *Inside the Environmental Movement: Meeting the Leadership Challenge.* Washington, DC: Island Press.

Walker, Jack L. 1983. "The Origins and Maintenance of Interest Groups in America." *American Political Science Review* 77: 390–406.

———. 1991. *Mobilizing Interest Groups in America: Patrons, Professions, and Social Movements.* Ann Arbor: University of Michigan Press.

E-philanthropy

"E-philanthropy" is the use of the Internet to foster charitable aid or donations that promote human welfare. It includes efforts that build and enhance relationships with supporters of nonprofit organizations using an Internet-based platform, including the online contribution of cash or real property or the purchase of products or services to benefit a nonprofit organization. In addition, e-philanthropy includes the storage and usage of electronic data or the use of electronic methods to communicate with donors and others and to support fundraising activities.

The term is often used interchangeably with "Internet fundraising," though the latter term is limited to fundraising efforts. Since the late 1990s, a growing number of nonprofit organizations have been turning to the Internet to improve supporter relationships, find new efficiencies in their operations, advocate on issues, and better inform their key publics as well as raise funds. The use of the Internet for philanthropic purposes transcends the geographical boundaries that have traditionally circumscribed a nonprofit organization's reach and brings into question the jurisdictional authority in regulating these activities. Lawmakers, however, are only now coming to grips with the legal ramifications of these online activities.

The National Association of State Charity Officers (http://www.NASCOnet.org) issued a document known as the *Charleston Principles: On Charitable Solicitations Using the Internet* in 2001. These principles, which stem from a dialogue that began in October 1999 among state charity officials, provide guidelines and standards for charities, professional fundraisers and counsels, and commercial coventurers to help state officials enforce regulations more efficiently and effectively as they relate to e-philanthropy. Initiatives such as this, and others around the world, will continue to drive the search for new regulatory solutions to the problems raised by the use of new technology in fundraising and philanthropy.

On one hand, traditional regulatory measures dealing with the activities of charities are being shown to be inadequate for dealing with the Internet activities of nonprofit organizations. On the other hand, regulatory measures designed to deal with Internet technology have tended to be more effective in the private and public sectors than in the voluntary sector.

In addition to the efforts of governments, the e-philanthropy Code of Ethics, a self-regulatory model, was established by ePhilanthropy Foundation, a nonprofit foundation based in Washington, D.C., in 2000. The ePhilanthropy Foundation believes that if nonprofit organizations voluntarily follow these principles, they can be confident that their online efforts are consistent with sound ethical practices—and,

more important, will send a signal to donors that they are knowledgeable about and committed to the ethical use of the Internet in their cultivation and solicitation of support.

As nonprofit organizations began to recognize that they could effectively and efficiently use Internet-based services, they began to integrate the new methods with the use of other, more traditional and proven fundraising techniques. More and more organizations have copied this integrated pattern. Many e-philanthropy techniques and tools have been developed to cover the wide range of philanthropy activities, including cultivation and stewardship of donor relationships, invitations to advocate on behalf of a charitable cause, and the solicitation of contributions online.

Taking the time to plan ahead can often mean the difference between making costly errors and developing a successful e-philanthropy strategy. The exact mix of strategies and techniques that will work are as varied as the number and types of nonprofits that deploy them. Generally, e-philanthropy techniques fall into six categories:

1. Communication, education, and stewardship
2. Online donations and membership
3. Event registrations and management
4. Prospect research
5. Volunteer recruitment and management
6. Relationship building and advocacy

As the tools and services for each organization will vary widely, organizations should always evaluate options and test assumptions. Incremental improvements and the gradual introduction of new services will help supporters and staff become accustomed to using the new technology and communicating via the Internet. Only by testing, however, can the organization learn which techniques perform the best.

E-philanthropy came of age on September 11, 2001. In the days and weeks following the terrorist attacks on the United States, the world turned to the Internet as a vehicle for its charitable response to the tragic events. The level of online philanthropic activity in the weeks following these events was so amazing that the experience has become a defining moment in American philanthropy. In the two months following the disaster, more than 1.3 million contributors donated over $128 million online. Online donations were made to both for-profit and nonprofit Web sites. In the case of for-profit Web sites—for example, banking sites or the sites of private technology corporations—the prior relationship that online customers already had with the for-profit companies provided both the comfort level and mechanism donors needed to create an unprecedented outpouring of online giving. The American Red Cross reported that for the first time in its history online, electronic donations had outnumbered those given via their 800 number, by a three-to-one margin. The short time frame in which so many gifts were made online helped to coin a new phrase under the rubric of e-philanthropy—"flash philanthropy."

But it is important to realize that nonprofit organizations around the world are using the tools surrounding e-philanthropy to raise money and improve donor relations without a shocking world tragedy. Organizations that have no connection to emergency relief are raising money as well. Flash philanthropy is just one part of the phenomenon of e-philanthropy.

The movement of nonprofits to use the Internet for e-philanthropy was furthered by the launch of http://www.networkforgood.org—a joint for-profit effort led by AOL Time Warner Foundation and AOL; the Cisco Foundation and Cisco Systems; and Yahoo! in partnership with more than twenty nonprofit foundations and associations. This multifaceted and free charity portal was aimed at empowering nonprofits and donors to make use of the Internet to benefit charitable causes.

The true power of e-philanthropy-based methods lies in their ability to do more than simply act as a novel way in which to raise money. It is in the areas of communication and relationship building that the Internet is having its most significant impact in philanthropy. In fact, these are the real drivers of fundraising success both offline and online. The Internet is viewed by many as an ideal platform from which to reach, inform, and engage potential donors, many of whom may be beyond the radar of normal fundraising channels. Charities should approach the Internet as a communication and stewardship tool first and a fundraising tool second.

The Internet gives donors easy access to numerous philanthropic choices. As the e-philanthropy revolution builds steam, more and more people have turned to the Web to fulfill their charitable intentions. As e-philanthropy has emerged, organizations have discovered that consistent and deliberate e-mail communication and a well-organized and informative Web site have become the keys to success.

E-philanthropy techniques have brought to the nonprofit world an unprecedented opportunity to leverage technology for the benefit of the charity and the convenience of the donor. Every organization spends time and resources recruiting and retaining charitable support. This support is based on relationships and fulfilled missions. Hundreds of options exist for using the Internet in each of the six categories of e-philanthropy outlined above. The Internet enhances the efforts of nonprofit organizations by providing efficient and effective communication tools tied to robust, secure online services. These services, in turn, empower donors to utilize information and support charitable causes anytime and anywhere.

Ted Hart

References and further reading

ePhilanthropy Foundation Homepage: http://www.homestead.com/ephilanthropyfoundation

Johnston, Michael. 1999. *The Fund Raiser's Guide to the Internet*. New York: Wiley.

Warwick, Mal, Theodore R. Hart, and Nick Allen, eds. 2002. *Fundraising on the Internet: The ePhilanthropy Foundation.Org Guide to Success Online*. 2d ed. San Francisco: Jossey-Bass.

Ethics and Philanthropy

In their simplest formulations, ethics (being good) and philanthropy (doing good) seem closely related. However, the relationship is complex, both conceptually and in practice. As philanthropy expert Paul Ylvisaker warned, "When you put two words like ethics and philanthropy together, you're in trouble: each of them resists definition, and when combined they can be totally elusive" (1999, 318). The connection was noted as far back as Aristotle's *Nichomachean Ethics* (Book 4, Chapters 1 and 2), which discussed "liberality" (philanthropy in general) and "magnificence" (large-gift philanthropy) as moral virtues. Many other philosophical and religious traditions have affirmed this connection; for example, the Bible clearly views charity and philanthropy as moral imperatives.

It is hazardous to define "ethics," since philosophers have been debating its meaning and source for 2,000 years (Becker and Becker 1992). The common understanding is that ethics is the study of the moral rightness or wrongness of human actions. Some philosophers have placed more emphasis on ethics as a body of thought, others on ethics as a thoughtful framework for moral action.

"Philanthropy," literally "love of humankind," connotes altruism, generosity, and effort to benefit humanity. For example, Robert Payton defined philanthropy as "voluntary service, voluntary association, and voluntary giving for public purposes" (1988, 1). As its etymology shows, "philanthropy" is not a neutral word: it envisions acts motivated by selfless love for others, especially "others in general" rather than the beggar at one's feet.

The most visible form of philanthropy is that of major gifts of money and other resources. Gifts that are large, have some social distance between giver and receiver, and are intended to have significant and long-lasting effects are more likely to be called philanthropic than, for example, weekly contributions to one's church or clothing given to a needy neighbor, often termed "charity." How does ethics relate to "philanthropy" in this sense?

From the perspectives of three major ethical theories (Aristotle, Immanuel Kant, and the utilitarians), the moral status of such acts is not self-evident. This is especially clear in Kant, who held that the maxim or principle underlying one's action was all-important: An apparently philanthropic act done from a base motive would be immoral, not moral. Aristotle bases the morality of philanthropic and other acts partly in the subjective realm: To be virtuous, an act must not only be of a certain type, it must also come from a man who knows what he is doing and chooses the act as good; further, the act must emanate from a "formed and stable character" of virtue developed over time by acts of that type. Only the utilitarian approach gives clear support to a presumption of morality on objective grounds: Whatever the character or intent of the

actor, an act is good if, on balance, it brings more pleasure than pain to all affected people. From the utilitarian viewpoint, it doesn't matter whether John D. Rockefeller's philanthropy was altruistically motivated by his lifelong Baptist faith and a genuine love of humankind or driven by cold, calculated economic and public relations concerns. All that matters is whether his acts brought more pleasure than pain to the millions of people affected. In other words, the ethics of large-gift philanthropy depends on the ethical framework used to make the assessment.

There is more consensus on whether to give in the first place. Virtually all philosophical and religious traditions hold that some giving is required at least from people of means. This moral obligation flows from the nature of humans, society, and property. Human beings are inescapably interdependent, from birth and nurturing to old age. This social dimension of human existence creates ethical responsibilities to each other, some of which are carried out through formal mechanisms of taxation and government programs but others of which depend on individual, thus ethical, decision making. Also, in most philosophical and religious traditions, property is not an absolute, unconditional value or right; in certain circumstances, others have prior moral claims on some of "our" property.

Not only individuals but also institutions do philanthropy. The latter include grantmaking foundations, corporations, federated funds such as United Way, and churches. As with individual philanthropy, ethics looks at both subjective and objective aspects of institutional giving. In one sense, ethical assessment is simpler here. Most institutional philanthropy—two-thirds, in the United States—comes from private foundations, which are required by federal law to give about 5 percent of their asset value in grants every year, so the ethical question of *whether* to give doesn't even arise. Also, institutional philanthropy, unlike individual philanthropy, is usually accompanied by public documents about mission, values, and purpose, which facilitates assessment of intent.

However, there is always room for discussion and debate about "real" intent, perhaps especially with corporate giving. On the objective side, assessing the effect of institutional philanthropy is ethically somewhat complex, even using the utilitarian standard of the greatest good for the greatest number. For example, most grantmaking foundations focus on short-term start-up grants, whereas grantseeking nonprofits typically want operating funds. Both sides offer persuasive professional and even ethical reasons for their preferences. Another example is the collective impact or nonimpact of institutional philanthropy in various areas of need. Funders have devoted billions of dollars to improving health care, eliminating poverty, alleviating racial tensions, advancing education, and promoting international understanding. In all these areas, funders must choose between root causes and immediate needs, with ethical arguments on both sides. To move this tension up one level, what would our ethical judgment be if all or nearly all institutional philanthropy went to basic research on such things as language systems, climate change, and interstellar physics? It is clear that funders have the legal freedom to give as much as they wish to any cause within the broad legal definition of "charity," but do funders also have total ethical freedom in their giving? Critics of philanthropy have long raised questions about the purposes and effects of institutional giving, and many of these questions have been ethical in nature.

Ethics has relevance not only to individual and institutional philanthropy but also to philanthropic work. In the United States, most such work is carried on by nonprofit organizations recognized as "charities" under Section 501(c)(3) of the federal Internal Revenue Code (IRC). Included are churches, universities and schools, hospitals, environmental agencies, international relief efforts, and countless social assistance and advocacy groups. "Philanthropy" here refers not to donors but to organizations doing what donors support. In what sense does ethics apply to the work of these organizations?

Although one must reject the common but misguided notion that philanthropic organizations uniquely represent society's moral element—all major human groups, families, businesses, governments, and nonprofits are to some extent moral agents—there is a sense in which philanthropic organizations have special ethical dimensions because of their mission, clients, supporters, and staff.

An organization manufacturing rubber bands has certain ethical responsibilities related to product safety, decent treatment of employees, honesty in dealing with clients, and so forth. But an organization whose mission relates to human rights, education, health care, or counseling assumes, by the fact of its mission and work, expanded ethical responsibility. The fact that most nonprofits focus on human and social welfare issues makes it clear why these organizations are properly seen as having special ethical dimensions.

Closely allied to the organization's mission and work is the type of staff required by that work. Since philanthropic organizations are centered in the professions—religion, medicine, education, social work—staff members bring with them a tradition of ethics and ethical codes, unlike workers in many for-profit companies and even government agencies. Thus the ethical valence of philanthropic work is further reinforced by the internalized values of professional staff members in these organizations.

Not only the missions and staffs but also the clients of philanthropic organizations have ethical relevance. The organization-client transactions of Safeway and Macy's entail basic considerations of honesty and product safety, but buying and selling apples and socks are not transactions fraught with ethical challenge. By contrast, the clients of many philanthropic organizations—children, poor people, victims of discrimination, the physically or psychologically ill—are highly and continually vulnerable. Agencies working with such clients have great power over them and thus great ethical responsibility to them.

There are other ethical dimensions of philanthropic organizations. Board members have ethical and legal responsibilities to monitor management, exercise due diligence over financial matters, avoid conflicts of interest, and above all, ensure that the organization fulfills its charitable purpose. Fundraisers are ethically bound to use appropriate techniques, refrain from excessive pressure, maintain the confidentiality of private information, and respect donor intent as to the use of funds. Volunteers must behave in accordance with the mission and work of the agency—for example, in mentoring children through Big Brothers

Big Sisters or in helping distraught callers to a suicide prevention hotline.

Michael O'Neill

See also Moral Philosophy and Philanthropy
References and further reading
Becker, Lawrence C., and Charlotte B. Becker, eds. 1992. *The Encyclopedia of Ethics.* New York: Garland.
Boris, Elizabeth T., and Teresa J. Odendahl. 1990. "Ethical Issues in Fundraising and Philanthropy." In *Critical Issues in American Philanthropy: Strengthening Theory and Practice,* edited by Jon Van Til, 188–203. San Francisco: Jossey-Bass.
Briscoe, Marianne G., ed. 1994. *Ethics in Fundraising: Putting Values into Practice.* San Francisco: Jossey-Bass.
INDEPENDENT SECTOR. 1991. *Ethics and the Nation's Voluntary and Philanthropic Community: Obedience to the Unenforceable.* Washington, DC: INDEPENDENT SECTOR.
O'Neill, Michael. 1997. "The Ethical Dimensions of Fund Raising." In *Critical Issues in Fund Raising,* edited by Dwight F. Burlingame, 58–64. New York: Wiley.
———. 2001. "Administrative Ethics in Nonprofit Organizations." In *Handbook of Administrative Ethics,* 2d ed., edited by Terry L. Cooper, 623–628. New York: Marcel Dekker.
Payton, Robert. 1988. "Philanthropy in Action." In *Philanthropy: Four Views,* edited by Robert Payton, Michael Novak, Brian O'Connell, and Peter D. Hall, 1–10. New Brunswick, NJ: Transaction.
Ylvisaker, Paul. 1999. "Ethics and Philanthropy." In *Conscience and Community: The Legacy of Paul Ylvisaker,* edited by Virginia M. Esposito, 318–328. New York: Peter Lang.

European Foundations

Although the general-purpose grantmaking foundation is often considered to be a twentieth-century American invention, endowments established for educational, religious, and other public purposes have existed in Europe for nearly 2,500 years. The antecedents of contemporary foundations in both the United States and Europe can be traced to ancient beginnings. Plato set aside funds to sustain the Academy after his death. Epicurus wrote a will leaving properties that supported his school for some 600 years. Theophrastus made a bequest to maintain the Lyceum of Aristotle. And throughout the ancient world there were countless other less famous institutions; most common among them were the many en-dowed hospices situated along pilgrimage routes and at temple sites.

The vast wealth of imperial Rome enabled emperors such as Antoninus Pius (86–161) and Marcus Aurelius (121–180) to establish foundations for the assistance of orphans and poor children. Lesser officeholders and private individuals in the farthest reaches of the empire also created endowments, embellishing their towns with civic monuments and supporting games and festivals. Pliny the Younger (62–113) left one of the fullest accounts of his giving, which was concentrated in his native town of Como. He endowed Como's library and public baths and promised to donate one-third of the expenses of a new school if the students' parents would contribute the rest. Other Romans undertook large-scale public works projects, often constructing and endowing public baths or building bridges, aqueducts,

Epicurus (342?–270 B.C.); undated engraving (Bettmann/Corbis)

theaters, race courses, and markets. When he died in 180, Herodes Atticus, the tutor of Marcus Aurelius, left an endowment to provide yearly a fixed sum of cash (one *mina*) to each Athenian citizen.

These ancient benefactors expected their gifts to be honestly managed and hoped that their institutions would last in perpetuity. Gradually, a body of law took shape that protected donors' intentions; by the first century, Roman law recognized the "legal personality" of these incipient foundations. The Emperor Constantine and the other Christian emperors of the Byzantine east continued to encourage charitable activity, promulgating protective laws while founding their own charitable institutions. In the sixth century, the Emperor Justinian granted the first recorded tax exemptions, offered assistance for the construction of new charitable institutions, and voiced continuing concerns about sound and honest management of charities while asserting the emperor's responsibility for overseeing charitable institutions. At the same time, the founding charters *(typika)* of monasteries and hospitals began to set out extremely detailed statements of charitable purpose, often specifying numbers of staff and their particular duties.

During the fourth century, Basil the Great, bishop of Caesarea, had established one of the most renowned foundations of any era, the Basileas. It was an institution, though called a hospital, that had much wider purposes: sheltering travelers, taking in the poor and elderly, and housing lepers and those with other illnesses. A Byzantine chronicler was so impressed that he compared the Basileas to the pyramids of Egypt, the gates of Thebes, and the other great wonders of the world. Other philanthropic institutions also flourished in the eastern half of the Roman Empire, some of them surviving well into the fifteenth century. They grew more specialized: *Xenones* or *xenodichia* served as hostels for travelers and pilgrims and could be found in cities and provincial towns; *ptocheia* were established for the poor and others who could not work; *gerocomeia* housed the elderly; and *orphanotropheia,* as the name suggests, took in orphans.

While the East flourished, the economy of the western half of the Roman Empire deteriorated. There, monasteries began to play a major role in confronting rural poverty and meeting the needs of trav-

elers. Arguably, these were the first foundations in Western Europe. They possessed many of the traits of the modern foundation: created by deed or charter and governed by an explicit body of rules, usually Benedictine or Augustinian monastic regulations; holding assets, albeit in the form of income-producing land; reflecting the pious intentions of donors; and pursuing charitable objectives through regular distributions to the poor, hospitality for travelers, care for the sick, and regular prayer for all.

With the gradual expansion of commerce and the revival of towns beginning in the eleventh and twelfth centuries, endowments of many and diverse types were created. Hospices and hospitals sprang up along trade, pilgrimage, and crusade routes. Although a number of these early hospitals cared for lepers, more often than not hospitals were intended to offer hospitality rather than medical care. The early founders were princes and other nobility, but soon their charitable establishments were augmented by those set up by an increasingly prosperous merchant class. Their foundations included homes for the elderly, specialized hospitals for the blind, beguinages for unmarried women, orphanages, and schools.

Charitable activity also began to take collective and communal forms in the twelfth and thirteenth centuries. Religious confraternities, trade or craft guilds, and urban parishes organized a variety of institutions to serve their memberships. They might provide funds for burials and funeral masses, financial assistance to widows and orphans, and in-kind distributions to the poor; some operated their own hospitals and almshouses. Managed by laymen, and accountable variously to clerical supervisors and increasingly to municipal officials, these institutions signaled an increasing secularization of charitable purposes and a growing sense of governmental responsibility for regulating charitable practices.

Common alms funds, which were overseen by municipal authorities and received private bequests and donations, began to appear in the fourteenth century. They can be viewed both as rudimentary community foundations and as primitive municipal welfare offices. They helped poor pupils to attend school, made cash and in-kind donations to the needy, and provided low-interest loans to workers. In some instances, they also supervised the accounts and activities of older charitable institutions.

The process of secularization and increasing governmental regulation and control accelerated in the sixteenth century, partly a product of the Reformation and Counter-Reformation and partly the work of humanist lawyers and reformers. Many older foundations had seen their revenues decline. Their charitable purposes became outmoded and their administration became lax and inefficient. Some sixty or seventy cities sought to reform these medieval charitable structures, centralizing assistance to the poor and assuming control of the hodgepodge of medieval institutions. Both King Francis I of France and Emperor Charles V took measures in their respective territories to bring about such wholesale reforms. For the most part, however, supervision of charitable institutions remained a local matter, the responsibility of municipal governments.

The most enduring national reform initiative from this era, certainly the one with the greatest influence on American charity, was the Elizabethan Statute of Charitable Uses (1601). It set out standards of public benefit and created a framework for ad hoc commissioners to investigate charitable abuses and enforce reforms. This supportive legal framework shaped England's burgeoning philanthropic sector in the seventeenth and eighteenth centuries. Approximately half of the new trusts created in the eighteenth century were set up to assist the poor; others paid apprenticeship fees, supported schools, made loans to workers, paid dowries, or left land for public purposes. England's culture of philanthropy came to differ significantly from that on the continent: Charitable purposes were defined in expansive terms following the 1601 statute; trusts and endowments could be relatively easily set up; legal mechanisms protected donors' intentions and prevented abuses; and Chancery Court proceedings were being continually simplified.

During the eighteenth and nineteenth centuries, the course of state-building on the European continent yielded philanthropic sectors with very different shapes and sizes. In France and several other Catholic countries with strong monarchies, patterns of state centralization began to curtail the role of private foundations as early as the seventeenth century. Neither French Physiocrats such as A. J. R. Turgot nor the even more radical Jacobins of the revolutionary era saw any public use for foundations. They were troubled by the "dead hand" of resources held in trust and suspicious of any mediating institutions that might stand between the individual citizen and the central state. Church and other charitable assets were seized and sold off, and intermediary associations and foundations were banned by the Le Chapelier Act of 1791. In France, foundations were effectively curtailed for nearly two centuries until the passage of new legislation in 1987. These revolutionary ideas also influenced other countries. The charitable sector has had a limited role in Belgium since the early nineteenth century, and a liberal, secular regime in Spain passed laws in 1823 and 1836 dissolving that nation's medieval foundations and banning new ones.

The English and French foundation sectors represent the two extremes of European historical experience. Other countries fall somewhere in between. Never having suffered the bitter struggles of the Reformation and later religious wars, Denmark and Sweden arrived at an accommodation between church and state that allowed older foundations to survive and, ultimately, for supportive legal structures to emerge. In the nineteenth century, foundations became important instruments for popular social movements to advance their causes, and both countries have a substantial philanthropic heritage.

It is more difficult to generalize about foundations in Germany and Italy. Prior to national unification, their respective stories are rooted in extremely diverse municipal and regional contexts. By the end of the nineteenth century, however, Germany was experiencing a period of foundation growth spurred on by wealthy industrialists who created recognizably modern foundations to support higher education, research, and new policy approaches to the problems of industrial society. Two world wars, hyperinflation, reconstruction, and a half century of national division put an end to these promising beginnings. Northern Italy in the nineteenth century continued its long-standing practices of civic engagement, sustaining its older charitable institutions, witnessing new acts of public patronage, and benefiting from a robust associational life. Mutual aid societies and cooperatives flourished in the north. In the much poorer south, civil society and foundations remained underdeveloped.

The second half of the twentieth century, but especially the 1980s and 1990s, have been an extraordinarily expansive period for European civil society generally and for the foundation sector in particular. Foundations have proliferated in a Western European environment that has benefited from increasing economic prosperity and political stability and that is now searching for institutional alternatives and adjuncts to "statist" approaches to many different public tasks, whether providing new approaches to social welfare delivery, health care, arts and culture, or education. Foundations have also been rediscovered in Eastern Europe following the demise of totalitarian regimes and the rapid attempts to construct market-driven economies and civil societies.

Today, both the role of foundations and the scale of their activities differ markedly from country to country. With the exception of the United Kingdom, where almost all the foundations are grantmaking, the majority of foundations in Europe either operate their own programs or have a mixed style of operating programs and making grants to other organizations. Their predominant fields of activity also vary considerably. Education, research, and social services are the principal areas of interest for foundations working in Austria, Belgium, Britain, Germany, Greece, Italy, Switzerland, and Turkey. Health and medical research are of primary interest to foundations in France, where the Institut Pasteur and the Institut Marie Curie have such distinguished histories. Arts and cultural foundations predominate in Spain, and Ireland expends a disproportionate amount on housing issues.

By 2001, there were an estimated 80,000–90,000 foundations in Europe. Country by country, the raw numbers range from highs of 20,000–30,000 foundations in Sweden and 14,000 in Denmark, most of them quite small, to lows of a mere 30 in Ireland and a few hundred in Belgium and France. The sectors have remained smallest in Austria, Belgium, France, Greece, Ireland, Luxembourg, and in Central and Eastern Europe. The sectors are slightly larger in Portugal, Spain, and Turkey. In sheer numbers of foundations, the sectors are moderate-sized in Finland, Germany, the Netherlands, Norway, and the United Kingdom. The numbers have grown largest in Italy, Lichtenstein, Sweden, and Switzerland. Foundation assets per capita tell a slightly different story. They are highest in Lichtenstein because of offshore assets held in foundations chartered there; next highest in Italy because of the banking assets that went into private foundations during the 1990s; and next highest in the United Kingdom and Germany, where substantial corporate assets have gone into foundations.

Although this overall growth reflects general economic prosperity and, in some cases, the advent of new democratic regimes, it has been further spurred in recent years by country-specific factors. Legal changes in Italy (1990), Spain (1994), and Portugal (1977) have aided the growth of the sector in those nations. Financial and technical assistance from the United States and Western Europe have been instrumental in building foundations and civil society organizations in Central and Eastern Europe. Where the sectors are small and growth is minimal, namely Austria, Belgium, and France, the reasons are largely legal and bureaucratic and reflect long historical experience.

Divergent national experiences make it risky to talk about twenty-first-century "European" foundations. The word "foundation" in its linguistic variations—*fondacion, fundaçao, fonds, stichting, Stiftung, stiftelse, saatio*—refers to widely differing sorts of institutions. Many organizations that are called "foundations" are actually membership associations with few assets; some depend heavily on government subventions, and some function as private investment trusts for families and have only limited charitable purposes. Increasingly, though, the term is being used to refer to institutions that share certain characteristics and are accepted as important players in democratic societies. Foundations, whether old or new, are now understood to be entities that hold some sort of asset, have been formally created by deed or charter, are legally separate from government, are privately governed, distribute no profits, and are able to serve important public purposes.

James Allen Smith

References and further reading

Anheier, Helmut K., and Stefan Toepler, eds. 1999. *Private Funds, Public Purpose: Philanthropic Foundations in International Perspective.* New York: Kluwer Academic/Plenum.

Cavallo, Sandra. 1995. *Charity and Power in Early Modern Italy: Benefactors and Their Motives in Turin, 1541–1789.* New York: Cambridge University Press.

Constantelos, D. J. 1991. *Byzantine Philanthropy and Social Welfare.* New Rochelle, NY: Aristide Caratzas.

Geremek, Bronislaw. 1994. *Poverty: A History.* Oxford, UK: Blackwell.

Hands, A. R. 1968. *Charities and Social Aid in Greece and Rome.* Ithaca, NY: Cornell University Press.

Henderson, John. 1994. *Piety and Charity in Late Medieval Florence.* Chicago: University of Chicago Press.

Mollat, Michel. 1986. *The Poor in the Middle Ages: An Essay in Social History.* New Haven, CT: Yale University Press.

Owen, David. 1964. *English Philanthropy, 1660–1960.* Cambridge: Harvard University Press.

Schluter, Andreas, Volker Then, and Peter Walkenhorst, eds. 2001. *Foundations in Europe: Society, Management and Law.* London: Directory of Social Change.

Schneewind, J. B., ed. 1996. *Giving: Western Ideas of Philanthropy.* Bloomington and Indianapolis: Indiana University Press.

F

Faith-Based Initiatives
See Charitable Choice

Federated Fundraising
Federated fundraising organizations provide support for community-based programs and services throughout the United States and are associated with core values of voluntarism. For most of the twentieth century, federated fundraising in this country was identified with the community chest/United Way system. The first community organization of this type in the United States appeared in Denver, Colorado, in 1887. Jewish federations also emerged in the late nineteenth century; however, they focused on a specific group of donors rather than the whole geographic community and, unlike United Ways, never established a prominent connection to corporate and workplace giving.

United Way's primacy in the field of federated fundraising was generally accepted until a new pluralism in fundraising organizations and activist causes developed after the social upheavals of the 1960s. Local United Ways faced intense challenges from a changing workplace and a greatly expanded field of financial federations. The historical evolution of financial federations was therefore characterized by a growth of diversity in the latter half of the twentieth century. This growth gave way to new issues of accountability and management in the 1990s. At the be-

ginning of the twenty-first century, new issues are emerging.

From Community Federations to United Funds
Although the combined fundraising appeal is viewed as particularly American, it came to Denver from England. At a time of social and economic change, religious and business leaders were influenced by the "Liverpool system" and in 1887 planned a joint campaign for fifteen social service agencies (Watson 1922). The Charity Organizations Society foundered after a few years, but in the early twentieth century federated fundraising campaigns appeared in cities across the country, including Elmira, New York; San Antonio, Texas; and later, Cleveland, Dayton, and Cincinnati, Ohio (Lubove 1969). Jewish federations arose in Boston in 1895 and spread elsewhere. Some community-wide federations later made special arrangements with these Jewish organizations and other religious groups.

What has been described as the first modern financial federation was created in 1913 by the Chamber of Commerce in Cleveland (Lubove 1969; United Way of America 1977). The Cleveland Federation of Charities and Philanthropies involved a larger group of city officials and businessmen and, unlike the Charity Organizations Society, employed professional staff. In addition to joint fundraising for a selected group of charities, the Cleveland Federation soon encompassed monitoring of agency budgets and consideration of community-wide service needs.

During World War I, financial federations spread along with war chests. By 1919, there were thirty-nine federated campaigns in the United States and Canada and their numbers were increasing rapidly (Brilliant 1990). By the 1920s, the core elements of federated fundraising had been established: a single community-wide campaign for a member group of local social welfare agencies; review of agency budgets with regard to efficient use of funds and community needs; increased involvement of professional staff along with community volunteers; and a strong connection to business, with a promise that donors would have "immunity" from other appeals from agencies in the combined campaign (Watson 1922). In some cities, there were separate councils of social agencies concerned with broader community needs; despite tensions, they usually worked closely with financial federations.[1] By 1918, professionals in councils and federations had sufficient common identity to form the American Association for Community Organization. This national organization later became the United Way of America.

As corporate contributions became increasingly important to federation campaigns, the tax status of these gifts began to matter. During the Great Depression, corporate leaders and federated funds were successful in obtaining legislation that established a charitable deduction for corporate contributions of up to 5 percent of profits (Brilliant 1990). Federated campaigns organized special mobilizations in the Depression, but after the federal government took over direct relief, federated funds shifted to family services and character-building agencies (United Way of America 1977). Meanwhile, as federations became more professional, their structures also changed. By this time, most had evolved from true partnerships with member agencies into what were defined later as "independent" federations with strong central management organizations (Provan 1983). Corporate donors were major stakeholders; many staff professionals, in federations as well as councils, were social workers.

Fundraising in the workplace became increasingly significant after the 1930s. Informal appeals to employees for mutual support (for birthdays or illness, for example) existed before then; in World War I more organized war-related appeals were held. In the 1920s, John L. Lewis promoted aid to workers in the miners union through a "check-off" for Red Cross donations (Brilliant 1990). Early in the Depression, a foreman obtained permission from the Cincinnati Milling Machine Company to solicit contributions from workers as they received their pay envelopes and other chests. By then, formal workplace campaigns had already taken place in Indianapolis (Aft 2003). However, at a time when residential campaigns were generally preeminent, Rochester, New York, was the exemplar for the "business type" campaign. Building on the war chest concept, by 1931 Rochester had developed a carefully structured campaign focused on workplace solicitation, including a suggested amount of deduction from wages of one hour's full earnings a week for ten weeks (Association of Community Chests and Councils 1932).

World War II brought about more changes. In 1941, two labor leaders were put on the national federation board (Community Chests and Councils); in 1943, federal legislation established payroll withholding for taxes. During a period of labor unrest, contracts negotiated in the late 1940s by the United Automobile Workers union and the Ford Motor Company in Michigan included a check-off (withholding from pay) for contributions to federated funds, along with the check-off for union dues. In an effort to consolidate charitable appeals, a new unified statewide fund included national agencies and health causes. In October 1949, the local Detroit United Foundation/Torch Drive used this United Fund model successfully to support the Michigan Heart Association and a Red Cross chapter in workplace solicitation (United Way of America 1977). In the 1950s, newly defined United Funds spread across the country, promising to eliminate multiple appeals in the workplace. Restrictions on workplace organizing in the Taft-Hartley Act of 1947 permitted some "beneficent" activities, but in the next decades limited charitable access generally meant United Way monopoly in workplace fundraising.

Federations, the Combined Federal Campaign, and Inclusiveness

After World War II, health-related appeals expanded along with medical knowledge. The American Cancer

Society, the American Heart Association, and the March of Dimes became major competitors with federated community-wide campaigns. Health charities formed their own federations, and by the 1960s, "health wars" erupted. Some other national agencies, such as the American Red Cross, were ambivalent about joining local federations in this period (Brilliant 1990).

Meanwhile, the federal government began to bring order to the many campaigns in its workplaces across the country. These campaigns would later develop parallel to, but structurally different from, those in corporate workplaces. Years of incremental initiatives led to a first Combined Federal Campaign (CFC), which began in 1964 with four groups: National Health Agencies, United Funds/community federations, a loose group of (two) International Voluntary Agencies (later the International Service Agencies), and the American Red Cross (where not part of a local community federation). By 1971, the CFC was permanent. It had national policies and oversight but functioned through local campaigns. United Ways managed campaigns; funds were distributed by formula and designation, and United Ways received the largest amounts (Brilliant 1990; U.S. Office of Personnel Management 2002).

Through the mid-1970s, United Funds (now United Ways) still largely followed the model of earlier decades. Community-based federations undertook fundraising and provided for citizen reviews for budgeting and allocation of funds, including some planning for local human service needs—either through their own organizations or through related community councils. Most United Ways funded a standard core of member agencies—many with national affiliations: family service agencies, recreational and character-building services (YMCAs and YWCAs, Girl Scouts, Boy Scouts, and Boys and Girls Clubs) as well as the Salvation Army, the American Red Cross, and some local agencies and health causes, such as the American Cancer Society. United Ways still enjoyed a monopoly in corporate workplaces; they generally avoided controversial causes and served both as buffer and connection between corporations and community human services.

Although federated funds evinced a notable degree of continuity, the social transformations of the 1960s caused enormous changes in the society around them. Federal funds supported new programs and also a new role for government in community planning. United Ways were criticized for including only a small part of all community services and for their elite leadership. Moreover, as civil rights gained new recognition, coercive techniques of fundraising became less acceptable to workers; they were challenged successfully in the CFC (Brilliant 1990). New and emerging advocacy federations, such as Women's Way in Philadelphia, began to seek entry to local United Ways or more directly to the workplace itself. Pressure from competitive funds developed in California from such groups as Associated In-Group Donors–United Givers and the Brotherhood Crusade of Los Angeles (a Black United Fund) (Brilliant 1990).

By the early 1980s, significant changes occurred first in the national CFC, and later in state and local employee campaigns. Although the U.S. Supreme Court stopped short of mandating a fully "open" federal workplace campaign in 1985, an accumulation of lower court decisions and congressional action in the end resulted in a restructured, more open campaign, including hundreds of groups with different viewpoints (U.S. Office of Personnel Management 2002; National Committee for Responsive Philanthropy 1987, 1989, 1990). Although a National Labor Relations Board decision in 1982 had affirmed exclusive access for United Ways in corporate workplaces (Brilliant 1990), the growing demands for choice in giving continued. The United Way was soon forced to modify its paradigm, first to include donor designation (both within the United Way member group and for outside causes) and later to highlight new modes of giving for areas defined as community priorities, such as child welfare or crime. At the end of the twentieth century, about sixty corporations also allowed workplace access to other federations, and United Way was placing more emphasis on large individual gifts (Billiteri 2000; Varchauver 2000; United Way of America 2001).

In the last decade of the twentieth century, problems multiplied. As designations grew in number and amounts, the citizen review process lost its preeminence. United Ways' stewardship role of funds was undermined by serious charges against the chief executive of United Way of America, William Aramony, in 1992 (Glaser 1993), and in subsequent years by the malfeasance of professionals in local United Ways (for example, United Way of the National Capital Area in 2002). Corporate demands for accountability increased, and United Way of America attempted to standardize reporting methods and centralize payroll deductions of local United Ways (Beene 2001; Strom 2002).

Alternative Funds, a New Pluralism, and Future Issues

Beginning in the mid-1960s, there was an explosion in the number of voluntary agencies in the United States (Weisbrod 1988), and growth in charitable organizations continued into the twenty-first century. Most charitable organizations are not part of federated funding groups; nonetheless, the number and variety of groups defined as "alternatives" to the United Way system has expanded constantly. The National Committee for Responsive Philanthropy helped to create the alternative funding movement, serving as an umbrella organization for traditional health funds as well as for advocacy and social justice groups such as women's funds, Black United Funds, and environmental groups.

Although alternative funds raise a relatively small amount of money compared to United Ways, their continuing growth threatens United Way hegemony in workplace giving (Beene 2001; United Way of America 2001). United Way claims to have 17 million givers; however, in the workplace fewer donors are giving larger (average) gifts. In fall 2001, alternative funds raised more than $222 million (National Committee for Responsive Philanthropy 2003); for essentially the same period, the approximately 1,400 United Ways reported revenues of $3.95 billion (United Way of America 2003). There is, however, some duplication in these figures since United Way revenues include funds designated to other groups.

In the late 1980s, the burgeoning group of progressive workplace funds and federations created their own national trade association, the National Alliance for Choice in Giving (NACG). In 2002, NACG had fifty-two member organizations with campaign revenues of over $13.5 million (National Alliance for Choice in Giving 2003). NACG included an Asian

Pacific Community Fund, the United Latino Fund, two women's federations, and some other social justice funds. Most of its members were progressive, true member-based federations, such as community-based Community Shares and state environmental federations (or Earth Shares). These social change federations are in local, state, and federal public employee campaigns; a few have even replaced United Ways as managers of these campaigns. However, they have less access to the corporate workplace.

The universe of alternative funds is larger than National Alliance membership. Among other alternative funds are some from the old CFC and from state employee campaigns, including the International Service Agencies, the former National Health Agencies, now affiliated with local health federations and known as Community Health Charities, and America's Charities, formerly the National Service Agencies and now a federation with more than 100 diverse members. In addition, there are a variety of other loosely affiliated federations, such as Independent Charities of America, which targets corporate access, as well as United Arts Funds, Black United Funds, more than ninety women's funds in the national Women's Funding Network (National Committee for Responsive Philanthropy 2003; Women's Funding Network 2003), and a new Union Community Fund, which directly challenges United Way–labor relationships. These last three groups have social change ideologies. Three women's funds, and some arts funds, function as federations.

In the early years of the twenty-first century, the growing numbers of federations and funds constitute a diverse, highly competitive marketplace. United Ways still dominate corporate workplaces but have changed. They now are more like foundations than federations; they provide only a small amount of support for affiliated agencies and are shedding the concept of membership. They are trying to recapture the community problem-solving role they enjoyed in the middle years of the last century and seeking new methods of outcome-related accountability. In addition, United Way and other workplace federations are operating in a highly uncertain business environment characterized by less manufacturing and more service-oriented businesses, continuing globalization of industry, and destabilized workforces (dispersed workers and displaced workers). These factors make fundraising more difficult.

Finally, increased donor choice, together with the emerging use of high tech e-giving, suggests even greater transformations ahead. Personal relationships between donor and recipient will surely be weakened. Questions must be raised about whether e-giving could eliminate the need for workplace campaigns or result in less money for competing causes, which now include more than health and welfare agencies. Moreover, quixotically, as federations market their diverse ideologies and purposes there will almost certainly be a felt need to re-create a new sense of local community. Meanwhile, the United Way and some other groups, such as the women's funds, are spreading their nets internationally.

Eleanor L. Brilliant

Notes

1. Names have changed frequently in this area of philanthropy: financial federations became community chests, United Funds, and later the United Way; councils of social agencies have used even more names over time and in different places, including health and welfare councils, planning councils, and community councils.

References and further reading

Aft, Richard. 2003. Interview with author, February 25.

Association of Community Chests and Councils. 1932. *Community Chest Campaigns.* New York: Association of Community Chests and Councils.

Beene, Betty S. 2001. "Perceptions of Organizational Structure and a Nonprofit System's Operations in a Changed Environment: A Descriptive Case Study." Ph.D. dissertation, George Washington University.

Billiteri, Thomas J. 2000. "United Ways Seek a New Identity." *The Chronicle of Philanthropy,* March 3, 1, 21–26.

Brilliant, Eleanor L. 1990. *The United Way: Dilemmas of Organized Charity.* New York: Columbia University Press.

Glaser, John S. 1993. *The United Way Scandal: An Insider's Account of What Went Wrong and Why.* New York: Wiley.

Lubove, Roy L. 1969. *The Professional Altruist: The Emergence of Social Work as a Career, 1889–1930.* New York: Atheneum.

National Alliance for Choice in Giving (NACG). 2003. Appendix A, "NACG: A Brief History," and attached documents, including "Chronology of Workplace Giving Federation and Fund Development, 1971–2001," and "Democratizing Philanthropy in the American Workplace."

National Committee for Responsive Philanthropy. 1987. *The Workplace Giving Revolution.* Washington, DC: National Committee for Responsive Philanthropy.

———. 1989. "President Signs CFC Legislation; Ends 11-Year Charity Drive Battle?" *Responsive Philanthropy* (Winter).

———. 1990. *Special Report on Workplace Giving Alternatives: 10% and Growing.* Washington, DC: National Committee for Responsive Philanthropy.

———. 2003. Charts with data on amounts raised by non–United Way, alternative funds and federations, provided to the author.

Provan, Keith G. 1983. "The Federation as an Interorganizational Linkage Network," *Academy of Management Review* 8 (1): 79–89.

Strom, Stephanie. 2002. "Questions Arise on Accounting at United Way." *New York Times,* November 19.

United Way of America, http://national.unitedway.org (cited January 19, 2003).

———. 1977. *People and Events: A History of the United Way.* Based on the manuscript of Elwood Street. Alexandria, VA: United Way.

United Way of America, Task Force on Strengthening the United Way System. 2001. *The Case for Action.* Draft Report (Spring).

U.S. Office of Personnel Management, Combined Federal Campaign. "Charitable Fundraising within the Federal Service," http://www.opm.gov/cfc/html/cfc_hist.htm (cited May 26, 2002).

Vorchaver, Nicholas. 2000. "Can Anyone Fix the United Way?" *Fortune Magazine,* December 27, 171.

Watson, Frank Dekker. 1922. *The Charity Organization Movement in Social Work.* New York: Macmillan.

Weisbrod, Burton A. 1988. *The Nonprofit Economy.* Cambridge: Harvard University Press.

Women's Funding Network. 2003. Membership List, February.

Filer Commission

The Commission on Private Philanthropy and Public Needs, known as the Filer Commission because of its chairman, John H. Filer (chairman and CEO of Aetna Life and Casualty, Hartford, Connecticut), was incorporated in September 1973. It was the second of two commissions initiated by John D. Rockefeller III that focused on charitable tax deductions and the role of philanthropic activity in American life (the first was the Peterson Commission). The Filer Commission idea grew out of discussions in

Rockefeller's philanthropic advisory group about possible new tax reform legislation in the early 1970s.

Initially conceived as an advisory committee to the House Ways and Means Committee, the privately funded commission was launched with the support of the U.S. Treasury Department. Leonard L. Silverstein, a well-known tax expert and Washington attorney for the Rockefeller family, was executive director. In February 1974, Gabriel Rudney, an economist, was loaned from the Treasury Department's Office of Tax Analysis to be director of research. In its final report, the commission listed twenty-eight members, including businessmen, civic leaders, former government officials, representatives of religious groups, a union leader, and one foundation executive. There were three black commissioners and one Hispanic member; four commissioners were women. A large separate advisory group had less diversity in its membership.

The commission brought in outside experts and members of the advisory committee to inform discussions around key topics such as the structure of tax preferences in the law, the impact of tax incentives on giving, nonprofit accountability and the role of the Internal Revenue Service, and regulatory alternatives. More than ninety papers were commissioned on these and related topics, including the history and role of philanthropy and voluntary activity, as well as descriptions of specific subsectors of the voluntary "third sector" in the United States. In 1975, the commission issued a report called *Giving in America: Toward a Stronger Voluntary Sector*, which made recommendations regarding new and continuing tax incentives, nonprofit accountability and regulatory policy, and the creation of a permanent national Commission on the Voluntary Sector, which some considered its most important recommendation. After the report was issued, a follow-up group continued meeting with Treasury officials. The Treasury Department published the six volumes of the commission's *Research Papers* in 1977, but that same year the follow-up advisory committee was disbanded as part of the new Carter administration's move to streamline government.

The commission's major accomplishments have been summed up as: (1) producing the first extensive body of research on the third sector, including econo-metric studies of motivations for giving; (2) drawing attention to the significance of the third sector in American life and inspiring a new academic field of nonprofit research; (3) providing arguments for preserving tax preferences for charitable donations and preventing more draconian changes in the tax laws; and (4) influencing some philanthropic reforms, such as reducing the excise tax on foundation income (to 2 percent), and (for a brief period after 1981) allowing nonitemizers to take charitable tax deductions. The commission did not deal with more fundamental issues related to social needs and private-public relationships.

There was, however, an unexpected and significant outcome of the commission process. After the commission was called elitist and criticized for inadequate representation of women and minorities, a "Donee Group" was formed. This marked a beginning of recognition for new perspectives and alternative voices in the American philanthropic arena. Additional papers and a separate "Donee Group Report" were funded by the commission and also included in the commission's *Research Papers*. The group was formalized as the National Committee for Responsive Philanthropy in 1976 and still exists. After Rockefeller's death in 1978, another voluntary organization, INDEPENDENT SECTOR, was created; it undertook some of the functions proposed for the permanent national commission, such as encouraging research, gathering data, and convening foundations and other nonprofit organizations around common issues.

Eleanor L. Brilliant

References and further reading
Brilliant, Eleanor L. 1990. *Private Charity and Public Inquiry: A History of the Filer and Peterson Commissions.* New York: Columbia University Press.
Commission on Private Philanthropy and Public Needs. 1964–1980. Ruth Lilly Special Collections and Archives, University Library, Indiana University–Purdue University, Indianapolis, Indiana.
———. 1975. *Giving in America: Toward a Stronger Voluntary Sector.* Washington, DC: Commission on Private Philanthropy and Public Needs.
———. *Research Papers.* 1977. Washington, DC: U.S. Department of Treasury.
Council on Foundations Records. 1973–1978. Series 2, Commission on Private Philanthropy and Public Needs files. Rockefeller Archive Center, Pocantico Hills, New York.

Eisenberg, Pablo. 1983. "Accountability, Accessibility and Equity in Philanthropy: Filling the Research Gap." In *Working Papers for the Spring Research Forum: Since the Filer Commission*. New York: INDEPENDENT SECTOR, May 3, 139–162.

Hall, Peter Dobkin. 1992. *Inventing the Nonprofit Sector and Other Essays on Philanthropy, Voluntarism and Nonprofit Organizations*. Baltimore: Johns Hopkins University Press.

Harr, John Ensor, and Peter J. Johnson. 1991. *The Rockefeller Conscience*. New York: Charles Scribner's Sons.

Knauft, E. B. 1983. "Functions of the Nonprofit Sector: The Place of the Filer Commission in the Scope and Activity of the Third Sector." In *Working Papers for Spring Research Forum: Since the Filer Commission . . .* New York: INDEPENDENT SECTOR, May 3, 119–137.

Rockefeller, John D., III. Papers. Rockefeller Archive Center, Pocantico Hills, New York.

Schwartz, John J. 1994. *Modern American Philanthropy: A Personal Account*. New York: Wiley.

Food and Antihunger Charities

Donating food to the needy is surely one of the oldest forms of giving, and it is one of the most common forms of charity in the United States. A 1992 national survey of registered voters found that 79 percent had donated food, money, or time to at least one of the thousands of food kitchens, pantries, and other nonprofits providing food relief (Eisinger 1998). Despite the economic growth of the late 1990s, direct-service food charities, which grew rapidly in number and size during the 1980s, continued to expand. Critics worry that this growth represents a deterioration in state responsibility for citizens. Others see the food charity sector as a complement to government services.

Direct-service food charities include food kitchens (or "soup kitchens"), which serve sit-down meals, and food pantries, which provide bagged or boxed goods. Food banks receive massive quantities of food from corporate donors and government-purchased surplus and serve as suppliers to these other organizations. Food rescue organizations collect surplus foods from farms or markets for pantries and kitchens. The most exhaustive survey of food charities, conducted in 2000 by the U.S. Department of Agriculture (USDA), found approximately 5,300 food kitchens, 32,000 pantries, 400 food banks, and more than 200 food res-

cue and other emergency food providers operating in the United States (Ohls and Saleem-Ismail 2002). These organizations encompass nonprofits ranging from small, all-volunteer food pantries to food banks with large budgets, professional staff, sophisticated food storage facilities, and distribution systems serving large geographic regions.

In addition to these charities, more than 100 nonprofits, which largely grew out of the gay and lesbian community and have their own national association, provide tailored, home-delivered food services to AIDS patients. Finally, thousands of child-care and drop-in centers, after-school programs, domestic violence shelters, youth clubs, private schools, and other nonprofits—some with national associations of their own—utilize millions of dollars in federal reimbursements each year, in addition to philanthropic resources, to serve meals to children, the elderly, and the homeless.

According to the survey cited above, approximately two-thirds of pantries and kitchens are associated with religious organizations, whereas food banks are less likely to be religiously affiliated. Over one-half of all kitchens and pantries rely solely on volunteers. In 2000, the average kitchen served more than 100 lunches per day and the average pantry served fifteen people each week. However, it is hard to generalize about the size of these charities because of the vast variation in makeup. It is worth noting that the geographic distribution of these nonprofits, compared to the need, is uneven. The USDA survey found emergency food services less commonly in rural areas despite high rates of poverty in rural America.

Food charity organizations utilize both private and public sources for funding and food. Although the government's food and nutrition programs dwarf these charities both in the value of benefits and number of participants, a small subset of people eligible for government aid appear to prefer private food assistance alone, perhaps on account of its relative ease. Even then, clients of food charities are also truly recipients of government support, as the majority of these providers make extensive use of the Emergency Food Assistance Program and other state and federal sources of commodities.

In subsistence or primitive societies, giving food was a means of securing one's own future: Monday's donor might be Friday's recipient in a community of hunter-gatherers. In modern economies, however, donations of food are less likely motivated and regulated by rules of reciprocity. Indeed, donors may be far removed from recipients. Volunteering to feed the poor may be deemed a charitable requirement for religious adherents or a response to perceived social injustice or governmental indifference for political activists. The pantries and free meals provided by the Catholic Worker movement provide an example of a combination of both motives.

The omnipresence of food charities can partly be attributed to modern agricultural science and the magnitude of the U.S. food market, both of which provide an abundance of opportunities for inventive activists to secure donations. In some communities, groups called "gleaners" gain permission to scour fields for marginal produce farmers would not bother to sell. Other sources of food contributions come from damaged goods (such as dented cans), perishable foods that cannot be sold (such as overstocked vegetables), and government commodities that USDA buys from agribusiness and gives to schools and charities. Leftover produce, baked goods, and all manner of items from restaurants and hotels are also part of the enormous food rescue strategy of many urban food kitchens and homeless shelters. Some food rescue operations have even added job-training programs that utilize donations from the hospitality business to train low-income adults for catering or cooking careers.

Although religious and political identities provide potential donors, advances in agriculture generate large surpluses, and the sheer size of the U.S. food economy provides an abundance of cast-off food, it is important to recognize that the design of the modern food charity system is also heavily conditioned by political factors dating back at least to the 1930s. During the Great Depression, enormous crop and livestock surpluses threatened the stability of agricultural markets. It was not politically tenable for vast quantities of food to be purchased by the government and then dumped to save agribusiness while many U.S. citizens were going hungry. In response to what observers have forever since called the paradox of hunger amidst plenty in the United States, the federal government began experimenting with purchasing mass quantities of surplus commodities for distribution, often by nonprofits, to the poor. Another political factor quickly came into play when retailers felt that commodity programs threatened their business. Pressure from store owners, plus concerns over corruption and the inadequacy of food commodities, led to experimentation with vouchers that the poor used to purchase certain items at stores (an early form of what is now the food stamp program).

Over the following decades, public interest in hunger waxed and waned. The emphasis in federal antihunger policy vacillated between commodity and voucher systems. In addition, new federal and state partnerships to deliver surplus food, and finances for food purchases, were developed. However, weak congressional interest and poor program design frequently resulted in low participation in voucher and commodity programs compared to the need. Arbitrariness in what was supplied and how it was rationed also plagued the commodity programs.

Increased interest in malnutrition in the United States from foundations, politicians, the media, and activists in the late 1960s and early 1970s finally cemented the establishment of food stamps as a universal program, making it the nation's primary safety net for nutrition assistance to the poor. Still more programs were developed to target commodities or federal reimbursements to specific subgroups, such as food delivery for the home-bound (Meals on Wheels), congregate meals for the elderly and children, and vouchers and food packages for pregnant women, infants, and young children. Most notably was the creation of the school meals system, which provides both public and private nonprofit schools with surplus commodities and reimbursements for purchased meals.

In the 1980s, cutbacks in federal programs, high unemployment, the deinstitutionalization of the mentally ill, and renewed interest in government-purchased commodities as a way to support agricultural interests spurred an increase in the number of food charities. Eventually, the professionalization of the sector developed with the advent of food banks and their own peak associations. Why the sector did not

Homeless people line up for a free Christmas dinner at the Los Angeles Mission on Christmas Eve 1990. (Joseph Sohm; ChromoSohm Inc./Corbis)

decline during the drop in poverty and unemployment in the 1990s is not clear, but increased use, especially by families and the employed, is a common finding of informal surveys of these nonprofits. Once viewed as a temporary measure, the food charity sector—which delivered 3 billion tons of foodstuff in 2000—appears both permanent and still growing.

Nonprofits as policy advocates and researchers, as well as providers of government-funded services, have a profound effect on federal nutrition programs, which now number fifteen, with total spending at $30 billion annually. At the national level, America's Second Harvest serves as the peak association for the vast majority of food banks, whereas the Food Research and Action Center serves as the major hub for the policy and advocacy work of what has been dubbed the "hunger lobby"—concerned nonprofits, policy activists, and other interests. The hunger lobby includes dozens of groups at the state and national levels that influence the budgeting, reimbursement rates, and policy making for all these direct and indirect federal government services. At the local level, some food banks and policy activist organizations also serve an advocacy role both for individual families (for example, navigating food stamp applications) and for the community as a whole (for example, influencing social policy). Other nonprofit associations playing a major policy role in federal nutrition programs represent interests such as child- and adult-care providers, school food service employees, and food manufacturers.

Douglas R. Hess

References and further reading

America's Second Harvest, http://www.secondharvest.org.

Berry, Jeffery. 1984. *Feeding Hungry People: Rulemaking and the Food Stamp Program.* New Brunswick, NJ: Rutgers University Press.

Eisenger, Peter. 1998. *Toward an End to Hunger in America.* Washington, DC: Brookings Institution.

Food Research and Action Center, http://www.frac.org.

Nord, Mark, Nader Kabbani, Laura Tiehen, Margaret Andrews, Gary Bickel, and Steven Carlson. "Household Food Security in the United States, 2000." Food and Rural Economics Division, Economic Research Service, U.S. Department of Agriculture, http://www.ers.usda.gov (cited February 2002).

Ohls, James, and Fazana Saleem-Ismail. 2002. "The Emergency Food Assistance System—Findings from the Provider Survey, Volume 1: Executive Summary." Food and Rural Economics Division, Economic Research Service, U.S. Department of Agriculture.

Poppendiek, Janet. 1986. *Breadlines Knee-Deep in Wheat: Food Assistance and the Great Depression.* New Brunswick, NJ: Rutgers University Press.

———. 1998. *Sweet Charity?: Emergency Food and the End of Entitlement.* New York: Penguin.

Riches, Graham, ed. 1997. *First World Hunger: Food Security and Welfare Politics.* New York: St. Martin's.

Ford, Henry (1863–1947), and Ford, Edsel (1893–1943)

Henry Ford and his son Edsel were both automobile manufacturers and generous givers. By putting the nation on wheels, they transformed its social fabric; in their philanthropy, they sought to preserve the past and jointly founded one of the world's largest private charitable foundations.

Henry Ford was born on July 30, 1863, in Dearborn, Michigan, the son of William and Mary Litogot Ford. He was an inveterate tinkerer, and sometime during the spring of 1896 he succeeded in building the quadricycle, a buggy powered by an internal combustion engine. Ford failed in his first two attempts to commercialize his vehicle. It was not until 1903 that the Ford Motor Company was established with the clear mission of building a motor car for the multitudes. By 1921, Ford had captured 55 percent of the U.S. market for automobiles. His first major philanthropic project was the establishment of Henry Ford Hospital in Detroit in 1915, which aimed to provide medical care to all at a reasonable charge. Although he was a notorious anti-Semite, Ford was generous to African Americans, in terms of both offering good jobs and in philanthropy.

The ruling passion of Henry Ford's last thirty years was the preservation of the past. In 1923, he embarked upon his first major venture in historical preservation, the Wayside Inn near South Sudbury, Massachusetts. The inn, immortalized in a poem by Henry Wadsworth Longfellow, was in imminent danger of demolition when Ford purchased and refurbished it.

Ford's crowning achievement was the creation of the Edison Institute in Dearborn, consisting of Greenfield Village, the Edison Institute Museum, and

Scientist George Washington Carver of Tuskegee Institute, flanked by Henry Ford (left) and his son, Edsel Ford, receives Henry Ford's gift of a fully equipped laboratory for food research and experiments. (Bettmann/Corbis)

the Edison Institute Schools. He filled his museum with millions of artifacts, ranging from old buttons to working locomotives. He moved every historical building that caught his fancy to Greenfield Village, including the Wright brothers' bicycle shop and the buildings at Menlo Park, New Jersey, where Thomas Edison had operated his first laboratory. Ironically, Henry would not allow automobiles on the grounds of the Edison Institute, which in 1953 renamed its museum in his honor.

Edsel Ford joined the Ford Motor Company after graduation from high school in 1912 and became president by age twenty-five in 1919. He began his philanthropy by sponsoring the polar expeditions of

Commander Robert Byrd, who became the first to reach the North Pole by airplane. Edsel supported the Detroit Institute of Arts, where his greatest gift consisted of twenty-seven fresco murals by Diego Rivera. Edsel was also deeply involved in the founding and operation of the Edison Institute.

In 1936, Edsel and Henry Ford launched the Ford Foundation. Undertaken as part of Henry's estate planning, the foundation was initially small and local in scope. The deaths of Edsel in 1943 and Henry in 1947 dramatically changed this picture. Between the two of them, they had owned nearly all of the stock of the Ford Motor Company. They left about 10 percent of that stock to their heirs; the remaining 90 percent went to the Ford Foundation. This windfall made the Ford Foundation the largest and most influential charitable foundation in the United States, a position it was destined to hold for nearly the remainder of the twentieth century.

Edsel died from cancer at the age of forty-nine on May 26, 1943. Henry lived on until April 7, 1947. Both Henry Ford and his son, Edsel, believed in a brand of philanthropy that focused on giving a "hand up" rather than a handout. They offered these hands up on a massive scale: From 1917 to 1943, nearly one-third of Henry Ford's net taxable income went to charities. And in launching the Ford Foundation, they guaranteed that their philanthropic influence would extend indefinitely into the future.

Joel J. Orosz

References and further reading

Collier, Peter, and David Horowitz. 1987. *The Fords: An American Epic.* New York: Summit Books.

Greenleaf, William. 1964. *From These Beginnings: The Early Philanthropies of Henry and Edsel Ford, 1911–1936.* Detroit: Wayne State University Press.

McDonald, Dwight. 1956. *The Ford Foundation: The Men and the Millions.* New York: Reynal.

Nielsen, Waldemar A. 1985. *The Golden Donors: A New Anatomy of the Great Foundations.* New York: E. P. Dutton.

Orosz, Joel J. 2002. "Henry and Edsel Ford." In *Notable American Philanthropists: Biographies of Giving and Volunteering,* edited by Robert T. Grimm Jr., 92–98. Westport, CT: Oryx Press.

Ford Foundation

Since its founding in 1936, the Ford Foundation has made more than $12.5 billion in grants and program-related loans. For most of the period following World War II, it was the largest foundation in the United States. An independent, nonprofit institution, the foundation's goals are "to strengthen democratic values, reduce poverty and injustice, promote international cooperation, and advance human achievement" (Ford Foundation 2003). Its program and structure reflect a belief that the best way to confront challenges is by supporting the efforts of those closest to the problems. About half of the foundation's grant budget is devoted to international issues, most of which are administered by a long-standing network of offices in Africa, Asia, Latin America, the Middle East, and Russia. The foundation is headquartered in New York City.

Over time, the Ford Foundation has successfully helped to establish and cultivate a global network of human rights organizations and promoted democratization in many countries. In the United States, it has fostered inner-city revitalization and the development of the public broadcasting system and pioneered programs that led to the creation of the National Endowment for the Arts. Along with other foundations, it established a network of international agricultural research centers that helped to foster and spread the "Green Revolution," and since the 1980s it has supported the spread of community-based management of natural and agricultural resources worldwide. It has played a major role in the development of several generations of leaders in the United States and abroad. Its most recent initiative in this regard is its International Fellowship Program, which will provide $280 million over ten years in graduate fellowships for thousands of individuals from around the world, including many members of marginalized groups.

Today, most grants are made within the context of larger initiatives. The foundation uses a wide range of approaches that include research, program-related investments, and grants contributing to everything from small projects to endowment campaigns. In the 1950s and 1960s, particularly outside the United States, the Ford Foundation worked as an operating foundation by providing technical assistance to government agencies. It now works almost exclusively through making grants, largely to nonprofit organizations and universities. The foundation remains committed to diversity internally, in grantee organizations and in the fields it supports.

When Henry Ford and his son, Edsel, established the foundation in 1936, it initially made grants on a modest scale in Michigan. Following the deaths of Edsel and Henry in the 1940s, and the settling of their estates, the foundation's assets grew dramatically through several gifts of Ford Motor Company stock. In 1950, with Henry Ford II as chairman of the board, the foundation formally separated from Ford family control. In 1955, the trustees announced a long-range policy of diversification of foundation holdings through the sale of Ford Motor Company stock, which led to tremendous growth and relative stability in the portfolio. Members of the Ford family remained on the board until 1976.

The foundation's board of trustees sets institutional policy and delegates authority for grantmaking and operations to the president and staff. Within budgetary parameters set by the board, program staff have considerable autonomy in making grants.

Alan Divack and Rusty Stahl

References and further reading

Ford Foundation. 2003. "Who We Are," http://www.ford found.org/about/mission.cfm (cited January 20, 2004).

Greenleaf, William. 1958. *The Ford Foundation: The Formative Years.* Unpublished manuscript, Ford Foundation Archives.

Macdonald, Dwight. 1956. *The Ford Foundation: The Men and the Millions.* New York: Reynal.

Magat, Richard. 1979. *The Ford Foundation at Work: Philanthropic Choices, Methods and Styles.* New York: Plenum.

Forten, James (1766–1842)

Known as a colored man of wealth and intelligence and a philanthropist, James Forten applied his energy and resources to abolish slavery. Born in Philadelphia to free African Americans Thomas and Margaret Forten on September 2, 1766, James Forten was exposed to sail making in early life by observing his father, who died of an unknown cause when his son was just seven.

Forten received his early education at the Friends' African School under Jacob Lehre. At the age of fourteen, he left school to join Captain Stephen Decatur Sr., on the privateer *Royal Louis* to fight the British in the Revolutionary War. The ship was captured on its second voyage, and Forten survived seven months on the British prison ship *Jersey.* Released by the British in 1782, Forten soon began working—as his father had—for Robert Bridges as a sail maker. In 1786, at the age of twenty, he was promoted to foreman, overseeing both black and white workers. Bridges retired in 1798 and arranged for Forten to purchase the business. By 1832, James Forten employed about forty workers and had amassed a fortune of about $100,000.

Forten used his influence as a businessman, activist, and philanthropist to promote abolition, women's rights, and equal rights for blacks. He often spoke at public gatherings where freedom or equality was at issue and helped draft several petitions to legislators to end discriminatory legislation prevailing at the time. Forten openly opposed the 1793 Fugitive Slave Act of Pennsylvania, which allowed alleged runaway slaves (and often free blacks) to be returned to masters in southern states. In 1813, when a bill was before the Pennsylvania Senate to bar the immigration of free blacks from other states, he wrote and published a pamphlet entitled *Letters from a Man of Colour,* successfully persuading lawmakers to uphold the words of equality in the Constitution and defeat the bill.

He became a fierce opponent to colonization—a movement designed to repatriate blacks to West Africa—and founded and served as president of the American Moral Reform Society, a group promoting education, temperance, economy, and universal liberty. A friend of noted abolitionist William Lloyd Garrison, Forten also supported Garrison's antislavery publication *The Liberator* with funding and by soliciting subscriptions. With Garrison and others, Forten helped found a chapter of the American Anti-Slavery Society in Philadelphia in 1833.

James Forten and his wife, Charlotte Vandine, had three daughters (Mary Isabella, Margaretta, and Sarah) and three sons (Robert Bridges Forten, Thomas Francis Willing Forten, and James Forten Jr.). He died on March 4, 1842, at the age of seventy-six.

Steve Gilliland

References and further reading

Doughty, Ester M. 1968. *Forten the Sailmaker: Pioneer Champion of Negro Rights.* Chicago: Rand McNally.

Logan, Rayford W. 1982. "James Forten." In *Dictionary of American Negro Biography,* edited by Rayford W. Logan and Michael R. Winston, 234–235. New York: W. W. Norton.

Thomas, Lamont D. 2002. "Paul Cuffe and James Forten." In *Notable American Philanthropists: Biographies of Giving and Volunteering,* edited by Robert T. Grimm Jr., 61. Westport, CT: Oryx Press.

Winch, Julie. 2002. *A Gentleman of Color: The Life of James Forten.* New York: Oxford University Press.

Foundation Center

Founded in 1956, the Foundation Center is a leading authority on institutional philanthropy. Describing itself as the "Gateway to Philanthropy," the Foundation Center is dedicated to serving grantseekers, grantmakers, researchers, policy makers, the media, and the general public by supporting and improving institutional philanthropy and promoting understanding of the field. The Foundation Center fulfills its mission by providing educational and research support and broad-based access to information pertaining to the nonprofit sector.

The center collects, organizes, and disseminates information about philanthropy in the United States, conducts and facilitates research on trends in the field, and provides education and training for grantseekers. It accomplishes these goals through a variety of training programs and publications. Headquartered in New York City, the Foundation Center maintains field offices in Atlanta, Cleveland, San Francisco, and Washington, D.C. It operates a network of five professionally staffed libraries and learning centers with comprehensive research collections and offers information free of charge. Additionally, the libraries offer free and fee-based educational programs on topics including, but not limited to, grantseeking, proposal writing, and foundations, and they collaborate with representatives from the nonprofit sector to present programs of interest to the philanthropic community. Foundation Center publications include *The Foundation Center's Guide to Proposal Writing, The Foundation Directory,* and *The National Directory of Corporate Giving,* among others.

In addition to the five libraries, the Foundation Center supports a network of 217 Cooperating Collections located in public libraries and nonprofit resource centers. The Cooperating Collections offer free access to core Foundation Center print and electronic resources, and many sponsor local training programs.

The Foundation Center's educational programs are not limited to those offered throughout the United States at on-site locations. The center's content-rich Web site has become the principal means by which it delivers information and services to the nonprofit community and the general public. It assembles news from foundations, corporations, public charities, and other members of the nonprofit sector; publishes trend analysis; provides searchable access to Foundation Center databases, including *Literature of the Nonprofit Sector, The Foundation Directory Online,* and *Foundation Fundamentals;* supplies access to its Online Bookshelf; and offers instruction and technical assistance in the online Learning Lab. A range of available electronic research tools includes Foundation Finder, Sector Search, Grantmaker Web Sites, and 990-PF Search. Visitors requiring additional assistance can send e-mail reference questions to an online librarian.

The premier source for current news on philanthropy, the online journal *Philanthropy News Digest (PND)* containing job postings, conference notices, and a message board, is available via the center's Web site, as is the *RFP Bulletin,* which contains abstracts of requests for proposals from private funders and governmental agencies. Site visitors can obtain in-depth information by and about private foundations through links to its GrantSmart Web site; connections to the Associates Program Online extranet, a controlled-access site, enables direct communication with center staff.

The Foundation Center funds more than half of its expenses through income earned from publications and services. Approximately 600 foundations and corporations provide annual support, and special project grants fund the development of new services. The Foundation Center is not a membership organization; donors to the center, however, receive discounts on fee-based services and publications.

Lisa Browar

References and further reading
Foundation Center, http://www.fdncenter.org.

Foundation Payout

Foundation payout has been called the "engine that drives philanthropic grantmaking" (Rosa 2001, 4). Indeed, payout refers to the amount distributed annually by foundations and other grantmakers—typically as grants. Only private foundations, though, are required by law to meet specific payout guidelines. The Internal Revenue Code (IRC) specifies that the minimum payout required of a private foundation is 5 percent of net investment assets. This 5 percent payout is called a "qualifying distribution" and includes grants as well as administrative expenses related to program, program-related investments, and amounts set aside for future charitable projects.

The payout requirement of 5 percent sets a mandatory minimum distribution for all private foundations, assuring that a minimum amount of cash and/or property is distributed for charitable purposes each year. The rate is reasonable enough to allow for adequate support of charitable activities by foundations while still allowing foundations to maintain their ability to exist over the long term. The payout requirement must be met no later than twelve months following the end of the tax year in question. Any shortfall is subject to a penalty of 15 percent of the undistributed amount in addition to the required distribution. Private foundations may pay out an amount in excess of their required distribution without penalty, carrying such amounts forward and applying them in up to five later years.

Payout is calculated as 5 percent of the average value of the private foundation's assets, including the fair market value of all investment assets (based on readily available market quotations), the foundation's monthly cash balances, and all other assets not used directly in carrying out the foundation's tax-exempt purpose. Distributions by the foundation counting toward the 5 percent requirement are defined by the IRC as qualifying distributions and include any amount paid to accomplish the foundation's charitable purpose, including grants, reasonable administrative expenses, and program-related expenses. If the foundation has prior approval from the Internal Revenue Service (IRS), some amounts set aside for specific projects in the future may also count as qualifying distributions. Foundations may meet their payout requirements with distributions of cash and/or property.

Prior to 1969, the IRC did not specify a required amount of payout, rather holding that a private foundation would lose its tax-exempt status if it accumulated, in aggregate, income that was unreasonable to carry out charitable activities. Deemed vague and ineffective, this rule was changed by Congress through the Tax Reform Act of 1969, which not only established the initial payout requirements for private foundations, but also stipulated rules against excess business holdings and self-dealing. The act also created the excise tax on private foundation income and the requirements for private foundations to report annually to the IRS (via Form 990 PF). Until 1981, foundations were required to pay out the equivalent of their adjusted net income if such an amount was greater than the required payout percentage. This requirement greatly influenced the investment activities of foundations and was ultimately removed in 1981. The payout rate changed several times between 1969 and 1981 (ranging between 4.125 percent and 6 percent) before ultimately settling on 5 percent in 1981.

Debate about the most appropriate rate of payout for private foundations is common within the foundation community. During the late 1990s, the National Network of Grantmakers and the National Committee for Responsive Philanthropy led a campaign to encourage private foundations to voluntarily raise the rate of payout to 6 percent. This campaign was generally unsuccessful in the wake of poor stock market performance and lowered foundation investment returns in the early 2000s. Generally, foundations agree that the 5 percent payout rate is adequate to make charitable distributions and maintain the assets of the foundation over the long term.

Kym Mulhern

References and further reading

Freeman, David, and the Council on Foundations. 1991. *The Handbook on Private Foundations.* New York: Foundation Center.

Hopkins, Bruce. 1998. *The Law of Tax-Exempt Organizations.* New York: Wiley.

Rosa, Julio, ed. 2001. *Payout for Change.* San Diego: National Network of Grantmakers.

Foundations

See Community Foundations; Grantmaking; History of American Foundations; Institutional Foundations

Foundations and the Labor Movement

See Union Movement and Philanthropy

Franklin, Benjamin (1706–1790)

Recognized as one of America's most important founding fathers, Benjamin Franklin is hailed for his work as an author, printer, scientist, and diplomat. He is less recognized as an important early figure in American philanthropy, even though he constantly exhibited and promoted the value of collective voluntary action and associational life.

Born to Josiah and Abiah Folger Franklin in 1706, Benjamin Franklin grew up in Boston. Although the rest of his male siblings received training in trades, Franklin obtained some schooling in preparation for a career in the ministry. Unable to pay for more education, twelve-year-old Franklin apprenticed at his brother's printing business and pursued self-education in his spare time. In 1723, Franklin moved to Philadelphia, where he ultimately became famous for his *Poor Richard's Almanac* and the newspaper the *Pennsylvania Gazette*. In 1730, he began a common-law marriage with Deborah Reed. The couple had two children, and Franklin also fathered one illegitimate child. In the 1740s and 1750s, Franklin's wealth allowed him to focus on science. He became famous for numerous discoveries and inventions, including advances in the study of electricity.

While Franklin was becoming a successful businessman, he started the Junto Club in 1727. Influenced by Daniel Defoe's *An Essay upon Projects* (1697) and Cotton Mather's *Bonifacius: An Essay upon the Good* (1710), this mutual benefit society comprised Philadelphia tradesmen who attended a weekly meeting for socializing, self-improvement, and the betterment of their city. On the latter aspect, Franklin and his group implemented—over subsequent decades—numerous community improvements. With an ever-growing city and a weak government, they brought about the Library Company of Philadelphia (the first American subscription library), paved roads, a volunteer fire department, a city police force, and street lighting. Demonstrating his love of science, in 1744 Franklin founded the American Philosophical Soci-

Benjamin Franklin (1706–1790) (Perry-Castaneda Library)

ety, an association of scientists who shared ideas and results in the hope of producing benefits for society at large. Franklin also devoted substantial time to the creation of the Philadelphia Academy (later the University of Pennsylvania), which opened in 1751. Through innovative fundraising, offering private donors a matching grant from the Pennsylvania Assembly, Franklin also opened the Pennsylvania Hospital in 1752.

As the American Revolution developed, Franklin served in the Second Continental Congress and then traveled to France to acquire that country's crucial support for the colonists' cause. After the war, Franklin participated in the Constitutional Convention of 1787. That same year, he served as the president of the Pennsylvania Society for Promoting the Abolition of Slavery. Originally a slave owner, he became an abolitionist late in life. At his death in 1790, Franklin's will established two funds (for Boston and

Philadelphia) that would offer loans to young apprentices for the next 200 years. Unfortunately, Franklin could not have anticipated the societal changes that brought about the dramatic decline in apprenticeships, and thus his funds' inability, at times, to help anyone. Although Franklin is praised for exhibiting the virtues of associational life, philanthropist Julius Rosenwald and others have criticized his last charitable act as a prime example of the perils of "dead-hand" philanthropy.

Robert T. Grimm Jr.

References and further reading

Brands, H. W. 2000. *The First American: The Life and Times of Benjamin Franklin.* New York: Doubleday.

Grimm, Robert T, Jr. 2002. "Benjamin Franklin." In *Notable American Philanthropists: Biographies of Giving and Volunteering,* edited by Robert T. Grimm Jr., 99–103. Westport, CT: Oryx Press.

Wright, Esmond. 1986. *Franklin of Philadelphia.* Cambridge: Harvard University Press.

Friendly Societies

Friendly societies evolved in the nineteenth century in the industrial cities of Europe. As the name implies, the societies institutionalized networks of friends, neighbors, and coworkers. An important purpose was to pool resources and to manage the most damaging risks a working-class family could encounter—an incapacitating illness, a severe accident, or even the death of the breadwinner. Many households in the new factory towns had no extended families to help and no investments or possessions to sell if a tragedy befell the primary wage earner.

The lack of family help or financial reserves was also acute among immigrants in the United States, whether they settled in the cities or rural areas. Friendly societies, or fraternal societies, as they were called in the United States, held out the promise of creating new communal bonds and financial support systems. Shared experiences took the place of kinship ties. The same religion, the same nationality, or work in the same industry generated trust on which the new self-help or mutual aid endeavors could be built.

Over the years, the small-scale efforts were replaced by large health and life insurance programs as well as pension plans offered by the private sector.

Governments also took over some of the societies' roles through social security systems and publicly funded health care programs. However, some friendly or fraternal societies have remained financially viable into the present time.

In Britain, a series of laws provided the legal and organizational framework. The Friendly Societies Act of 1974 defines friendly societies as "voluntary, mutual organizations whose main purposes are assisting members (usually financially) during sickness, unemployment or retirement, and the provision of life insurance." The Friendly Societies Act of 1992 provides a comprehensive legal framework for the purposes and powers of friendly societies as well as for the organizational structure and mechanisms for governmental oversight.

In the United States, federal law regulates the tax-exempt status of all nonprofit entities, including fraternal societies, and state laws cover incorporation issues. Table 1 shows the two types of fraternal societies recognized by the Internal Revenue Service (IRS). Section 501(3)(8) entities under the Internal Revenue Code (IRC), called fraternal beneficiary societies and associations by the IRS, are primarily set up to manage personal risks through fraternal insurance programs and to provide for the elderly through annuity plans while also promoting brotherhood or sisterhood bonds through local lodges, clubs, or chapters. They may also conduct charitable or educational activities, contributions to which are tax-deductible if they are dedicated for purposes covered by 501(c)(3).

Section 501(c)(10) organizations, so-called domestic fraternal societies and associations, cannot offer insurance or other benefit plans to their members. Their major purpose is to offer conviviality through their lodge system or other local arrangements. Net earnings may go to charitable causes or other activities, and contributions are tax-deductible if they fall under the 501(c)(3) purposes.

There are similarities and differences between British friendly societies and American fraternal beneficiary societies. Both types of organizations subscribe to the self-help and mutual-aid principle in managing certain household risks, such as severe illnesses, catastrophic accidents, or the death of a family member. In addition to life and health insurance

Table 1 Fraternal Societies in the Internal Revenue Code

Section Code	Types of Organizations	Nature of Activities	Contributions Tax-Deductible?
501(c)(8)	Fraternal beneficiary societies and associations	Lodge providing for payment of life, sickness, accident, or other benefits to members.	Yes, if made for certain Sec. 501(c)(3) purposes*
501(c)(10)	Domestic fraternal societies and associations	Lodge devoting its net earnings to charitable, fraternal, and other specified purposes. No life, sickness, or accident benefits to members.	Yes, if made for certain Sec. 501(c)(3) purposes*

*Sec. 501(c)(3) purposes: religious, educational, charitable, scientific, literary, testing for public safety, to foster national or international amateur sports competition, or prevention of cruelty to children or animals.
Source: U.S. Internal Revenue Service, *Tax-Exempt Status for Your Organization,* Publication 557 (Washington, D.C.: U.S. Internal Revenue Service, 2001), p. 57 (http://www.irs.gov/forms_pubs/).

plans, some societies offer mortgages and annuities to their members. In both countries, early societies included a strong community-building dimension. Trust was important for a breadwinner to hand over a share, even a small one, of his meager income to a common pool in the expectation of some benefit in the unknown future. Even today, friendly or fraternal societies market themselves as deserving of trust by highlighting their longevity and the size of their membership.

A noteworthy difference between the British and American societies can be observed in the leadership as well as in the background of the members. In Britain, some of the impetus to form friendly societies came from the outside. One study found that members of the ruling elite perceived the poor as a threat to their own privileged lifestyle and supported self-help efforts as a way to reduce poverty (Gosden 1961). Favorable legislation encouraged industrial workers to join friendly societies, and trade unions, which did not enjoy such a favorable status, used the friendly society legislation to strengthen their own organizations (ibid.).

In contrast, the leadership to form fraternal societies in the United States came from the ranks of the members, who were farmers, professionals, and businessmen in addition to industrial workers. Also, some fraternities modeled their organizational structure on the secrecy and rituals of the Freemasons. Over the years, two types of fraternities evolved: "fraternal secret societies," which did not offer insurance benefits to their members, and "fraternal benefit societies," which focused on insurance programs. The different paths are reflected in the distinction made by the IRS between fraternal beneficiary societies and domestic fraternal societies.

The number of fraternal societies presently in the United States is difficult to gauge. The National Taxonomy of Exempt Entities—Core Codes, developed by the National Center for Charitable Statistics, has separate codes for fraternal beneficiary societies and domestic fraternal societies but publishes the data under the broad category of mutual/membership benefit organizations, which includes a diverse field of Section 501(c)(5) to 501(c)(27) entities. The comprehensive inventory of fraternal organizations taken by Alvin Schmidt in 1980 identifies about 450 societies. The number is not exact because information about some fraternities is difficult to obtain. They may not exist anymore, or they may be protective of their secret status and reluctant to share information.

In contrast, other fraternal societies make good use of the Internet as a marketing tool. This is seen as a necessity to attract new members. Whether a society falls into the fraternal benefit camp, the fraternal secret group, or somewhere in between, many have experienced stagnation or even a decline in membership. Future viability and vitality will depend on the ability of these societies either to make their present mission appealing to the next generation or to adapt their mission to meet new needs.

Siegrun Fox Freyss

References and further reading

Beito, David T. 2000. *From Mutual Aid to the Welfare State: Fraternal Societies and Social Services, 1890–1967.* Chapel Hill: University of North Carolina Press.

Gosden, P. H. J. H. 1961. *The Friendly Societies in England, 1815–1875.* Manchester, UK: Manchester University Press.

———. 1973. *Self-Help: Voluntary Associations in Nineteenth-Century Britain.* London: Batsford.

Hernandez, José Amaro. 1983. *Mutual Aid for Survival: The Case of the Mexican American.* Malabar, FL: Krieger.

Hopkins, Eric. 1995. *Working-Class Self-Help in Nineteenth Century England: Responses to Industrialisation.* Houndmills, UK: Palgrave Macmillan.

Hunt, Kimberly N. 2002. *Encyclopedia of Associations,* 38th ed. Vol. 1, *National Organizations of the U.S.* Farmington Hills, MI: Gale Group.

Registry of Friendly Societies, http://www.fsa.gov.uk/pubs/additional/rfsweb.pdf

Schmidt, Alvin J. 1980. *Fraternal Organizations.* Westport, CT: Greenwood.

Fraternal Societies

See Mutual Benefit Organizations

Fundraising

Fundraising can be traced back to biblical times (for example, the building of the tabernacle in Exodus), to classical Greece and Rome, to accounts of the Middle Ages, and to charitable acts and activities of Elizabethan England. In a mostly European and Judeo-Christian context, America grew up with the spirit of philanthropy. Private gifts from the wealthy in countries of origin helped to develop and sustain not just America's colonies but also its early institutions. Government support was also highly influential, but private generosity built the foundations of a philanthropic tradition in the United States.

Some authorities consider the fundraising efforts for the establishment of Harvard College in 1641 as the foundation of professional fundraising. Others also point to the College of William and Mary in Virginia, and still others believe that Jane Addams and the establishment of Hull-House in Chicago in 1889 signaled the beginning of organized philanthropy and fundraising.

Although philanthropy played a significant role in the history of the United States, fundraising as an organized and organizational function only dates back to the early 1900s. The early twentieth century is usually identified as the starting point of the professionalization of fundraising. This was partly due to the growth of paid staff, which changed the philanthropic landscape from one directed by volunteers to one of professionals who then directed volunteers. Scott M. Cutlip, who wrote the most definitive history of fundraising in the United States, said, "Organized philanthropy supported by systematic fundraising is a twentieth-century development in the United States. Philanthropy, in America's first three centuries, was carried along on a small scale, largely financed by the wealthy few in response to personal begging appeals" (Cutlip 1990 [1965], 3). According to Cutlip, World War I provided the foundation for organized fundraising; others, however, believe that the YMCA movement, which began in the early 1900s, actually provided the roots for modern fundraising. Some researchers identify distinct eras in twentieth-century fundraising, delineating both change and continuity in a historical context, but others give generational views or ignore the historical context altogether.

Much of what is considered to be standard practice in fundraising actually began as innovative techniques created to meet certain needs. Prior to World War I, fundraising was still quite unorganized and haphazard. Philanthropy was usually the domain of the wealthiest. During this period, the need to reduce the requests to the few identifiable donors caused federated fundraising agencies to emerge. Eventually, fundraising began to involve increasing numbers of citizens, particularly in the area of social welfare where organizations and people had already been active (for example, in black churches and through women volunteers). At this time, fundraising was the function of nonspecialists and volunteers.

Among those who began to lay the groundwork for formalized fundraising were Lyman L. Pierce and Charles Sumner Ward, who have been credited with developing the campaign method for the Young Men's Christian Associations (YMCAs). Others active during this era were individuals who served as leaders of alumni associations, such as William

Lawrence, volunteer president for Harvard's association. Included in this era should be evangelists such as Dwight L. Moody and Frederick T. Gates. The latter was able to solicit John D. Rockefeller for a major gift to establish a major institution—the University of Chicago. The first commercial fundraising firm was established by Frederick Courtenay Barber in 1913, but because he charged a commission, his place in the historical annals is usually discounted. The progenitors of today's consulting firms were established in approximately 1919.

In spite of ongoing activity prior to World War I, fundraising was mostly associated with YMCAs. Only as Ward and Pierce began to tutor others did the understanding of fundraising as a function and service expand. Ward is quoted in Cutlip as having said, "I would leave this work immediately if I thought I were merely raising money. It is raising men that appeals to me" (1990 [1965], 43). The American Red Cross War Council was created at the beginning of the war with the purpose of conducting fundraising for relief efforts. Ward and Pierce, on loan from the YMCA, were hired to help with this effort, and they raised record amounts of money. Another significant figure emerged during this time, John Price Jones, the first to combine experience in newspapers and public relations with fundraising. The YMCA's form of fundraising, which focused on Christian values and stewardship, and Jones's businesslike approach to fundraising now joined to provide a foundation for modern fundraising—a combination of vision and mission with commercial overtones.

After World War I, consultants became more predominant in fundraising. In September 1919, the firm of Ward, Hill, Pierce and Wells was established. This team included recognizable, famous names, and therefore business was brisk. Others who had gained experience in the YMCA and Red Cross campaigns now became the first wave of fundraising counsel—the pioneers. At this time several changes took place in the fundraising field. First, the fixed fee, rather than commission-based fundraising, became accepted. Second, in spite of the name recognition of many who established or worked for fundraising firms, the idea that the consultant must remain in the background so that attention could be focused on the organization

came into fashion. Third, the literature in fundraising received a boost in 1966 when Harold "Si" Seymour, who worked for the John Price Jones company, codified a standard practices volume that became the first training manual in fundraising history (Seymour 1993).

This era of fundraising consultants slowed down with the Great Depression. The campaigns, which had taken an identifiable format, faded, although Americans still gave, particularly for relief programs. Philanthropy now ceased to be the domain of the wealthy, and the average citizen joined with government to provide relief. Because these were desperate days, fundraising practices took on some questionable aspects. As a result, the American Association of Fundraising Counsel (AAFRC) was established in 1935 to preserve the integrity and promote the dignity of fundraising. The founders of the AAFRC, pioneers of fundraising as an organized activity, attempted to position fundraising as a philanthropic effort, an endeavor that saw a merging of ideological and philosophical ideals with sound business practices.

Fundraising matured greatly between the two world wars. At the beginning of World War II, the Red Cross began a blood donor program; this was the result of increasing government intervention in relief funding, which meant the Red Cross's traditional services were no longer required. Because the Red Cross adapted to change and raised great sums of money, Cutlip called it the greatest fundraiser of modern times (1990 [1965]).

After World War II, the example of the Red Cross caused many other institutions to begin raising money, and for the first time in-house staff began to be hired. This was particularly true for colleges and universities, where administrators saw the need for more funds and increased goals and recognized the need for professionalism to accomplish this. During the post–World War II period, the need for fundraising campaigns soared and organizations began to seriously compete for charitable dollars. Much happened in fundraising, perhaps too much and too fast. There was little understanding of professional fundraising in the general public. America's ongoing discrepancy of opinion and feeling—sympathy for causes but antipathy for fundraisers—may have begun at this point. Lack of standards caused an understandable mistrust of fundraisers, although the public usually exercised its charitable impulses anyway.

The 1950s saw an increase in federal funding programs. The government poured out funds in greater amounts than philanthropy had contributed, yet when the funding programs closed down, private donors who had become accustomed to government programs were not ready to close the gap. The nation did not recover from this effect until the late 1970s.

In 1960, an influential and significant organization was established to serve the growing number of practitioners—the National Society of Fund Raisers, renamed the National Society of Fund Raising Executives in 1978 and renamed again in 2001 as the Association of Fundraising Professionals (AFP). This organization ushered in the era of staff fundraisers, which continues until today. Nonprofit organizations set up development departments and conducted annual and capital campaigns, many of them multimillion-dollar ones. The practice of placing resident consultants from fundraising firms at institutions began to fade with this influx of permanent staff, and consultants became campaign advisers instead. More associations were also founded during this era, with the most recognizable being the Association for Healthcare Philanthropy, established in 1967. One final landmark of the 1960s was the Tax Reform Act of 1969, which subjected charitable organizations to new regulations.

An expansion of fundraising strategies, such as telethons and door-to-door methods, characterized the 1970s. The Council for the Advancement and Support of Education was formed in 1974, and in that same year The Fund Raising School was established by Hank Rosso, Joe Mixer, and Lyle Cook. This was probably the first formalized training available for fundraising practitioners. In the 1970s there was also an increase in government oversight. These highlights of fundraising history show that the knowledge about philanthropy and the organizations that employ fundraisers increased considerably.

The 1980s brought an influx of fundraisers into the nonprofit arena. Much of this was due to government funding cutbacks. Public educational institutions began to seek support from private funds, something many initially resisted, and the race to compete became fierce. The fundraising function was internalized by this time, with consultants serving an advisory role. In 1980, INDEPENDENT SECTOR was established. This organization has been successful in representing donors and fundraisers and has served in an advocacy role. Its formation marked a turning point for donors and fundraising professionals, who began to work more collaboratively to achieve their mutual goals.

Many changes occurred in fundraising in the 1990s, including the following:

- Increased professionalism in fundraising, with a proliferation of courses and training programs
- Development of a body of research and literature providing a theoretical and practical base for the profession
- Intensified demand for accountability by nonprofits
- Consistent increases in philanthropic giving (although never higher than 2 percent of the gross domestic product [GDP])
- Growth in the number of nonprofit organizations
- Greater public interest in philanthropy and understanding of the nonprofit sector
- More scrutiny of the sector and its organizations, and therefore increased criticism
- A vast jump in the number of publications related to the nonprofit sector and philanthropy
- A shift in how individuals enter the profession; that is, increased participation in formal educational programs in fundraising as a way of entering the profession
- Greater use of technology in fundraising, particularly the Internet
- Changes in the characteristics and behaviors of donors

The professionalization of fundraising began to receive serious attention in the 1990s. Considerable headway has been made in the fundraising field to bolster the argument that it is a profession. There is a growing, credible pool of knowledge on which fundraisers base their practice; professional development opportunities are numerous; the need for special skills is readily acknowledged; collegiality is generally an expected behavior and organizations such as AFP and other professional associations foster this; ethical practice is a qualification for membership in professional associations; and more attention is placed on the service aspect of fundraising than ever before.

Most people enter the fundraising field because it is an environment that serves human needs—needs that are not served by the business and government sectors. People want to heal, to educate, to preserve cultures, to shelter the abused, to inspire, and to preserve. Other objectives may certainly be worthwhile, such as career advancement, involvement in a specific field of interest, and working in a field that has such a significant impact on nonprofit causes, but belief in the causes that a fundraising professional serves is of primary importance. Fundraising should touch souls, not just of those served, but of the professional as well. Fundraising, or development, as some prefer to call it, is a fundamental part of the process that makes institutions successful.

For the fundraiser, satisfaction is derived from results, often intangible or invisible for some time into the future, not from recognition. An orientation to public service is critical and should be a significant motivation for entering the profession. Idealism and enthusiasm must be balanced with accountability, businesslike behavior, and practical action. At the bottom of all is this reality: Most work in the nonprofit sector, whether it is advocacy, healing, educating, entertaining, preserving, or some other activity, will not just happen unless someone brings in money. And the more fundraising is integrated into the entire organization, the more successful it will be.

In this integration process, the roles fundraising plays in an organization can be several. Kathleen S. Kelly's (1998) qualitative study on fundraising roles explaining how practitioners carry out job responsibilities identified four variations in practitioner behavior—liaison, expert prescriber, technician, and problem-solving process facilitator. The liaison role is a traditional one in which the practitioner coordinates, facilitates, and interprets when organizational representatives meet with prospective donors. The expert prescriber assumes responsibility for raising money and does it with great skill, but others are left out of the process. The technician is not part of the management team but produces and implements the techniques and strategies needed in the process, such as use of the Internet for fundraising. The problem-solving process facilitator is a member of the management team and is knowledgeable about as well as involved in the organization's management.

Although Kelly called for more research to verify and substantiate these findings, seasoned professionals would acknowledge that every fundraiser must, at one time or another, function in all four roles. Perhaps this is one of the challenges of fundraising as a career. But it is also one of its benefits. Various roles are appropriate for various organizations, and a person's strengths can be utilized in more than one way.

Lilya Wagner

References and further reading

Broce, Thomas E. 1986. *Fund Raising*, 2d ed. Norman: University of Oklahoma Press.

Ciconte, Barbara Kushner, and Jeanne G. Jacob. 1997. *Fund Raising Basics: A Complete Guide.* Gaithersburg, MD: Aspen.

Cutlip, Scott M. 1990 [1965]. *Fundraising in the United States: Its Role in America's Philanthropy.*, New Brunswick, NJ: Transaction.

Duronio, Margaret A., and Eugene Tempel. 1996. *Fund Raisers: Their Careers, Stories, Concerns, and Accomplishments.* San Francisco: Jossey-Bass.

Gurin, Maurice G. 1985. *Confessions of a Fund Raiser.* Rockville, MD: Taft Group.

Kelly, Kathleen S. c. 1998. *Effective Fund-raising Management.* Mahwah, NJ: Lawerence Erlbaum Associates.

———. 1998. "Four Organizational Roles of Fundraisers: An Exploratory Study." Paper presented at the Association for Research on Nonprofit Organizations and Voluntary Action, 27th Annual Conference, Seattle, November 5.

Mixer, Joseph R. 1993. *Principles of Professional Fundraising.* San Francisco: Jossey-Bass.

Olcott, William A. 1998. *Make a Note of It: Wit and Wisdom from Fund Raisers for Fund Raisers.* Chicago: Bonus Books.

Tempel, Eugene R., Sara B. Cobb, and Warren F. Ilchman, eds. 1997. "The Professionalization of Fundraising." *New Directions for Philanthropic Fundraising* no. 15 (Spring).

Rosso, Henry A. 1996. *Rosso on Fund Raising: Lessons from a Master's Lifetime Experience.* New York: Jossey-Bass.

Schwartz, John J. 1994. *Modern American Philanthropy: A Personal Account.* New York: Wiley.

Seymour, Harold J. 1993. *Designs for Fund-Raising,* 2d ed. Rockville, MD: Fundraising Institute (a division of The Taft Group).

Wagner, Lilya. 2001. *Careers in Fundraising.* New York: Wiley.

Fundraising as a Profession

Fundraising in the twenty-first century is practiced according to proven technical standards and guided by generally accepted ethical standards. Fundraising is more formal and pervasive in the U.S. philanthropic world than in most other countries but is growing globally as well.

Historically, fundraising was an informal, volunteer activity, and informal, volunteer fundraising at the grassroots level continues today. However, formal, organized fundraising, involving volunteers and managed by paid professionals, has become an important structure in nonprofit organizations. Fundraisers today, whether volunteer or paid, use a variety of techniques that evolved from early practices. The case statement, a presentation of needs for potential donors, is a key tool. The technique was being used as early as 1643, when two volunteers used a piece called "America's First Fruits" as a case statement to raise funds in England for Harvard College. Benjamin Franklin raised funds for libraries, a hospital, and a university by asking colonists to give according to their means and seeking the largest gifts first. Two important technical standards used today, the gift range chart and sequential solicitation, evolved from this practice. Many of the management practices used in modern fundraising can be traced to Charles Sumner Ward and Lyman L. Pierce, who raised funds for the Young Men's Christian Association at the turn of the twentieth century. Their "campaign" methods were followed by others, and fundraising at the turn of the twenty-first century is indebted to their innovations.

The last quarter of the twentieth century saw a doubling in the number of nonprofit organizations in the United States and significant growth in paid professional fundraising. Fundraising began as a consultant relationship to nonprofit organizations but is primarily an organization-based practice today. The Association of Fundraising Professionals (AFP) (formerly the National Society of Fund Raising Executives) grew from 1,899 members in 1979 to 24,429 members in 2000. It has chapter members in the United States, Canada, Mexico, and around the globe. Similar organizations exist in Austria, Australia, Argentina, Brazil, Germany, New Zealand, South Africa, Switzerland, and other countries. What began as a male-dominated activity has become a female-dominated activity today. More than 60 percent of those doing fundraising are women, and women are entering the field at a rate of three to one compared to men. Although women did much of the fundraising work for charitable organizations forty or fifty years ago, they did so as volunteers; today, they have professional careers in fundraising that often require college degrees.

Scholars from such disciplines as history, marketing, sociology, psychology, and philosophy have built a knowledge base to support the technical and ethical standards that fundraisers practice. Sophisticated marketing techniques often influence direct mail, telemarketing, and e-mail solicitation of small gifts from large numbers of individuals around the globe. Standards exist for approaching professionally run corporate giving and foundation grantmaking programs, and theoretical models, such as the philanthropic identification model (Schervish 1997), support fundraising structures.

Fundraisers disagree about whether fundraising is a profession or a field striving toward being a profession. Fundraisers are not yet able to control entry to the field as some professions can, and only the most senior practitioners have the influence and autonomy that is usually accorded a profession. But on many other fronts, fundraisers have achieved professional status. They tend to have a service mentality and are more generous than other individuals with their time and money. They utilize a growing body of knowledge. And there are university-based programs to help new fundraisers become educated about philanthropy, the nonprofit sector, nonprofit management, donor behavior, and fundraising.

Common to all fundraisers around the globe is the acceptance of a code of ethics. The AFP code of ethical standards was adopted in 1964. Fundraising groups around the world have adopted or adapted the AFP code, and the AFP Ethics Committee penalizes those who violate it. But not all fundraisers belong to a professional organization, and volunteers and amateurs practice in the same arenas as those who consider themselves professionals.

At the beginning of the twenty-first century, the profession faces opportunities and challenges. Growing wealth and income in the United States and other countries have created opportunities for increased philanthropy, and nonprofit organizations are recruiting fundraisers to secure philanthropy. The supply of available fundraisers, however, cannot meet the demand. This has meant both increased salaries for fundraisers and increased needs for training and acculturation as practitioners from other fields have been recruited to fundraising positions.

There is evidence that the traditional models of fundraising are challenged by new donors. In the past, the philosophy of fundraising was based on a worthy case for support, and fundraisers represented organizations with a good cause in search of donors. Today, in contrast, donors with an interesting idea or project often seek a willing organization to carry it out. Concepts such as venture philanthropy, social entrepreneurship, and supply-side philanthropy are becoming more widespread and need careful study by fundraisers.

Eugene R. Tempel

References and further reading

Burlingame, Dwight F., and Lamont J. Hulse. 1991. *Taking Fundraising Seriously.* San Francisco: Jossey-Bass.

Duronio, Margaret A. 1997. "The Fund Raising Profession." In *Critical Issues in Fund Raising,* edited by D. F. Burlingame, 37–57. New York: Wiley.

Duronio, Margaret A., and Eugene R. Tempel. 1997. *Fund Raisers: Their Careers, Stories, Concerns, and Accomplishments.* San Francisco: Jossey-Bass.

Schervish, Paul G. 1997. "Inclination, Obligation, and Association: What We Know and What We Need to Learn about Donor Motivation." In *Critical Issues in Fund Raising,* edited by D. F. Burlingame, 110–138. New York: Wiley.

Tempel, Eugene R., and Matthew J. Beem. 2002. "The State of the Profession." In *New Strategies for Educational Fund Raising,* edited by M. Worth. Washington, DC: American Council on Education/ Greenwood Publications.

Wagner, Lilya. 2002. *Careers in Fundraising.* New York: Wiley.

G

Gallaudet, Thomas Hopkins (1787–1851)

Born in 1787 in Hartford, Connecticut, Thomas Hopkins Gallaudet is most remembered for his charitable work in educating the deaf. He attended Yale and the Andover Theological Seminary and intended to become an itinerant preacher until, upon returning to his boyhood home in 1814, he encountered his neighbor's nine-year-old deaf daughter, who was unable to read or communicate in any way. Cognizant of the value of quality education, Gallaudet was inspired to learn how to teach the deaf.

His neighbor convinced him to travel to Europe to study how the deaf were taught in England and France. In London, Gallaudet met the Braidwood family, who ran a school for the deaf, but they insisted that Gallaudet would have to spend three years learning their secret method and then swear to keep the secret to himself. Dissatisfied with this option, Gallaudet sought the guidance of Abbe Sicard, head of the Institut Royal des Sourds-Muets in Paris, who was in London to demonstrate his school's method. Sicard was willing to teach the method to Gallaudet. In France, Gallaudet made close acquaintance with two deaf faculty members at the Institut Royal—Laurent Clerc and Jean Massieu—the former of whom would return with him to Hartford.

The school that Gallaudet established is unique in the history of charitable institutions because his was the first to receive funds from a state legislature (Fenner 1944, 51). That money, combined with support from private subscriptions, led to the opening of the first permanent school for the deaf on April 15, 1817. Originally named the American Asylum at Hartford for the Education and Instruction of the Deaf and Dumb, the school today is known as the American School for the Deaf. Gallaudet served there as principal from 1817 until 1830 and then resigned in order to write children's books and return to preaching.

As Gallaudet entered the twilight of his life, two of his sons took up his beloved cause of educating the deaf. Thomas, the eldest son, founded St. Ann's Church for the Deaf in New York; the younger son, Edward Miner Gallaudet, founded the Columbia Institution for the Education of the Deaf and Dumb and Blind in Washington, D.C. The only location for higher education of deaf students in the world, the Columbia Institution was later named Gallaudet University in honor of Thomas Hopkins Gallaudet. He only accepted having the school named after him because of a petition signed by graduates urging him to do so. Gallaudet continued to champion various education reforms, especially that of professionalizing the vocation of teaching. He served as chaplain at the Retreat, a Harvard insane asylum; while there, Gallaudet came to believe that proper education in hygienic facilities could help prevent insanity among the young (Fenner 1944, 56).

Thomas Gallaudet (1787–1851) (Corbis)

Well-regarded by his peers, humble in his actions, and compassionate toward the disadvantaged, Gallaudet was a model for nineteenth-century Christian benevolence. He continued to write numerous articles and deliver lectures until his death on September 10, 1851.

Emily M. Hall

References and further reading
Degering, Etta. 1968. *Gallaudet, Friend of the Deaf.* New York: D. McKay.

Fenner, Mildred Sandison, and Eleanor C. Fishburn. 1944. *Pioneer American Educators.* Port Washington, NY: Kennikat.

Neimark, Anne E. 1983. *A Deaf Child Listened: Thomas Gallaudet, Pioneer in American Education.* New York: Morrow.

"Thomas Hopkins Gallaudet." Gallaudet University Web site, http://pr.gallaudet.edu/visitorscenter/GallaudetHistory/ (cited December 13, 2002).

Garcia, Hector Perez (1914–1996)

Dr. Hector Perez Garcia led the Latino civil rights movement a decade before there was national recognition of minority rights. Having grown up in a hostile Texan border town, Dr. Hector, as he was commonly known, held fast to the founding documents of American democracy. Spurred by his deeply held belief in equal rights for all under the laws of the nation, he was moved to action by the injustices he experienced as a young man and, later, as a military physician.

Born in 1914 in Llera, Tamaulipas State, Mexico, Garcia was four years old when his family immigrated to Mercedes, Texas, to flee the Mexican Revolution. He and five of his siblings earned medical degrees at a time when the average Mexican American in Texas earned only a third-grade education. By the time the United States had entered World War II, Dr. Hector had earned his M.D. and completed his surgical residency. As an army doctor stationed in Italy, Garcia was awarded a Bronze Star medal with six battle stars. Upon the conclusion of the war, he returned to Texas to help veterans receive their military benefits. To many Mexican American veterans who could not access the military health system, Dr. Hector was more than a medical adviser, he was an advocate.

The story of Army Private Felix Longoria exposed the pervasive and accepted bigotry of Texans in the national media. Private Longoria had died during a volunteer mission in the Philippines in 1944 and was scheduled by his family to be reinterred in his Texas hometown. Yet, when his wife tried to have his funeral services at the local cemetery, the funeral director upheld the long-standing policy of separate facilities for Mexican Americans. Private Longoria had died serving his country yet was barred from a respectful funeral service on account of racial prejudice. His wife could not stand for it and immediately contacted Dr. Hector, who had by this time established himself as a champion of veteran rights in the community. After involving the national press, Dr. Hector received the support of then-Senator Lyndon Baines Johnson. With the backing of Senator Johnson, Private Longoria was eventually buried at Arlington National Cemetery.

Mrs. Longoria's experience in putting her husband to rest was simply one of the many indignities that

Mexican Americans endured in 1940s Texas. In order to ensure civil rights for all veterans and their families, Dr. Hector founded the American G.I. Forum. The agency started with veteran rights as its focus but quickly expanded to include other basic interests such as access to education, human rights, and voting rights.

During the Johnson presidency, Dr. Hector served on the U.S. Commission on Civil Rights. He was appointed U.S. alternate ambassador to the United Nations in 1967. Among his numerous awards, Dr. Hector received the Medal of Freedom in 1984, becoming one of only three Hispanics to receive this honor.

Until his death on July 26, 1996, Dr. Hector continued to serve as a Latino advocate. Two years later, Congress chartered the American G.I. Forum, placing the agency side by side with organizations such as the American Legion. The Mexican government bestowed the Aztec Eagle, its highest award, upon him in the same year. The American G.I. Forum is now headquartered in Denver, Colorado. Its membership, which exceeds 160,000, carries the civil rights torch—lighted by Dr. Hector—to this day.

Susan Haber

Mary Garrett (1853–1915) (Bettmann/Corbis)

References and further reading

Avila, Alex. 1997. "Freedom Fighter." *Hispanic* (January/February): 18.

Harris, Joyce Saenz. 1990. "Hector P. Garcia: When It's Time to Pull Some Strings, They Call Him 'Dr. Hector'; Civil Rights Leader and Founder of the American G.I. Forum." *Dallas Morning News,* August 19, 1990, 1E.

Hector Perez Garcia. Papers. Mary and Jeff Bell Library, Special Collections and Archives Department, Texas A&M University, Corpus Christi, Texas, http://www.sga .utmb.edu/ulams/drgarcia.

Garrett, Mary Elizabeth (1853–1915)

Mary Elizabeth Garrett was born in Baltimore, Maryland, on March 5, 1853. A strong supporter of education for women, she was instrumental in building institutions that encouraged financial and political independence for women and "used her wealth as a bargaining chip to push for women's suffrage and to advance women's roles in medicine and higher education" (Sander 2001). Her parents were both from mercantile families in Baltimore, and her father was president of the Baltimore and Ohio Railroad. Garrett studied with private tutors and traveled widely abroad with her parents, sometimes serving as her father's secretary.

Garrett was a volunteer to the Woman's Industrial Exchange, a national effort to improve women's financial status through the sale of clothing, baked goods, and other items made by women. She became the founding director of the Woman's Industrial Exchange of Baltimore in 1880. Garrett inherited one-third of her father's fortune as Baltimore and Ohio Railroad titan upon his death in 1884, becoming at age thirty-one one of the wealthiest single women in the United States. She then began to fund other philanthropic interests. Along with a group of women friends who shared her interest in education, social change, and philanthropy, including M. Carey Thomas, Mary Mackall Gwinn, Elizabeth T. King, and Julia Rogers, she helped to establish Bryn Mawr

School for Girls, a girls' college preparatory school, in 1885. Named after the women's college of which Thomas was then dean, Bryn Mawr School increased the educational opportunities for young women in Baltimore. Garrett donated $400,000 for the project and was involved in the school's construction.

Garrett was also instrumental in opening Johns Hopkins Medical School in 1889, making her gifts contingent on the school being open to women from the beginning. This was the university that, ten years earlier, in 1877, had rejected her friend Thomas from attending classes. Garrett's first offer of a donation of $35,000 with these contingencies was rejected. This did not stop her from fighting for admission of women to the medical school. Thomas's father and Garrett's father were both trustees of Johns Hopkins; Gwinn's father was the executor of Johns Hopkins's will. Garrett and Thomas organized the Women's Medical School Fund in 1890 with notable key women supporters such as First Lady Caroline Scott Harrison; writer Sarah Orne Jewett; Jane Stanford, wife of Leland Stanford (the founder of Stanford University and a U.S. senator); and abolitionist Julia Ward Howe, among others.

Garrett's practice of "coercive philanthropy," making gifts with conditions and restrictions, eventually had results. When she personally added to her initial gift offer more than $300,000, the school finally accepted her conditions and agreed to enroll women. Her stipulations for her final gifts to Johns Hopkins included equal admissions policies and privileges for women and men in medical education; the admissions prerequisite of a bachelor's degree with a background in the sciences and languages; and a graduate, four-year degree program. Her coercive philanthropy had the effect of raising the qualitative level of U.S. medical schools in the late nineteenth century, which until then included few requirements and provided limited medical training.

In 1906, Garrett became a director of Bryn Mawr College. She gave approximately $350,000 to the college in her lifetime, most of it after 1894, when Thomas was named college president. Her contributions constituted 10 percent of Bryn Mawr's annual budget, made up for deficits, and supported many endeavors at the college (Horowitz 1994, 257, 276).

Garrett was also a suffragist. She was active in the fundraising effort for a permanent endowment for the National American Woman Suffrage Association, raising $12,000 a year for five years. In addition, she served as chairperson of the finance committee of the national College Women's Equal Suffrage League.

In her lifetime she donated more than $1.5 million to causes promoting women's suffrage and high standards for education for women and men. Garrett died of leukemia in 1915, leaving her mansion to the Hopkins School of Medicine. In 1923, the mansion became the first home of the Baltimore Museum of Art. She left the remaining $500,000 of her fortune to M. Carey Thomas.

Rebecca Roth

References and further reading
"Garrett, Mary Elizabeth." Women in American History, Encyclopedia Britannica, http://search.eb.com/women/articles/Garrett_Mary_Elizabeth.html.
"History of Bryn Mawr," http://www.brynmawr.pvt.k12.md.us/about/history.aspx (cited December 3, 2002).
Horowitz, Helen Lefkowitz. 1994. *The Power and Passion of M. Carey Thomas.* Urbana: University of Illinois Press.
James, Edward T., Janet Wilson James, and Paul S. Boyer, eds. 1971. *Notable American Women, 1607–1950: A Biographical Dictionary.* Vol. 2. Cambridge: Belknap Press of Harvard University Press.
"Mary Garrett." http://www.mdarchives.state.md.us/msa/speccol/photos/philanthropy/html/mgarrett.htm (cited December 3, 2002).
McCall, Nancy, and Elizabeth M. Peterson. 2002. "Mary Elizabeth Garrett." In *Notable American Philanthropists: Biographies of Giving and Volunteering*, edited by Robert T. Grimm Jr., 107–112. Westport, CT: Oryx Press.
Rossiter, Margaret W. 1982. "Doctorates for American Women, 1868–1907." *History of Education Quarterly* 22 (Summer): 159–183.
Sander, Kathleen Waters. 2001. "Trailblazer for Women Doctors: Mary Garrett and the Women's Medical School Fund Transformed Medical Education." *The Baltimore Sun*, March 4, 1C.
Worthington, Janet Farrar. 1998. "The Other Feminist." *Hopkins Medical News* (Fall): http://www.hopkinsmedicine.org/hmn/F98/feminist.html (cited December 3, 2002).

Garvey, Marcus Mosiah, Jr. (1887–1940)

Marcus Mosiah Garvey Jr. was born in 1887 to Marcus Mosiah Garvey Sr. and Sara Jane Richards in St. Ann's Bay, Jamaica. His father was a mason and his

Marcus Garvey Jr. (1887–1940) (Library of Congress)

America over the next few years, Garvey published many pamphlets and articles in order to cultivate and express his thoughts on the plight of blacks throughout the world. It was not until coming to the United States on March 24, 1916, however, that his homegrown ideology became an accepted philosophy, "Garveyism." A fusion of personal success with racial uplift, it quickly grew in popularity among American blacks.

In July 1918, Garvey organized the New York chapter of the Universal Negro Improvement Association (UNIA). This organization began with thirteen members in a small Harlem lodge and within five years catapulted to a million members. Garvey preached economic independence and the return to Africa as a solution for "Negro" preservation. In August 1919, the UNIA laid the foundation for a steamship company, the Black Star Line (BSL), which made several voyages to the Caribbean and Central America. The purposes of BSL were to supply a means of transportation for the "Back to Africa Movement" and to give blacks an entity in which they could invest and take pride. The UNIA also created the Negro Factory Corporation to promote businesses within the black community. The Universal Black Cross Nurses, Universal African Motors Corps, and the Black Flying Eagles were prominent examples.

The first to introduce large-scale ethnic pride philanthropy, Garvey was not only a motivator and leader but an excellent fundraiser in the black community and also among whites. He was able to raise funds for the UNIA's capital fund program from prominent people such as the president of Columbia University, banker William C. Ritter, physicians, and many other philanthropists. Through his charismatic personality, Garvey was able to make several tours throughout the United States to raise funds in order to support racial pride among black races.

Garvey was immensely popular and able to motivate the masses emotionally and financially. U.S. government officials feared his efforts and the influence he had in the black community. On January 12, 1921, he was arrested and convicted for alleged mail fraud. He spent two years in an Atlanta prison and was then deported back to Jamaica.

After his deportation, Garvey went to London to establish a temporary Universal Negro Improvement

mother a domestic worker. Coming from extremely modest means, Garvey was forced to leave school at the age of fourteen to work as a printer's apprentice. As a captivating black leader who organized the first American black nationalist movement and "awakened a race consciousness that made Harlem felt around the world" (Powell 1938, 71), Garvey was able to establish and fund several nonprofit organizations and schools in order to propel blacks to the forefront of the world society during the early part of the twentieth century.

Mostly self-taught, his early education was obtained from Standard 6, a Church of England school in Jamaica. As a young adult in London, he attended Birbeck College. There, and in Jamaica and Central

Association headquarters. Between 1928 and 1935, he traveled back and forth from London to Jamaica and published a newspaper called *New Negro World*. In 1935, Garvey, with his wife and children, settled in London. He died there on June 10, 1940.

Mamie L. Jackson

References and further reading

Hill, Robert A., ed. c. 1983. "The Marcus Garvey and Universal Negro Improvement Association Papers." Vols. 1–7. Berkeley: University of California Press.

"History." Marcus Garvey Cultural Center, University of Northern Colorado, http://www.unco.edu/garvey/history.htm (cited October 27, 2001).

"The Marcus Garvey and UNIA Papers Project." University of California at Los Angeles, http://www.isop.ucla.edu/mgpp/default.htm (cited October 27, 2001).

Powell, Adam Clayton, Sr. 1938. *Against the Tide: An Autobiography*. New York: Richard R. Smith.

Gates, William H., III (1955–), and the Bill and Melinda Gates Foundation

William H. Gates III, history's youngest self-made billionaire and cofounder of Microsoft Corporation, did not intend to pursue philanthropy actively until he retired, but his visits to Africa and a 1993 World Development Report about massive health inequalities around the globe led him to found the world's largest foundation, the Bill and Melinda Gates Foundation ($23 billion in assets in 2002). By the age of forty-five, Bill Gates had already donated—in today's dollars—more than seven times what Andrew Carnegie gave in his lifetime.

Bill Gates was born to William and Mary Maxwell Gates on October 28, 1955, in Seattle, Washington. His father was an attorney with Preston, Gates and Ellis, and his mother, now deceased, was a schoolteacher, a University of Washington Regent, and chairwoman of United Way International. Bill Gates, or "Trey," as his family called him, grew up with two sisters and attended public elementary school and the private Lakeside School, where he and close friend Paul Allen discovered computers. By the age of thirteen, they were earning money writing programs, a passion they continued through college. As a junior at Harvard University, Gates wrote a version of the pro-

gramming language BASIC for personal computers, then dropped out to found Microsoft with Allen. Gates continues as chairman and chief software architect of Microsoft Corporation.

In 1994, Gates married Dallas native Melinda French, a program manager at Microsoft. They have three children, Jennifer (1996), Rory (1999), and Phoebe (2002). At a bridal luncheon for the couple, Bill Gates's mother challenged them: "From those who are given great resources, great things are expected" (Strouse 2000, 61). As the thirty-eight-year-old Bill told *Playboy* magazine later that year, he intended to eventually give away 95 percent of his wealth, but not until he was in his fifties. He did, however, establish the William H. Gates Foundation in 1994, focusing on global health and projects in the Pacific Northwest, which his father managed out of cardboard boxes in his basement. In 1997, Gates tapped former Microsoft executive Patty Stonesifer to head a second foundation, the Gates Learning Foundation, dedicated to providing computers with Internet access to every public library serving low-income communities in the United States and Canada. Despite some critics' concerns that this initiative was aimed merely at creating future Microsoft customers, the foundation pursued its goal of Internet access in every community by 2003.

In 1993, Bill Gates was "stunned" by a World Development Report that showed that 11 million children die every year from preventable causes (Gates 2002). Further reading and visits to Africa in the mid-1990s brought home to the Gateses the health inequalities of developing nations. "The world's poorest 2 billion people desperately need health care, not laptops," Bill Gates said (Sims 2000). Bill and Melinda Gates had found a focus for their philanthropy. "I saw a cause I believed in. Seeing how urgent the needs are changed my time line," Gates said ("Saint Bill," 2001, 16). In 1999, the two Gates foundations were folded into the Bill and Melinda Gates Foundation, which focuses on four areas: global health, education, libraries, and Pacific Northwest giving.

The informal structure of the original organizations remain. Bill and Melinda Gates personally read and approve all grants of more than $1 million, and both travel and speak widely on behalf of the founda-

Bill Gates (right) tours a library that has received a gift of Gates Foundation–funded computers. (Reuters/Jeff Christensen; Reuters/Corbis)

tion. Meanwhile, day-to-day operations are handled by cochairs Stonesifer and William Gates Sr., an "all-in-the-family approach" to grantmaking (Strouse 2000, 61). There is no outside board of directors, and Stonesifer works without pay in a nondescript office building near a dock on Lake Union in Seattle. The staff is lean in comparison with many other major foundations because it uses outside experts to supplement internal expertise as needed.

The foundation does not generally fund operating costs or endowments. It "prefers to attack problems by developing 'tools' that will have long-lasting impact"—such as AIDS vaccines or inexpensive ways to prevent diarrhea (McCarthy 2000, 154). The foundation focuses on issues where it can use the "catalytic

dollar," leveraging additional private and public funding from partners that may range from developing country governments and United Nations' agencies to corporations and academic institutions (Strouse 2000, 62). The Gates Foundation also uses the "push" and "pull" approach to innovation, for example, by "pushing" new advances in AIDS research through grants for scientific work that otherwise would not happen and "pulling" investments by pharmaceutical companies by promising distribution avenues once such research is successful (ibid., 63). The work of the Gates Foundation has not been without its critics. Some individuals charge that the foundation is a public relations ploy to soften Bill Gates's image after the U.S. government's antitrust lawsuit against Microsoft in

2000. One thing is certain: It is too early to assess the long-term impact of the world's largest foundation—or its richest donor.

Meanwhile, Gates generally avoids discussing the motivations for his philanthropy. He credits the example of his parents and the counsel of such philanthropic luminaries as Vartan Gregorian, president of Carnegie Corporation of New York. He may simply be driven by the realization that he can make a difference. As he told eighty world leaders at a United Nations General Assembly Special Session on Children, "I hadn't planned on getting involved in philanthropy until later in life; when I was in my sixties; when I could devote full time to it. But the more I learned, the more I realized there is no time. Disease won't wait. . . . I believe together we will take care of our children. We can do it—and nothing on earth is more important" (Gates 2002).

Mary Jane Brukardt

See also Law of Charity
References and further reading
"The Bill Gates Interview." 1994. *Playboy,* July, 55.
Cowley, Geoffrey. 2002. "Bill's Biggest Bet Yet." *Newsweek,* February 4, 44.
Gates, Bill. 2002. "U.N. Secretary General's Luncheon," a speech presented at the United Nations, New York, May 9.
McCarthy, Michael. 2000. "A Conversation with the Leaders of the Gates Foundation's Global Health Program: Gordon Perkin and William Foege." *The Lancet,* July 8, 153–155.
McMahon, Patrick. 2001. "Melinda Gates Approaches Giving Aggressively." *USA Today,* July 31, A8.
"Saint Bill." 2001. *The Economist,* June 16, 16.
Sims, David. 2000. "Media Agape at Gates' Conversion." *The Industry Standard* (electronic version), November 6, http://www.thestandard.com/article/0,1902,19959,00.html (cited August 9, 2002).
Strouse, Jean. 2000. "How to Give Away $21.8 Billion." *The New York Times Magazine,* April 16, 56.

Gifts

See Philanthropy and the Good Samaritan; Stewardship

Girl Scouts of America

See Low, Juliette Gordon

Girard, Stephen (1750–1831)

Stephen Girard was born as the second of ten children on May 20, 1750, in the Bordeaux region of France. His father was a former French naval officer who operated a successful shipping business. Girard eventually became a multimillionaire in the United States through his successful shipping business and other ventures. He is most remembered for the will he left at his death, which gave a large portion of his estate to the City of Philadelphia. These funds eventually were used to establish Girard College, a K–12 college preparatory boarding school.

Girard spent much of his youth at the shipyards and developed an early interest in navigation. At age fourteen, expressing a desire to escape the limited opportunities he perceived among family and friends in Bordeaux, he convinced his father to let him sign on as a cabin boy in one of the family's merchant ships. By the early 1770s, Stephen had left the family business, earned his master's license, and was responsible for large cargoes on transatlantic voyages. In 1774, Girard had to sell his cargo for a huge loss on the French Caribbean island of St. Dominique. Fearful of imprisonment for debt if he returned to France, he became a sailor on a boat to Britain's American colonies. Disgraced, penniless, and cut off from his family, the twenty-four-year-old Girard disembarked in New York, eager to earn enough money to pay off his creditors and return to his previous business.

Revolutionary fervor enveloped New York in 1774. Merchants chafed at the restrictions and duties that England imposed upon colonial shipping. The times were ripe for a daring sea captain to profit from the circumstances. Girard never lacked courage and began to engage in smuggling ventures. By the time the British imposed a wartime blockade, Girard was an adept blockade-runner and privateer. Operating now out of Philadelphia, he amassed enough money to pay off his debts, marry, and assume a comfortable lifestyle.

By 1782, Girard joined his brother in the shipping business. They profited handsomely from innovations such as warehousing nonperishable products, insuring cargo, and paying captains by the trip, increasing their desire to make quick voyages. The success of Girard's shipping business gave him the financial opportunity

Stephen Girard (1750–1831) (Corbis)

to diversify. In the early 1800s, he owned extensive property in Philadelphia, coal mines, a stake in potential railroads, and the largest bank in Pennsylvania. By the early 1820s, some estimate Stephen Girard's financial holdings to have been in excess of $40 million—an immense fortune at that time.

At home, Girard maintained a decent library and was well read in Enlightenment philosophy and political theory. He supported Thomas Jefferson for the presidency in 1800 and contributed to Republican candidates throughout his life. His personal relationships evinced his devotion to Enlightenment reason. He considered merit, not need, the basis for all business dealings, even when it came to paying his house staff. He did not recognize biblical truths and considered much of Christian ethics to be only a rationalization of weakness. As a self-made man, he expected others to exert the effort necessary for their own success.

The controversial will he left at his death was but the final act in a long series of philanthropic activities.

Girard joined the Masonic Order and donated time and money to its charitable causes. During his lifetime, he supported numerous other charitable groups, such as the Society for the Relief of Distressed Masters of Ships and Their Widows, the Public School Fund of Philadelphia, the Pennsylvania Institution for the Deaf and Dumb, organizations tending to animal welfare, and the Orphan Society.

When Philadelphia suffered from terrible yellow fever epidemics in 1793, 1797, 1798, 1802, and 1820, Girard became a pivotal figure. Doctors of the time seemed powerless to stem the spread of the disease, prescribing explosions of gunpowder in town squares and the bleeding of patients. Infected sufferers were scorned and sometimes driven out of town. Philadelphia purchased an old mansion on the city's outskirts on Bush Hill to house yellow fever "patients," who were ensconced there while they waited to die. Girard, who visited Bush Hill for the first time in September 1793, found this solution unacceptable. It seemed at once to exacerbate the fears of residents and visitors and to relinquish control over life and death to some power that man did not understand. He donated money to improve the provisions of the makeshift Bush Hill Hospital and spent countless days there tending to the patients and the business needs of the facility. Although many other men of means left the city, Girard actually bathed and cared for the victims.

His greatest charitable concern, however, was to aid the orphans who roamed the city streets, stealing, begging, and prostituting themselves while subject to the taunts and blows of passersby. In Philadelphia, as in other major U.S. cities in the early 1800s, there were high numbers of abandoned children. Epidemics, the death of mothers in childbirth, and an unprecedented rise in illegitimate births, which coincided with the decline in Christian morality and the rise of liberalism in early nationhood, took their toll. As early as 1810, Girard conceived of founding a large boarding school to shelter and educate these children.

When he died in 1831, Stephen Girard left $140,000 to various relatives, provided for the lifetime support of a onetime slave and long-term housekeeper, and distributed about $1 million among the various charities that he had supported during his life.

The bulk of his estate, approximately $7 million, he donated to the City of Philadelphia to found a school for poor boys. Reflecting Girard's adherence to the liberal philosophical doctrines of the Enlightenment, he prescribed that the school's instructors be chosen on merit to teach their practical knowledge of geography, grammar, reading, writing, mathematics, astronomy, and experimental philosophy. He prohibited the teaching of religion or the hiring of any priest or minister as a teacher.

As Girard expected, his heirs challenged the will, using his expressions against religious teaching as a means to attack the document's validity. They hired the noted Daniel Webster to represent them, and the case made its way to the U.S. Supreme Court in 1844. The great orator told the court that "public policy" required that the will be voided, noting that its irreligious sentiments threatened morality and encouraged license.

Justice Joseph Story's decision for the Court was an important legal pronouncement on the law of philanthropy in the United States. First, the Court confirmed that in order to receive property, the benefactor of a will must be a legal entity—that is, either a person or a corporation. Second, a corporation may take public or private form, but either way it is bound to act in strict accordance with the decedent's or testator's intent if it accedes to the funds. Third, the Court found the will not to be inconsistent with public policy and therefore ruled that the state (the City of Philadelphia) was able to take the bequest if it was willing to follow Girard's instructions for its use. In 1848, Girard College opened its doors. Today, Girard College continues as a private but full-scholarship K–12 boarding school, with a college preparatory curriculum, for children of limited financial means.

Mark McGarvie

See also Law of Charity
References and further reading
Abbott, Edith. 1963. *Some American Pioneers in Social Welfare.* New York: Russell and Russell.
Adams, Donald R. 1978. *Finance and Enterprise in Early America: A Study of Stephen Girard's Bank, 1812–1831.* Philadelphia: University of Pennsylvania Press.
———. 1978. "Portfolio Management and Profitability in Early-Nineteenth-Century Banking." *Business History Review* (Spring): 61–79.
Girard, Stephen. Papers. Girard College, Philadelphia, and Archives and Manuscripts, Pennsylvania Historical and Museum Commission, Harrisburg, PA.
Husband, Joseph. 1920. *Americans by Adoption.* Boston: Atlantic Monthly Press.
Keats, John. 1978. "Consider the Curious Legacy of Stephen Girard." *American Heritage* (Fall): 38–47.
McGarvie, Mark D. 2002. "Stephen Girard (1750–1831), Merchant, Misunderstood Republican Idealist, Donor of a Landmark Bequest, and Founder of Girard College." In *Notable American Philanthropists: Biographies of Giving and Volunteering,* edited by Robert T. Grimm Jr., 116–121. Westport, CT: Oryx Press.
Miller, David S. 1988. "The Polly: A Perspective on Merchant Stephen Girard." *The Pennsylvania Magazine of History and Biography,* April, 189–208.
Minnigerode, Meade 1927. *Certain Rich Men.* New York: Putnam's.
Taylor, Michele Taillon. 1997. "Building for Democracy: Girard College, Educational and Architectural Ideology." Ph.D. dissertation, University of Pennsylvania.
Vidal, Girard, et al. v. Philadelphia, 43 U.S. 126 (1844).

Global Nonprofit Sector

The global nonprofit sector consists of the vast assortment of hospitals, universities, social clubs, professional organizations, day-care centers, environmental groups, family counseling agencies, religious congregations, sports clubs, job training centers, human rights organizations, soup kitchens, homeless shelters, foundations, and other organizations that occupy the social space between the market and the state in countries throughout the world. Despite their diversity, these entities share important common features that justify thinking of them as a distinctive set of institutions, an identifiable social "sector" (Salamon et al. 1999). In particular, they are all

- *organizations,* that is, they have some structure and regularity to their operations, even if they are not formally or legally constituted;
- *private,* that is, they are not part of the apparatus of the state, even though they may receive support from governmental sources;
- *not profit distributing,* that is, they are not primarily commercial in purpose and do not

exist primarily to distribute any profits they may earn to their managers or to a set of "owners" but rather devote them to furthering the organization's mission;

- *self-governing,* that is, they have their own mechanisms for internal governance, are able to cease operations on their own authority, and are fundamentally in control of their own affairs;

- *voluntary,* that is, membership in them is not legally required or otherwise obligatory.

Although it has been common to think of such institutions as peculiar to the United States, in fact they are present in many countries, though their scale and importance have been obscured by a widespread lack of basic data and information. Fortunately, this situation has been improving in recent years as researchers gain a clearer picture of the immense scope of the global nonprofit sector.

Historical Background

The presence of nonprofit-type institutions throughout the world is by no means just a recent phenomenon. To the contrary, these institutions have deep historical roots in a wide range of societies and cultures. In part, these roots are religious. Virtually every major religious tradition emphasizes the obligation individuals have to make charitable contributions (Constantelos 1978, 222–225; White 1987, 214–216). Institutions to collect and make use of these contributions have long existed in a wide assortment of settings. The Koran, for example, mentions the obligation to give no less than thirty-two times, and Islamic *waqfs,* or charitable endowments, predate their Western foundation counterparts by several centuries. Indeed, one school of thought sees religion as perhaps the most potent source of incentives to forge such institutions. According to this so-called supply-side theory, the formation of such institutions requires social entrepreneurs, and religious convictions motivate such entrepreneurs to come forward not only to fulfill religious obligations but also to win adherents to a particular creed (James 1987). This leads to the conclusion that such institutions are likely to be most prevalent where religious diversity, and religious con-

flict, heighten the need of religious groups to maintain and extend their member base.

But religion is by no means the only source of the impulse to form nonprofit institutions. Social movements, the desire to secure a range of "collective goods" not otherwise available from the market or the state, patronage from powerful donors or political elites, cultural or professional interests, and many other factors have also played a role at different times and places. The result is a richly varied international structure of private nonprofit institutions.

Though they have deep historical roots, however, nonprofit organizations seem to have grown enormously in recent years. Indeed, a veritable "global associational revolution" appears to be under way in many parts of the world, a massive upsurge of organized private, voluntary activity (Salamon 1994). Though the evidence is admittedly far from precise, such organizations appear to have expanded impressively over at least the past three decades in Western Europe, North America, and the Far East; in Latin America, Africa, and South Asia; in Central Europe; and in the Middle East, Central Asia, and China. In fact, the rise of the nonprofit sector may well prove to be as significant a characteristic of the late twentieth and early twenty-first centuries as the rise of the nation-state was of the late nineteenth and early twentieth.

That these organizations are developing so rapidly seems due to four interrelated developments. The first is the widespread questioning of the capacity of states to handle the combination of social welfare, development, environmental, and related functions that have been thrust upon them in recent years. Closely related is the growing realization that the market cannot solve these problems either. Because of their unique combination of private structure and public purpose, their generally smaller scale, their connections to citizens, their flexibility, and their capacity to tap private initiative in support of public purposes, nonprofit organizations have surfaced as strategically important participants in the worldwide search for a "middle way" between sole reliance on the market and sole reliance on the state to cope with social, economic, and environmental problems (Giddens 1998, 78).

Also contributing to the growth of civil society organizations have been the dramatic breakthroughs in information technologies. These developments have awakened people to the realization that their circumstances may not be inevitable, that opportunities may be better elsewhere, and that change is possible. This awareness has stimulated citizen activism, awakened gender, environmental, and ethnic consciousness, and prompted heightened interest in human rights. In addition, these technologies have vastly simplified the task of forming and sustaining the resulting organizations.

A third factor contributing to the surge has been the worldwide spread of literacy and the emergence in distant regions of educated elites with the skills to organize nonprofit groups. The lack of economic opportunity and the presence of political repression in many places have stimulated individuals in this group to form nonprofit organizations as a response. The educated elites thus form a key leadership cadre for the growing sector that has been so striking a feature of recent global life.

These impulses have been encouraged, finally, by a variety of external actors that have provided important moral and material support for the expansion of the global nonprofit sector. Included have been liberal elements in the Catholic Church, which, for example, played an important role in stimulating the formation of grassroots community groups throughout Latin America in the aftermath of the Castro revolution of 1960, Western charitable foundations committed to grassroots democracy and poverty alleviation, and multinational corporations eager to rally organized citizen support in order to ensure a "license" to operate in faraway lands.

Terms and Concepts

Despite their growing presence and importance, nonprofit organizations remain the lost continent on the social landscape of our world, largely invisible to most policy makers, business leaders, the press, the public at large, and even many people within the sector itself. Even the most basic information about these organizations—their numbers, sizes, activities, economic weight, finances, and roles—has been lacking in most places, and a deeper understanding of the factors that contribute to their growth and decline has been almost nonexistent. Instead, social and political discourse has been dominated by a "two-sector model" that acknowledges the existence of only two major social sectors outside of the individual and the family—the market and the state, or business and government—but not of a "third sector" made up of private nonprofit institutions.

In part, this lack of information reflects the considerable conceptual confusion that has long persisted about the defining features of this range of organizations. Indeed, a plethora of terms denoting the types of organizations that constitute the sector adds to the confusion. Each of these terms—"nonprofit organization," "charity," "voluntary organization," "nongovernmental organization (NGO)," "social economy," and "civil society"—highlights a particular feature of this class of organization while downplaying others, and each therefore focuses attention on a particular subset of entities. Different constituencies therefore favor different conceptions of the field.

The common term used in the United States, and in economic discourse, is "nonprofit" organization or sector. This term emphasizes what is often a central feature of these organizations—that they do not exist to earn a profit. But strictly speaking, nonprofit organizations in most countries are permitted to earn a profit; what is typically forbidden is the distribution of such profits to a group of owners or members. Many of those who object to the negative connotations of the term "nonprofit" prefer to refer to these organizations as "charities" or "voluntary organizations." This terminology is most common in the Anglo-Saxon countries, where the Elizabethan Statute of Charitable Uses first gave legal standing to a broad class of organizations serving what were considered to be "charitable" purposes. But the term "charity" has come to suggest that these organizations are supported chiefly by private charitable gifts, and the term "voluntary" has come to suggest that they are staffed chiefly by volunteers. Neither of these conditions turns out to hold in a substantial number of cases. What is more, the term "charity" has come to have a connotation of paternalism that is also resisted by many activists in the field.

These considerations have led many, particularly in the developing world, to coin the term "nongovernmental organization," or NGO, to refer to this range of nonstate/nonmarket institutions (see, for example, Fisher 1993, 8–10). This term conveniently emphasizes the position of these organizations outside the sphere of state action, and in many cases opposed to it. It has also served to identify a particular class of these organizations, those engaged in grassroots development work with a significant empowerment component, and thus to differentiate them from the more traditional charitable and assistance-oriented institutions that exist in third world countries, often as a residue of the colonial era. But these restrictions make the term "NGO" a highly subjective one dependent on an observer's judgment about the objectives the organization is really pursuing.

A somewhat different concept has surfaced in continental European treatments of this set of institutions. Here the focus has been on a broader set of institutions imbued with a solidarity, or social, perspective. The term most often used to depict these institutions is the French term *economie sociale,* or "social economy." Included within the economie sociale are not only associations and foundations but also mutuals and cooperatives, organizations that violate the prohibition on the distribution of profit that is so central to the nonprofit concept. Advocates of this conceptualization emphasize that although mutuals and cooperatives distribute profits to their members, they are still not primarily profit-oriented institutions but rather "place service to [their] members or the community ahead of profit" (Defournoy and Develtere 1999). This definition brings the social economy concept much closer to the nonprofit one, though this depends on how strictly one interprets the strictures on service over profit (for example, is a huge French mutual insurance company truly a part of the social economy, or is it in the business sector?).

Finally, in the wake of the citizen movements that led to the collapse of the Communist regimes in Central Europe and Russia in the late 1980s and early 1990s, another term—"civil society"—has gained currency to depict this range of institutions. This concept, which has its philosophical roots in the Scottish Enlightenment and in the work of Hegel (Seligman 1992), was used by advocates of reform in Central Europe to justify the creation of a sphere of social action, and an accompanying set of organizations, that

citizens could enter outside of state ownership and control. The term has since been extended to refer to any social institution, indeed any form of individual or joint action, that is not primarily or exclusively economic in orientation and that engages individuals in their capacity as citizens or that supports them in this capacity. So defined, however, the term embraces an immense array of social phenomena—not just voluntary associations and foundations, but also a free press (which can also be a part of the business sector) and an independent judiciary (which can also be a part of government).

Scope and Structure

In the face of this definitional turmoil, a group of researchers affiliated with the Johns Hopkins Comparative Nonprofit Sector Project has identified a set of structural or operational features that seem to capture most of the key ideas embodied in the preceding concepts but that translate them into objective and operational terms suitable for empirical analysis (Salamon and Anheier 1997). This definition identifies nonprofit organizations as social institutions that share the five crucial characteristics noted earlier—they are organizations, whether formal or informal; they are private, that is, not part of the structures of government; they are not profit distributing, or at least do not primarily operate to distribute profits to their owners or members; they are self-governing and in reasonable control of their fate; and they are voluntary in the sense that individuals are free to join them or not.

This definition embraces a broad array of the institutions commonly considered to be part of the "third" or "nonprofit" sector. It includes NGOs as well as more charitably oriented institutions, advocacy agencies as well as service providers, and organizations oriented chiefly to the poor as well as others that serve a broader clientele (for example, symphonies or operas). As applied in practice by the Hopkins researchers, it even includes some mutuals and cooperatives where community objectives clearly outweighed profit-seeking ones in the opinion of local researchers.

Armed with this definition, the Hopkins team, including local associates in more than thirty countries, developed the first systematic, empirical picture of this "global nonprofit sector" in some thirty-five nations (Salamon et al. 1999; Salamon et al. 2003). The resulting data have already transformed the traditional understanding of this set of institutions internationally. Four of these findings seem especially worth noting here.

Scope

In the first place, these data make clear that the global nonprofit sector is a considerable economic force. In the thirty-five countries for which data have been assembled through the Hopkins Comparative Nonprofit Sector Project (see Figure 1), nonprofit organizations as defined above had estimated expenditures of US$1.3 trillion as of the late 1990s. What this means in practice is that if this set of institutions, in just these thirty-five countries, were a separate national economy, it would be the seventh largest economy in the world, ahead of Italy, Brazil, Russia, Spain, and Canada and just behind France and the U.K.

The nonprofit sector in these thirty-five nations looms large in employment terms as well, with a total workforce of 39.5 million full-time equivalent workers, including both paid and volunteer staff. This means that nonprofit organizations employ 4.4 percent of the economically active population, or nearly one out of every twenty economically active persons, in these countries. This is ten times more people than are employed in the utilities or textile industries in these countries, five times more people than are employed in the food-manufacturing industry, and 20 percent more people than are employed in the entire transportation and communications industry. Of these 39.5 million full-time equivalent employees, 22.7 million, or 57 percent, are paid employees, and 16.8 million, or 43 percent, are volunteers. These nearly 17 million full-time equivalent volunteers translate into 170 million actual people involved with these organizations, however, since the typical volunteer works only three to five hours each week.

Variations

Although the nonprofit sector is a generally larger presence than is commonly recognized, its scale varies considerably from place to place. Thus, as Figure 1 shows, the nonprofit workforce—volunteer and paid—varies from a high of 14 percent of the economically active population in the Netherlands to a low of 0.4 percent in Mexico.

These data also make clear that the nonprofit sector is by no means exclusively, or even chiefly, an American phenomenon, as is sometimes believed. To the contrary, four of the countries for which data were assembled—the Netherlands, Belgium, Ireland, and Israel—have larger proportions of their economically active populations employed by nonprofit organizations than does the United States. With volunteers added, three countries—the Netherlands, Belgium, and Ireland—still outdistance the United States with regard to the share of their economically active populations engaged with the nonprofit sector. Especially notable is the huge scale of the nonprofit sector in many supposedly "welfare states" of Western Europe. This suggests that our conception of the Western European welfare state may be seriously flawed: What exists in many of these countries is not a "welfare state" but a "welfare partnership" in which government provides the funding for welfare services but relies extensively on private, nonprofit institutions to deliver the needed services.

Activities

Most of the total workforce of nonprofit organizations—60 percent—is primarily engaged in *service* activities, that is, the delivery of direct services such as education, health, housing, economic development, and the like. Of these, by far the most important are education and social services. At the same time, at least a third of the sector's workforce is engaged in essentially *expressive* functions such as culture, the arts, religious worship, and the representation of political perspectives or occupational or professional interests.

Generally speaking, volunteers are proportionately more likely to be engaged in the sector's expressive functions and paid staff in its service functions, though the majority of the workforce in both categories of activity is paid staff. Differences also exist among countries in the extent to which service or expressive functions absorb the largest share of the nonprofit workforce. Thus, although service functions dominate in most places, in the Nordic countries the expressive functions are clearly the most important.

Figure 1 Civil Society Organization Workforce as Percent of Economically Active Population, by Country

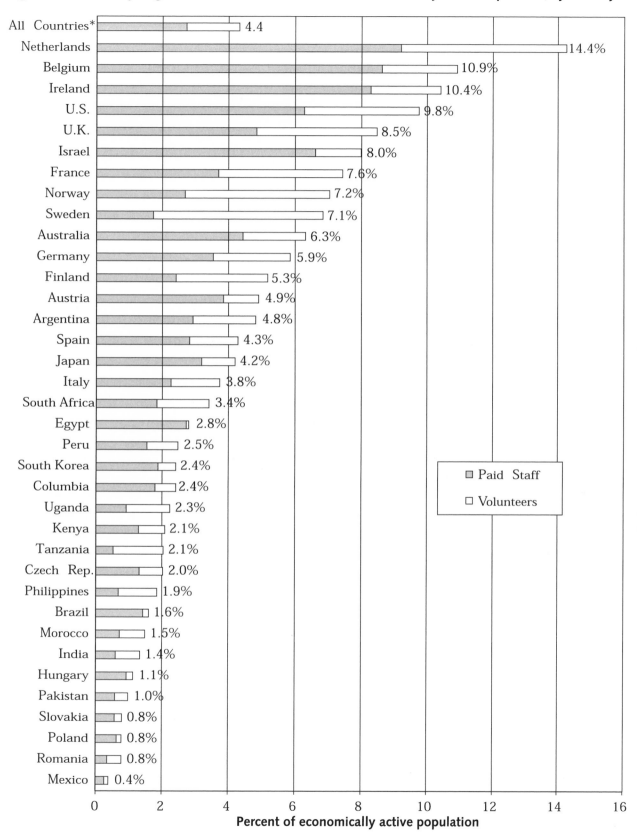

* 36-country unweighted average Source: *Global Civil Society: Dimension of the Nonprofit Sector*, Vol. 2

This reflects the fact that the Nordic welfare states have vested more responsibility for human service delivery, and not just finance, in the hands of government agencies. Contrary to widespread belief, however, a substantial nonprofit sector still exists in the Nordic countries, but it is largely volunteer based and concentrated in the expressive functions, including sport and recreation.

Revenues

A fourth, somewhat surprising finding of this research is that private philanthropy—including contributions from foundations, individuals, and corporations—accounts for a considerably smaller share of nonprofit revenue than is widely recognized. In particular, philanthropy ranks third behind service fees and government support in the financing of nonprofit organizations around the world, with an average of 12 percent of the revenue as opposed to 53 percent from fees and 35 percent from government. In no country, in fact, does private philanthropy constitute the major source of nonprofit income, and this includes the United States, where fees and charges dominate. The one major deviation from the general pattern is in Western Europe, where public-sector payments outdistance fees and charges in the revenue base of the nonprofit sector.

When volunteer inputs are factored into the equation and treated as a part of charitable contributions, this overall pattern changes somewhat. With volunteers included, the philanthropic share of total nonprofit support swells from 12 percent to 30 percent. In other words, contributions of time, even when valued conservatively, outdistance contributions of cash to nonprofit organizations by 2.5 to 1. Even with volunteers included, however, fees and charges remain the major source of nonprofit income in most places, accounting, on average, for 43 percent of the total support.

Issues for the Future

For all its recent dynamism and growth, the global nonprofit sector remains a fragile organism, vulnerable to external threats, unsure of its sources of support, imperfectly rooted and legitimized, and not sufficiently appreciated or understood even by many of its own supporters. As a result, the success of the global associational revolution, and the potential contribution it can make to the solution of social and economic problems, are far from assured. Serious challenges exist. What is more, these challenges take a number of different forms.

First there is the challenge of legitimacy. Information about the global nonprofit sector remains highly fragmented and incomplete, public awareness is limited, and legal structures are often not very supportive. In some countries, for example, the formation of associations requires an affirmative act from whatever ministry has responsibility for its field of endeavor.

Second is the challenge of effectiveness. Training of third-sector leaders is still in its infancy in many places and the support institutions for these organizations have only begun to develop. Given the important social responsibilities nonprofit organizations are assuming globally and the complexity of the organizations that are resulting, it is imperative that the same kind of training that is available for business and government leaders be established for civil society organizations as well.

A third critical challenge is sustainability. Philanthropy alone does not seem capable of generating the support these organizations need to perform the social roles of which they are capable and to carry out the important work they do both in financial and human terms. Boosting such support, but also supplementing it from other sources, thus becomes an important priority.

Finally, there is the challenge of partnership, the need to connect civil society organizations to other major social actors in business and government. This is important not only for reasons of fiscal health but also because of the need for collaborative approaches to the serious problems that confront societies. In such an environment, a "new governance" is needed, one that goes beyond older notions of conflicts among the three sectors (government, business, and nonprofit) and instead emphasizes the opportunities for collaboration (Salamon 2002).

Conclusion

The nonprofit sector is thus a major social and economic force throughout the world at the present time.

Once considered to be present only in a handful of countries, these organizations stand revealed as a global force, with a significant presence in virtually every country and region. This is not to say that important variations are not present in the size, composition, and financing of this set of institutions from country to country. To the contrary, the variations are immense, reflecting the distinctive cultures, traditions, and political histories of different places. Indeed, one of the strengths of the comparative approach is precisely that it highlights these differences and brings them into better focus. Nevertheless, the ubiquity of the global civil nonprofit sector turns out to be one of its most salient features.

Lester M. Salamon

References and further reading

Anheier, Helmut K., and Lester M. Salamon, eds. 1998. *The Nonprofit Sector in the Developing World: A Comparative Analysis.* Manchester, UK: Manchester University Press.

Constantelos, Demetrios J. 1987. "Charity." In *The Encyclopedia of Religion,* edited by Mircea Eliade, 222–225. New York: Macmillan.

Defourny, Jacques, and Patrick Develtere. 1999. "The Social Economy: The Worldwide Making of a Third Sector." In *L'economie sociale au Nord et au Sud,* edited by J. Defournoy, P. Develtere, and B. Foneneau, 1–30. Brussels: DeBoeck.

Fisher, Julie. 1993. *The Road from Rio: Sustainable Development and the Nongovernmental Movement in the Third World.* Westport, CT: Praeger.

Giddens, Anthony. 1998. *The Third Way: The Renewal of Social Democracy.* Cambridge, UK: Polity Press.

James, Estelle. 1987. "The Nonprofit Sector in Comparative Perspective." In *The Nonprofit Sector: A Research Handbook,* edited by Walter W. Powell, 397–415. New Haven, CT: Yale University Press.

Kramer, Ralph. 1989. *Voluntary Agencies in the Welfare State.* Berkeley: University of California Press.

McCarthy, Kathleen D., Virginia A. Hodgkinson, Russy Sumariwalla, and Associates. 1992. *The Nonprofit Sector in the Global Community: Voices from Many Nations.* San Francisco: Jossey-Bass.

Salamon, Lester M. 1994. "The Rise of the Nonprofit Sector." *Foreign Affairs* 73, no. 4 (July/August): 109–122.

———. 2002. *The Tools of Government: A Guide to the New Governance.* New York: Oxford University Press.

Salamon, Lester M., and Helmut K. Anheier. 1997. "Toward a Common Definition." In *Defining the Nonprofit Sector: A Cross-National Analysis,* edited by Lester M. Salamon and Helmut K. Anheier, 29–50. Manchester, UK: Manchester University Press.

Salamon, Lester M., Helmut K. Anheier, Regina List, Stefan Toepler, Wojciech Sokolowski, and Local Associates. 1999. *Global Civil Society: Dimensions of the Nonprofit Sector.* Baltimore: Johns Hopkins Institute for Policy Studies.

Salamon, Lester M., Regina List, Stefan Toepler, Wojciech Sokolowski, and Local Associates. 2003. *Global Civil Society: Dimensions of the Nonprofit Sector.* Baltimore: Johns Hopkins Institute for Policy Studies.

Seligman, Adam. 1992. *The Idea of Civil Society.* New York: Free Press.

White, Charles. 1987. "Almsgiving." In *The Encyclopedia of Religion,* edited by Mircea Eliade, 214–216. New York: Macmillan.

Goff, Frederick Harris (1858–1923)

Frederick Harris Goff was a lawyer and banker who is considered the innovator of the community trust. Born in Blackbury, Illinois, to Frederick C. and Catherine Brown Goff on December 15, 1858, he moved with his family to Cleveland, Ohio, in 1864 after a short residence in Evanston, Illinois, and, as a teenager, to Kansas.

As a youth, Goff worked as a crew member on a Great Lakes vessel and as an assistant to a survey team. After his brief stay in Kansas, he returned to Cleveland, where he attended the Hudson Street School. In 1874, he went to Ann Arbor, where he completed high school and enrolled in the University of Michigan. After graduation in 1881, he returned to Cleveland and studied for the bar. He was admitted in 1883 or 1884.

Goff quickly developed an expertise in corporate reorganization and estate law. He first served as a partner in the firm Carr and Goff. In 1890, he was a partner in Estep, Dickey, Carr, and Goff and later in Kline, Tolles, and Goff. His rise to legal prominence was rapid and his reputation and ability such that John D. Rockefeller purportedly asked him to serve as his legal counsel. Goff is said to have refused the offer because of his desire to remain in Cleveland.

By 1900, Goff was a highly regarded and wealthy member of Cleveland's legal community. He changed careers, however, in 1908, sacrificing a good deal of his annual income to become the president of the Cleveland Trust Company, a position he held until his death. Under his guidance, Cleveland Trust became the city's largest bank, increasing its assets by nearly 600 percent.

Goff's business activities were linked to and complemented by involvement in civic issues. In 1903, he became mayor of Glenville, the upper-class suburb east of the city in which he resided. As mayor he ended gambling at the local harness racing track, thereby angering some of the well-to-do racing fraternity but paving the way for the suburb's annexation to Cleveland. In 1907, as the legal representative of the major private traction company in Cleveland, he handled negotiations with the city's reform mayor, Tom L. Johnson, centering on municipal ownership of the city's street railways. Initially adversaries, Goff and Johnson became close friends. The plan they negotiated was a masterful compromise between private ownership and public benefit and control. Later, in World War I, Goff served as vice chairman of the Capital Issues Committee in President Woodrow Wilson's War Finance Corporation.

The experience that Goff had gained as an estate lawyer and banker, and his interest in civic betterment, formed the basis of his most noteworthy achievement, the creation of the community trust. As a lawyer Goff had been troubled by the creation of legacies and trusts locked to purposes that were antiquated or no longer viable. He first dealt with the issue as the head of the Cleveland Trust Company, where he created a series of "living trusts" through which donors oversaw the disposition of portions of their funds during their lifetime.

He moved the concept further in 1914 and created the Cleveland Foundation, the nation's first community trust. The trust pooled individual bequests and had a governing board to determine the best use of the funds for the civic good. The board (or distribution committee) of the Cleveland Foundation was originally composed of five members: Two were appointed by the bank (in this case, Cleveland Trust) that held the principle and three by public officials.

Goff married Frances Southworth in 1894. They had three children: Frederika, William S., and Frances M. He died on March 14, 1923, and is buried in Cleveland's Lake View Cemetery.

John Grabowski

See also Community Foundations
References and further reading
Frederick Harris Goff: A Memorial. 1924. Cleveland: Cleveland Trust Co.
"Goff, Frederick H." 1987. In *The Encyclopedia of Cleveland History,* edited by David D. Van Tassel and John J. Grabowski, 2d ed. Bloomington: Indiana University Press, http://ech.cwru.edu/ech-cgi/article.pl?id=GFH1 (cited January 20, 2004).
Grabowski, John. "Frederick Harris Goff." In *Notable American Philanthropists: Biographies of Giving and Volunteering,* edited by Robert T. Grimm Jr., 121–124. Westport, CT: Oryx Press.

Goodrich, Pierre Frist (1894–1973)

An intensely private man, Pierre Frist Goodrich deeply believed in the power of education, ideas, and liberty. He was a gifted lawyer, an astute businessperson, and an accomplished philosopher and philanthropist who believed in funding efforts to explore the concept of liberty.

Goodrich was born in the small western Indiana community of Winchester in 1894 to Cora and James Goodrich. After graduation from Winchester High School, he attended Wabash College in Crawfordsville, Indiana, where he graduated Phi Beta Kappa in 1916 with a bachelor's degree in humanities. He than matriculated to Harvard Law School and attended for one year before spending two years serving his country in World War I as a second lieutenant in the Army Quartermasters Corps. He returned to Harvard and finished his law degree in 1920.

After graduation, Goodrich returned to Winchester and began to practice law, forming an association with John Macy under the firm name Macy and Goodrich. He also began to take part in the many business ventures of his family, such as the banking, utility, and grain companies. In 1923, Goodrich moved to Indianapolis and became a member of the firm Haynes and Mote, which became Mote and Goodrich after the 1923 death of Paul Haynes. Goodrich quickly became one of the most well-respected corporate lawyers in Indiana.

Goodrich regularly worked twelve-hour days and occasionally worked all day and night just to prove he could. This work ethic, coupled with his keen intellect, played an important role in the success of the Goodrich business empire. Goodrich became an innovator of various business practices that are now commonplace among similar companies. For instance, he initiated, at Peoples Loan and Trust, fee-based services long before any other bank considered the practice. At the Ayrshire Collieries Coal Corporation, he instituted the practice of reclaiming the strip-mined coalfields (not required by state and federal law for another thirty years). In another visionary act, Goodrich outlawed smoking in all of his office buildings in 1960.

In the mid-1940s, the success of the Goodrich family–owned businesses, which included Ayrshire Collieries Coal Corporation, Peoples Loan and Trust the Indiana Telephone Corporation, City Securities, and Central Newspapers, allowed Pierre Goodrich to pursue his intellectual and philanthropic interests. These were closely interrelated, which spurred his involvement with the Great Books Foundation, the Foundation for Economic Education, the China Institute of America, the Mont Pelerin Society, and the Institute of Humane Studies. Goodrich also was dedicated to several local nonprofit organizations. He was a longtime Wabash College trustee, founder of the Winchester Community Foundation, and a participant in many other local nonprofit organizations supporting music and education.

Goodrich created his lasting legacy, the Liberty Fund, in 1960 in Indianapolis. According to James Buchanan, advisory general director of the Study of Public Choice at George Mason University and 1986 Nobel laureate in economics, "Liberty Fund is the permanent embodiment of Pierre Goodrich's faith in the power of ideas and his personal belief that ideas are more exciting and more important than things" (Starbuck 2001, xvi). The *Liberty Fund Basic Memorandum* written by Goodrich serves as the detailed operating manual for the foundation. In the 129-page confidential memorandum, Goodrich stated that he created the fund with the intent that "some hopeful contribution may be made to the preservation, restoration, and development of individual liberty through investigation, research, and educational activity" (ibid., 414).

Currently, the Liberty Fund conducts more than 175 conferences a year that allow scholars from around the world to congregate, study, and discuss issues related to liberty. The conferences are based upon the great works and ideas of the past, with topics ranging from "Jefferson, Madison, and the Constitution of a Liberal Republic" to "Liberty in Melville's *Moby Dick*." The fund also publishes approximately twenty classic books a year, including *American Political Writing during the Founding Era: 1760–1805* and *Union and Liberty: The Political Philosophy of John C. Calhoun*.

Goodrich passed away on October 25, 1973, with little publicity in comparison to some of his contemporary philanthropists but with an enduring legacy in the Liberty Fund.

W. David Lasater

References and further reading

Hubbard, Kin. 1929. *The Indiana Biographical Association*. James O. Jones.

"Liberty Fund." 2000. Brochure. Indianapolis: Liberty Fund.

The National Cyclopedia of American Biography. 1980. N.p.: James T. White.

"Pierre F. Goodrich Dies; Business Executive Had Diversified Career." 1973. *Indianapolis Star*, October 26, A1.

Starbuck, Dane. 2001. *The Goodriches: An American Family*. Indianapolis: Liberty Fund.

Governance of Nonprofits

Governance is the process of providing strategic leadership to a nonprofit organization. It entails the functions of setting direction, making policy and strategy decisions, overseeing and monitoring organizational performance, and ensuring overall accountability. Nonprofit governance is a political and organizational process involving multiple functions and engaging multiple stakeholders.

The meaning of "governance" is relatively different for nonprofit and governmental settings. Public-sector (government) governance refers to the political process of policy and decision making for communities and political jurisdictions, whereas nonprofit governance refers to the process of providing leadership, direction, and accountability for a specific nongovernmental, not-for-profit organization.

In the United States and many other nations, an incorporated nonprofit organization must have a governing board and, as a matter of law, this board constitutes "the organization." It is common for boards to hire staff to actually do the work of the organization, often with support from volunteers. Nonetheless, it is the governing board that ultimately is accountable for all acts undertaken in the name of the organization, whether or not those acts are formally approved or implemented by the board itself. This accountability exists regardless of the size or nature of the organization and regardless of whether the organization employs staff, and members of nonprofit governing boards must recognize that they have certain legally enforceable duties and obligations by virtue of their membership on the board. (These duties and obligations are relevant only to the official governing board itself and do not apply to nongoverning bodies such as advisory boards or councils.)

Nonprofit governance is primarily the province of an organization's governing board, often known as a board of directors or board of trustees. However, in larger organizations that employ staff, it is not unusual for others to be a part of the governance process as well. In particular, it is common for the chief executive or staff officer of the organization to play a very active role.

Governance, Strategy, and Leadership

Effective governance is integral to the success of the nonprofit organization. Governance is essentially a decision process grounded in the assumption that organizations can cause desired results to occur by choosing appropriate courses of action. Fundamentally, governance and strategic leadership are about making informed organizational choices: choices about why the organization exists, what the board wants to accomplish, the best ways to achieve those results, the resources it will need to do these things and how it will secure them, and how the board will know whether the organization is making a difference. Strategy is the process of selecting among competing courses of action and implementing them to achieve chosen goals and outcomes. The process involves gathering information and using it to inform the decision process, with the expectation that effective strategy choices will result in organizational success. Unlike the for-profit world, where these choices

are largely grounded in options for making money for someone, nonprofits essentially always begin with a focus on doing good—and making choices about how best to have an impact.

Effective governance and strategy are integral to the sustainability and long-term effectiveness of a nonprofit operating in today's complex and competitive world. To succeed, nonprofits (like all organizations) must continuously renew the link between what they do and the needs and interests of the community they serve. They must ensure they are providing the services needed and valued by their clients and constituents in ways that are consistent with the organization's core values and principles. As the organization serves its clients, governance involves making judgments about how well or poorly the organization is doing and then making choices about how it can be more effective.

Approaches to Understanding Governance

Much has been written in recent years about the organization and practice of nonprofit governance. This writing typically has taken one of two general approaches. The first is the normative approach, which tends to be prescriptive about how nonprofit governance *should be* organized and practiced. The second approach is descriptive or analytic and focuses on explaining how nonprofit governance *actually is* practiced in nonprofits. Each approach has positive and negative aspects.

The Normative Approach

The normative literature on nonprofit governance offers recommendations and prescriptions for how governing boards ideally should work. All are grounded in the core principle that the governing board has (and should have) the authority and accountability for organizational decisions and actions (Houle 1997; Carver 1997). The board is the premier authority to which all other actors in the organization are responsible and accountable. In other words, these models assert that it must be the board that governs the organization; all other actors (such as executive directors, staff members, and volunteers) are subordinate to it, and their roles in the governance process are to support the board.

It is recognized that many boards do not operate as these models prescribe, and the orientation of this literature is that governing boards are more effective when they implement these prescriptions for design and practice. Overall, these models encourage governance approaches by which a board will govern without falling into either of the traps of becoming (1) a meaningless "rubber stamp" to the chief executive's or others' decisions or (2) too operationally involved and thus micromanaging the affairs and operations of the organization. According to these models, both types of dysfunctional behavior reflect a lack of understanding or competence by the board and/or the executive about the board's function of governance and how it must be executed.

In general, these models explain that an effective board will

1. determine the mission, vision, values, strategic directions, and goals for the organization (using the principles and methods of rational strategic planning);

2. establish policies to guide all subordinate organizational decisions and actions to implement the chosen mission, goals, etc.;

3. serve as a key and relatively independent link connecting the organization and its primary stakeholders, and monitor the organization's overall operating environment to ensure that the organization is attentive and responsive to it;

4. supervise, monitor, and assess the performance of the organization with regard to its chosen mission, goals, directions, and policies, particularly through the systematic management of the chief executive's performance.

The normative approaches place a strong emphasis on the rational process of strategic planning as the way to set direction and enable strong organizational performance (Bryson 1995; Allison and Kaye 1997). Such strategic planning involves a logical process of making informed choices. Specific direction, goals, and priorities are determined through a process that starts with a clear understanding of the organization's

mission, the needs and interests of its owners (the community or a group of members), and the conditions of the organization and its operating environment. Through a rational assessment of the strengths and weaknesses of the organization, and the opportunities and threats posed by these conditions and the organization's future operating environment, the governing board (usually with the advice of executive staff, sometimes with advice from volunteers or other key stakeholders) will make choices about what to accomplish (that is, it sets goals) and how to best achieve them (that is, it identifies strategies).

Performance goals are established as a part of this process and serve as the basis for assessing the organization's performance. The formal document that articulates this information is the *strategic plan*, and this plan becomes the guide for management and staff. The logical culmination of this planning cycle occurs when, after allowing a time period to execute the plans (often annually), the board (usually with executive involvement) reviews and assesses the organization's performance and uses this information to refine or change its plans for the next cycle. The effective board also will use this information to evaluate and document the performance of the organization and its chief executive and to administer rewards or sanctions based on their assessment of performance.

Critics of the normative literature argue that it tends to be overly rational and restrictive and observe that such models reflect neither the reality nor the range of possibilities that may be appropriate to the complex world of nonprofit organizations (Herman and Heimovics 1991; Holland 2002). Some highlight the complexity of community organizations and explain that the behavior of boards and other decision makers in such settings is not necessarily rational. Others point to the reality that it is chief executives who often are expected to lead the governance process. Some question whether it is realistic to believe that organizations have goals; only the people associated with them have goals, and their goals often differ from those of the organization. It also has been observed that, regardless of their desirability, few organizations actually implement these processes as designed. In the "real world" of nonprofits, factors such as interpersonal and organizational politics, time and other resource constraints, lack of knowledge and skill, low motivation, incomplete execution, and many other dynamics often interfere with and sometimes entirely derail such well-intended and well-designed processes. It has been argued that it is more useful to understand and articulate the actual dynamics of boards; as a result, several writers have taken the descriptive approach.

The Descriptive Approach

The governance literature that takes a more descriptive or analytic approach focuses on the ways that nonprofits actually implement the governance process. While acknowledging the legal reality that the governing board holds ultimate accountability for the organization's behavior, the advocates of this approach strive to be more realistic in explaining the less precise yet very real dynamics of the typical nonprofit's governance process and to accurately reflect what happens when the messiness of nonprofit organizational life interacts with the organization's governance processes.

The descriptive writing on governance documents the reality that, regardless of the specific balance of roles, governance responsibility usually is shared between the board and the chief executive, often with important involvement from other key stakeholders (Herman and Heimovics 1991). It is relatively unusual for the governance process of a nonprofit organization to be as board-driven as the normative perspective advocates. In reality, nonprofit boards play a range of roles with varying degrees of engagement or involvement in governance. Likewise, in reality, chief executives also play a range of roles with varying degrees of engagement and involvement. These executives (and sometimes other staff, as well) are quite heavily involved in the governance and strategy development of their organizations, often at the insistence of the board. Neither they nor their boards believe they are usurping or interfering with the legitimate work of the board. Indeed, they often are seen as advancing governance by bringing a complementary perspective, important information, and essential leadership to the process.

Recent research describes a range of ways that boards and executives share strategy-setting and deci-sion-making roles in nonprofit governance, sometimes involving other stakeholders (see, for example, Bradshaw et al. 1992; Taylor et al. 1996). In general, there are four typical patterns of involvement: (1) in many established nonprofits, governance has evolved to the point that the chief executive dominates the governance process by developing decisions that the board merely ratifies; (2) in many large nonprofits that are dominated by professional work (such as hospitals), the professional staff tends to dominate the governance process, and the chief executive and board take leadership roles only on certain administrative and infrastructure matters; (3) in smaller and more volunteer-driven organizations, it is more common to see boards driving and dominating governance and the chief executive only staffing the process; and (4) in organizations such as advocacy and community-based, grassroots nonprofits, it is not uncommon to observe a collegial or collective governance approach that actively involves most or all of the organization's significant stakeholders in governance decisions. Depending upon the circumstances, any of these may be appropriate.

In varying settings and at different times, governing boards may be the actual *decision makers, decision influencers,* or *ratifiers* of decisions of others (Galbraith 1983). Some of the variables that appear to affect such patterns include organizational size, history, culture, the professional content of the organization's work, and the organization's stage of development as well as the interests and competence of the board, its members, and the chief executive.

Some scholars and writers (such as Mintzberg 1994) have taken issue with whether it is realistic to expect organizations to take the rational approach to strategic decision making that is prescribed by normative writers. These writers observe that strategic plans often have rather little impact on organizational action and rarely provide the intended strategic guidance. It has been noted that major changes in strategy often are triggered by dramatic circumstances, not an orderly choice process.

Likewise, it is not very common for nonprofit boards to use strategic plans as the basis for systematic organizational performance evaluation (Murray and Cutt 2000). Further, even when evaluations are implemented, it is only occasionally true that they result in any overt change in the strategy and policy decisions of an organization's governing board. Nonetheless, recent research affirms a positive relationship between strategic planning processes and nonprofit organization effectiveness, suggesting that the rational approaches do have value for some organizations that use them well (Stone et al. 1999).

Interestingly, several of the descriptive scholars have gone on to write in a rather normative tone, drawing on their findings about common practices to explain what should be done to enhance nonprofit board effectiveness. These emerge as relatively prescriptive reports, grounded in the judgment that the most common practices reflect the best practices of effective nonprofit organizations. This may or may not be valid, and there is little reason to assume that certain approaches or strategies are valuable simply because they are common in practice.

The Relationship between Governance, Board Effectiveness, and Nonprofit Effectiveness

It is widely accepted that effective governance is integral to organizational effectiveness and success, whether in the business or nonprofit worlds. Organizations that fail to act strategically to adapt to a changing environment become irrelevant. Of course, governance alone does not accomplish anything—it is the effective execution of a well-chosen strategy that gains the results the organization seeks. Governance is at the front end of the process and provides the focus for all that follows.

However, in spite of legal requirements for governing boards, there has been debate in recent years about whether governing boards are actually necessary or add value to the organization's effectiveness (Ryan 1999). Nonprofit experts have long argued that board effectiveness is essential to nonprofit effectiveness, generally for the reasons that governance and strategy are understood to be essential to organizational success. Most nonprofit boards and executives share this view, though there are those who have come to question the value of boards in today's complex and fast-changing world. Board detractors complain that boards interfere with organizational agility and responsiveness, meddle in matters about which they

know little, and interfere with staff work. Board proponents argue that competent and well-designed boards work in partnership with talented executives to add unique value that enhances organizational agility and responsiveness, focus on the matters they are best equipped to decide, and meet organizational needs the staff is not equipped to address. Both perspectives have anecdotal evidence to support their positions.

Recent research on boards affirms that board effectiveness is positively related with nonprofit organizational effectiveness (Herman and Renz 2000; Green and Griesinger 1996), and there is direct evidence that organizations with effective boards are more successful than others. In fact, one recent study found a clear link between improved board performance and organizational financial performance (Jackson and Holland 1998). However, none of these studies explains which causes which. Does board effectiveness lead to organizational effectiveness, or vice versa? In all likelihood, these are very interrelated. It is entirely likely that effective organizations make sure they develop effective boards, and that these effective boards do all they can to develop an effective organization.

Boards of Directors

The board of directors (sometimes known as the board of trustees or the governing board) is the primary group of people entrusted with and accountable for the leadership and governance of the nonprofit corporation. Governance is a central responsibility of the board, yet the typical board's work goes beyond that of governance alone. For example, it is common for boards and their members to also serve as

- ambassadors who build relationships and generate goodwill;
- sponsors and representatives who advocate on behalf of the organization;
- trusted advisers and consultants who offer guidance and serve as sounding boards for the chief executive and staff;
- resource developers who help the organization secure essential resources.

In certain membership organizations, board members may also serve as representatives who advocate on behalf of particular constituencies or membership groups in the governance process. However, this is not an appropriate role for a member of the board of a typical nonprofit organization.

Legal Duties

In the United States, the board of directors of a nonprofit corporation has the ultimate responsibility and accountability for the conduct and performance of the organization. Boards regularly delegate the work of the organization to executives, staff, and volunteers, yet they cannot delegate or reassign their responsibility for that work. Nonprofit corporations are entities authorized by a state to be formed for the purpose of engaging in public service, and each such corporation must have a governing body that oversees and ultimately is legally accountable for the organization.

Over the past decade, there has been an increase in the attention paid to the legal responsibilities of nonprofit boards and their members. Both federal and state authorities have placed increased emphasis on the need for nonprofit boards to be accountable for the quality of their governance and oversight of their organizations. The increasingly competitive and demanding environment of nonprofits, including increased competition between nonprofits and for-profit businesses, likely will lead to even more legal accountability. Nonprofit boards have roles that go far beyond those legally required, yet there is no question that boards must be very attentive to the performance of their legal responsibilities.

From a legal perspective, the nonprofit board and its members, individually, have three fundamental duties:

1. Duty of care, which is taking the care and exercising the judgment that any reasonable and prudent person would exhibit in the process of making informed decisions, including acting in good faith consistent with what the individual board member truly believes is in the best interests of the organization. The law recognizes and accepts that board members may not always be correct in their choices or decisions but holds them accountable for being attentive, diligent, and thoughtful in considering and acting on a policy, course of action, or other decision. Active preparation for and participation in board meetings where important decisions are to be made is an integral element of the duty of care.

2. Duty of loyalty, which calls upon the board and its members to consider and act in good faith to advance the interests of the organization. In other words, board members will not authorize or engage in transactions except those in which the best possible outcomes or terms for the organization can be achieved. This standard constrains a board member from participating in board discussions and decisions when he or she as an individual has a conflict of interest (that is, personal interests that conflict with organizational interests).

3. Duty of obedience, which requires obedience to the requirements of applicable laws, rules, and regulations as well as honoring the terms and conditions of the organization's mission, bylaws, policies, and other standards of appropriate behavior.

Board members are obligated to honor these standards with regard to all decisions and actions of the board, and those who do not may be subject to civil and even criminal sanctions (including sanctions imposed by the Internal Revenue Service [IRS] in cases of inappropriate personal benefit).

Core Responsibilities

Much has been written on the core responsibilities of the nonprofit board, and no one list is universally applicable to all nonprofit organizations. According to a list articulated for BoardSource (formerly the National Center for Nonprofit Boards), it is the board's responsibility to

1. determine and articulate the organization's mission, vision, and core values;
2. recruit and select the organization's chief executive;

3. support and assess the performance of the organization's chief executive;

4. ensure that the organization engages in planning for its future;

5. determine the set of programs that the organization will deliver to implement its strategies and accomplish its goals and monitor the performance of these programs to assess their value;

6. ensure that the organization has financial and other resources adequate to implement its plans;

7. ensure the effective management and use of the organization's resources;

8. enhance the organization's credibility and public image;

9. ensure organizational integrity and accountability;

10. assess and develop the board's own effectiveness.

Fiduciary Responsibility

Boards and board members often are reminded that they have a fiduciary responsibility to the organization and, ultimately, to the larger community within which they serve. At its core, fiduciary responsibility is the responsibility to treat the resources of the organization as a trust, and the responsible board will ensure that these resources are utilized in a reasonable, appropriate, and legally accountable manner. Although the phrase often is used to refer especially to financial resources, it applies to the stewardship of all of the assets and resources of the organization.

The appropriate exercise of fiduciary responsibility includes the following:

1. Adoption of a set of policies to govern the acquisition and use of financial and other resources

2. Establishment, on a regular basis (usually annual), of a budget that allocates financial resources to the programs and activities that will accomplish the organization's mission, vision and goals, and outcomes (preferably, in alignment with a strategic plan)

3. Development and implementation of an ongoing system for monitoring and holding staff and volunteers accountable for their performance with regard to these policies and budgets

4. Development and implementation of an ongoing system to monitor, assess, and report on the overall fiscal condition and financial performance of the organization

5. Implementation of an external independent review process (that is, an audit) on a regular basis (usually annual) to assess the organization's fiscal condition and health, including the effectiveness of its systems and policies for the protection and appropriate use of financial resource

Unfortunately, many boards operate in much less systematic ways to ensure fiduciary accountability, and some become very enmeshed in the details of the organization and its management. In reasonably healthy organizations with competent staff, such micromanagement is counterproductive. It can create an inability to see the forest for the trees (that is, the board becomes so caught up in details that the important trends and issues are overlooked or obscured) and disrupts and alienates the executives and staff who experience the interference.

Typical Structures and Characteristics of Nonprofit Boards

Nonprofit boards have specific positions (officers) and work units (committees and task forces) that help the board organize and accomplish its work. The typical nonprofit board in the United States has twelve to twenty-four members, and the average board size is seventeen members. Boards must meet regularly, but the frequency of meetings varies from quarterly to bimonthly or monthly.

Officers

The officers of the typical nonprofit organization are the key leaders for the organization. In most states of the United States, a nonprofit corporation must have certain officers. The most common positions are board chair (or president), vice chair (or vice president), secretary, and treasurer. The board chair is the chief voluntary officer of the organization and is responsible for organizing and conducting the meetings of the board. Further, it is the chair's responsibility to facilitate the board's work as a team and to ensure that meetings and other board activities are conducted in an effective manner. It is common for the board chair to oversee the performance of the organization's chief executive on behalf of the board, although some organizations elaborate the process by involving both the chair and the executive committee in executive performance management.

Committees and Task Forces

Boards engage in much of their work as a full group and, ideally, all members work as a team to accomplish the work of the board. Nonetheless, most boards also develop committees and task forces to help the board do its work, and these entities are part of the governance system of the organization. For most boards, some of these units are permanent or "standing" structures, whereas others accomplish a specific task and then disappear. It is increasingly common for boards to refer to the permanent structures as committees and to the limited-term entities as task forces or ad hoc committees, although some organizations do use the labels interchangeably. It is common for board committees to be comprised entirely of board members, but it is increasingly common to also invite non-board members with unique expertise or knowledge to serve. Often, the standing committees are specified in the organization's bylaws, which explain their duties and responsibilities.

For boards with elaborate committee systems, the following are among the most common types of committees:

1. *Executive Committee:* This committee is typically comprised of the officers and sometimes also includes committee chairs or selected other board members. It usually has the authority to act on behalf of the board between meetings and to address organizational emergencies. Some executive committees have the authority to act independently, but many are required to have their actions reviewed and ratified by the full board.

2. *Nominating Committee:* This committee has the responsibility for recruiting candidates for board and committee membership and preparing a slate of candidates or nominees for consideration and action by the full board. Some also nominate officers. It is increasingly common to define this committee's responsibilities to include a year-round cycle of board development activities, including new member orientation, member self-assessment, board self-assessment and development, and the development of board training programs and retreats. When operating with this enlarged portfolio, such committees often are called board development committees.

3. *Fundraising or Development Committee:* This committee usually is responsible for working with staff and board to organize and implement the organization's fundraising events and activities, including the solicitation of major gifts and grants.

4. *Finance Committee:* This committee is responsible for planning, monitoring, and overseeing the organization's use of its financial resources, including developing a budget to allocate the organization's funds. It develops for board action the financial policies the organization requires. Unless the organization has a separate audit committee, the finance committee also oversees and reviews the organization's independent audit.

5. *Personnel Committee:* This committee usually is responsible for planning, monitoring, and overseeing the organization's use of its human resources (paid and volunteer). It develops needed personnel policies, including policies guiding performance management and supervision, employee compensation and benefits, and handling of grievances.

6. *Program Committee:* It is common for nonprofits to have one or more committees

to oversee the organization's system(s) for delivering quality services to clients and to ensure that these services are provided in a timely and responsible manner. This committee may handle certain relations with community leaders and interest groups that have key interests in the programs of the organization and plan for program development or refinement to meet future needs.

It is important that committees and task forces do only work that legitimately is the responsibility of the board, taking care that these structures do not interfere with the operations of the organization. Many boards have too many committees, and it has become a trend among some boards to minimize the number of standing committees and use task forces as needed to address issues of strategic importance.

David Renz

See also Nonprofit Governing Boards

References and further reading

Allison, Michael, and Jude Kaye. 1997. *Strategic Planning for Nonprofit Organizations.* San Francisco: Jossey-Bass.

Bradshaw, P., Vic Murray, and J. Wolpin. 1992. "Do Nonprofit Boards Make a Difference? An Exploration of the Relationships among Board Structure, Process and Effectiveness." *Nonprofit and Voluntary Sector Quarterly* 21: 227–249.

Brudney, J. L., and Vic Murray. 1998. "Do Intentional Efforts to Improve Boards Really Work?" *Nonprofit Management and Leadership* 8: 333–348.

Bryson, John. 1995. *Strategic Planning for Public and Nonprofit Organizations.* San Francisco: Jossey-Bass.

Carver, John. 1997. *Boards That Make a Difference,* 2d ed. San Francisco: Jossey-Bass.

Galbraith, Jay. 1983. *Designing Complex Organizations.* Reading, MA: Addison-Wesley.

Green, J. C., and D. W. Griesinger. 1996. "Board Performance and Organizational Effectiveness in Nonprofit Social Service Organizations." *Nonprofit Management and Leadership* 6: 381–402.

Herman, Robert D., and Richard Heimovics. 1991. *Executive Leadership in Nonprofit Organizations: New Strategies for Shaping Executive-Board Dynamics.* San Francisco: Jossey-Bass.

Herman, Robert D., and David O. Renz. 2000. "Board Practices of Especially Effective and Less Effective Local Nonprofit Organizations." *American Review of Public Administration* 30: 146–160.

Holland, Thomas. 2002. "Board Accountability: Lessons from the Field." *Nonprofit Management and Leadership* 12: 409–428.

Holland, Thomas P., and D. K. Jackson. 1999. "Strengthening Board Performance: Findings and Lessons from Demonstration Projects." *Nonprofit Management and Leadership* 9: 121–134.

Houle, Cyril O. 1997. *Governing Boards: Their Nature and Nurture.* San Francisco: Jossey-Bass.

Ingram, Richard T. 1996. *Ten Basic Responsibilities of Nonprofit Boards,* 2d ed. Washington, DC: National Center for Nonprofit Boards.

Jackson, D. K., and Thomas P. Holland. 1998. "Measuring the Effectiveness of Nonprofit Boards." *Nonprofit and Voluntary Sector Quarterly* 27: 159–182.

Mintzberg, Henry. 1994. *The Rise and Fall of Strategic Planning.* New York: Free Press.

Murray, Vic, and James Cutt. 2000. "An Overview of Rhetoric and Reality of Organizational Performance Evaluation by Nonprofit Boards." Unpublished paper presented at Innovation, Change, and Continuity in Nonprofit Organization Governance conference, Midwest Center for Nonprofit Leadership, University of Missouri–Kansas City, April 6–7.

Murray, Vic, and Bill Tassie. 1994. "Evaluating the Effectiveness of Nonprofit Organizations." In *The Jossey-Bass Handbook of Nonprofit Leadership and Management,* edited by R. D. Herman, 303–324. San Francisco: Jossey-Bass.

Ryan, William P. 1999. "Is That All There Is?" *New England Nonprofit Quarterly* 6, no. 2 (Summer): 8–15.

Stone, Melissa Middleton, B. Bigelow, and W. Crittenden. 1999. "Research on Strategic Management in Nonprofit Organizations." *Administration and Society* 31, 378–423.

Taylor, Barbara E., Richard P. Chait, and Thomas P. Holland. September–October, 1996. "The New Work of Nonprofit Boards." *Harvard Business Review* 74 (5): 36–43.

Government–Nonprofit Sector Relationship

The government-nonprofit relationship is at the center of a host of major, high-profile policy concerns in the United States. President George W. Bush's Faith-Based and Community Initiative has been hotly contested, in part because of disputes on the appropriateness of government funding of sectarian organizations. The successful implementation of welfare reform hinges to a great extent on the capacity of nonprofit service agencies funded by government to place welfare recipients in permanent jobs. The enduring concerns on the disposition of money raised by the American Red Cross and other charities in the wake of the September 11, 2001, tragedy is directly related to the proper role of government in maintaining accountability over nonprofit organizations. And the widespread concern about the decline in American civic life is rooted in part on the argument that without participation in voluntary associations and groups, the engagement of Americans in the "public sphere" will continue to erode. Central issues of the twenty-first century, including democratic participation and social rights, are directly connected to the government-nonprofit relationship.

The government-nonprofit relationship has important implications for policy and practice. In brief, government and the nonprofit sector interact along three dimensions: legal structure, the policy role, and the service delivery role. In regards to the legal structure, nonprofits exist within legal rules and regulations established by government. These rules profoundly affect the character of nonprofit organizations and their accountability to government. Second, nonprofit organizations are deeply involved in trying to influence public policy. Indeed, one of the key reasons for the importance placed upon nonprofit organizations by many scholars and policy makers is their ability to represent citizen interests before government (Berger and Neuhaus 1977; Meyer 1982). This representative role includes a wide variety of nonprofits—from local chapters of the Parent-Teacher Association to the World Wildlife Fund and the Children's Defense Fund. Third, nonprofits are increasingly essential to the delivery of an array of public services, especially in the social and health areas. Often, these nonprofit agencies are supported extensively by public funds. However, many of the smaller nonprofit service agencies frequently depend upon private, donated funds. Good examples include soup kitchens, food banks, and emergency shelters. President Bush's Faith-Based Initiative would increase the service delivery role of nonprofit agencies even further by encouraging many faith-based organizations to expand their services and apply for government funding.

Along each dimension, the relationship between government and nonprofits has become more com-

President George W. Bush speaks at a conference on faith-based and community initiatives in Philadelphia, December 12, 2002. During his speech, Bush rebuked Senate Majority Leader Trent Lott for recent comments appearing to endorse the past segregationist policies of Senator Strom Thurmond. (Reuters/Kevin Lamarque/Corbis)

plicated and intensive in the past twenty-five years. In part, this shift is related to the sheer increase in the size and scope of the nonprofit sector. The number of 501(c)(3) organizations under the Internal Revenue Code (IRC) is up over fivefold since 1967 (INDEPENDENT SECTOR 2002). Many nonprofit agencies providing services such as health care and foster care receive millions of dollars in public funds. This growth has generated public pressure to monitor and evaluate the performance of these organizations and to ensure greater financial and operational accountability. Performance-based contracts between government and the nonprofit service agencies have now become the norm for many federal, state, and local funding programs.

Further, the growth of the sector has brought increased scrutiny to the tax benefits received by nonprofit organizations and to the services they offer, especially to ensure that services are consistent with an organization's mission and tax status. For example, many policy makers and scholars argue that nonprofits should provide a certain level of charity care if they are to retain their nonprofit tax status. Members of Congress, including Republican Representative Ernst Istook of Oklahoma, have proposed legislation that would restrict the political activity of nonprofit organizations, contending that publicly chartered charities should not engage in any significant amount of political activity.

Each dimension of the government–nonprofit sector relationship is also quite varied. The legal frameworks governing the role of nonprofit organizations and their prerogatives have varied considerably over time (Hall 1987). Indeed, in the nineteenth century, the boundary between ostensibly public and private organizations was quite blurry. Substantial variation also exists from state to state on the laws regulating nonprofit organizations and the procedures necessary to obtain tax-exempt status.

The types of nonprofits taking an interest in influencing public policy range from neighborhood associations, interest groups, and grassroots organizations to umbrella coalitions of social service agencies and social movements such as the AIDS movement. The latter pressured government to respond to the growing AIDS crisis in the 1980s. The resultant AIDS policy provided extensive funding to nonprofit AIDS service agencies and also enlisted AIDS advocacy organizations in an ongoing relationship with government.

This AIDS example is typical of a larger and more widespread pattern where the growth of government facilitates the expansion of the policy and service role of nonprofit organizations. At the state level, for instance, the number of advocacy organizations representing human service agencies has increased sharply in recent years as government contracting of nonprofit agencies has risen. Moreover, some scholars have theorized that the growth of advocacy organizations was directly tied to the growth of the state (Salisbury 1984; Walker 1991; Skocpol 1999).

The use of nonprofit agencies by government to provide public services has a long history in the United States. But the extent of government funding of nonprofit agencies in a whole range of service categories—from home health to museums to child welfare—has increased sharply since the 1960s. Further, the growth of government funding for public services has been a central factor in the big jump in the number of nonprofit organizations. Just since 1977, for example, the number of nonprofit social service agencies has tripled (Smith 2002).

The tools by which government supports this public service function of nonprofit organizations have greatly diversified. Initially, government support for nonprofit organizations expanded primarily through direct grants and subsidies. However, in recent years, government has supported nonprofit service agencies through loans, tax credits, vouchers, and tax-exempt bonds. For example, nonprofit child-care agencies are supported primarily through vouchers and tax credits (and client fees) rather than through direct government grants.

The growing interconnections between government and the nonprofit sector have focused sharp attention on this relationship in terms of its impact on government, nonprofit agencies, and society more generally (Smith and Lipsky 1993; Grønbjerg 1993; Salamon 1987; Saidel 1991; DeHoog 1984). Nonprofits are especially attracted to government funding because of the relative scarcity of private donations, particularly in many controversial or complex services such as programs for the mentally ill. Government funding often allows nonprofits to pursue their mission and have an impact on the broader community. However, in the process of receiving government funding, nonprofits may be encouraged (and sometimes forced) to become more formalized as organizations, including adopting a higher level of professionalization. The receipt of government funds may convey enhanced organizational legitimacy, which may then be useful in obtaining additional public and private grants as well as attracting new board members, volunteers, and staff. Government funding draws nonprofits into the public policy process and gives them a stake and a voice in important policy concerns related to their organization's services.

But these very benefits can also lead to negative consequences. Managing contracts is a very time-intensive and complicated task, especially in the current era of government accountability and performance management (Smith 2002; Grønbjerg and Smith, forthcoming; Kettl 2000). Increasingly, government contracts and grants do not provide adequate support for the program administration. The result is to squeeze nonprofits financially; indeed, many contracts actually lose money for the organization if all of the administrative and overhead costs are considered (Smith 2002).

But the implications of government funding and contracts for nonprofits go well beyond the direct financial consequences. Government funding of nonprofits in social and health policy tends to be targeted on certain people or services and can be accompanied by a range of program and budgetary requirements and expectations. Consequently, the management flexibility of nonprofit executives and staff may be significantly circumscribed. Conflicts may arise between nonprofits and government as nonprofits strive to serve a community of interest as they define it in order to fulfill their mission and government attempts to treat citizens with equity (Smith and Lipsky 1993). The proliferation of more indirect means of government funding, such as vouchers and tax credits, may under some circumstances lessen this inherent dilemma. However, some types of tax-credit and voucher programs are also subject to extensive government regulation (Smith 2002).

Government funding may also encourage nonprofits to organize themselves internally in line with government expectations and funding streams (Grønbjerg 1993). This type of management structure may help nonprofits cope with the demands of government funding but may actually undermine the sustainability of nonprofits by discouraging revenue diversification and long-term strategic planning. Also, substantial government funding may inadvertently weaken the governance capacity of nonprofit boards because board members are often unprepared to oversee the complexity of government funding. Further, board members may believe that substantial private fundraising is unnecessary if government is providing most of the funding (Smith and Lipsky 1993).

Nonprofits are particularly attractive to government agencies as public service providers for several reasons. First, purchasing services from nonprofit organizations may allow government to more quickly start services than if it had to provide these services internally. Second, nonprofit agencies are usually nonunion and thus may offer government officials greater flexibility in program design and implementation. Third, and related to these considerations, contracting may appear to be cheaper than providing government services (although the transaction costs of contracting may actually mean that it is more expensive than direct public services). Fourth, government funding of nonprofits may be a way for government to support a favored constituency group or association. This may also help government win support of public programs in times of fiscal distress or problems.

In practice, these putative advantages of government support of nonprofits may be difficult to realize. Once funding is awarded, governments find it difficult to move money around and reallocate it to other organizations, partly because nonprofits will mobilize politically if they believe their funding is threatened. Further, government officials are faced with a principal-agent problem (Pratt and Zeckhauser 1985; Donahue 1989). That is, government, as the "principal," relies upon nonprofit organizations to be their agents. But in this situation, government may find it difficult to know whether the agent is implementing policies according to the objectives and priorities of government.

Government also faces pressures to respond to emergent needs, which is complicated by the investment of government in existing programs and services. Faced with this challenge, government officials may be tempted to further regulate existing contracts and grants in order to achieve new priority objectives. And while contracting shifts the risk of program implementation to the nonprofit agency, government may find it difficult to take full credit for successful programs; in the long run, government-supported activities may undermine support for government, even among citizens who benefit from them (Smith 1993).

The impact of government funding and policy on nonprofit organizations is perhaps most evident in organizations that depend heavily upon government dollars, especially in highly visible services such as child protection, mental health, and job training. But government policy also affects many other types of nonprofit organizations, even those without substantial public funding, such as arts and culture organizations. Many museums, orchestras, and zoos receive direct and indirect public subsidies. These subsidies have greatly encouraged the growth of such institutions in the past twenty years and has facilitated their investment in new physical infrastructure. This growth and development leads to greater formalization of programs and services, which in turn leads to changes in the management and mission of these organizations.

The increasingly intertwined and complicated relationship between government and nonprofits presents many daunting challenges that will need to be addressed if government and the nonprofit sector are to have a productive and a mutually satisfactory relationship. The growing dependence of government on nonprofit agencies—many of them relatively young and undercapitalized—means that government has a great interest in the management infrastructure of nonprofit organizations. Thus, government and the nonprofit sector need to work together to develop innovative ways of supporting and enhancing nonprofit management capacity. Needed reforms and initiatives include more flexible payment systems, new technical assistance strategies and models, and realistic and appropriate performance measures.

Nonprofits, for their part, need to improve their strategic planning, strengthen their board governance, and diversify their funding sources. Also, many nonprofit agencies receiving government funds are actually not very well connected to their communities. Thus, they are often quite vulnerable to government influence and pressure. And the lack of strong community connections may seriously hamper an agency's resource and board development strategies. Nonprofits also need to recognize that in an era of tight government budgets, creative partnerships between nonprofits, including mergers and formal collaborations, may be necessary. The successful adoption of these initiatives will require a new way of thinking among nonprofits, that is, a shift away from the focus on organizational growth and development to think more broadly about community needs and problems.

Further, nonprofits need to become better advocates for their own organizational interests as well as those of the community. Many nonprofits—especially those receiving government funds—are reluctant to undertake political advocacy owing to concerns about the potential impact of advocacy and lobbying on their tax status and their existing or future government contracts and grants (Berry 2003). But nonprofits could do much more advocacy without jeopardizing their tax situation or their relationship with government. Nonprofit staff and volunteers, including board members, need to be much more knowledgeable about the laws and regulations governing advocacy and must become more proactive in developing both collective and individual strategies to effectively represent their interests.

To be sure, some nonprofit organizations exist independent of government. But these organizations tend to be small, with little capacity to influence public policy, provide extensive services to people in need, or promote citizen participation in societal affairs. Thus, if we as a society want nonprofit organizations that are sustainable and vital, we need to be prepared to invest in both the public and nonprofit sectors and squarely address the challenges in managing the relationships across sectors.

Steven Rathgeb Smith

References and further reading
Berger, Peter L., and Richard J. Neuhaus. 1977. *To Empower People.* Washington, DC: American Enterprise Institute.
Berry, Jeffrey, with David A Arons. 2003. *A Voice for Nonprofits.* Washington, DC: Brookings.
DeHoog, Ruth Hoogland. 1984. *Contracting for Human Services: Economic, Political, and Organizational Perspectives.* Albany: State University of New York Press.
Donahue, John D. 1989. *The Privatization Decision.* New York: Basic Books.
Grønbjerg, Kirsten. 1993. *Understanding Nonprofit Funding.* San Francisco: Jossey-Bass.
Grønbjerg, Kirsten, and Steven Rathgeb Smith. Forthcoming. "The Scope and Theory of Government-Nonprofit Relations." In *The Nonprofit Sector: A Research Handbook,* 2d ed., edited by Walter W. Powell and Richard Steinberg. New Haven, CT: Yale University Press.
Hall, Peter Dobkin. 1987. "A Historical Overview of the Private Nonprofit Sector." In *The Nonprofit Sector: A*

Research Handbook, edited by Walter W. Powell. New Haven: Yale University Press.

INDEPENDENT SECTOR. 2002. *The New Nonprofit Almanac and Desk Reference.* Washington, DC: INDEPENDENT SECTOR.

Kettl, Donald F. 2000. *The Global Public Management Revolution.* Washington, DC: Brookings.

Meyer, Jack A., ed. 1982. *Meeting Human Needs: Toward a New Public Philosophy.* Washington, DC: American Enterprise Institute.

Pratt, Jon W., and Richard J. Zeckhauser, eds. 1985. *Principals and Agents: The Structure of Business.* Boston: Harvard Business School Press.

Saidel, Judith. 1991. "Resource Interdependence: The Relationship between State Agencies and Nonprofit Organizations." *Public Administration Review* 51 (November–December): 543–553.

Salamon, Lester M. 1987. "Partners in Public Service: The Scope and Theory of Government-Nonprofit Relations." In *The Nonprofit Sector: A Research Handbook,* 99–117. New Haven, CT: Yale University Press.

Salisbury, Robert H. 1984. "Interest Representation: The Dominance of Institutions." *American Political Science Review* 78 (1): 64–76.

Skocpol, Theda. 1999. "How America Became Civic." In *Civic Engagement in American Democracy,* edited by Theda Skocpol and Morris P. Fiorina, 27–80. Washington, DC: Brookings.

Smith, Steven Rathgeb. 1993. "The New Politics of Contracting: Contracting and the New Nonprofit Role." In *Public Policy for Democracy,* edited by Helen Ingram and Steven Rathgeb Smith, 198–221. Washington, DC: Brookings.

———. 2002. "Social Services." In *The State of the Nonprofit Sector,* edited by Lester M. Salamon, 149–186. Washington, DC: Brookings.

Smith, Steven Rathgeb, and Michael Lipsky. 1993. *Nonprofits for Hire: The Welfare State in the Age of Contracting.* Cambridge: Harvard University Press.

Walker, Jack L. 1991. "Interests, Political Parties, and Policy Formation in the American Democracy." In *Federal Social Policy: The Historical Dimension,* edited by D. T. Critchlow and Ellis W. Hawley, 141–170. University Park: Pennsylvania State University Press.

Grantmaking

The term "grantmaking" describes the core business of charitable foundations, namely, awarding gifts of cash (grants) to private, not-for-profit organizations in support of projects meant to enhance the common good. Whether conducted by the trustees of small, unstaffed foundations or by paid staff at larger foundations, grantmaking implies an element of choice on the part of grantmakers. In short, grantmakers decide which of the nonprofit organizations applying for grants receive them, for which purposes, and for what amounts. This ability to choose grantees confers considerable power on grantmakers, which leads to temptations for poor behavior on their part. The power imbalance has led to the development of "A Grantseeker's Bill of Rights" defining basic standards of professional grantmaking behavior.

History

Although the history of charitable bequests is a long one, traceable at least as far back as ancient Greece, the history of grantmaking is a relatively recent phenomenon. The reason for this apparent dichotomy is simple. Most of the early philanthropic institutions—ancient Roman municipal endowments, medieval British ecclesiastical foundations, colonial American charitable societies—were limited by their donor or by state charter to the support of specified institutions or causes. Trustees of such "proto-foundations" had little or no discretion in their giving; their role was to ensure that the donor's or state's giving directions were faithfully followed. Such giving was charitable, to be sure, but it was not grantmaking, for the trustees lacked the ability to make alternate choices as to recipients.

In grantmaking, some degree of flexibility is essential as times and conditions change and in light of the success, or lack thereof, of a foundation's original plan. For example, the Magdalen Society, one of the earliest proto-foundations in the United States, was founded in Philadelphia in 1800 to "ameliorate the distressed condition of those unhappy females who have been seduced from the paths of virtue, and are desirous of returning to a life of rectitude" (Weaver 1967, 22). Despite their best efforts, the trustees of the Magdalen Society could not find many prostitutes "desirous of returning to a life of rectitude," and the Magdalen Society was eventually reorganized as today's White-Williams Foundation, focusing on youth development, which in the year 2000 became the first private foundation in the United States to celebrate its bicentennial.

Although some nineteenth-century charitable institutions gave their trustees a degree of discretion in making grants, the advent of grantmaking on a broad and systematic scale did not occur until the establishment of the great general-purpose foundations, the Carnegie Corporation of New York (1911) and the Rockefeller Foundation (1913). These foundations were unprecedented in the United States in terms of both the size of their assets and the scope of their ambition. They pioneered a new approach to philanthropy, one that did not tie the organization to fixed charitable purposes but rather allowed their trustees—and even the hired staff—discretion in selecting, and, from time to time, changing, the causes that the foundation supported. Grantmaking, with all of its human ingenuity and human frailty, became the core activity of general-purpose foundations.

Grantmaking Styles

The style of grantmaking adopted by general-purpose foundations depends upon the theory of change that they embrace. A theory of change is a set of beliefs about the most effective ways to create social movement toward the common good. Over the years, two broad camps developed in the American foundation world. One camp believes that foundations should remain flexible in order to seize upon unforeseeable opportunities. They should avoid rigidity in thinking and methods of operation. The other camp believes that foundations should create their own opportunities in a systematic fashion. In order to do this, they must be highly strategic, focusing with discipline upon defined targets. Out of these two great camps arose four main grantmaking styles. Each style has its own particular strengths and weaknesses and its own set of vexing tradeoffs. Therefore, although individual foundations may prefer one style over another for their own operations, it is impossible to say that any one of these styles is more effective than any other. The four styles, and their various characteristics, are as follows:

1. *Passive* foundations have enormous flexibility and a great breadth of interests. They are able to quickly seize opportunities and to change directions as circumstances evolve. Passive foundations usually do not have a strategic plan, however, so they do not typically have a strong sense of direction. Nor can they go into much depth on any one subject. They accept unsolicited proposals—in fact, they make no efforts to solicit proposals at all—and merely fund the best of those proposals that they receive.

2. *Proactive* foundations also have considerable flexibility and a breadth of interests, but they also announce defined areas of operation. Within these areas of interest, they may do some strategic planning and go into some depth. They may even solicit some proposals through a "request-for-proposals" process. Proactive foundations, however, always remain substantially open to receiving unsolicited proposals and to seizing unexpected opportunities.

3. *Prescriptive* foundations have only a limited amount of flexibility and breadth of interests. They have chosen to become quite focused in their operations and very strategic in their planning. This strategic stance allows them to go into considerable depth within their restricted areas of operation, but it also makes them less able to respond to unexpected opportunities. Prescriptive foundations solicit most of their proposals through carefully defined request-for-proposals processes and generally do not have much flexibility, or even interest, in responding to unsolicited proposals.

4. *Peremptory* foundations have very little flexibility and a very limited breadth of interests. They create a highly disciplined strategic plan from which they do not deviate. This plan allows them to go into enormous depth in very tightly defined areas of operation. The tradeoff is that they have almost no ability to respond to unforeseen opportunities. They solicit all proposals through requests for proposals (or sometimes choose grantees without requiring them to even apply). Most peremptory foundations will not even

consider unsolicited proposals, much less fund one. (Orosz 2000, 25–27)

Given the fact that the names of all these styles start with the letter P, their qualities can best be understood by constructing a "Four-P Continuum" (ibid., 26). This continuum, shown in Figure 1, suggests that each of the four styles has strengths and weaknesses that make them appropriate and useful in some grantmaking contexts but inappropriate and useless in others. This tradeoff holds true, as well, for six qualities of foundation work that are valued, to a greater or lesser degree, across the charitable foundation field. These qualities are flexibility, breadth, opportunism, discipline, strategy, and depth. It is instructive to convert the Four-P Continuum into a matrix expressing the level of these qualities within each grantmaking style (see Table 1).

As the matrix demonstrates, grantmaking styles inevitably entail tradeoffs. Passive foundations have great flexibility to seize opportunities but lack the discipline to be strategic and focused. Peremptory foundations have the discipline to be highly strategic but lack any flexibility to seize opportunities. Moreover, a foundation cannot move from one style to another without giving something up. A passive foundation, for example, cannot become more strategic without becoming less flexible, cannot achieve greater depth without sacrificing breadth, and cannot become more disciplined without sacrificing the ability to seize opportunities. Thus there is no one "ideal" style of grantmaking. Each style has strengths that make it appealing, but each also has drawbacks that make it unappealing.

Figure 1 Four-P Continuum

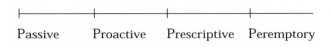

Passive   Proactive   Prescriptive   Peremptory

The Human Factor: Attributes and Temptations

There is no "hard science" of grantmaking; it is more of an art or a calling than it is a science or a profession. At every stage in the grantmaking process, from the theory of change on the front end, to the yes or no decision at the midpoint, to the management and closing of the project at the end, human personalities and judgments intrude and determine the course that the grant will take. Therefore, as Alan Pifer, a former chief executive officer of the Carnegie Corporation of New York, noted, the "human factor" is the most important element in grantmaking (Pifer 1973, 3). What attributes should a grantmaker possess? Many have attempted to create checklists of such attributes, and the terms chosen vary from list to list. At least six of these attributes, however, appear to be absolutely essential. They are as follows:

1. *Integrity:* All transactions between grantmakers and grantseekers ultimately depend upon trust. A mendacious grantmaker, therefore, ultimately cannot be effective.
2. *People skills:* Grantmaking is a human enterprise, and it is absolutely essential that grantmakers be empathic and respectful listeners, articulate speakers, clear writers, and intuitive and sensitive observers.

Table 1 Four-P Continuum Matrix

	Passive	*Proactive*	*Prescriptive*	*Peremptory*
Flexibility	Great	Considerable	Some	Little
Breadth	Great	Considerable	Some	Little
Opportunism	Great	Considerable	Some	Little
Discipline	Little	Some	Considerable	Great
Strategy	Little	Some	Considerable	Great
Depth	Little	Some	Considerable	Great

3. *Analytical ability and creativity:* Program officers must have the ability to analyze ideas, test their internal logic, and rate their external value. At the same time, program officers must have the ability to grasp the possibilities of ideas, to envision how they might develop, and to take leaps of faith. Effective grantmakers, in short, possess a good balance of "head" and "heart."

4. *Spirituality:* Grantmaking, at its best, demonstrates a love for fellow humans, provides an avenue to transform faith into action, and satisfies a craving to connect to others in a profound way.

5. *Sense of balance and proportion:* Grantmakers are offered endless opportunities to do good; if all were accepted, the foundation would quickly run out of money and the grantmaker would quickly run out of time. Grantmakers must learn how to say no to good ideas from worthy applicants and to avoid becoming personally overcommitted, overstressed, and overwhelmed.

6. *Compassion:* Grantmaking is more than the making of grants. It is also the breaking of hearts. Many, if not most, of the proposals that must be declined come from good people who are doing good things, and the last thing an applicant needs when absorbing this disappointment is to have a grantmaker heap insult upon injury by being disrespectful or insensitive. (Orosz 2000, 48–52)

Grantmakers also face a number of temptations as they go about their duties. Their success depends upon their ability to resist the blandishments of temptations such as those listed below:

1. *Succumbing to flattery:* Grantmakers typically receive very little criticism, whether constructive or otherwise, but receive a great deal of flattery from individuals and organizations hoping to get grants. Grantmakers need to develop an "internal gyroscope" to gauge the true value of their performance because outside feedback is an unreliable guide.

2. *Becoming arrogant:* The paucity of criticism and the abundance of flattery can cause grantmakers to begin to believe that they truly are as good as the flatterers say, and this can lead to a sense of power or even infallibility. Grantmakers must consciously struggle against this temptation in order to keep their perspective and effectiveness.

3. *Becoming cynical:* It necessary to discount the flattery in order to counter the arrogance, but this discounting can be taken to an extreme. Grantmakers who do this are likely to think that every kind word they receive is undeserved and that the only reason that they receive praise is that they work for a foundation. Believing none of the flattery, therefore, is just as dangerous as believing all of it.

4. *Forgetting the stewardship:* Grantmakers are notorious for forgetting that they are employed by a foundation and starting to think that the foundation's money is their own. They must remember that their role is one of stewardship of money for the benefit of society. This cannot be done if they make grantseekers feel as if the proposal request is a plea for a personal loan.

5. *Believing that all grantseekers are unworthy:* When a grantmaker becomes too analytical—that is, when the "head" takes over the "heart"—it seems that all grantseekers are unworthy.

6. *Believing that all grantseekers are worthy:* The mirror image of the previous peccadillo is to have one's "heart" completely rule one's "head." All foundations receive more proposals than they can possibly fund. Grantmakers who find so much value in every proposal that they want to fund all of them are doing a service to no one. Program officers simply must make hard decisions and disappoint good people.

7. *Taking the easy way out:* Grantmakers soon discover that well-written proposals are

easier to fund than poorly written ones, but it is not always the case that well-written proposals describe better *ideas* than poorly written ones. The danger is that grantmakers, who always carry a heavy workload and are always pressed for time, will be tempted to fund well-written proposals that describe mediocre ideas over poorly written proposals that describe great ideas. Excellence in grantmaking is no accident; it is achieved by a lot of hard work. Program officers who merely develop mediocre ideas could (and should) be replaced by cash machines. (Orosz 2000, 39–45)

A Grantseeker's Bill of Rights

Grantseekers are on the other side of the equation from grantmakers. Given the power disparities between the two, it might be more accurate to say grantseekers are on the other side of the tracks. Grantmakers who do not have the proper human attributes, or who succumb to the temptations of philanthropy (or both), can exacerbate these disparities and treat grantseekers very poorly. It is important to note that grantseekers have rights as well as obligations. In fact, the rights have been systematized in "A Grantseeker's Bill of Rights." The rights are as follows:

1. The right to receive a clear statement of the foundation's funding interests
2. The right to have all communications answered
3. The right to an explanation of, and an estimated timeline for, the foundation's proposal review process
4. The right to a prompt acknowledgment of receipt of the proposal
5. The right to have all proposals read in full and seriously considered
6. The right to a timely and unambiguous funding decision
7. The right to receive an explanation of the reasoning behind funding decisions
8. The right to have all requirements for the grant relationship clearly spelled out, in writing (including the right to have any

components of the grant *required* by the foundation *paid for* by the foundation)
9. The right to have all reports completely read and carefully considered
10. The right to be informed if continued funding is a possibility (Orosz 2000, 46–47)

Living up to the standards presented in "A Grantseeker's Bill of Rights" is an essential element of professional practice for any grantmaker, but not an onerous task. It simply requires a commitment to open and honest communication with all grantseekers.

A Grantmaker's Bill of Rights

Although grantmakers have the advantage in the power disparity, the grantmaking process is an equation, and grantseekers, too, have an obligation to behave honorably toward grantmakers. Moreover, grantmakers also have rights as well as obligations. These rights have been systematized in "A Donor's Bill of Rights," developed and endorsed by several prominent nonprofit and fundraising organizations. Donors' rights are listed below:

1. The right to be informed of the organization's mission, of the way the organization intends to use donated resources, and of its capacity to use donations effectively for their intended purposes
2. The right to be informed of the identity of those serving on the organization's governing board, and to expect the board to exercise prudent judgment in its stewardship responsibilities
3. The right to have access to the organization's most recent financial statements
4. The right to be assured that their gifts will be used for the purposes for which they were given
5. The right to receive appropriate acknowledgement and recognition
6. The right to be assured that information about their donations is handled with respect and with confidentiality to the fullest extent provided by the law

7. The right to expect that all relationships with individuals representing organizations of interest to the donor will be professional in nature

8. The right to be informed whether those seeking donations are volunteers, employees of the organization, or hired solicitors

9. The right to have the opportunity for their names to be deleted from mailing lists that an organization intends to share

10. The right to feel free to ask questions when making a donation and to receive prompt, truthful, and forthright answers (Light 2000, 66–67)

Living up to "A Donor's Bill of Rights" is an essential element of professional practice for any grantseeker, but not an onerous task. Grantmakers and grantseekers alike must strive for open and honest communications with each other.

Conclusion

Grantmaking is the essential core skill in the operation of charitable foundations across the United States. It is crucial, therefore, that it be done wisely and well. The ultimate end of charitable foundations—positive social change—will never happen unless there is all-around excellence in grantmaking. Or, to put it negatively, shoddy grantmaking leads directly to shoddy outcomes. The last word on this subject belongs to the Greek philosopher Aristotle, who stated in Book 2 of *Nicomachean Ethics*, "Anyone . . . can give away money or spend it; but to do all this to the right person, to the right extent, at the right time, for the right reason, and in the right way, is no longer something easy that anyone can do. It is for this reason that good conduct [in such matters] is rare, praiseworthy, and noble" (Orosz 2000, 1).

Joel J. Orosz

See also History of American Foundations
References and further reading
Council on Foundations. 1986. *Principles and Practices for Effective Grantmaking,* rev. ed. Washington, DC: Council on Foundations.
Ford Foundation, http://www.grantcraft.org.
Kibbe, Barbara, F. Setterberg, and Cole Wilbur. 1999. *Grantmaking Basics: A Field Guide for Funders.*
Washington, DC: The David and Lucile Packard Foundation and the Council on Foundations.
Light, Paul C. 2000. *Making Nonprofits Work: A Report on the Tides of Nonprofit Reform.* Washington, DC: Aspen Institute and Brookings Institution Press.
Orosz, Joel J. 2000. *The Insider's Guide to Grantmaking: How Foundations Find, Fund, and Manage Effective Programs.* San Francisco: Jossey-Bass.
Philanthropic Research, Inc. "Doing Business As Guidestar," http://www.guidestar.org.
Pifer, Alan. 1973. "President's Message." *Annual Report of the Carnegie Corporation of New York.* New York: Carnegie Corporation of New York.
Weaver, Warren. 1967. *U.S. Philanthropic Foundations: Their History, Structure, Management and Record.* New York: Harper and Row.

Grantseeking

Grants represent a small but significant portion of support available for eleemosynary endeavors. They are awarded by two types of entities: foundations and government agencies or programs. Foundation grants constitute approximately 10 percent of private philanthropy, as tracked by the American Association of Fundraising Counsel's *Giving USA*. Grant funding awarded by government sources has not been quantified but represents a relatively small portion of public funds.

The foundation world is divided into two categories, private and public. The category that a particular foundation falls into depends on the source of the funds that compose its asset base. Private foundations, those in which the assets derive from private sources, are divided into three types. The two of greatest interest to grantseekers are the independent foundation and the corporate, or company-sponsored, foundation. Independent foundations, also called family foundations, make up 88 percent of all private foundations in the United States. The third type of U.S. legal entity classified as a private foundation is an operating foundation, a public charity that operates its own program and does not generally make grants to other organizations. The balance of foundations are public, and of these, the category of greatest interest to grantseekers is that of the community foundations, entities that exist to support activities in a specifically delimited geographic area. Public foundations also include women's funds and other funds related to specific populations and activities, such as funds created by the sale of hospitals that become "new health" or "health care conversion" foundations.

According to the *Catalog of Federal Domestic Assistance,* the federal government provides fifteen different kinds of financial support, of which only two are grants. Formula grants are allocations of money to states, counties, or municipalities that provide support for initiatives mandated by law and open to local interpretation. Currently there are 173 such programs. Project grants represent the other category, and there are currently 889 different programs that include support of a wide variety of activities—fellowships, research, construction, experimentation and demonstration, evaluation, and planning.

The Grantseeking Process

The process by means of which grants are sought and won has seven steps.

Step 1: Initiation

What constitutes the first step depends on whether the grantseeker is taking an active or responsive role. If the grantseeker is initiating the process, the first step consists of conducting research on grant opportunities. The repository of much information on private sector grantmaking is the Foundation Center Library, with national, regional, and local collections as well as substantial information available through the Foundation Center's Web site at http://www.fdn center.org. If the grantseeker is investigating public-sector opportunities, one place to start is the *Catalogue of Federal Domestic Assistance,* which details all forms of public funding. If the grantseeker is responding, he or she will mostly likely do so in response to a request for proposals (RFP) in which the grantmaker invites grantseekers to compete to accomplish a specific goal.

Step 2: Preliminaries

In the case of proactive grantseeking, research consists of identifying those foundations and corporate entities that make grants to support work in the discipline of the eleemosynary organization, such as education, social services, or the arts; in the geographic area in which the organization is located; and for a purpose consistent with the endeavor being contemplated, for example, a special project, scholarship, capital ex-

pense, or general unrestricted operating funds. Once appropriate foundation prospects are identified, representatives of the grantseeking organization map their contacts, reviewing the names of individuals who are involved in the foundation to identify relationships that exist between grantmaker and grantseeker.

If the grantseeker is reacting, the preliminary step usually consists of either speaking with a representative of the foundation informally or attending a formal technical assistance session sponsored by the grantmaker. In either case, the grantseeker should learn about the purpose of the request for proposals and the eligibility and selection criteria.

Step 3: Introduction

For grantseekers taking the initiative, the introductory phase consists of a meeting between representatives of the grantseeking and grantmaking organizations. At this meeting, the grantseeker learns the details of the specific grantmaker's decision-making process and presents information to position his project or activity as attractive to the grantmaker. Ideally, this meeting results in the grantmaker inviting the grantseeker to submit a formal proposal.

For grantseekers responding to a grantmaker's RFP, the introductory phase consists of the preparation and submission of a letter of intent (LOI), usually a brief document outlining the plan for the project and the ways in which the grantseeker's project addresses the grantmaker's agenda. Usually, grantmakers screen and review LOIs and invite some applicants to continue to the next phase of the competition.

Step 4: Development of the Plan

The preparation of a grant proposal or request is an exercise in planning and positioning. The development of a compelling, cogent proposal involves securing and documenting the "buy-in" of key participants, forecasting schedules, estimating resources required, and calculating costs. In addition, the project or organization must be positioned so that it is presented as an attractive opportunity or partner for the grantmaker.

Step 5: Submission

Once the proposal or formal request document has been prepared in compliance with the criteria outlined by the grantmaker, the grantseeker must submit it in a timely fashion.

Step 6: Advocacy

In competitive situations, decision makers often may be swayed by further advocacy on behalf of the grantseeking organization. Once a proposal has been submitted, grantseekers work to convince decision makers or those who influence decision makers that their application merits support.

Step 7: Stewardship

Once a grant has been awarded, the funds have been disbursed, and project implementation is in process, the relationship between grantseeker and grantmaker moves to another level. Regular communication in the form of timely reports and updates from grantseeker to grantmaker pave the way for positive responses to future requests.

Documents Associated with Grantseeking

To maintain preferential tax status, grantmakers must have documentation of grant requests. A proposal is the primary record of a grantseeker's appeal for a grant and generally consists of nine components, as follows:

1. The background of the organization: the organization's mission, experience, and qualifications for conducting the project
2. The statement of need, or problem description: an outline of the circumstances that make the project necessary or desirable
3. Objectives: the changes toward which the work described is aimed
4. Methods: the activities by means of which change will be effected, and often, a timeline for events related to the project or activity
5. Outcomes: the results hoped to be accomplished through the project or activity
6. Personnel: the people who will conduct the project and their qualifications
7. Evaluation: the plan by means of which the grantseeker will determine the effectiveness of the project or activity
8. Future funding: the plan for support after the grant being sought runs out

9. Budget: the revenue and expense plan to support the activities

Proposals are often preceded by an introductory cover letter and an executive summary providing an overview of the proposal. Grantseekers also often include appendices and attachments to the proposal for documents supporting or amplifying their argument.

As noted above, prior to developing and submitting a proposal, grantseekers often submit a letter of intent, which is customarily structured as a mini-proposal. Another document grantseekers often prepare during the preliminary phase of the process is a "white paper," a discussion of issues of shared interest for both grantmaker and grantseeker.

Susan L. Golden

References and further reading

Brown, Larissa Golden, and Martin John Brown. 2001. *Demystifying Grant Seeking.* San Francisco: Jossey-Bass

Burke, Jim, and Carol Ann Prater. 2000. *I'll Grant You That.* Portsmouth, NH: Heinemann.

Carlson, Mim. 1995. *Winning Grants Step-by-Step.* San Francisco: Jossey-Bass.

Clarke, Cheryl A. 2001. *Storytelling for Grantseekers.* San Francisco: Jossey-Bass.

Golden, Susan L. 1997. *Secrets of Successful Grantsmanship.* San Francisco: Jossey-Bass.

Hall, Mary. 1988. *Getting Funded,* 3d ed. Portland, OR: Continuing Education Publications.

Kiritz, Norton J. 1980. *Program Planning and Proposal Writing.* Los Angeles: The Grantsmanship Center.

McIlnay, Dennis P. 1998. *How Foundations Work.* San Francisco: Jossey-Bass.

New, Cheryl Carter, and James Aaron Quick. 1998. *Grantseeker's Toolkit.* New York: Wiley.

Orosz, Joel J. 2000. *The Insider's Guide to Grantmaking.* San Francisco: Jossey-Bass.

Grassroots Associations

A grassroots association (GA) is a local, nonprofit, volunteer group using the associational form of organization, which typically involves a set of volunteer members and one or more elected volunteer leaders pursuing the group goal. GAs are the most frequent form of nonprofits in the United States and often form a local base for national or international associations.

Although poor in average economic resources, they are rich in volunteerism and hence philanthropy.

The group goal may be any one (or more) of a wide range of possible objectives but most commonly concerns leisure or occupational interests. Although some GAs have nonmember service goals (for example, Parent-Teacher Associations and Lions Clubs), most focus on member service, peer-helping, or self-help goals (for example, lodges of Freemasons, local trade unions, Boy Scout troops, bowling leagues, or Alcoholics Anonymous chapters). In either case, voluntary altruism is present in the sense that members are helping other people outside their own immediate families.

GAs first began to flourish around 8000 B.C. in settled, horticultural, preliterate societies, which contrasted with the earlier nomadic, hunting-gathering, preliterate bands that had dominated most of human existence. These early common interest associations were men's clubs, secret societies, age group clubs, or economic guilds. Later, in ancient agrarian civilizations such as Egypt, China, Greece, and Rome, local religious congregations and occupational guilds existed from about 3000 B.C. With the coming of industrial society in the United States, as in Great Britain and elsewhere in Europe from about A.D. 1800, GAs became even more common as factory workers unions and employers associations began to flourish. But there were also now political parties, road associations, sects and cults, social clubs and fraternities, arts associations, social movement groups (for example, antislavery and women's suffrage groups), health and service associations, amateur sports and hobby clubs, and so on. The twentieth century was the heyday of American GAs, with some decline of traditional GAs in its latter decades and a trend toward self-help and support groups. The concept of the GA in social science seems to date from early in the twentieth century, especially with the Progressive movement, although the broader concept of association saw some use earlier.

Prevalence and Interorganizational Relations

The raw numerical prevalence of GAs in U.S. states, counties, municipalities, and other territorial units is strongly affected by the population of the unit in question. The population-standardized prevalence has been about 30 GAs per 1,000 population in the latter part of the twentieth century, making the United States a leader, but not foremost, in GA prevalence. Given the current U.S. population, one can estimate that there could well be more than 8 million GAs in the nation. A higher population-standardized prevalence in individual territorial units results from such factors as a higher degree of permissiveness of political control (civil liberties), higher levels of modernization and socioeconomic status, greater prevalence of nonassociational organizations (businesses, government agencies, nonassociational nonprofits), more ethno-religious heterogeneity, more aggregate resource mobilization (such as technical assistance or umbrella groups), more aggregate social cohesion (informal social bonds among people), and unique cultural or historical factors.

About half of the GAs in the United States are monomorphic, that is, not affiliated with a higher-level territorial unit such as a parent or umbrella group. The other half are polymorphic with affiliation to a state, regional, national, or international umbrella group or federation. Many GAs also have local affiliations with a nonprofit, governmental, or for-profit organization that provides space for meetings or other activities and may sponsor or control the GA in some ways. Church-based or school-based GAs are common examples. Nonreligious GAs with $5,000 or more in annual revenues are required to register with the Internal Revenue Service (IRS), and nonreligious GAs with $25,000 or more in annual revenues are required to file annual financial reports with the IRS (Form 990). About 10–20 percent of GAs are registered with the IRS and have formal tax-exemption letters. The polymorphic GAs receive tax exemption through their parent/umbrella organization. Aside from these three kinds of affiliations, most GAs have little in the way of direct interorganizational relationships. Nonetheless, GAs are typically affected by competition for members in the sociodemographic pool of eligible potential members in their communities.

Impact and Effectiveness

GAs may have either or both of two types of impact: an internal impact, on their members, or an external impact, on their environments—both social and biophysical. GAs tend to have the internal impact of social support, peer helping, and self-expression and sometimes the related external impact of nonmember helping or service (for example, post-disaster aid, firefighting, emergency medical services, or crime control). They usually have the internal impacts of providing both experiential knowledge of group processes and information related to their activities. Many GAs also provide information to nonmembers. Most provide some sociopolitical activation to members, resulting in psychological empowerment and more individual political activity. Many also have the external impact of creating sociopolitical influence, sometimes affecting public issues. GA volunteer activities generally have an imputed (attributed) economic value in U.S. society of roughly $200 billion annually at present, and GAs also sometimes help members with job contacts and job skills. Many GAs specifically provide economic system support (for example, farmers groups, unions, merchant associations, and professional groups). GAs often promote greater happiness/satisfaction and physical and mental health. This is especially true for self-help groups but to some extent for GAs generally. The large and varied cumulative impact of GAs is significantly related to the fact that the United States is a participatory democracy with a large and active voluntary, nonprofit sector.

The effectiveness of GAs is influenced by several factors. Those that have greater impact tend to have (1) better resource mobilization for means (activities) and ends (goals) (for example, sufficient recruitment of active members, high internal activity, and sufficient internal funding); (2) better ideology, incentives, and values; (3) better maintenance, or internal control (for example, sufficient internal democracy, high internal cohesion, persistence over years); and (4) better, more fruitful relationships and interactions with their environment (for example, substantial autonomy, participation in a supralocal federation or umbrella group, informal cooperation with other local groups). Effectiveness factors for internal impact–seeking GAs also include having a member sponsorship system for new members, using comember peers as a reference group for personal change, having members feel accepted and affirmed as persons, and the like. Effectiveness factors for

external impact–seeking GAs also include creating a greater sense of local community, having an optimal mix of external and internal goals, avoiding internal divisiveness and factionalism, and so on.

Structure and Processes

As contrasted with paid-staff nonprofits, GAs tend to be characterized by founder or formational choices that lead to groups that have mostly member-benefit goals, an informal group style, high internal democracy, some sociodemographic membership criteria, and more diffuse goals. GAs tend to have internal guidance systems that involve stronger sociability incentives, stronger purposive incentives (satisfactions from pursuing group goals), stronger service incentives, and weaker utilitarian incentives (money or goods received for work) than paid-staff nonprofits. GAs also tend, in comparison with paid-staff nonprofits, to have internal structures that emphasize mainly volunteer workers, informal tax exemption (no IRS registration), informal organization, internal democracy, member-benefit goals, linkage to a supralocal federation or umbrella group, substantial sociodemographic homogeneity, and few economic resources.

The internal processes of GAs (vs. paid-staff nonprofits) tend to emphasize evening and weekend timing of activities, intermittent activities, low external funding, broad and intermittent political activity, low or moderate prestige, informal recruitment, informal socialization of newcomers, volunteer termination of membership, and younger age of the group itself. Unlike paid-staff nonprofits, the leadership of GAs tends to be mainly elected (vs. appointed), unpaid, low in professionalism, higher in charisma, higher in consideration (attention to emotional needs) of followers, lower in supervision of followers, looser in priority setting, usually promoted from inside, low in selectivity, and higher in leader quality problems. GAs also tend to have fewer government relations than paid-staff nonprofits. Like paid-staff nonprofits, GAs tend to increase in internal complexity (bureaucratization, formalization, specialization, and so on) and size with age, although GAs are more likely to consciously resist increasing complexity than are paid-staff nonprofits.

Individual Participation and Exceptional Individuals

About 40 percent of U.S. adults report being active in one or more GAs, and 60–70 percent report being members of one or more (not counting local religious congregations, which would raise the figure by another 10–15 percent). Children aged twelve to seventeen also report high levels of membership and activity. The determinants of individual GA participation vary according to the measure of participation used. The number of GAs belonged to tends to be associated with particular variables. These include:

1. Contextual variables (higher average income or education of neighborhood, small community of residence, employment in a larger corporation)
2. Dominant-status sociodemographic variables (higher education, income, and occupational prestige if employed, marriage, full-time employment, more school-age children, moderate age)
3. Active-effective character on personality variables (greater sense of efficacy and internal locus of control, morality, empathy, emotional stability, self-esteem or ego strength, extraversion, emotional warmth, assertiveness)
4. Favorable attitudinal variables (greater perceived efficacy of GAs, greater perceived benefits of GA participation and fewer costs, more altruistic attitudes/values, greater sense of civic duty, greater perception of GA attractiveness)
5. Favorable situational variables (being asked or encouraged to join a GA, having friends or acquaintances in GAs)

Membership in a given GA is predicted by living close to the GA, having sociodemographic characteristics similar to members of that GA, having favorable attitudes toward the specific GA, and experiencing favorable situational variables (such as being asked to join the GA or having friends or acquaintances in the GA). Greater participation in a GA, once someone is a member, is predicted by higher socioeconomic sta-tus (education, income, occupational prestige), a more active-effective character on personality variables, more favorable general attitudes about GA participation, more favorable attitudes toward the specific GA (more perceived benefits and fewer costs from participation, greater satisfaction with participation), and more favorable situational variables. Greater length of membership in a GA is predicted by favorable specific attitudes about the GA (such as continuing to receive more benefits and less costs from participation, satisfaction with participation) and favorable situational variables. Deciding to exit a GA is predicted by less favorable specific attitudes toward the GA and less favorable situational variables (moving of residence, getting a new job, conflict with educational pursuits). In general, greater prediction of GA participation results from inclusion of predictors from more domains.

More GA membership and more participation in a GA once a member are positively associated with other socioculturally approved forms of leisure social participation, such as neighborhood interaction, friendship activity, political activity, outdoor recreation and sports activity, print media activity (for example, reading newspapers and books), informal helping behavior, volunteer program activity, and charitable giving. This positive association across types of socioculturally valued leisure activities in U.S. society represents a leisure general-activity pattern of broad importance.

Exceptional individuals tend to have more impact on GAs than on paid-staff nonprofits, making more of a difference to the success of the former. GA founders tend to be high in active-effective character and favorable attitudes toward GA participation, often being charismatic leaders. Some exceptional GA activists found several GAs in their lifetimes.

Values and Futures

GAs are shown to make cumulative positive contributions to U.S. society when evaluated by such standards as participatory democracy, political pluralism, quality of life, the general welfare, the public interest, civil society, and positive social capital. In an authoritarian state or dictatorship, by contrast, GAs are usually seen by the societal leadership as threatening and dangerous unless tightly controlled; hence such societies tend to suppress GAs and carefully control the ones allowed to exist. A small minority of GAs in the United States, perhaps 1–5 percent, are fundamentally deviant from societal norms in their principal goals and/or (especially) their means of accomplishing these goals (for example, delinquent youth gangs, witches' covens, some social movement groups, some communes, underground militias, nudist groups, some cults and sects, terrorist groups, hate groups). In general, these deviant GAs cause relatively little social harm, although some of them do substantial harm. They constitute collectively part of the price democratic societies pay for freedom of association and other civil liberties—that is, a voluntary society.

The future of GAs in the United States is, in one sense, guaranteed by the fundamentally democratic nature of the society. GAs will probably continue to flourish in the new century as in the prior one. However, there is likely to be a continuation of the decline of many traditional GAs and a rise of more social support and self-help GAs. There may also be a continuation of the shift of volunteering from GAs to volunteer programs (volunteer departments of paid-staff nonprofits, government agencies, or even certain for-profit organizations such as proprietary hospitals), as in the past few decades. If there is a catastrophe of national scope (for example, a plague or epidemic, an environmental disaster, or widespread terrorism), participation in GAs and numbers of GAs will likely decline.

David Horton Smith

See also Mutual Benefit Organizations; Nonprofit Sector; Voluntarism

References and further reading

Ellis, Susan, and Katherine Noyes. 1990. *By the People: A History of Americans as Volunteers,* rev. ed. San Francisco: Jossey-Bass.

Hall, Peter Dobkin. 1992. *Inventing the Nonprofit Sector and Other Essays on Philanthropy, Volunteerism, and Nonprofit Organizations.* Baltimore: Johns Hopkins University Press.

Milofsky, Carl, ed. 1988. *Community Organizations: Studies in Resource Mobilization and Exchange.* New York: Oxford University Press.

Putnam, Robert D. 2000. *Bowling Alone: The Collapse and Revival of American Community.* New York: Simon and Schuster.

Smith, David Horton. 1994. "Determinants of Voluntary Association Participation and Volunteering: A Literature Review." *Nonprofit and Voluntary Sector Quarterly* 23 (3): 243–263.

———. 2000. *Grassroots Associations.* Thousand Oaks, CA: Sage.

Wuthnow, Robert. 1998. *Loose Connections: Joining Together in America's Fragmented Communities.* New York: Free Press.

Gratz, Rebecca (1781–1869)

Rebecca Gratz was a devout Jew who dedicated her life to serving those less fortunate. Born the seventh child of twelve to a wealthy and well-connected Philadelphia family on March 4, 1781, Gratz became a beloved legend for her charitable deeds and devotion to her community. Most likely educated at the Young Ladies Academy in Philadelphia, she was familiar with literature, geography, philosophy, some Christian teachings, and republican political values of post–Revolutionary War America. Through her studies, she developed a strong sense of patriotism. Though she never married, she helped establish charitable organizations and educational centers with funds provided by her father and brothers.

At the age of twenty, she helped to establish the Female Association for the Relief of Women in Reduced Circumstances. The organization provided goods and services directly to women whose families were suffering after the Revolutionary War. Fourteen years later, in 1815, Gratz helped to establish the nondenominational Philadelphia Orphan Asylum. Serving as its secretary, she was able to champion her causes in a quiet way through the publicly distributed minutes of the meetings. Forty years later, Gratz would be instrumental in establishing the Jewish Foster Home and Orphan Asylum. The asylum provided an answer for orphans who were the result of the rise in Jewish immigration and poverty in the Philadelphia area of the time. Gratz was persuaded to assume the role of vice president.

By the end of 1817, Gratz had established an informal Hebrew school in her home for anyone desiring to attend, including her nieces and nephews. Although the school did not endure, the idea of the Hebrew home school was paired with the Protestant

Sunday school to create the Hebrew Sunday School in 1838. Gratz served as its superintendent and assisted in the development of its curriculum.

In 1819, Gratz established the Female Hebrew Benevolent Society, the first independent Jewish women's organization. The group's mission was carried out primarily in Philadelphia and eastern Pennsylvania but was as far reaching as Alabama and Kentucky. Gratz was often referred to as "the foremost Jewess of her day," and many believe that her beauty, wit, and devotion to her faith inspired Sir Walter Scott's heroine Rebecca in his novel *Ivanhoe*. Gratz died on August 27, 1869, having outlived all of her siblings save for her youngest brother, Benjamin. Today, she is recognized as one of the most important women in U.S. history.

Kristine M. Haskett

References and further reading

Ashton, Dianne. 2002. "Rebecca Gratz: 1781–1869." In *Notable American Philanthropists: Biographies of Giving and Volunteering*, edited by Robert T. Grimm Jr., 129–133. Westport, CT: Oryx Press.

Henry, Sondra, and Emily Taitz. 1986. *Written Out of History: Our Jewish Foremothers*. Fresh Meadows, NY: Bilblio.

Jewish Virtual Library, http://www.us-israel.org/jsource/biography/Gratz.html.

Jewish Women's Archive, http://www.jwa.org/.

Wagenknecht, Edward. 1993. *Daughters of the Covenant*. Amherst: University of Massachusetts Press.

Guggenheim Family

The Guggenheims had more diverse interests—art, aerospace, literature, and science—than most of the great philanthropic families. The Guggenheim fortune began with Meyer Guggenheim (1828–1905), who emigrated to America from Switzerland in 1848. Guggenheim began his career operating a pushcart in the streets of Philadelphia; he then invented a stove polish that didn't blacken hands and used the profits from this invention to invest in Colorado silver mines. By 1895, Guggenheim had become an international entrepreneur, with mines in the U.S., Mexico, and Latin America.

In 1895, Guggenheim's competitors decided to form American Smelting and Refining, a giant copper trust that Guggenheim refused to join. Guggenheim and his rivals then fought a business war, which ended in 1901 when Guggenheim took over American Smelting and Refining. Later named Asarco, the firm remained the source of the Guggenheim mining fortune.

Meyer Guggenheim had seven sons. Four of them formed foundations. The smallest was formed by Murry Guggenheim, who started a small foundation that provided free dental care for the poor. The other three foundations, those of Daniel, Solomon, and Simon Guggenheim, discussed immediately below, are more substantial.

Daniel Guggenheim (1856–1930) first practiced philanthropy after the San Francisco earthquake of 1906, when he sent $500,000 in cash, which was hauled around the San Francisco streets in two pushcarts and dispensed to the unfortunate. But his great love was airplanes. When the Daniel Guggenheim Fund for the Promotion of Aeronautics was created in 1926, notes Guggenheim family biographer John H. Davis, it was seen by the philanthropic world as "little more than a manifestation of technological exhibitionism." When President Calvin Coolidge heard that someone was giving $2.5 million to make airplanes go faster, he said, "What's the use of getting there quicker if you haven't got anything to say when you arrived?"

But during the foundation's short life (it was liquidated in 1930, shortly after Guggenheim's death), it funded important advances. Guggenheim money funded the research of Robert Goddard, the pioneering American rocket designer, and Theodore von Karman, who helped develop the DC-3. Guggenheim money also helped fund the first commercial passenger flight in 1929.

Solomon Guggenheim (1861–1948) spent his first sixty-five years leading an utterly conventional life, delighting in fancy clothes, stately mansions, and Old Master paintings. In 1937 Guggenheim met Baroness Hilla Rebay von Ehrenwessen, who spent several weeks painting his portrait. She convinced him that modern art, specifically the works of Wassily Kandinsky, László Moholy-Nagy, and Rudolf Bauer, was important.

By 1939, Guggenheim had accumulated several hundred modern paintings, and created "The Solomon R. Guggenheim Collection of Non-Objective Art," an exhibition that toured in several cities. In 1944, he decided to create a museum in New York City and hired architect Frank Lloyd Wright to design the building. But while land had been purchased for the museum and Wright had completed his design, construction had not started by Guggenheim's death.

Simon Guggenheim (1867–1941) became a philanthropist when his oldest son, John Simon Guggenheim, died at seventeen after complications from pneumonia.

He consulted with American Smelting and Refining general counsel Carroll Atwood Wilson, who recommended consulting Swarthmore College president Frank Ayledotte and Henry Allen Moe. Wilson, Ayledotte, and Moe were all Rhodes scholars, and they helped to create the John Simon Guggenheim Memorial Foundation in 1925 as a Rhodes-like organization that awards one-year fellowships to scholars in a wide variety of fields. Under Moe's leadership, the Guggenheim Foundation gave fellowships to most of the American composers, painters, and novelists who flourished between 1925 and 1975.

Of the second generation of Guggenheims, the most important is Harry Guggenheim (1890–1971), son of Daniel. He succeeded his uncle as president of the Solomon R. Guggenheim Foundation and overcame very high obstacles imposed by New York City planners to ensure that construction of the museum was begun in 1956 and completed in 1959. Guggenheim also continued his father's interest in aeronautics, being the principal patron of Robert Goddard. Together with his wife, Alicia Patterson, Guggenheim helped create *Newsday;* the wealth from this newspaper was used to create the Alicia Patterson Foundation and the Harry Frank Guggenheim Foundation, which studies ways of preventing violence.

Marguerite "Peggy" Guggenheim (1898–1979), was the daughter of Benjamin Guggenheim, who drowned on the Titanic. Though her estate never amounted to more than $450,000, she nonetheless proved one of the most dynamic and influential patrons of modern art. Her "Art of This Century" gallery (1942–1945) discovered many important American modernists, most notably Jackson Pollock. She also was a patron of (and eventually married) surrealist Max Ernst. Her collection and her Venice mansion were absorbed by the Solomon R. Guggenheim Foundation after her death.

Martin Morse Wooster

References and further reading
Davis, John. H. 1978. *The Guggenheims.* New York: Morrow.

Gill, Anton. 2002. *Art Lover.* New York: Harper Collins, 2002.

Guggenheim, Peggy. 1979. *Out of This Century: Confessions of an Art Addict.* New York: Universe Books.

Lomask, Milton. 1964. *Seed Money.* New York: Farrar, Straus.

Weld, Jacqueline Bograd. 1986. *Peggy: The Wayward Guggenheim.* New York: Dutton.

Wooster, Martin Morse. 1997. "The Guggenheim Foundation's Slide towards Irrelevance," *Foundation Watch.*

GuideStar

The GuideStar Web site, http://www.guidestar.org, is an online database providing information about nonprofit organizations classified as public charities, private foundations, or private operating foundations under Section 501(c)(3) of the Internal Revenue Code (IRC). The database derives most of its information from digitized copies of the tax filings of these nonprofits and from other public documents. Nonprofits are also encouraged to join the GuideStar project by submitting additional information. Over half a million tax forms are entered into the database annually with the intention of keeping three years of tax filings available online. The Web site crossed the 2 million visitor mark in the year 2000.

The Web site is the major project of Philanthropic Research, Inc. (PRI), located in Williamsburg, Virginia. Arthur W. Schmidt, who continues to serve as its president, formed PRI in 1994. PRI is registered as a public charity. Its own entry in the database is a model of the information PRI would like to have for every entry. The mission statement of PRI is to promote philanthropy by providing information to donors, nonprofit boards, grant administrators, the government and the general public. PRI states that the "progress in American philanthropy and nonprofit practice is constrained by the absence of information about the practices of nonprofit organizations" (GuideStar). It earns more than one-third of its revenues from the sale and licensing of information derived from its database but provides the Web site as a public service.

Fred Westcott

References and further reading
GuideStar, http://www.guidestar.org.

Habitat for Humanity International

Habitat for Humanity International is a grassroots, nonprofit organization that builds houses. Founded in 1976 by evangelical Christians Millard and Linda Fuller, the organization is headquartered in Americus, Georgia, but has more than 1,500 separately incorporated local affiliates throughout the United States and 300 additional affiliates located within eighty-three different countries. Habitat International provides leadership, coordination, promotional, and some financial resources to the affiliates, and the affiliates, through volunteer labor, accomplish most of the actual building. To date, Habitat has built or renovated approximately 125,000 houses worldwide (of which about 40,000 are in the United States), and in doing so, the organization estimates that it has housed close to 625,000 people. This success seems to be accelerating. It took fifteen years for Habitat to build its first 10,000 homes. The next 10,000 took only two years, the following 10,000 took fourteen months, and the organization expects eventually to begin building 20,000 homes per year.

Certain organizational characteristics account for this success as well as for securing Habitat's place among the best known and most widely respected nonprofits in the United States. The first of these is its emphasis on "partnership," a word used ubiquitously at Habitat. Rather than mere clients, the lower-income people whom Habitat serves (that is, the "homeowners") are considered partners in the sense that they contribute to the building of their own homes through their hours of "sweat equity," and ultimately, they purchase these homes. No doubt this self-help quality largely accounts for Habitat's popularity. Moreover, Habitat creates other partnerships that make it possible for the homeowners to purchase their homes. Specifically, typically middle-class volunteers provide much of the labor the organization needs, local governments help make inexpensive or foreclosed properties available, and construction-related organizations provide labor and building materials at reduced prices or as donations. As a result, the homes are very inexpensive (the average Habitat home in the United States is $46,000).

Another important characteristic of Habitat is its reliance on nonsectarian religious values that enable it to cull volunteer and financial support from a wide array of American congregations. For instance, the notion that religious faith must be acted out in pragmatic ways is a major theme at Habitat that is attractive to various religious communities. Likewise, Habitat's "theology of the hammer" denotes the prevalent attitude within the organization that theological differences are far less important than the value of service to others that different faith traditions have in common.

Finally, Habitat has effectively packaged and promoted its volunteer opportunities such that they appeal to a broad range of people. Its Covenant Church pro-

Former president Jimmy Carter and former first lady Rosalynn Carter saw lumber for a house for Habitat for Humanity. The Carters lead the Jimmy Carter Work Project (JCWP) for Habitat for Humanity International one week each year. (Mark Peterson/Corbis)

gram taps the support of church-based constituencies. Its Campus Charters mobilize college students, especially those seeking an alternative spring break experience. The Global Village program attracts those who can afford the time and money to volunteer for two- and three-week periods in a developing country. Former president Jimmy Carter and his wife, Rosalynn, have been visible spokespeople for the Habitat cause. Special events, such as the annual, week-long Jimmy Carter Work Project, are important for building many houses at one location and, since they gain significant media attention, for raising the public's awareness of housing issues and of Habitat itself. These characteristics and initiatives—along with the hands-on, tangible, and at times exciting nature of Habitat projects—have helped the organization grow significantly during its first quarter century of operation.

Jerome P. Baggett

References and further reading

Baggett, Jerome P. 2001. *Habitat for Humanity: Building Private Homes, Building Public Religion.* Philadelphia: Temple University Press.

Fuller, Millard. 2000. *More than Houses: How Habitat for Humanity is Transforming Lives and Neighborhoods.* Nashville: Word Publishing.

Gaillard, Frye. 1996. *If I Were a Carpenter: Twenty Years of Habitat for Humanity.* Winston-Salem, NC: John F. Blair.

Habitat for Humanity International, http://www.habitat.org (cited August 16, 2002).

Hart Case

See Law of Charity

Health and Nonprofits

Overwhelming size, diverse makeup, constant change, and controversy—these descriptors characterize the intersection of the health industry and the nonprofit sector. Nonprofit healthcare organizations generate a sizable proportion of the nonprofit sector's revenues, and they do so in a highly competitive, capital-intensive industry. The nonprofit healthcare subsector includes a diverse mix of service providers—long-term care facilities, hospices, community clinics, mental health facilities, and health plans. Additionally, related organizations include advocacy, research, and professional service organizations. Few industries experience the level of public scrutiny currently focused on health care. Health services costs and financing, consumer safety, patient privacy, and research and treatment ethics all currently drive changes in the constitution of the industry, intersector dynamics, and government regulation. Additional causes of change drivers include medical and information technology capabilities. Health care is an integral part of the nonprofit sector, although its presence is constantly challenged and its makeup constantly changing. This discussion focuses on the health services industry; professional services organizations such as the American Medical Association exert strong influences on the industry, as do research, patient support, and advocacy organizations.

Historical Development

Organizations offering new services often organize as nonprofit entities—for example, the first institutionalized U.S. hospitals and the first prepaid healthcare plans were nonprofit organizations (Metcalf 2002). Recent examples of this phenomenon include outpatient dialysis, hospice, and home healthcare services. The industry's roots lie with the private physician, a largely unconnected network of services provided by individuals, and public policy that allocates care of the needy and sick to their families. This system left a rapidly expanding, unmet need during the Industrial Revolution,which was eventually addressed by charitable facilities (almshouses) that sought to address the needs of the poor. Such facilities originally provided little health care and simply served as a shelter for those in need or whom society deemed unseemly. Only after the understanding of contagious disease developed did facilities resembling contemporary hospitals develop. Still, hygiene and treatment capa-

bilities of the time resulted in such inpatient facilities being viewed as "death houses," and their use was limited to individuals who had no alternatives for care. Some religious orders, however, saw the suffering of the sick poor as a way to provide good works in the service of God. This provided the origins of an orderly and educated approach to nursing and the church-sponsored hospitals that still dominate the industry.

The situation changed dramatically early in the twentieth century. Improvements in hygienic and surgical practices and the discovery of antibiotics and vaccines changed the hospital environment from one of resigned death to one of optimism and cures. This change shifted the focus of health care for all individuals from the physician's office and the patient's home and more toward the hospital—the age of scientific medicine had arrived. This shift, made possible by technologic advances, was facilitated by changes in healthcare financing and public policy.

In 1929, the Great Depression forced hospitals to experiment with health insurance plans. One of these, at Baylor University Hospital in Dallas, Texas, developed into the model for the Blue Cross Hospital Insurance. The nonprofit Blue Cross plans, and later the medical expenses Blue Shield plans, can be credited with revolutionizing access to health care for middle-class Americans. Such plans were broadly established by the mid-1920s. Initially, covered individuals primarily financed their own insurance plans. This changed, however, in 1939 during World War II when worker shortages resulted in employers adding healthcare coverage to their employee benefit packages. More middle-class Americans now had financial access to better-quality medical care—and expectedly, its use increased.

The federal government was also involved in this major expansion of the healthcare industry. Through funding initiatives and tax policy, the U.S. government has impacted industry growth and the ownership mix in health care—primarily through its access to capital (Needleman 2001). The most obvious of these include:

1. The Hill-Burton Hospital Construction Act of 1946, which intended to expand access of hospital facilities to unserved or underserved

geographic areas. This act was tremendously successful in increasing hospital capacity, particularly for nonprofit facilities, by financing capital expenses and included a requirement for charity service to the facility's community.

2. The Medicare and Medicaid programs. Medicare has consistently provided incentives to private, for-profit industry entry by providing a known funding source for services (such as hemodialysis). More recently, however, Medicare and Medicaid funding constraints have pushed out some for-profit managed care plans.

3. The Health Maintenance Organization Act of 1973, which hoped to contain health costs by supporting the development of health maintenance organizations (HMOs).

4. The Internal Revenue Service's withdrawal of an organization's 501(c)3 charitable tax-exemption status. Such tax concerns, particularly when combined with an organization's concerns about access to capital, have either mandated or resulted in organizations' conversion from nonprofit to for-profit status.

This abbreviated history of nonprofit healthcare organizations almost directly mirrors the history of the sector overall—the two are inseparably intertwined. What remains unstated, and perhaps unknown, is how the dynamic nature of the ethics, technology, and politics differentially impact the sectors.

Scope of the Healthcare Industry's Nonprofit Sector

Healthcare services are a dominant subsector of nonprofit organizations. They have the largest total revenue of all nonprofit subsectors and the largest number of paid employees, and they pay the most in wages and salaries.

Given the rapid growth in other nonprofit subsectors, growth of any sort has been minimal in the number of healthcare organizations. Hospitals constitute the bulk of nonprofit healthcare organizations, and trends in both the subsector and its relationship to the

overall nonprofit sector mirrors this fact. Sixty-one percent (2,998 of 4,908) of the United States' community hospitals were nonprofit organizations in 2001 (American Hospital Association 2002). By contrast, only 24 percent (1,156 of 4,908) were state or local government owned, and 15 percent (754 of 4,908) were investor owned. Although some growth occurred in the number of for-profit hospital facilities in the late twentieth century, this growth slowed by the beginning of the twenty-first century. During this same period, the numbers of public and nonprofit facilities declined substantially (Salamon 1999).

Health services organizations generate the largest total revenue of all nonprofit subsectors (49 percent [326.3 billion of 664.8 billion total for the entire sector] in 1997) (Weitzman et al. 2002). They generate this revenue primarily from fees (89.1 percent in 1997), which strikingly differentiates them from other nonprofit subsectors (Weitzman et al. 2002). Trends in revenue mirror the decline in reimbursements from government and managed care plans. Given the dominance of health care in most areas, it received only 10 percent of the private contributions in 1998—a proportion that has remained relatively stable during the past three decades.

To provide perspective on the impact of the nonprofit healthcare subsector, the Bureau of Labor reports that approximately 9.3 percent (10.3 million people in 2001) of all U.S. nonfarm private-sector workers were employed in health service positions. Within the nonprofit sector, health services employed 43 percent of the sector's paid employees in 1998; of these, 72 percent were employed by hospitals (see Table 1). This percentage is down from the past as more health care is delivered outside hospital walls. The health services subsector paid 54 percent ($141 billion of the nonprofit sector's total $259 billion) of total wages and salaries within the nonprofit sector. Hospital employees earned 77 percent of the healthcare service's wages. Although this percentage is lower than previous years, this reflects the change in how healthcare services are delivered, as other nursing and personal care facilities and other health services have increased their shares of the subsector's wages. Volunteers play a relatively small role in the healthcare sector when compared to the large number of employed

Table 1 Employment within the Health Services Subsector (1998)

Health Service Category	Number (1,000)	Percent (within subsector)
Nursing and personal care facilities	572.5	12
Hospitals	3,347.2	72
Other health services	557.3	12
Medical and dental clinics	204.0	4
Total	4,681.0	100

Source: Adapted from Weitzman 2002, 41.

staff. Still, 11.4 percent of adults report volunteering to a health-related organization during 1998, with 69.4 percent of these volunteers giving time to nonprofit health organizations (15.7 percent to for-profit and 14.5 percent to public organizations) (Weitzman et al. 2002).

The Mixed Healthcare Services Market

Communities and patients or clients often have inaccurate perceptions of the ownership status—and the subsequent impact of that status—of their healthcare service organizations. In a 1998 survey, the Kaiser Family Foundation found that approximately half of respondents thought that the majority of health services (hospitals, nursing homes, and health insurance plans) were for-profit companies (Kaiser Family Foundation 1998). For example, 49 percent of respondents responded that most hospitals were for-profit entities when in reality only 15 percent are. Interestingly, however, the public often favors nonprofit ownership when asked if it impacts their choice of healthcare service providers, but a majority believe that for-profit facilities are more efficient and provide better quality care. Nonprofit providers are viewed as being more community oriented and as low-cost providers. Research supports the belief that for-profits are more efficient service providers, depending upon the service. Research also supports the perception that nonprofits tend to charge patients less for comparable services and that nonprofits are more community oriented. Although research has rarely found that for-profit providers provide higher quality care, it has consistently found that nonprofit providers offer higher quality care for some services. Although

researchers do disagree, a general interpretation of research findings suggests that either ownership does not impact care quality or that nonprofits provide better quality care (Schlesinger and Gray in press).

Explanations and justifications for a mixed healthcare market abound. Some theorists point to economic theory and a functional market's requirement for full consumer information as the justification for government intervention through favorable tax treatment of nonprofit healthcare facilities. Consumers' heavy reliance on trust and their inability to fully judge service quality in the transaction between consumer and provider underlies this market failure. Others look at historical trends in access to capital to explain the relative proportions of ownership forms over time (Needleman 2001). Both the charitable roots of health services and public policy impacted access to capital. Another method of explaining the mixed market focuses on the particular service's life cycle (Schlesinger and Gray in press). New, low-demand, relatively high-cost services are commonly organized as or by nonprofit organizations. As demand for such services increases beyond these organizations' capacity, incentives for entry by investor-owned firms increase. Certain events—such as regulatory, legislative, or financing changes—can dramatically stimulate growth in the number of for-profit providers and subsequently increase competition for existing nonprofit providers. Price competition forces for-profit and nonprofit organizational behavior to converge, and as performance pressures rise, organizations merge or leave. This pressure impacts for-profit providers more heavily than nonprofit providers, resulting in an increase in the proportion of nonprofit providers in a service. Recent examples of this cycle include long-term care facilities, psychiatric hospitals, and home healthcare services.

Current Challenges

Many of the difficulties faced by nonprofit health organizations challenge the industry as a whole. Demographic trends, such as an aging population and shifts in the ethnic composition of clientele, result in both increased demand for services and changes in the types of services required. Some healthcare facilities are now operating at or close to capacity; additionally, many facilities face aging physical plants. Financial constraints due to inadequate Medicare and Medicaid reimbursements, managed care, and competitive markets force difficult decisions on who to serve, what services to offer, and how to deliver those services. Services to the underinsured, uninsured, and unprofitable services become greater burdens on facilities when operating margins are small. Volatile equity markets create additional pressures. Advances in both medical technologies and information systems require additional capital investments. Labor shortages cause increases in labor costs to facilities and force some facilities to curtail services. Regulatory changes, such as the Health Information Protection and Portability Act of 1996, force facilities to adjust operating procedures and often require financial investments.

Challenges specific to nonprofit health organizations mirror those seen elsewhere in the nonprofit sector but are often intensified by the healthcare market. Questions exist as to whether there should be a continued role for nonprofit facilities in health services and specifically whether public policy should continue to support their existence (Needleman 2001).

The profit motive and its potentially distorting impact on socially desirable outcomes in human health are a constant concern to individuals and policy makers. Access to health care remains a national concern. Nonprofit institutions, on average, provide more charity care and charge lower fees for their services. Service quality may also be impacted by the need to meet shareholders' influence to increase profits. Again, if there is a difference in quality, nonprofit providers tend to provide higher quality services. Competition does tend to drive a convergence in the behavior between for-profit and nonprofit institutions, but most studies find that ownership differences persist even in intensively competitive markets. For example, research suggests that the gap in charity care provision between nonprofit and for-profit facilities is widening (Schlesinger and Gray in press).

Critics of the nonprofit presence often target nonprofit hospitals, which appear very similar to their for-profit counterparts, as economic drains on communities—"investments" that do not provide adequate returns to their community "investors." Beyond Internal Revenue Service (IRS) challenges to 501(c)3 status, some local communities view these facilities' tax-exempt status as a drain on the community and have challenged this status in court, with the result that several hospitals now pay their municipalities direct payments in lieu of taxes to preempt such challenges. Facilities, at a minimum, now painstakingly document activities that benefit their communities (for example, charity care and health education).

One factor in the community benefit issue is an institution's commitment to its community. Locally owned nonprofit facilities show greater commitment to their local communities, which results in institutions that view their mission as serving not just their patients but their community. System affiliation, increasingly relevant as nonprofit facilities merge or join networks, does impact organizational behavior. Effects are larger on for-profit than nonprofit organizations, and they tend to magnify the ownership-related performance differences.

The increasingly complex nature of health services delivery and current fiscal constraints have caused the need to develop creative arrangements to ensure access to capital or simply to ensure institutional survival. Hospitals have both created and, in some cases, later devolved comprehensive vertical healthcare delivery systems that included everything from physician practices to long-term-care facilities. Joint ventures between for-profit and nonprofit providers, created with various legal and organizational arrangements, challenge the IRS to define organizational boundaries and when a nonprofit's activities will benefit private parties. Nonprofit to for-profit ownership conversion has become relatively commonplace. Nonprofit health insurance organizations (for example, Blue Cross and Blue Shield organizations) used conversion to mutual ownership as a means to increase access to equity. Some hospital trustees have questioned the relative benefit of such large amounts of community assets being held as hospital physical plants. Such questioning has led to experiments where a hospital's physical assets are sold to create a foundation to address community health in ways other than directly providing health care—with mixed success.

Autumn Workman

References and further reading

American Hospital Association. 2002. "Fast Facts on U.S. Hospitals from *Hospital Statistics*™." Available at http://www.hospitalconnect.com/aha/resource_center/fastfacts/fast_facts_US_hospitals.html (cited May 19, 2003).

Goddeeris, John H., and Burton A. Weisbrod. 1998. "Conversion from Nonprofit to For-Profit Legal Status: Why Does It Happen and Should Anyone Care?" In *To Profit or Not to Profit: The Commercial Transformation of the Nonprofit Sector*, edited by Burton A. Weisbrod, 83–104. Cambridge: Cambridge University Press.

Gray, Bradford H., and Mark Schlesinger. 2002. "Health." In *The State of Nonprofit America*, edited by Lester M. Salamon, 65–106. Washington, DC: Brookings Institution Press.

Kaiser Family Foundation. 1998. "Survey of Americans about Health Care and the Stock Market." January. Menlo Park, CA: Kaiser Family Foundation. Available at http://www.kff.org/content/archive/1359/facts.html (cited November 5, 2003).

Marmor, Theodore R., Mark Schlesinger, and Richard W. Smithey. 1987. "Nonprofit Organizations and Health Care." In *The Nonprofit Sector: A Research Handbook*, edited by Walter W. Powell, 221–239. New Haven, CT: Yale University Press.

Metcalf, Marcia. 2002. "The McNerney Forum: Advancing the Role of Nonprofit Health Care." *Inquiry* 39 (2): 96–100.

Needleman, Jack. 2001. "The Role of Nonprofits in Health Care." *Journal of Health Politics, Policy and Law.* 26 (5): 1113–1130.

Salamon, Lester M. 1999. *America's Nonprofit Sector: A Primer*, 2d ed. New York: The Foundation Center.

———. 2001. "The Nonprofit Sector at a Crossroads: The Case of America." In *Third Sector Policy at the Crossroads: An International Nonprofit Analysis*, edited by Helmut K. Anheier and Jeremy Kendall, 17–35. New York: Routledge.

Schlesinger, Mark, and Bradford H. Gray. Forthcoming. "Nonprofit Organizations and Health Care." In *The Nonprofit Sector: A Research Handbook*, edited by Walter W. Powell and Richard S. Steinberg. New Haven, CT: Yale University Press.

Sloan, Frank A. 1998. "Commercialism in Nonprofit Hospitals." In *To Profit or Not to Profit: The Commercial Transformation of the Nonprofit Sector*, edited by Burton A. Weisbrod, 151–168. Cambridge: Cambridge University Press.

Van Til, Jon. 2000. *Growing Civil Society: From Nonprofit Sector to Third Space*. Bloomington: Indiana University Press.

Weitzman, Murray S., Nadine T. Jalandoni, Linda M. Lampkin, and Thomas H. Pollak. 2002. *The New Nonprofit Almanac and Desk Reference: The Essential Facts and Figures for Managers, Researchers, and Volunteers.* San Francisco: Jossey-Bass.

Higginson, Henry Lee (1834–1919)

Henry Lee Higginson was a complex personality who overcame a variety of personal disappointments in his early life to ultimately achieve lasting recognition as a successful banker, founder of the Boston Symphony Orchestra, and patron of Harvard University. Born in New York City on November 18, 1834, Higginson and his family moved to Boston four years later after his father lost a large sum of money in the panic of 1837.

Higginson experienced a series of failures in his early adult life. His desire to study at Harvard was cut short after only a few months on account of illness. He aspired to be a concert pianist, a dream that was tragically halted by inept medical treatment for a hand injury. His subsequent attempts at business also proved fruitless.

With the onset of the Civil War, he followed the path of many of his Boston social elite, abolitionist peers, joining the ranks of the Union Army in a crusade to extinguish slavery. Although he served honorably, glory and higher rank eluded him. He was gravely wounded in his only battle and sustained a prominent scar on his cheek from that action. That scar and the title of major were very personal badges of honor that remained with him for the rest of his life.

This string of personal setbacks culminated just after the Civil War in a disastrous attempt to operate a Georgia cotton plantation with recently freed slaves as paid laborers. Higginson and his partners lost more than $90,000 in the venture, a gigantic sum for that era, and were forced to sell the business.

Higginson's life began to take a positive turn in 1868 when, at the age of thirty-four, he somewhat reluctantly joined his family's banking firm. Here, his steady character, honesty, and skill in dealing with the firm's clients brought him wealth, recognition, and stability. In 1873, after only five years with the firm and with a fortune estimated at between $750,000 and $1 million, he began to realize some of his earlier dreams of collaborating with the arts and higher education.

As the driving force and sole underwriter of the Boston Symphony, Higginson created the first permanent symphony orchestra in the United States in 1881. In the course of his nearly forty-year relationship with the symphony, Higginson donated more than $1 million. His work on behalf of the symphony was equaled by his efforts in furthering education, predominantly at his alma mater, Harvard. In addition to financing the Harvard Student Union Building, he endowed a professorship and secured the properties that became the sites of the school's medical and business schools. Higginson also donated much of his personal art collection to the Harvard University Museum of Fine Arts.

Perhaps his most personal donation came in the form of Soldiers Field, which he presented to the university in memory of six fallen comrades who were killed in action in the Civil War. Higginson believed that on the playing grounds of Soldiers Field, the future leaders of our country would be molded through the competition and teamwork associated with sports. Higginson lost consciousness during surgery on November 14, 1919, and was buried one day before what would have been his eighty-fifth birthday.

Douglas M. Czajkowski

References and further reading
Czajkowski, Douglas. 2002. "Henry Lee Higginson (1834–1919), Banker and Founder of the Boston Symphony Orchestra." In *Notable American Philanthropists: Biographies of Giving and Volunteering,* edited by Robert T. Grimm Jr., 145–147. Westport, CT: Oryx Press.
Higginson, Henry Lee. 1866. "Charles Russell Lowell." *Harvard Memorial Biographies.* Cambridge: Sever and Francis.
Meyerhuber, Carl I., Jr. 1974. "Henry Lee Higginson and the New Imperialism." *Mid America* 56 (3): 182–199.
Perry, Bliss. 1921. *Life and Letters of Henry Lee Higginson.* Boston: Atlantic Monthly Press.

Higher Education and Philanthropy

See Women, Higher Education, and Philanthropy

Hispanic Philanthropy

Who Are Hispanics?

The term *Hispanic* refers to people in the United States who are descended from Latin American, Spanish-speaking cultures. Hispanic is an ethnic category, not a racial one; Hispanics may be of any race. Hispanics often refer to themselves as Latinos, which is derived from the Spanish word for Latin American, *Latinoamericano.* The term *Hispanic* is more popular with government and other agencies that follow the lead of the U.S. Census Bureau. The bureau established "Hispanic origin" as a new demographic category in the 1970s, thereby bringing the term into widespread use.

Hispanics are the largest of the nation's racial and ethnic minority groups, and this group is growing relatively fast. The U.S. Census Bureau estimates that by 2050, Hispanics will number 98.2 million, comprising 24.3 percent of the U.S. population (U.S. Census Bureau 2000). Hispanics are a young population. The proportion under eighteen years of age is 35 percent, compared to 25.7 percent for the nation as a whole (Guzmán 2001, 7).

Hispanics are a long-established part of U.S. life and culture. Some Hispanic families have been rooted in the Southwest since the seventeenth century. One out of five Hispanics lives in western states, but every state has a Hispanic population, ranging from 5,500 Hispanics in Vermont to 11 million in California. Chicago, Houston, and San Antonio have more than half a million Hispanic residents each. A new pan-Hispanic or Latino ethnic identity is emerging in the United States, encouraged not only by U.S. political culture and institutions, but also by the desire for cultural identity among children born of intermarriage among Hispanic national origin groups and by increased mass marketing to Hispanics by commercial advertisers.

Hispanics, on average, are poorer, less educated, and unemployed more often than the rest of the U.S. population. Despite above-average labor-force participation rates, Hispanics' poverty rate of 21.4 percent is nearly triple that of non-Hispanic whites (Ramírez and de la Cruz 2003, 6). Among Hispanics between sixteen and twenty-four years of age, 27.8 percent have dropped out of high school (National Center for Education Statistics 2001). Of the Hispanic youth who have graduated from high school, only 16.5 percent have continued on to college and earned a bachelor degree (FIFCFS 1997, 92). Despite those disadvantages, the number of wealthy individuals in the

Hispanic population is increasing. Typically, they are newly successful business entrepreneurs. Thus, in addition to Hispanics' traditional forms of giving, volunteering, and social responsibility, there is growing potential for major philanthropic gifts, including giving by newly affluent Hispanics of humble origins.

Do Hispanics Give and Volunteer as Much as Other People?

Periodic surveys conducted by INDEPENDENT SECTOR find that Hispanics give less to nonprofit organizations, and less often, compared to U.S. residents in general. For example, one survey found that while 72 percent of U.S. households contributed money to charity, only 53 percent of Hispanic households did. Of those who gave, Hispanics on average tended to give smaller percentages of their household income (Hodgkinson and Weitzman 1992). But those findings can be misleading, as the following paragraphs explain.

Ethnicity does not cause Hispanics to be less philanthropic. Other factors account for Hispanics' lower reported rates of giving and volunteering to nonprofit organizations. Some are due to the population characteristics described above. Hispanics have less income and wealth, on average, and have larger families to support. Hispanics have less formal education and so are less familiar with the idea of public support for nonprofit organizations. Many Hispanics are immigrants from other countries with different traditions of giving and helping.

In most Latin American countries, churches are practically the only formal organizations that receive voluntary contributions from the public at large. Instead of giving cash gifts to officially recognized public charities (other than churches), Latin Americans are more accustomed to giving cash and other assistance to individuals who are members of the donor's extended family or kinship network.

Hispanics give and volunteer at about the same rate as everyone else in the United States, if (a) we define giving and volunteering broadly enough to include informal assistance given through personal networks and (b) we disregard differences in giving explained by differences in income, education, and recency of immigration. A survey of Californians by Michael O'Neill and William Roberts (2000) found that when giving and volunteering are broadly defined and the influence of income, education, and immigration is statistically controlled, there are no significant differences in how often, and how much, Hispanics give and volunteer in comparison to other Californians. Another study by Rodolfo O. de la Garza and Fujia Lu reached similar conclusions for Mexican Americans—the largest national origin segment of the nation's Hispanic population (Campoamor, Díaz, and Ramos 1999).

Distinctive Philanthropic Traditions

Hispanics give as much as anyone else, all things considered. But Hispanics give in different ways. Hispanic cultures have different philanthropic traditions, according to a research team led by Bradford Smith (Smith, Shue, Vest, and Villarreal 1999). Their study of Guatemalans, Mexicans, and Salvadorans living in the San Francisco Bay area found, for example, that the Mexican tradition of god-parenthood is an important vehicle for involving nonrelatives in patterns of giving within extended family and kinship networks of individuals. Those networks facilitate philanthropy both large and small. For example, informal networks facilitate the transfer of large amounts of money and goods from immigrants in the United States to small rural communities in Mexico. Mexican immigrants in the study sometimes shared their homes with relatives and friends in need. However, the Mexicans rarely contributed time or money to nonchurch and non-Mexican organizations outside their personal networks.

Guatemalans in the study had a tradition of providing food and lodging to newly arrived immigrants from their home country. In contrast to Mexicans, the Guatemalans were more likely to help nonrelatives whom they did not know well. The Guatemalans also tended to fault mainstream U.S. philanthropic and nonprofit organizations for being impersonal, greedy, and ignorant of Guatemalan traditions of community responsibility.

Salvadorans were found to give to well-established mainstream nonprofits in the San Francisco Bay area, even though Salvadorans in the study expressed distrust of large charitable organizations. Salvadorans also practiced a tradition of sheltering other Salvadorans in need.

Despite variations in their national cultural traditions, the three groups had some philanthropic behaviors in common. The Guatemalans, Mexicans, and Salvadorans all contributed relatively little time and money to mainstream charities, except for churches. All three groups typically sent money to family, kin, and communities outside the United States. They provided caretaking services to the young and old, instead of leaving their care to government, nonprofit, or commercial agencies more commonly used by other U.S. residents. Relatively affluent members of all three groups tended to help newcomers to the United States. Charity among the Hispanics studied included an element of traditional Latin American *personalismo*, in which personal, intimate, one-to-one relationships shaped the nature and extent of giving. And finally, all three groups tended to distrust formal institutions, including philanthropic and nonprofit organizations, as well as the government and large firms.

What Fundraising Strategies Work with Hispanic Donors?

Researchers and other writers (Campoamor, Díaz, and Ramos 1999; Wagner and Deck 1999) report that Hispanic philanthropy reflects strong traditions of compassion and social responsibility, combined with distrust of formal institutions other than the church. However, in a study that included many U.S.-born Hispanics, de la Garza and Lu did not find the distrust noted by others (Campoamor, Díaz, and Ramos 1999).

Hispanics appear to have much in common with other potential donors. When deciding whether to give to nonprofit organizations, Hispanics are probably influenced most by people they trust. Immigrants and other Hispanics are less experienced and educated, on average, about the U.S. nonprofit sector. Their experiences in other countries could discourage trust in both government and private organizations in the United States. Hispanics would therefore tend to rely more on trusted members of traditional extended family and kinship networks when deciding whether to give, and to whom.

Trustworthy leaders of nonprofits based in local Hispanic communities may be better positioned to cultivate and promote U.S.-style philanthropic gift giving by Hispanic donors (as I proposed in Wagner and Deck 1999). But interviews of affluent Cuban Americans and other donors by Ana Gloria Rivas-Vázquez warn us not to overgeneralize (Campoamor, Díaz, and Ramos 1999). Rivas-Vázquez demonstrates that Hispanic philanthropy is shaped by a wide variety of worldviews, interests, priorities, community commitments, and experiences, as well as the variety of national cultural and ethnic traditions noted by other observers. The effects of Hispanic ethnicity and cultural diversity on U.S. nonprofits and philanthropy, and the implications for fundraising among today's and tomorrow's Hispanic donors, remains a source of unanswered questions for future research.

Mike Cortés

References and further reading

Campoamor, Diana, William A. Díaz, and Henry A. J. Ramos, eds. 1999. *Nuevos Senderos: Reflections on Hispanics and Philanthropy.* Houston: University of Houston/Arte Público Press.

Federal Interagency Forum on Child and Family Statistics (FIFCFS). 1997. *America's Children: Key National Indicators of Well-Being.* Washington, DC: FIFCFS.

Gallegos, Herman E., and Michael O'Neill, eds. 1991. *Hispanics and the Nonprofit Sector.* New York: Foundation Center.

Gibson, Campbell, and Kay Jung. 2000. *Historical Census of Population Totals by Race, 1790 to 1990, and by Hispanic Origin, 1970 to 1990, for the United States, Regions, Divisions, and States.* Population Division Working Paper No. 56. Washington, DC: U.S. Census Bureau.

Guzmán, Betsy. 2001. *The Hispanic Population: Census 2000 Brief.* Washington, DC: U.S. Census Bureau.

Hodgkinson, Virginia A., and Maury A. Weitzman. 1992. *Giving and Volunteering in the United States: Findings from a National Survey.* Washington, DC: INDEPENDENT SECTOR.

National Center for Education Statistics. 2001. *Dropout Rates in the United States: 2000.* Washington, DC: U.S. Department of Education. Downloaded from http://nces.ed.gov/pubs2002/droppub_2001 (cited October 20, 2003).

O'Neill, Michael, and William Roberts. 2000. *Giving and Volunteering in California.* San Francisco: University of San Francisco Institute for Nonprofit Organization Management.

Ramírez, Roberto R., and G. Patricia de la Cruz. 2003. *The Hispanic Population in the United States: March 2002.*

Current Population Reports. Washington, DC: U.S. Census Bureau.

Smith, Bradford, Sylvia Shue, Jennifer Lisa Vest, and Joseph Villarreal. 1999. *Philanthropy in Communities of Color.* Bloomington: Indiana University Press.

Therrien, Melissa, and Roberto R. Ramírez. 2001. *The Hispanic Population in the United States: March 2000.* Current Population Reports. Washington, DC: U.S. Census Bureau.

U.S. Census Bureau. 2000. "Projections of the Total Resident Population by Five-Year Age Groups, Race, and Hispanic Origin with Special Age Categories: Middle Series, 2050–2070." Table NP-T4-G, Population Projections Program, Population Division. Washington, DC: U.S. Census Bureau. Downloaded from http://www.census.gov/population/projections/nation/summary/np-t4-g.pdf (cited on October 20, 2003).

Wagner, Lilya, and Allan Figueroa Deck, eds. 1999. *Hispanic Philanthropy: Exploring the Factors That Influence Giving and Asking. New Directions for Philanthropic Fundraising* 24 (Summer).

History of American Foundations

Philanthropic foundations are nongovernmental, not-for-profit organizations, with financial assets provided by a donor or donors, managed by trustees and officers, and expending its income on programs and projects formed to maintain and aid socially useful purposes. The modern U.S. foundation as an instrumentality for such giving has developed into what is in many ways a unique and complex social, economic, and political institution, though it has deep roots in the past.

Forerunners of present-day foundations can be traced far back in history to ancient China, Egypt, and other civilizations of the Near East. Plato's Academy, for example, was established in 347 B.C. with a bequest that helped to sustain its existence for some 800 to 900 years. The early records of the Hebrew people of the eastern Mediterranean show that they, too, set aside funds for worthy causes. By about A.D. 150, the growth of the Roman Empire witnessed the founding and operation of organizations bearing many of the hallmarks of foundations. This development culminated in the decrees of Emperor Constantine in 324–327 that recognized the growing Christian church as, in essence, a foundation.

Fostered by these early decrees and others promulgated by later state rulers of Christendom, the medieval Roman Catholic Church became the overwhelming philanthropic institution of the period in Western Europe. In Eastern Europe, the Greek Orthodox Church played a similar role. Although numerous charitable organizations were set up under church auspices, emphasis in giving tended to be placed upon spiritual rather than secular purposes. The Islamic world, from the time of its founding by Mohammed in the seventh century to the present, has witnessed the establishment of numerous foundations (entitled *wakif*) for worthy charitable and philanthropic purposes

England and Europe

England's religious break with the Roman Catholic Church in the 1500s was accompanied by significant changes in English political, economic, and social structure. The change fostered an ever-increasing number of foundations under state rather than religious control and, at the same time, more foundations established for and devoted to secular rather than spiritual purposes. The wording of the 1601 Elizabethan Statute of Charitable Uses, uniformly referred to as the cornerstone of English law concerning foundations, clearly reveals this change. In contrast, other Western European countries, particularly France, adopted legal and economic measures that inhibited rather than encouraged the founding and operation of foundations.

In ensuing centuries, Communist governments of Central and Eastern Europe adopted measures that essentially outlawed the formation or operation of foundations. European colonies established or controlled by England tended to follow its example of fostering foundations. The reverse was true, to a greater or lesser degree, by colonies established by the French and other countries sharing the French attitude.

The United States

The assemblies of the future U.S. states adopted English procedures regarding the few foundations established during colonial times, and these were carried over following independence. A few individuals, such as Benjamin Franklin and Stephen Girard, set up foundations prior to the Civil War. After the war, rapid accumulation of wealth provided the means for the first of the large U.S. foundations, with their wide-ranging national and international scope, to be established. Early notable ones were the Peabody Education Fund, founded in 1867, and the Russell Sage Foundation, founded in 1907. It was not, however, until the inauguration of the philanthropies of Andrew Carnegie and John D. Rockefeller, capped by the Carnegie Corporation of New York in 1911, with initial assets of $125 million, and the Rockefeller Foundation in 1913, with a corpus eventually totaling more than $180 million, that the modern U.S. philanthropic foundation came into its own.

Some observers have advanced the theory that people create foundations and other nonprofit organizations for nonaltruistic and selfish reasons, such as self-glorification or a desire to avoid taxes. Although these factors may play a part in philanthropy, most observers maintain that other, more significant factors are at work. The latter believe that foundations are the modern expression of a real spiritual, religious, or humanitarian desire to perform good deeds with accumulated wealth. This rationale was advanced by Andrew Carnegie in his book *The Gospel of Wealth* (1900) and was shared to a large degree by John D. Rockefeller. This "gospel" holds that the socioeconomic-political system, that is, the capitalistic system, prevailing in the late nineteenth and early twentieth centuries provided an increasingly better way of life for the masses. This period also saw, however, the accumulation of great wealth by a relatively few individuals. These persons had three choices: leaving their wealth to heirs, giving it away for charitable purposes upon their death, or establishing foundations in their lifetime. Carnegie and Rockefeller chose the third way as the best means of disposing of their wealth, hoping to use it for the benefit of mankind. Influenced by such thinking and example, other wealthy individuals funded sizable foundations in the early decades of the twentieth century. Examples include the Commonwealth Fund (1918), the Duke Endowment (1924), the W. K. Kellogg Foundation (1938), and the Olin Foundation (1938). By the 1930s, there were some 200 to 300 foundations of real significance

as to assets, grants, and scope of activities in the United States.

These foundations were independent organizations set up by individuals or family members. Sometimes called "family foundations" or "general-purpose foundations," they are the best known type of foundation in the United States and have the largest assets. Three other types of foundations, some with considerable assets, emerged in the twentieth century. These can be distinguished as: (1) company-sponsored or corporate foundations, (2) operating foundations, and (3) community foundations. Corporate foundations are those established by companies rather than private donors but are also devoted to philanthropic purposes. They are usually administered by those having an official relationship with the sponsoring business, and their grants are often concentrated in areas where the business or its transactions are located. The General Motors Foundation, for example, gives primarily in cities where the company has plants or significant operations. Operating foundations generally employ their own staff to carry out their programs, though they sometimes make grants to other entities. Many organizations, such as foundations supporting libraries, horticultural gardens, and museums, fall into this category. The Longwood Foundation's principal activity, for example, is the support it provides for the operation of horticultural gardens open to the public. Community foundations are located in cities or other specific areas. Their funds are usually derived from multiple sources and their grants are usually made in the areas where they are located. The New York Community Trust, for example, gives priority to the funding of projects having particular significance for the New York City area.

Foundations may be set up in one of three different ways. They may be: (1) perpetual—that is, the principal shall be held forever and only the income expended; (2) optional—with the option of expending principal as well as income; and (3) liquidating—where the principal and income must be expended by a specified time. Most foundations are of the perpetual or optional type. The Carnegie foundations generally fall into the former category, the Rockefeller foundations into the latter. The Julius Rosenwald Fund, which operated from 1917 to 1948, is a good example of the liquidating type. Regardless of type, all U.S. foundations have been afforded broad freedom of action in carrying out the purposes for which they were set up and in carrying out wide-ranging programs. In cases where the specified program of a foundation becomes outmoded, U.S. courts can apply the cy pres (as near as possible) doctrine. One of the best known examples of such application is the Bryan Mullanphy Fund, which was set up in the 1850s to aid poor travelers from St. Louis to settle in the West. Owing to the cessation of such emigrants, the fund was eventually allowed to provide aid for St. Louis travelers in general.

Most larger foundations and many smaller ones have embraced the concept of preventive rather than palliative giving. That is, rather than giving a coin to a beggar, foundations should attempt to change the conditions resulting in beggary. Concomitantly, their money should be used as venture or risk capital, that is, providing funds for worthwhile philanthropic projects that could only be financed with difficulty, or not at all, from other sources. Foundation giving on such principles has often been advanced as a major justification for their continued existence. Several examples of such venture-capital giving, among many that could be cited, are the Flexner Report of 1910, sponsored by the Carnegie Foundation for the Advancement of Teaching, which helped to revolutionize medical teaching and practice in the United States. Also, the discovery of the insulin treatment for diabetes by Dr. Frederick Banting was in large part the result of grants from several foundations. Another example is the Dorr Foundation's 1954 grant for the marginal white striping of a Connecticut highway, which led to a dramatic fall in accident rates on that highway and eventually to the adoption of such striping across the United States and Canada.

Following the Great Depression and after World War II, the United States witnessed a surge in the number of foundations being established. By the 1950s, more than 4,000 U.S. foundations were in existence with combined assets of about $3 billion, some seventy of the largest holding assets of $10 million or more each. By the year 2000, more than 40,000 foundations had been established with a wide geographical distribution across the United States and with combined assets of about $400 billion. The fifteen largest each held assets in excess of $2 billion or more, and the next ninety, in size of assets held, each had $420 million or more. Heading the list as the largest foundation in the United States, and for that matter, throughout the world, was the Bill and Melinda Gates Foundation, with assets of about $24 billion.

Accompanying this stupendous growth in numbers and assets was the change in the geographical distribution of U.S. foundations. Although foundations for many years were concentrated in the Northeast, the latest statistics show considerable expansion in the number of foundations founded and located in other sections of the country. Also, the foundation concept and method of operation has been copied by an increasing number of other institutions of various types in society. Although they do not meet the strict definition advanced earlier, colleges and universities, religious institutions, hospitals, labor unions, and even government institutions have named and incorporated foundations into their structures. Examples include the University of Mississippi Foundation, the Presbyterian Church (U.S.A.) Foundations, the Mayo Foundation, the Cesar E. Chavez Foundation, and the governmental National Science Foundation and National Endowments for the Arts and the Humanities. These entities have, in large measure, been brought into existence because of the greater amount of administrative flexibility and other benefits afforded them as the result of operating under the foundation concept.

Although most foundations are established under the laws of a particular state, they have been subject to relatively little state regulation. Because they were tax exempt until a national percentage tax was placed on them in the 1970s, more by accretion than by design governmental supervision of U.S. foundations has largely fallen under the oversight of the Treasury Department's Internal Revenue Service (IRS). Although there has been advocacy in the past few decades to create a new public or private supervisory body for foundations, patterned to a greater or lesser degree on the British Charity Commission, to date the movement has gotten nowhere. Despite broad freedoms in carrying out their programs and projects both in the United States and abroad, foundations have been subject to a number of critical public and private investigations in some periods. These have included studies of foundations and their operations. The more important ones include those undertaken by the governmental Walsh Commission (1915–1916), the Cox (1952–1953), Reece (1953–1954), and Patman (1961–1969) committees, the Treasury Department (1965), and the later the private Peterson (1969–1970) and Filer commissions (1973–1977). Much of the critical attitude evinced in such studies and investigations, together with that emanating from some of the media and portions of the public in general, can be traced in large part to a lack of information and knowledge concerning foundations, which, in turn, can be traced to a dearth of research and publications about them.

Perceiving this to be the situation, many U.S. foundation officials, particularly since the 1950s, have encouraged all foundations to provide more information about their aims and activities. Also, they have led in the establishment of organizations devoted to amassing information and producing publications about foundations. These have included the trailblazing Foundation Center and the Council on Foundations as well as programs at academic institutions for the study of foundations and other philanthropic organizations. Today, Harvard University, Duke University, Indiana University, the University of Mississippi, and some fifty other U.S. universities and colleges conduct such programs. Since the 1970s, several groups of scholars have been formed, such as the Association for Research on Nonprofit Organizations and Voluntary Action (ARNOVA) and the International Society for Third-Sector Research (ISTR), which includes members who engage in research and writing about foundations both in the United States and abroad.

Several other significant changes in U.S. foundations have occurred in the past fifty years, including the diversification of personnel by way of gender, race, and religion and an increase in the number, size, and scope of activities abroad. Up until World War II, the trustees and executives of foundations, particularly the larger ones, were in large measure white, Anglo-Saxon, Protestant, and male. Since that time, a virtual personnel revolution has taken place, much of it due to conscious efforts for change by foundation trustees and officers. In the past decade, a much more diversified personnel representation at all levels, but particularly at the trustee and executive level, has taken place in all foundations, not just those dealing with minority issues. A telling example of this change is the fact that in recent years the executive heads of some of the larger foundations have been women, nonwhites, foreign-born people making their home in the United States, and non-Christians.

The international activities of U.S. foundations are probably the most salient and far-reaching aspect of their development since World War II. Prior to that time, while some other motives, such as Andrew Carnegie's interest in his native Scotland, entered into such activities, a major hallmark for the relatively few foundations conducting programs and having a presence abroad was the fact that their founders had extensive business dealings there. Examples are Rockefeller in oil, Carnegie in steel, and George Eastman in photography. Two foundations, the Carnegie Corporation of New York and the Rockefeller Foundation, dominated the international programs conducted by U.S. foundations in this period. Probably the best known were Carnegie's various fellowship programs and peace efforts and Rockefeller's many health and nutrition programs. In the late 1950s and 1960s, there was a significant increase in the number of foundations entering this arena together with a stepping up of activity among those already engaged there. The Tinker Foundation, set up in 1959, began to conduct a sweeping program promoting a broader understanding of Spain, Portugal, and Ibero-America. The W. K. Kellogg Foundation in the 1960s enlarged its agricultural and health programs in the countries of South America.

U.S. foundation activities in the international arena have come in for a small amount of intermittent criticism at home and abroad. At home, the major criticism has been that foundation funds would be better spent alleviating problems in the United States rather than tackling foreign ones. Abroad, and concentrated in the years of the Cold War and since, there have been charges that some foundations are disguised agencies of the U.S. government. The major rebuttal in the first instance was that much of the money flowing into the foundation coffers abroad was derived from profits made there. As to the second, although it may be true that a very few foundations have been used as a "cover" for U.S. intelligence purposes abroad, the number of such foundations has been minuscule when compared to the total number operating there. Furthermore, such conduct was and has been roundly condemned by many other foundation and governmental figures.

Beginning with its reorganization in 1950 and continuing on into the 1980s, the Ford Foundation overshadowed all other U.S. foundations active abroad in terms of size, range, and scope. It concentrated a larger portion of its resources in foreign activities than any other American foundation. A burgeoning number of large and small foundations, however, are now devoting increasing resources abroad. Five large foundations in aggregate now exceed Ford giving abroad: the John D. and Catherine T. MacArthur Foundation, Pew Charitable Trusts, the Andrew W. Mellon Foundation, the Open Society Fund (founded by George Soros), and the Charles Stewart Mott Foundation. To encourage such activity among smaller foundations, the Rockefeller Foundations recently began conducting a course for them in the most effective methods to be utilized in foreign giving.

The two primary aims of international foundation efforts are to foster more democratic and stable societies abroad and to help to bring about a more peaceful world. In pursuing these ends, U.S. foundations have encouraged the creation of indigenous organizations all over the world that share these same goals and provide support for their operation. Since the 1980s, U.S. foundations with these ideals have expanded into Central and Eastern Europe. Although the former Communist governments of that region had adopted measures essentially outlawing the formation of domestic foundations, as well as prohibiting the operation of foreign ones within their borders, with the breakup and liberalization of such governments in the late 1980s a growing number of U.S. foundations began allocating funds for projects there.

Many programs, such as those of the Charles Stewart Mott Foundation, the Rockefeller Brothers Fund, the various Soros foundations, and the Ford Foundation, have fostered the creation of organizations in these countries resembling to a considerable degree the structure of U.S. foundations—for example, the Information Center for Foundations and Other Not-for-Profit Organizations in Prague, Czechoslovakia. With such efforts, sponsoring foundations hope to aid in the development of more democratic and freer societies in the region. Support has also been provided for the establishment of other regional and international organizations of this type, such as the European Foundation Centre and CIVICUS: World Alliance for Citizen Participation.

Joseph C. Kiger

See also Community Foundations; Grantmaking; Institutional Foundations

References and further reading
Andrews, F. Emerson. 1956. *Philanthropic Foundations.* New York: Russell Sage Foundation.
Carnegie, Andrew. 1900. *The Gospel of Wealth and Other Timely Essays.* New York: Century.
Fosdick, Raymond B. 1952. *The Story of the Rockefeller Foundation.* New York. Harper and Bros.
Fosdick, Raymond B., with Henry F. Pringle and Katherine Douglas Pringle. 1962. *The Story of the General Education Board.* New York: Harper and Row.
The Foundation Directory. Editions 1–21. 1960–1999. 21st ed., 1999. New York: Foundation Center.
Foundation News and Commentary. Vols. 1–42. 1960–1969. New York: Foundation Library Center. 1969–1971. New York: Foundation Center. 1971–2001. Washington, DC: Council on Foundations.
Fremont-Smith, Marion R. 1965. *Foundations and Government: State and Federal Law and Supervision.* New York: Russell Sage Foundation.
Keppel, Frederick P. 1930. *The Foundation: Its Place in American Life.* New York: Macmillan.
Kiger, Joseph C. 1954. *Operating Principles of the Larger Foundations.* New York: Russell Sage Foundation.
———. 1987. *Historiographic Review of Foundation Literature: Motivations and Perceptions.* New York: Foundation Center.
———. 2000. *Philanthropic Foundations in the Twentieth Century.* Westport, CT: Greenwood.
Lagemann, Ellen Condliffe. 1989. *The Politics of Knowledge: The Carnegie Corporation, Philanthropy and Public Policy.* Middletown, CT: Wesleyan University Press.
Nielsen, Waldemar. 1985. *The Golden Donors: A New Anatomy of the Great Foundations.* New York: Truman Talley, E. P. Dutton.
U.S. Department of the Treasury. 1977a. *Giving in America: Report of the* [Filer] *Commission on Private Philanthropy and Public Needs.* Washington, DC: Government Printing Office.

———. 1977b. *Research Papers Sponsored by the* [Filer] *Commission on Private Philanthropy and Public Needs.* 5 vols. Washington, DC: Government Printing Office.

Weaver, Warren S. 1967. *U.S. Philanthropic Foundations: Their History, Structure, Management, and Record.* New York: Harper and Row.

Whitaker, Ben. 1979. *The Foundations: An Anatomy of Philanthropic Societies.* New York: Pelican.

History of Philanthropy

The history of philanthropy within Western civilization, after a period of long neglect, has become a topic of serious scholarly investigation over the past twenty-five years. An extensive scholarship on human charitable and philanthropic practices and institutions is now developing because historians, as well as investigators in kindred disciplines such as anthropology, law, and religious studies, now recognize the vital, formative roles that dynamic gift exchange and charitable action can take in human communities over time. Newer studies emphasize philanthropy's dual capacity throughout history to affect and to effect systems of compassionate aid, ethics, government, status, and ritual. Consequently, widely accepted but vague definitions of "philanthropy," as merely "the love of mankind"—manifest especially through private and voluntary giving for public benefit—are now open to criticism, revision, and expansion. Historical discoveries are uncovering the wide variety of human behaviors, power relations, obligations, and ambitions to which the term "philanthropy" and its cognates once applied.

The historical dimensions of "philanthropy" are many. A human habit to conceive deities as givers of life and other benefits that must be acknowledged implies that principles of benevolent gift exchange fundamentally shape conceptions of the divine and form historic systems of religion and service. In these systems, the faithful emulate a generous God or gods by becoming givers themselves; giving is a religious duty and moral imperative of the highest order. This raises the question of whether philanthropic acts, especially those motivated by religious devotion, are ever the product of simple donor choice or voluntary subscription. Divinities, imagined as generous protectors of the most vulnerable members in human communities (orphans, widows, the sick, and so on), exhort the pious to exemplary charity for the weak. But changing popular convictions about the social utility or threat of the disabled can contradict such benevolent precepts. The history of philanthropy thus incorporates numerous, recurrent controversies over the real motives, right forms, and proper recipients of individual and collective aid.

Given some donors' expectations of recompense in this world or the next, philanthropy must be considered as a potential means to gratification, status definition, and power for individuals and social groups. Enduring early Christian reconceptualizations of charity as a donor's payment to gain personal atonement and sanctification force scrutiny of giving as essentially self-serving and disciplinary in nature. From the third century of the common era (200 C.E.), Christian theologians argued that pious benefactors might better themselves, seek eternal preferment, and win entry to heaven with worldly gifts of the right kind. Here, the interests of givers greatly outweigh the needs of receivers in shaping philanthropy's historical norms and forms. Medieval churchmen's redefinitions of alms deeds to include fraternal correction and corporal punishment of sinners also expressly connect philanthropy and police for the preservation of Christendom. Under this regime of philanthropy, the conservation of God's gift of grace, charity supreme, entails human generosity in the counsel, prosecution, and injury of sinners, whose evil acts diminish divine favor over all, threatening the salvation of others. The history of philanthropy must pay special attention to the dynamism of the subject demonstrated by past practitioners' conflicting definitions and constant reinterpretations of the term and its meanings.

Historically, the formation and expansion of political entities can be closely linked to how different competitors for civil power have employed their philanthropies as instruments of community consolidation, caste definition, imperial expansion, nation building, and colonialism. Concentrations of philanthropists and philanthropic institutions in ancient cities gave philanthropy a central role in the construction of civic culture and in the definition of civil society. Great territorial lords, such as kings from antiquity to early modern times, relied heavily on exclusive and ceremonial presents to display their nobility and set strict limits to their own ranks. Monarchs tried to portray kingship itself as the superintendence of generosity in all things. Imperialists from Augustus Caesar to Queen Victoria coveted stature as supreme donors, endowing their dominions with waterworks, schools, libraries, stadiums, and markets that are the impressive infrastructure of empire. Innumerable private contributors gave to nineteenth-century explorer clubs and resolute missionary societies whose labors drove expanding European and American colonial empires throughout the Southern Hemisphere. And the precocious rise of the nation-state in the Western world gave philanthropists a new and demanding focus for their care to which they quickly responded. In modern times, patriotic donors and the trustees of philanthropic institutions often funded or modified private charities to serve what they believed to be the best interests of the state. Such widespread "nationalization" of private Western philanthropy starting in the eighteenth century compounds the political significance of the subject. It requires deeper investigation of philanthropy's key role in building and changing power structures over time.

Within kingdoms and states, social ranks and classes have differentiated themselves and reinforced group identity through their charitable practices. Distinctive forms of mutual aid and voluntary association, such as early modern friendly societies that amalgamated members' small weekly donations to distribute upon unemployment or illness, have been crucial in sustaining laborers and working-class consciousness over time. Eighteenth-century non-noble businessmen capitalized upon their growing economic power and entrepreneurial skills to gain greater social recognition through their giving, especially by creating new charities, such as marine societies that trained orphans for naval or shipping careers. These new foundations more conspicuously served the economic and military interests of competitive nation-states while helping to advance the careers and fortunes of the donors. Operating settlement houses for needy transients and visiting the homes of the poor to distribute alms or advice also enabled nineteenth-century middle-class benefactors (male and female) to show off the virtuous habits of bourgeois domesticity

for wider public emulation. Middle-class women in Britain and the United States drew directly upon their experience running such charitable endeavors when they organized themselves in later suffrage campaigns to demand a vote in all elections—a transformation of experience demonstrating philanthropy's historical importance as an apprenticeship to power.

The multiplication of charity organization societies in Europe and America after 1860 came under the nearly complete direction of middle-ranking commoners. Here they promoted the belief that amateur, unfocused giving, especially indiscriminate largesse by society's elite, must be replaced by coordinated, disciplined, and economical aid programs accountable for the real improvement of those being helped. Middle-class charity organizers demanded and developed "scientific philanthropy" as the only acceptable model of effective modern giving and service. This recent reconceptualization of philanthropy on scientific grounds has driven the accelerating professionalization of giving, fundraising, and foundation management in modern times. Contemporary philanthropists, now operating in bureaucratically streamlined charitable organizations, have also used their gifts to encourage the professionalization of other fields most useful to them. Seeking to comprehend and repair society's problems more efficiently, major philanthropies have demanded and subsidized refinements in the social-scientific analytical skills applied by demographers, economists, sociologists, social workers, statisticians, and urban planners. The history of philanthropy must therefore push beyond descriptions of problems solved and people helped to include major alterations in socioprofessional ranks and status hierarchies caused by swifter circulation of gift capital and sharper competition over its efficient use.

The subversive, insurrectionary, and liberating potentials of philanthropy in history are plainly evident and demand new attention. Benevolent associations, be they apostles, chivalric brotherhoods, or humane societies of various kinds, have often become potent agencies of change, challenging the status quo, empowering the meek, and freeing the disadvantaged from oppression. For good or ill, brotherly bands have driven schismatic religious movements in ancient and modern times, using exemplary care of others to fracture and renew creeds. Over time, benevolent voluntary associations have extended civil rights and protections, for example, by aiding immigrants, working to free slaves, and demanding better treatment for the mentally ill. Nor should the simple, emancipating power of ordinary people to make last wills and testaments be overlooked. This right to testamentary charity, exercised even by females in more patriarchal times, enabled propertied individual donors to make ultimate distribution of their own worldly goods. Since as early as the sixteenth century, European women, especially spinsters and widows, have adeptly used their legal right to make will gifts so as to thwart kinsmen's efforts at controlling or despoiling them. Often with help from the independent philanthropic institutions their testamentary gifts enriched, aging benefactresses parlayed their estate donations into lifetime annuities invulnerable to family misappropriation and set up long-term pension plans under institutional guarantee for their unrelated girl-friends in surviving female support networks. Seen in this perspective, incidents of philanthropy have often liberated benefactors and beneficiaries from the dictates of authority and convention.

A chronological overview of successive, interconnected regimes of philanthropy offers further examples of themes necessary for full historical analysis of the subject.

Judaism's Philanthropies

Charity is a moral imperative deeply structuring the daily rituals by which Jews must demonstrate their fidelity to one God, essentially defined by his abundant giving to the people of Israel. The earliest books of the Bible, comprising the Torah, or fundamental Jewish law, and dating from 900 to 600 B.C.E., state God's possession of the universe and require the propertied to know themselves as merely stewards of the worldly goods donated for their use by Jehovah (Lev. 25:23: "for the land is mine, for you are strangers and sojourners with me"). Mosaic descriptions of the divine as the special guardian of orphans, widows, and refugees entail Israelites, in turn, to render material and spiritual assistance quickly to the bereft (Deut. 10:19: "Love the stranger therefore; for you were strangers in the land of Egypt"). Misanthropy is apostasy, unthinkable disobedience and renunciation of

God. Rendering divine justice (*tsedeq* in Hebrew) to the weak and needy informs Jewish conceptions of charity or good works *(tsedaqah)*, enhancing the imperative nature of such philanthropy.

From the eighth through the seventh centuries B.C.E., the tribes of Israel thus established compulsory systems of community tithing at weekly, annual, triennial, septennial, and quindecennial rhythms for the help of the impoverished, the indebted, and the enslaved. Rites of giving organized ancient Jewish calendars and spaces of worship. From the era of the second temple (536 B.C.E. to 70 C.E.), Jews provided chambers for the collection and distribution of charity within the hallowed inner sanctum of the Jerusalem temple and other synagogues. Donors could leave their gifts secretly in one room, while beneficiaries collected the offering in a second room, unseen by contributors and thus immune to any shame that might sully that exchange in the eyes of God. Philanthropy informed the entire architecture of Jewish shrines and communities.

Generations of rabbis taught their supporters to believe that biblical commandments entailed charitable assistance from rich to poor beyond customary gleanings and tithes for the needy. Lessons in this regard fill Talmudic literature compiled from 200 to 600 C.E. Voluntary givers who act anonymously, forswearing fame, who organize others in lasting systems of aid, and whose gifts reach recipients before they fall into destitution earn highest praise in this literature. Humane conduct of discretionary charity also long shaped the hierarchy of all Jewish virtues, as the later ethical writings of Maimonides (1135–1204 C.E.) attest. Charity here is not only an indispensable virtue in itself, it is the crucial action enabling other virtues of the Jews to manifest themselves: piety, compassion, love of justice, and devotion to communal survival.

At the turn of the common era, accumulating rabbinical judgments stipulated acceptable material limits to charitable behavior, prescribed annulments to tithes and jubilees for the needy under certain conditions, and condoned closer scrutiny and wiser selection of recipients by donors offering aid. Field corners to be left for poor gleaners, for example, were set precisely at one-sixtieth of the surface area of each farmer's holding. The superiority of tithes and chari-

Following ancient tradition, a kibbutz member (and rabbi) tithes some of his onions to the land, as the temple is no longer available. (Ted Spiegel/Corbis)

table acts accomplished at Jerusalem was reiterated. The hierarchical implications of Jewish charity, structuring social ranks and the protocols of priestly office, intensified to yield more seemly but also more debatable philanthropic acts. Jewish sectarians antedating the rise of Christianity took new inspiration from disputes over proper forms of giving. These controversies catalyzed broader dissent against established and intertwined political, religious, and charitable institutions. Breakaway Jewish sects, such as the apostolic movement of the Nazarene Jesus, employed a rebellious philanthropy to castigate opponents, succor new supporters, and win disciplined followers.

Greco-Roman Philanthropies

The ancient Greek word *philanthropia* can be translated as "love for mankind." But the Greeks and Romans assembled a much wider range of practical definitions for the term between 500 B.C.E. and the

beginning of the common era (1 C.E.). To the Greeks, philanthropy was first the attribute of gods, such as Prometheus, who took pity on lowly mankind and granted celestial gifts, in this case fire, given to relieve the darkness and raw misery of human existence. "Philanthropy" thus served as a special marker of godliness and divine benevolence and justified cosmic hierarchies with gods on top and subordinate humans below engaging in ritual worship of those deities. Ancient Mediterranean peoples, Jews, Greeks, Romans, and Christians, shared a conception of gods as great givers. From an early date in the West, philanthropy informed and shaped religious values and practices.

The utility of gifts to mark and legitimate status distinctions captivated classical scholars and monarchs who cooperated to place "philanthropy" among the regal attributes of mortal kings. With wise gifts to underlings, noble leaders could become gods on earth, legitimating their worldly rule and more effectively eliciting their subjects' obedience. The Greek philosopher and royal tutor Xenophon (c. 430 B.C.E.–c. 355 B.C.E.) extolled "philanthropist" as the best and most influential status for a true monarch. Later Hellenic kings and Byzantine emperors could thus be suitably addressed in Greek as "Your Philanthropy," a more flattering title than "Your Majesty" and one showing that imperial rulership flowed from great gifts. The Greeks and the Romans described philanthropy as a compelling force in the power politics of human communities wielded cunningly by those who sought to dominate classical polities. For both peoples, "philanthropy" also came to mean trustworthy conduct in diplomacy, especially through proper reception and treatment of ambassadors, honest negotiation of alliances, and fidelity to the details of written treaties. The term accumulated very strong, normative, political and diplomatic connotations.

Ancient city-state governments might confer "philanthropies," meaning honorary titles, special privileges, and fiscal exemptions, upon residents for their outstanding military, diplomatic, or cultural achievements. Town governors extolled generosity in private gifts for broad public benefit as a necessary virtue of fortunate citizens. Rich townsmen took up this obligation, competing for the sociopolitical advantages donors could claim though gifts to fund city arsenals, to build up protective walls, to distribute grain cheaply, to erect temples, and to stage impressive civic events such as drama festivals. The entire corpus of great Greek plays, still performed to rapt audiences today, owes its creation to a multitude of ancient presents made by Greek private donors who built theaters, gave patronage to playwrights, hired or coached actors, and subsidized drama contests. Greek municipalities relied heavily on such donations to fund civic amenities and sought to make them the perennial responsibility of wealthy private givers. Lacking any blood aristocracy transmitting and monopolizing status by inheritance, Greek urban communities conferred prestige on a succession of wealthier private citizens who excelled in the open, competitive art of giving. For ambitious townsmen, failure to participate in these philanthropic contests killed their charisma. Parsimony became ignoble suicide. Aspiring patrons of public life in the Greco-Roman world thus confronted philanthropy not as a choice but as a duty that could be legitimately coerced via peer pressure, popular demand, and the adjudications of civic law courts.

For the Greeks, "philanthropy" could also define the generous attitude of itinerant philosophers, such as Socrates, who shared their learning freely and "gave" correction to the arrogant and ignorant. Such generosity with their learning set philosophers apart (as more godlike) and introduced "philanthropy" as a signifier of superior human intellect and vision. This empowered the learned to probe convention, question established wisdom, and bid to direct education of the young. A jury of Athenian citizens condemned Socrates to death and executed him (in 399 B.C.E.) on a charge of "corrupting youth" through his gift for public teaching (supported by donations from students). This example demonstrates just how risky and dangerous the contentious lives of ancient "philanthropists" could become. Ancient idioms suggest that "philanthropy" could subdivide and factionalize as well as construct and sustain communities.

As conquerors, heirs, and cautious copiers of the Greeks, the Romans assumed better apprehension and regulation of philanthropy to be among their greatest obligations as a civilized people. Roman efforts to systematize a practical ethics of giving to preserve society itself can best be seen in the works of Stoic philosophers such as Seneca, including his *On Benefits*, composed circa 60 C.E. This thorough analysis of gifts made and acknowledged well or ill asserts a direct linkage between faulty giving by amateur benefactors and rampant ingratitude among beneficiaries. And ingratitude, according to Seneca, is a terrible thing threatening the integrity of Roman civilization itself, held together only by the "glue" of gratitude binding beneficiaries to benefactors at all levels of society. Prospective donors must be instructed in the politics and psychology of how to give rightly to generate maximum gratitude from receivers. Seneca's massive guidebook on the subject demands all patrons to choose their beneficiaries and their benefits with exacting premeditation. "No gift can be a benefit unless it is given with reason. . . . Thoughtless benefaction is the most shameful sort of loss" (Seneca 1989 [c. 60], 222).

Seneca requires donors to set clear priorities in giving. Selection and distribution of necessities for the needy must replace delivery of mere embellishments to life or frivolous entertainments. Indiscriminate Greek modes of giving are now condemned as grossly irresponsible, neither satisfying real public needs nor generating the deep gratitude between giver and receiver that holds entire communities together. Roman lawyers contributed to this timely, binding redefinition of philanthropy. They laid the basis for a Western law of wills and foundations in stratagems by which one generation of donors could secure funds in perpetuity for their own proper funeral and recurrent memorial rites. This arrangement better obligated successive generations of descendants to pious performance of these anniversary ceremonies.

According to Seneca, correct Roman givers must also scrutinize and choose their beneficiaries very carefully. The donor's easy comfort in judging the character of others in need becomes essential to the successful consummation of this highly political philanthropy. In Seneca, one thus finds classical anticipations of subsequent arguments that Western philanthropy must become a discriminatory science in which the calculations of the head regulate the impulses of the heart. Seneca's treatise also prefigures later contentions that the state itself must be construed as the ultimate beneficiary of all discrete acts of private philanthropy.

Christian Philanthropies

The Jesus movement was initially driven by iconoclastic, heart-felt forms of philanthropy. Historians of early Christianity have amassed evidence of a new church integrated by novel modes of giving inimical to Jewish, Christian, and Roman regimes of generosity in communal government. Ecumenical charitable practices appear to be the essential means by which Christians distinguished themselves from Jews, captured enthusiastic Greek disciples, built up church institutions, and blocked Roman attacks on the young sect. The striking variety of lessons about giving conveyed in early Christian literature attests to the importance of debates over proper charitable practices in the genesis of new faiths throughout the ancient world. Recent investigations of Christian origins intensify the importance of selflessness, voluntary poverty, alms deeds, and hospitality in the life of Jesus and the church his acolytes constructed. Here, church members' cathartic identification with small groups of brethren through loyal sharing and total devotion to care of the needy is seen as the foundation of a new creed.

In the Gospel of Mark (composed c. 65 C.E.), Jesus distinguishes himself by engaging in repeated acts of healing, exorcism, and miraculous provision of sustenance (see Mark 6:38–44 for the famous multiplication of loaves and fishes). Jesus also heals the withered hand of a suffering man in a synagogue on the Sabbath, asking rhetorically: "Is it lawful on the Sabbath to do good?" (Mark 3:4). He puts active service of human needs above rigid observation of Jewish law requiring rest on the holy day. Awed disciples and outraged Jewish priests witness Jesus' subversive intensification of the individual charitable imperative that Judaism first championed. Jesus amplifies these calls for a more comprehensive benevolence in Mark by demanding that each follower become a "servant of all" (Mark 9:35) and prepare for discipleship by giving away all personal possessions to the poor (10:21). This order contradicts Talmudic rulings that no benefactor ever part with more than a fifth of his wealth in doing good nor ever become a charge on the community as a whole. The disciple's willful impoverishment also makes rich, Greek-style largesse to gain honor impossible.

The Gospel of Luke (6:27–31) also communicates Jesus' command to love your enemies and to give to every beggar generously and without expectation of any return whatsoever. Early Christians' total disinterest in the character of their beneficiaries and in their capacity to acknowledge or repay a benefit broke all the rules Stoical Romans set for politically correct generosity. A parable told in Luke (10:29–37) recounts how a wounded Jewish traveler, untouchable by a Hebrew priest and a Levite punctiliously observing caste purity laws, is saved by the Samaritan, a foreigner, whose charity thus transcends boundaries of tribal identity and social rank. This is the Christian role model of transcendent compassion. The Christian God embodied in Gospel parables as the Good Samaritan advocates a more universal charity that is not self-seeking or ostentatious. Such early Christian ideas about alms defeat momentarily the self-promoting purposes seen in Greco-Roman giving.

Christian recruitment and growth in the power of church officials often proceeded through gifts to others: free weekly group meals to build solidarity, ransom payments to redeem captive brethren, and distribution of church alms in times of disaster. Converts to Christianity altered classical balances of power between benefactors and beneficiaries. The growing Christian church was not merely a refuge for the poor and miserable. Wealthier, more learned townsmen also joined new congregations, employing their administrative talents and personal gifts to strengthen and guide the church. Through their control of sacred offices, especially bishoprics, Christian notables competed directly with old pagan elites for the power and prestige within late antique cities. However, church officials, at the command of an authoritarian institution built to achieve doctrinal orthodoxy among adherents, also had to discipline their flocks. Christian authorities used pious giving to police ordinary believers while rewriting many times over their doctrines on the proper means and ends of philanthropy.

By presenting themselves through impressive acts of public welfare as "lovers of the poor," bishops relied upon acts of philanthropy to mobilize popular support for the extension of their own autocratic governing authority. Regular church food doles tended to keep the needy in one place, and ecclesiastical licensing of beggars helped to make the itinerant more tractable for intimidating call-up if need be to back their episcopal patrons in urban power struggles. Thus Christian bishops began to challenge pagan town governors' former monopoly over the maintenance of public order and its rewards. Such clerical generosity, however, was neither disinterested nor directed unconditionally to the relief of suffering. Institutionalized Christian philanthropy here appears as a vital means by which great rival social and religious factions vying for political power contested and supplanted one another, occasionally at the expense of the poor. Success in this spirited police action required clerical patrons to exercise their disciplinary skills via charitable acts and to modify discourse about the proper objectives of Christian charity.

Most crucial here was church supervision over the accumulation and strategic use of wealth, not direction for its abandonment. Selective charity gained significance as a means of personal preferment and containment of sin, habituating ordinary givers to the tutelage of their clerical superiors about salvation. Saint Augustine, bishop of Hippo in 396–430 C.E., asserted that "almsgiving without purpose of amendment is useless" (Augustine 1978 [421], 74). According to Augustine, acceptable methodical alms included reproaches to the immoral and physical punishment of sinners. A good almsgiver could be one "who corrects with blows or restrains by any kind of disciplinary measure another over whom he has authority" (ibid., 72). High clerics' advocacy of alms to protect and police entire Christian communities reconnected private philanthropy with the power politics of the public sphere.

Medieval and Renaissance Philanthropies

Later Roman and Byzantine emperors accepted Christianity in part because they recognized the abundant social services churches could provide to their poorest subjects and saw the utility of churchmen in the charitable maintenance of public order. Emperor Constantine's edict of 321 C.E. gave the Catholic Church the right to stand as heir and receive will gifts from all testators. Increased legacies to the church enabled construction of diverse affiliated charitable institutions, including hospitals, orphanages, almshouses, and monasteries. The collapse of the old urbanized Roman Empire in western Europe after 500 C.E. and the flight of populations to the countryside under the pressure of barbarian invasions demolished many of the established church charities. Rural monasteries as unrivaled institutional dispensaries of Christian charity would only endure as long as the bulk of the surviving western European population was rooted to the land under the feudal system.

However, a slow recovery of long-distance travel, trade, and town life gathering force after 1000 C.E. promoted population shifts back to cities and human abandonment of fixed monastic care networks. Rising town populations after 1200 C.E., with a disproportionate increase in the numbers of the poor, presented westerners with new dilemmas over the management and care of the needy and sick, whose numbers seemed to be dangerously increasing. Cities at this time became centers of innovative private initiative and institutional experiment in the practice of philanthropy. Urbanites took the lead through their own charities in prioritizing relief efforts and in discriminating more finely between the deserving and undeserving indigent. The miserable rapidly lost their once endearing status as the "poor of Christ."

In the towns of the Byzantine Empire, hospitals expanded to cope with an intensified urbanization of the population. They benefited from a propensity of Greek Christians to appreciate medicine as the finest form of love in action—philanthropy in a new and popular professional guise. Byzantine emperors permitted hospitals to accept gifts and legacies directly, freeing them from fiscal control by clerics and enabling them to pursue their own fundraising as secular foundations legally independent of the church. Emperors conferred exemptions from imperial taxation on these organizations, causing them to thrive. By medieval times, the noun "philanthropy" also came to mean the tax-exempt status imperial rulers conferred on select charities. From this early date, fiscal immunities became integral to the definition and ethos of Western philanthropic institutions.

In European cities of the era, the provision of care became an arena of contention between venturesome benefactors who sought both to help more of the needy and to validate their own particular conception of true Christian charity. Participants in these philanthropic experiments included the reform-minded mendicant orders of the Catholic Church, Franciscans (founded 1209 C.E.), and Dominicans (1216 C.E.), who embraced poverty, became beggars themselves, and sought to vivify Catholic philanthropy with a return to the self-abnegating, "Samaritan" behaviors of Jesus and his early apostles.

Urban lay confraternities of men and women became important contemporary competitors in collective efforts to practice a more meaningful charity. A confraternity was a club of ordinary citizens who joined together to accomplish pious and philanthropic works satisfying their need for immediate, personal enactments of neighborly Christian virtues. Some confraternities operated under priestly direc-

tion, but most had just a chaplain and were only loosely tied to clerical networks of influence. These voluntary associations used pooled, private donations to care directly for certain classes of the needy, to sponsor impressive rituals of communal peacemaking, and to patronize artists of all kinds. In Florence and other Italian Renaissance cities, volunteers flocked to confraternities, creating more than 100 such organizations by the fifteenth century. Adherents used these organizations in part to forge peaceable ties with other citizens across frightening boundaries of neighborhood and social rank. The psycho-social benefits accruing to donors and volunteers living in densely populated, conflicted cities became the chief motivating factors to innovative forms of secular philanthropic activity. But what the recipients of such aid actually got now depended more on what made donors feel better about themselves.

Mendicant and confraternal revisions of Christian charity encouraged a proliferation of more individual philanthropic ventures, often paid for by newly enriched Renaissance merchants and business entrepreneurs. Private foundations of all kinds developed under the patronage and investment of these men and their womenfolk. They showed a penchant for practical forms of endowed philanthropy to earn personal spiritual benefit, committing productive agricultural lands or funds in perpetuity to set up and run hospitals, orphan homes, charity schools, apprenticeship programs, and asylums for the elderly throughout the cities and towns of Europe. Unfortunately, rampant inflation, currency debasements, fluctuating real estate values, and theft or misuse of funds by trustees sapped the resources and utility of endowed European foundations in the sixteenth and seventeenth centuries. By the middle of the eighteenth century, the extravagance, obsolescence, and corruption of many endowments, among the most widespread forms of philanthropy, invited sweeping attacks on this venerable but outmoded agency of caring by statesmen, jurists, and determined charity organizers.

Early Modern Philanthropies

The famous Elizabethan Statute of Charitable Uses (1601) represents one royal government's effort to curtail the whim of patronage and arrest the rampant corruption of private charitable foundations. The wholesale confiscation and disbandment of Catholic charities by Tudor monarchs in the contemporaneous English Reformation made it imperative that all available philanthropic capital be employed productively to save the state the cost of supporting the old parish poor. The preamble to the Statute on Uses specified those charitable causes susceptible to legal endowment via trusts, including aid of the poor, care of veterans, advancement of learning, and promotion of religion. Parliament was determined to multiply the amount of private monies available to promote social welfare, so this bill stipulated in great detail how lawful commissions of inquiry under government aegis could be formed to discover "any breach of trust, falsity, non-employment, concealment or conversion" of endowed charitable funds. Delegating its powers of surveillance, the Elizabethan state partnered with lawyers and philanthropists in creating a more secure legal environment for the private service of public welfare. The statute not merely defined charitable uses but also announced the state's prerogative to police an early semblance of the nonprofit sector.

The Elizabethan Statute should be considered merely the earliest in a long series of royal edicts and parliamentary acts across Europe more carefully regulating charitable organizations and their property under state supervision. In the eighteenth century, new statutes of mortmain were enacted by many European kings and legislatures (England in 1735, France in 1749, Hapsburg Empire in 1755). The common purpose of this legislation was to restrict severely the capacity of donors to convey real estate or monies derived from landed wealth into the permanent endowments of charitable organizations. Such assets, it was argued, should not be locked in mortmain—immune to sale and market forces forever. These resources better belonged in the patrimonies of noble families and landed magnates whose dynastic material welfare and unimpeded commercial activity were more important to the sociopolitical stability of rapidly modernizing states. The creation of any new endowed foundations was also rendered far more difficult by this legislation, in part so as to diminish the amount of fixed charitable assets retarding development of more dynamic and productive commercial

markets bankrolling the modernization of the state and economy.

Statesmen contended that charities could better prosper through entirely ad hoc fundraising campaigns and more competitive solicitation of cash gifts from individual donors to meet immediate needs. Under a regime of more exacting charitable efficiency, donors themselves sought better investment of their gifts, ideally training needy people for productive self-sufficiency, which would be better for the social security of all. This historical process has been called a "capitalization of charity," a tendency among early modern European and American philanthropists after 1600 to construe charitable donations as their own voluntary capital placements entitling them to tangible returns and to some degree of lifetime control over the employment of funds they provided to entrepreneurs running innovative philanthropies.

The advent of charity as capital made the jobs of officers in philanthropic organizations harder. Charity as capital volatilized streams of private donations, accelerating the pace at which donors demanded hard evidence of positive welfare outcomes and shifted their support at will among numerous, more highly competitive relief organizations to maximize their gifts' public benefit. Charity as capital also promoted a reconceptualization of philanthropy itself as a choice, not necessarily a duty or moral obligation of the propertied. Philanthropy's ascription to voluntary action within the "voluntary sector" is thus a comparatively recent historical development. Charity administrators, especially a new cadre of middle-class trustees, now had to seek, elicit, and manage a mix of private donations, public subventions, and legitimate institutional earnings in order to accomplish their philanthropic missions. Thus, far from being outside the development of contemporary market economies and state instruments of police, post-Reformation European and American philanthropies, in their quest for operational efficiency, promoted the calculating and experimental attitudes of mind intrinsic to capitalism's success in well-governed polities.

Modern Philanthropies

The eighteenth century witnessed the interconnected capitalization, nationalization, and rationalization of philanthropy. This process was refined and globalized in the nineteenth century as leading benefactors promoted organized philanthropy as a science requiring higher degrees of expertise from its practitioners. Wholesale importation of efficient business methods into the running of charities, championed by early-twentieth-century American captains of industry such as Andrew Carnegie and John D. Rockefeller, resuscitated the endowed but newly agile foundation as a legitimate vehicle of modern scientific philanthropy capable of reinventing itself regularly to cure emergent social or cultural problems. The dynamism of the modern nonprofit sector may be recent history's most impressive contribution to philanthropy. However, the conscience of modern philanthropists and their lingering obligatory sense of giving as justice may be rooted more deeply in the subject's antiquity.

Kevin C. Robbins

References and further reading
Andrew, Donna. 1989. *Philanthropy and Police: London Charity in the Eighteenth Century.* Princeton: Princeton University Press.
Augustine, St. 1978 [421]. *Faith, Hope, and Charity.* Translated by Louis Arand. New York: Newman Press.
Brown, Peter. 2002. *Poverty and Leadership in the Later Roman Empire.* Hanover, NH: Brandeis University Press.
Cavallo, Sandra. 1995. *Charity and Power in Early Modern Italy: Benefactors and Their Motives in Turin, 1541–1789.* Cambridge: Cambridge University Press.
Constantelos, Demetrios. 1991. *Byzantine Philanthropy and Social Welfare.* New Rochelle, NY: Aristide Caratzas.
Cunningham, Hugh, and Joanna Innes, eds. 1998. *Charity, Philanthropy, and Reform.* London: Macmillan.
Davis, Natalie. 2000. *The Gift in Sixteenth-Century France.* Madison: University of Wisconsin Press.
Flynn, Maureen. 1989. *Sacred Charity: Confraternities and Social Welfare in Spain, 1400–1700.* Ithaca, NY: Cornell University Press.
Henderson, John. 1994. *Piety and Charity in Renaissance Florence.* Oxford: Oxford University Press.
Himmelfarb, Gertrude. 1991. *Poverty and Compassion: The Moral Imagination of the Late Victorians.* New York: Knopf.
Kloppenborg, John S., and S. G. Wilson, eds. 1996. *Voluntary Associations in the Greco-Roman World.* London: Routledge.
Lindberg, Carter. 1993. *Beyond Charity: Reformation Initiatives for the Poor.* Minneapolis: Fortress Press.
Loewenberg, Frank. 2001. *From Charity to Social Justice: The Emergence of Communal Institutions for Support of the Poor*
in Ancient Judaism. New Brunswick, NJ: Transaction Books.
Miller, Timothy. 1985. *The Birth of the Hospital in the Byzantine Empire.* Baltimore: Johns Hopkins University Press.
Rickett, C. E. F. 1979. "Charitable Giving in English and Roman Law. A Comparison." *Cambridge Law Journal* 38: 118–147.
Safely, Thomas. 1997. *Charity and Economy in the Orphanages of Early Modern Augsburg.* Boston: Humanities Press.
Seneca. 1989 [c. 60]. *Moral Essays.* Vol. 3, *On Benefits.* Translated by John Basore. Cambridge: Harvard University Press.
Veyne, Paul. 1976. *Bread and Circuses: Historical Sociology and Political Pluralism.* London: Penguin Books.
Weissman, Ronald. 1982. *Ritual Brotherhood in Renaissance Florence.* New York: Academic Press.
Wilson, Peter. 2000. *The Athenian Institution of the Khoregia: The Chorus, the City, and the Stage.* Cambridge: Cambridge University Press.
Winter, Bruce. 1994. *Seek the Welfare of the City: Christians as Benefactors and Citizens.* Grand Rapids, MI: Eerdmans.

Hogg, Ima (1882–1975)

Ima Hogg, philanthropist, collector, and patron of the arts, was the daughter of Texas governor James Stephen Hogg and his wife Sarah Ann. Fondly known as Miss Ima for most of her ninety-three years, she was born in Mineola, Texas, on July 10, 1882. She had three brothers. Miss Ima was eight years old when her father first took office as governor, and she spent many of her younger years in Austin, where the family resided.

Ima's mother died of tuberculosis in 1895 and Ima was sent to a boarding school at the Coronal Institute in San Marcos. In 1899, she enrolled at the University of Texas at Austin, and two years later she went to New York City to study music. She had played the piano since the age of three. When her father became ill in 1905, Miss Ima stayed by his bedside and nursed him until he died from a heart attack in 1906. The following year, she left for Europe to continue her music studies in Vienna and Berlin. When she returned to live in Houston, she gave piano lessons to a select group of students and subsequently founded the Houston Symphony

Orchestra, the beginning of her many philanthropic endeavors. She became ill in 1918 and spent the next two years in Philadelphia to receive care by a specialist in mental and nervous disorders, but returned to Houston in 1923.

The family oil business had finally struck oil near West Columbia, Texas, and Miss Ima was widely involved in philanthropic activities. She founded the Houston Child Guidance Center in 1929 to provide treatment and counseling for troubled children and their families. Miss Ima's older brother, William Clifford, died in 1930, leaving a bequest that facilitated Ima's establishment of the Hogg Foundation for Mental Hygiene, which later became the Hogg Foundation for Mental Health at the University of Texas. Miss Ima, a Democrat, played her hand in politics in 1943 and won an election to the Houston school board. There, she worked to create symphony concerts for children in school and to ensure equal pay for teachers regardless of sex or race.

Before Ima became ill and left for Philadelphia in 1918, she was the president of the Houston Symphony Society, a position she returned to in 1946 and would hold for ten more years. She became the first woman president of the Philosophical Society of Texas in 1948. Miss Ima had been collecting American art and antiques since the 1920s, and in 1966 she presented her collection, as well as Bayou Bend, the River Oaks mansion that she and her brothers had built in 1927, to the Museum of Fine Arts in Houston. Thousands of visitors are drawn to the Bayou Bend Collection annually to see one of the most distinctive collected works of its kind.

The Hogg family home at Varner Plantation near West Columbia was restored by Miss Ima in the 1950s and presented to the state of Texas as the Varner-Hogg Plantation State Historical Park. The next decade, she refurbished the Winedale Inn and gave it to the University of Texas. Winedale Inn was a stagecoach depot and livery at Round Top, Texas, in the 1800s. It now serves as a history center for the study of Texas's past where an annual fine arts festival is held. In 1969, the town of Quitman, Texas, launched the Ima Hogg Museum in her honor. The museum was originally her parents' home in Quitman.

In 1953, Miss Ima was appointed by Governor Allan Shivers to the Texas State Historical Survey Committee, a body that gave her an award in 1967 to recognize her astounding work and commitment in preserving Texas history. In 1960, she served by appointment from President Dwight D. Eisenhower as a planning member of the National Cultural Center in Washington, D.C., which is now better known as the Kennedy Center. Two years later, Ima Hogg was asked by Jacqueline Kennedy to serve on an advisory panel to help find historical furniture for the White House. Miss Ima's interest in gardens was also rewarded when the Garden Club of America honored her in 1959. Other honors she received came from the National Trust for Historic Preservation in 1966 and from the American Association for State and Local History in 1969.

Ima Hogg's contributions to the state of Texas and the University of Texas were recognized when she became the first recipient of the Santa Rita Award, given by the University of Texas system for her contributions to the university and higher education. The Academy of Texas honored Miss Ima, Oveta Culp Hobby, and Lady Bird Johnson as the first three women members in 1969. The academy honors outstanding recipients who expand and facilitate knowledge in any field of higher education. Miss Ima also received an honorary doctorate in fine arts from Southwestern University in 1971, and the following year she was recognized for her contributions to America's cultural heritage when she received the National Society of Interior Designers' Thomas Jefferson Award.

Ima Hogg left for London shortly after her ninety-third birthday to attend concerts and visit museums. She fell out of a taxi on the way to the theater, however, and broke her hip. She died soon thereafter, on August 19, 1975. She was buried on August 23 in Oakwood Cemetery, Austin. Her funeral was held at Bayou Bend, her beloved home, which she had long planned as a gift to the city of Houston. The Ima Hogg Foundation, a not-for-profit organization set up by Miss Ima in 1964 to enrich research, knowledge, and capacities for mental health, was the major benefactor in her will.

Mark Neumeister

References and further reading

Bernhard, Virginia. 1984. *Ima Hogg: The Governor's Daughter.* Austin: Texas Monthly Press.

———. 2002. "Ima Hogg." In *Notable American Philanthropists: Biographies of Giving and Volunteering,* edited by Robert T. Grimm Jr., 147–151. Westport, CT: Oryx Press.

"Governor Daniel." Note from Ima Hogg, Page 1, Texas State Library. Texas State Library and Archives Commission, http://castor.tsl.state.tx.us/governors/modern/daniel-hogg-1.html (cited October 17, 2001).

"Hogg, Ima." The Handbook of Texas Online, http://www.tsha.utexas.edu/handbook/online/articles/view/HH/fh016.html (cited August 30, 2001).

Iscoe, Louise. 1976. *Ima Hogg: First Lady of Texas.* Austin: Hogg Foundation for Mental Health.

Hoover, Herbert Clark (1874–1964)

Herbert Clark Hoover, the thirty-first president of the United States, was born to Quaker parents in West Branch, Iowa, in 1874 but was orphaned at the age of ten with the death of his mother, his father having died from typhoid fever when Hoover was just six. After the death of his parents, he moved to Oregon to live and work with an uncle. Although Herbert Hoover did not attend high school, he was admitted to Stanford University in 1891 and graduated in 1895 with a degree in geology. He married his college sweetheart and fellow geology student Lou Henry in 1899, and together they had two sons, Herbert Jr. and Allan.

After establishing himself as a premier mining scout and amassing a fortune of approximately $4 million, Hoover focused on his career as a public servant. He helped to feed the hungry, house the homeless, and employ the unemployed with various programs both domestically and abroad. His philanthropy, supported by his personal beliefs and practices of individualism, also encompassed his various political roles. His emphasis on the benefits of voluntary service was pervasive throughout his career.

While running his mining business in London during the early 1900s, Hoover was a passionate observer of the society of several European countries at a crucial period in world history. As World War I broke out, he directed a program that helped thousands of stranded American tourists to find safe passage back to the United States. Because of this successful mission, Hoover left behind his lucrative mining business to head the Commission for Relief Belgium (CRB), which was created in 1914 to help feed millions of starving Belgians and French citizens. Hoover successfully directed this vast food administration program and was personally in charge of international diplomacy and fundraising (Eckley 1980, 28).

Hoover's work during his stint in Belgium earned him an appointment as U.S. food administrator in 1917 by President Woodrow Wilson. Hoover accepted the position, seeing it as an opportunity to volunteer alongside his fellow Americans in the war effort. A war-ravaged Europe awaited the support of the United States at the end of World War I. Hoover was commissioned by President Wilson to redefine the mission of the Food Administration to create a new agency, the American Relief Administration, which would help to reconstruct Europe, and eventually it became a private agency. Facing imperialistic ideas among the leaders of key European nations, Hoover focused on those who were most devastated by the war, the children. Millions of orphaned, malnourished, and diseased children, including those of the former enemy, Germany, were fed through his efforts.

In 1921, Hoover went on to become the secretary of commerce under President Warren Harding, a position he held for seven years. While in the cabinet, he consolidated organizations for the health and welfare of children into the American Child Health Association. He ran for president as a Republican in 1928 and won by 6 million popular votes and 375 electoral votes. Shortly thereafter, the stock-market crash of 1929 occurred. Hoover's idealist individualism, which led him to argue against federal aid to alleviate the Great Depression, contributed to his loss of favor among the American people, and thus, his loss in 1932 to Franklin D. Roosevelt.

Seeing his loss as emancipation, Hoover became an outspoken opponent of Roosevelt's New Deal and threw himself into his personal philanthropic interests. He served as chairman of Boys Club of America and helped to establish 500 new Boys Clubs during his tenure. He also served for nearly fifty years on the Stanford University board of trustees. In 1938, he returned to Europe to be recognized for his contributions following the war, but with a new war looming, Hoover returned to the United States and warned against involvement in the potential conflict. After the bombing of Pearl Harbor, he began to reevaluate how realistic world peace might be. Following World War II, President Harry S. Truman asked Hoover to conduct a study to assess worldwide food needs, and in 1946 he became the cofounder of the United Nations International Children's Emergency Fund (UNICEF). He went on to open several libraries and collections across the country (Eckley 1980, 46). Hoover did much of his giving in private and went on to write and publish a number of books and articles before his death on October 20, 1964.

Keight S. Tucker

References and further reading
Eckley, Wilton. 1980. *Herbert Hoover.* Edited by Kenneth E. Eble. Boston: Twayne.

Fausold, Martin L. 1985. *The Presidency of Herbert Hoover.* Lawrence: University Press of Kansas.

Hoover, Herbert C. 1951–1952. *The Memoirs of Herbert Hoover.* 3 vols. New York: Macmillan.

Nash, George H. 1983–1996. *The Life of Herbert Hoover.* 3 vols. New York: W. W. Norton.

"Herbert Hoover." White House Web site, http://www .whitehouse.gov/history/prsidents/hh31.html (cited October 17, 2002).

Howe, Samuel Gridley (1801–1876)

Samuel Gridley Howe pursued philanthropic causes throughout his lifetime—from doctoring the wounded in wartime to raising funds for European independence movements to advocacy for the disabled. Howe is best remembered as an innovator in education for the blind and deaf, a reformer of treatment for the mentally ill, and an advocate for the integration of blacks during and after the Civil War. In his twenties, he placed himself in harm's way to aid the Greeks in their fight for independence. A few years later, Howe worked to aid starving Polish refugees who were also fighting for independence. Directly after these events, he established the first school for the blind in the United States—the Perkins School for the Blind in Boston. His involvement in advocacy and social reform in many areas continued until the time of his death.

As a child, Howe loved playing a good joke on someone. Known as a prankster throughout his schooling, Samuel Gridley Howe came to channel that energy into philanthropic work in his native Boston and elsewhere throughout the nineteenth century. Born on November 10, 1801, Howe grew up knowing what it was like to be an outsider. His father was an ardent Jeffersonian Democrat, which set the family apart in the strongly Federalist Boston area. The family was not wealthy; consequently, Howe attended the Latin School and Brown University, neither of which was considered a first-rate learning institution at the time. A mediocre student at best, he was suspended on several occasions due to problems in his behavior. In 1821, Howe entered Harvard Medical School and soon went to study with Dr. Ingalls, a prominent Boston physician. In the medical profession, Howe found his calling.

The tumultuous international events of the 1820s also were an allure for the new doctor. In 1828, Howe traveled to Greece to aid the patriotic army in their fight for Greek independence. He found the experience enthralling and was soon fully engulfed in the struggle, nursing the wounded, raising money for the poor, even traveling back to the United States to rally Americans around the Greek cause. It was at this point in time that Howe's philanthropic roots were firmly planted. During these excursions back to the states, he actively raised money for the war effort in Greece. These fundraising trips were extremely successful; Howe raised thousands of dollars and became a hero in his local community for his efforts.

His experiences in Greece and other parts of Europe led him, in 1831, to become interested in establishing a school for the blind. A figure of some prominence in Boston, Howe saw the establishment of a school as the way to bolster his self-worth while simultaneously helping an underrepresented group in society. All through his life, Howe would struggle to reconcile his great need for recognition and importance with an unnaturally low self-esteem.

Howe began the project by visiting France, England, and Germany to see how the blind were educated in those countries. Ideologically opposed to the methods he observed there, Howe decided to forge new territory in the education of the blind and the deaf. But, in 1832, Howe faced an obstacle far greater than how to run his school—imprisonment in Berlin. He was imprisoned by the Germans while trying to bring relief to starving Polish refugees during their war for independence. Released shortly thereafter, Howe returned to Boston even more a hero than when he left. Many citizens of the city had started to call him a philanthropist, a term loaded with respect and social status. At the time, philanthropy in Boston was an activity of the very elite. His elevation into a higher stratum of people served further to legitimate his burgeoning work with the blind and deaf.

Howe revolutionized the way that the blind and, to some degree, the deaf came to be educated. He began by printing books in Braille upon his return to Boston in 1832, the same year in which he officially started the Perkins School for the Blind. He quickly printed the Bible, *Paradise Lost, Hamlet,* and *Pilgrim's Progress,* among other works (Sanborn 1891). He also improved the Braille typeset, making it easier to decipher, and began to train teachers to instruct students on the use of Braille books and other learning materials.

In 1843, Howe married Julia Ward. Between 1851 and 1853, they coedited *Commonwealth,* a Boston newspaper devoted to the antislavery movement. Julia was a published and well-respected writer in her own right. Together they had five children. Theirs was a stormy marriage; the two often lived apart for months at a time while Howe traveled the United States on speaking tours. These tours encompassed many topics, among them Howe's opposition to the Mexican War. Howe was a Whig by 1845 and also strongly opposed slavery. He became somewhat of a crusader for prison reform, too, especially when those imprisoned were fugitive slaves.

Howe increasingly lobbied for the abolition of slavery. As the Civil War approached, he wondered how best to contribute to the Union cause. Being too old at the age of sixty to work in the army hospitals, he decided to work with the Emancipation League, a group he had helped to found in Boston some time before. That group supported the enlistment of African American troops during the war and took up

the cause of black education after the war. Howe simultaneously served on the U.S. Sanitary Commission, lobbying for more health officers and better troop hygiene.

Howe additionally began to study the effects of institutionalization on the mentally ill. Suffering himself from lifelong depression, he was compelled to change what he saw as a flawed system. He determined that the large, state-run housing offered for the insane was wholly inadequate and, in fact, harmful to those in its care. Instead, Howe advocated for smaller housing units that focused on achieving independence for residents. He took the family as a model for charity and felt that the state-run institutions should be as parents to the mentally ill, helping those offspring to grow up and prepare for the real world, whether they reached that world or not. In 1865, Howe became the chairman of the Massachusetts Board of State Charities—the first board of its kind in the United States—and used the position as a platform to lobby for further housing reformation for the poor and insane (Spartacus 2002).

Howe did not forget his original desire to revolutionize the way the blind were taught. Throughout the middle part of the nineteenth century, Howe continued to study the most effective way to educate blind and deaf students. His greatest challenge, and arguably his greatest success, came in the form of Miss Laura Bridgman. Both blind and deaf since the age of two, Miss Bridgman presented a unique set of problems for Howe. Howe never believed in using sign language; he thought signs were too abstract to convey actual meaning to a deaf or blind and deaf person. Instead, he advocated for the use of finger spelling, where each word is spelled out into the hand of the deaf and blind person in order to convey a sentence or idea. Miss Bridgman eventually learned how to finger spell and became a prolific Braille reader. She was never, however, able to live on her own or interact with the seeing and deaf society. In that way, she did not fulfill the goals set out by Howe for his pupils.

Many of Howe's expectations went unfulfilled, mostly because he set goals that were unrealistic. He wanted to teach blind and deaf children according to their talents; in that way, he revolutionized their education by making these children more than the sum of their disabilities. He sought to narrow the gap between the blind and the sighted in society, a goal that he did achieve. But he ultimately wanted blind, deaf, and mentally ill children to learn how to function fully in society, which was impossible. As the children matured into adults, they simply had too many differences with "normal" society to be able to be fully integrated.

Even though many of his dreams were not realized, Samuel Gridley Howe will be remembered for his innovation in the areas of education for the blind and deaf, reformation of treatment for the mentally ill, and integration of blacks during and after the Civil War. He died in Boston in 1876 of a brain tumor. Interestingly, Howe left nothing to his wife and only $2,000 to Laura Bridgman in order that she be taken care of for the rest of her life at the Perkins School for the Blind (Gitter 2001).

Emily M. Hall

References and further reading

American Council of the Blind. *Organizational Profile.* Available at http://www.acb.org/profile.html (cited January 19, 2003).

Gitter, Elizabeth. 2001. *The Imprisoned Guest: Samuel Howe and Laura Bridgman, the Original Deaf-Blind Girl.* New York: Farrar Straus and Giroux.

Grant, Mary Hetherington. 1994. *Private Woman, Public Person: An Account of the Life of Julia Ward Howe from 1819–1868.* Brooklyn, NY: Carlson Publishing.

National Federation of the Blind. 2002. *About the NFB.* Available at http://www.nfb.org/aboutnfb.htm (cited January 18, 2003).

Perkins School for the Blind. *History.* Available at http://www.perkins.pvt.k12.ma.us/section.php?id=53 (cited January 18, 2003).

Sanborn, Franklin Benjamin. 1891. *Dr. S. G. Howe: The Philanthropist.* New York: Funk and Wagnalls.

Schwartz, Harold. 1956. *Samuel Gridley Howe, Social Reformer, 1801–1876.* Cambridge, MA: Harvard University Press.

Spartacus Educational. *Samuel Gridley Howe.* Available at http://www.spartacus.schoolnet.co.uk/USAShoweG.htm (cited September 28, 2002).

Human Services and Philanthropy

The human services field is of growing importance to ordinary Americans who now expect access to a broad range of personal support services. A large proportion of those services are delivered by nonprofit organizations (Salamon 1999; Smith 2002; Grønbjerg 2001). Moreover, human services nonprofits are numerous and account for the largest proportion of charitable nonprofits in the United States, although they are dwarfed in size by hospitals and institutions of higher education (Weitzman et al. 2002). The changing relationship between human services nonprofits and government has become a major driving force in the field. Meanwhile, the role of philanthropy and the extent to which charitable contributions support nonprofit human services organizations has been diminishing, and the influence that key philanthropic institutions had in the past is also declining.

Scope and Structure

There are no good data to document the overall size and composition of the human services field or of its nonprofit components. Indeed, even the definition of what constitutes human services is problematic. Some consider the field to include just four subfields—individual and family counseling, vocational rehabilitation, residential care, and day care (Salamon 1999; Smith 2002). Intermediary definitions add legal and various community services to this list (Weitzman et al. 2002). The National Taxonomy of Exempt Entities (NTEE) includes activities related to crime/legal assistance, employment/training, food/nutrition, housing/shelter, public safety/disaster, recreation, youth development, and traditional human services (Weitzman et al. 2002; Foundation Center 2002).

Using an intermediary definition of human services and data from the U.S. Economic Census, one study reported that the nonprofit social services field spent $66 billion on operations in 1997 (Weitzman et al. 2002, Table 4.2). If the broader definition of human services under NTEE and data from Form 990 financial information filed with the Internal Revenue Service (IRS) by charities are taken into account, total operating expenses reach $77 billion (ibid., Table 5.15), or just over 1 percent of the total national income ($7.3 trillion) in 1998. Both estimates likely undervalue the size of the nonprofit human services field.

Nor do these estimates address how important human services nonprofits are compared to government and for-profit organizations. Nonprofits accounted for 61 percent of total revenues and 55 percent of employees for 1994, using the narrow four-subfield definition of social services (Salamon 1999). A more recent analysis, which excludes government but adds a small number of miscellaneous social services entities, shows that tax-exempt entities accounted for 70 percent of nongovernmental social services wages and 57 percent of nongovernmental social services establishments in 1997 (Smith 2002).

The latter study also confirmed that nonprofits were key players in some social services fields, dominating individual and family services and vocational rehabilitation agencies and playing a major role in residential care facilities, accounting, respectively, for 91, 89, and 58 percent of employment. Nonprofits therefore significantly shape the service delivery system in those fields, although they lost ground in residential care facilities over the 1977–1997 period (going from 73 to 58 percent of employment). For-profit entities dominate other subfields, most notably day care (62 percent of employment), recreation, and legal services, and their share most likely has increased over the past twenty years (up from 44 percent of employment in day-care services). For-profits therefore exert a significant and growing influence on their nonprofit counterparts in these fields as all compete for clients, staff, and other resources and face similar institutional constraints (for example, professional standards in legal services, liability issues in recreation, and licensing requirements in day care). Of course, the nonprofit role in all of these fields would be more prominent if the value of volunteer labor in the form of foregone salary and wages were included.

The nonprofit human services field has grown considerably since at least the 1970s and probably for some time prior to that (Grønbjerg 2001). The number of nonprofit social services establishments and employees more than doubled over the 1977–1997 period (up by 125 and 135 percent, respectively) (Smith 2002). These organizations rely on a mix of revenues, although the specifics and trends are subject to dispute. Thus one study reported that social and legal services nonprofits received about half (52 percent) of total revenues from government in 1997, about a fifth each from fees (19

percent) and donations (20 percent), and the rest from a variety of other receipts (Weitzman et al. 2002, Table 4.3). Another, however, estimated that the revenue base of the nonprofit social services sector (excluding legal services and civic organizations) in 1996 was dominated by fees (43 percent) followed by government funding (37 percent), with private giving trailing at 20 percent (Salamon 1999). The latter figures may be the more accurate of the two but are still subject to substantial uncertainties (Paarlberg and Grønbjerg 1999).

The growth in nonprofit human services has been fueled by sources other than donations. Major shifts have occurred in the revenue profiles of member agencies of the United Way of Chicago, for example. The proportion of agencies relying on government funding for half or more of their revenues increased from zero percent in the 1950s to 84 percent in the mid-1990s, while the proportion obtaining half or more of their revenues from donations declined from 86 percent to 19 percent over the same period. There were no changes in primary reliance on fees and service charges.

More comprehensive data on nonprofit social and legal services organizations show no changes in government funding over the 1977–1997 period (from 54 to 52 percent of total revenues), but growing reliance on private-sector revenues (up from 10 to 19 percent of revenues) and declining reliance on donations (down from 32 to 20 percent) (Weitzman et al. 2002, Table 4.3). The overall growth in the four traditional nonprofit service fields over the 1977–1996 period is accounted for primarily by increases in commercial revenues (69 percent), followed by government (22 percent) and private giving (9 percent) (Salamon 1999). In other words, all three sources of revenues grew, but fees grew at a much faster rate than government funding, with private giving trailing far behind.

What these aggregate figures obscure, of course, is the great diversity in financial profiles among individual nonprofit human services agencies, including differences reflecting the mix of services provided and the size of operations. The aggregate figures are dominated by larger agencies because they account for the bulk of dollars involved, while the majority of human services organizations are quite small. Commercial activity is probably concentrated among larger non-profits (Crimmins and Kiel 1990), suggesting that the typical nonprofit human services agency relies more extensively on government and donation funding than is implied by the aggregate profile. There may also be regional variations in financial profiles (Salamon 1995), since local political cultures vary in their propensity to use public funding to finance services (Rosentraub 1991; Bielefeld and Corbin 1996) and regions differ in their historical patterns of nonprofit development (Nielsen 1979; Hall 1987; Wolpert 1989).

Nonprofit Human Services and Public Policy

At one level, the growth in human services and the continuing dominance of nonprofits in the field suggest that things are going well. However, a closer look points to the challenges posed by key public policy developments. Although nonprofit human services have benefited enormously from the pervasive and long-standing preference in the United States for privatizing public-sector activities, the mechanisms by which human services are privatized have changed and are now fundamentally different from even the recent past.

There have been three major waves in privatization of human services (Grønbjerg and Smith 1999). During the first wave, which lasted until the early 1960s, modest public subsidies were available for private orphanages, old people's homes, and the like. Public-sector oversight consisted mainly of occasional investigations and scrutiny by ethnic or religious institutions (Morton 1993; Brown and McKeown 1997; Hacsi 1997).

During the 1960s and 1970s, a new pattern emerged as public funding increased dramatically for welfare services. New or expanded federal programs required state and local matching funding and diminished the role of local authorities. Much of the new funding was channeled toward nonprofit service providers, with some federal programs virtually mandating funding for nonprofits, but the format shifted from annual subsidies to production-related grants and contracts. This made it easier for the larger and more distant levels of government now involved to maintain formal accountability.

The large volume of funding served to establish numerous and close ties between the two sectors, and nonprofit agencies and their coalitions became directly involved in the policy-making process. Their political influence reflected their expertise in documenting the impact of policy changes, the extent to which public agencies depended on them to deliver mandated services, as well as their own motivations for playing an active role because of the stakes they had in the process. The more formalized funding structures created growing transaction costs related to grant or contract renewals, compliance, and reporting systems—to the point that these absorbed considerable management efforts by both public and nonprofit agencies (Grønbjerg 1993). In addition, the growth in government financing shifted costs away from donors, although the latter were still very important to nonprofit agencies because of the flexible funding they provided.

During the third wave of privatization, beginning in the mid-1980s, some programs that previously had provided significant funding for human services nonprofits declined or stagnated (for example, social services block grants) while others (such as foster care, child welfare, Head Start, substance abuse, and health) increased. In addition, the funding mechanism changed for several programs (for example, child welfare, substance abuse) as states began to switch to Medicaid financing in order to maximize federal support or adopted managed-care models to contain costs. This shift increased compliance costs and revenue uncertainties for provider agencies.

The Personal Responsibility and Work Opportunity Reconciliation Act of 1996, also known as the Welfare Reform Act, and the "devolution" of responsibilities from the federal government to states and local communities created other challenges. These programs allow greater flexibility in structuring services to meet mandated program goals, but large, multiservice agencies are likely to benefit most since they can more easily shift their many funding sources among program activities. They also have powerful board members, strong connections to political actors, and close linkages to lobbying organizations. The typical small, focused nonprofits tend to be undercapitalized, cannot easily alter their service mix, and are politically weak, but they often provide niche services targeted at specific neighborhoods or client groups. Recent developments that favor faith-based agencies have further shifted the political landscape. So have efforts to require (or strongly prefer) the delivery of services through local area service networks, with the associated system of lead agencies, subcontracts, and potentially major problems of collaboration and governance (Milward and Provan 2000; Bickers 1999).

Overlaying these trends is increased reliance on performance contracts by government agencies. These contracts specify levels of compliance with welfare reform and workforce development standards. Designed to improve efficiency and effectiveness, these developments constitute a major cultural challenge for nonprofits—forcing them to downplay their traditional pride in quality services and good-faith efforts in favor of market-like behavior. The system also invites competition by for-profit agencies that claim they can provide the specified outcomes and services at a lower cost (Frumkin and Andre-Clark 2000). For that reason, performance contracts may squeeze nonprofit agencies financially by limiting their ability to cross-subsidize operations and meet broader service missions. This, combined with a shift from producer to consumer subsidies in public welfare spending, results in more uncertain and fragile revenue streams for human services nonprofits and a blurring of the line between nonprofit and for-profit providers.

Human Services and Philanthropy

These developments in public funding of human services suggest the need to look more closely at the role of philanthropy, which historically has been a major source of support for human services nonprofits. However, that role has been diminishing, and philanthropy may no longer provide a safety net. *Giving USA* (AAFRC 2002) reported that human services nonprofits (broadly defined) received only about 10 percent (or $21 billion) of giving from all sources in 2001, roughly the same percentages they have received since the early 1970s, even though government funding for the field expanded dramatically during that period.

Assessing the importance of different types of philanthropic support for human services is more difficult because of a lack of adequate data. Individuals are the largest source of donations overall, accounting for 76 percent of the $212 billion in total giving in 2001 (ibid.), but most of these donations benefit congregations. Twenty-five percent of U.S. households made donations to human services in 1995, a smaller proportion than those donating to religion (48 percent) or health (27 percent) (Hodgkinson and Weitzman et al. 1996, 26). However, human services receive only about 10 percent of all individual contributions, slightly more than health and education (about 8 percent), but far less than religion (about 60 percent). Given the difficulty of obtaining good data on individual contributions (Rooney et al. 2001), it may not be useful to place great confidence in these numbers.

More important may be the greater competition for individual donations and major shifts in the capacity and interests of individual donors. The U.S. income structure has become more bifurcated in recent years, reflecting the loss of well-paying manufacturing and mid-level management jobs. The almost obscene growth in corporate executive compensation along with corporate mergers and acquisitions has increased the number of individuals with significant assets. Because high-income families tend to support cultural, educational, and environmental fields, these shifts in income and the estimated $10 trillion in intergenerational transfers over the next twenty years (Avery 1994) will likely benefit the latter fields more so than the human services nonprofits.

Certainly, competition for individual donations (and for fundraising expertise) appears to be growing and is now increasingly focused on wealthier donors where the return on fundraising costs can be maximized. Nonprofits that wish to avoid control by elite interests and seek donations from the less wealthy must compete for visibility and loyalty in an arena that is increasingly dominated by slick public relations efforts. Many have sought to target special donor markets or cultivate new constituency groups, but highly sophisticated efforts are likely to be beyond the scope of the vast majority of human services nonprofits. They are too small and have too limited management capacity and lack the cachet of major cultural or educational institutions.

Other sources of philanthropic funding, such as United Way, corporate, and foundation support, impact the human services field by how they determine priorities and underwrite research to influence social policy. In addition, their service grants support agencies and programs that are an integral part of the human services system. However, there is little systematic knowledge of how this diverse cast of philanthropic funders views the human services environment or makes funding decisions.

The role of United Way organizations, traditionally a major source of donations for human services agencies, appears to be diminishing. In 2000–2001, some 1,900 United Way organizations, in close collaboration with local businesses, raised $3.9 billion (United Way of America 2002). In return for their support, local corporate leaders sit on United Way boards and serve on volunteer committees that determine priorities and allocate funds. Traditionally, local human services agencies became member agencies of the local United Way and agreed to curtail their own efforts to raise funds (at least from businesses). As member agencies, they received allocations as long as they remained members in good standing. In fact, the United Way system is one of the major ways in which U.S. corporations support human services, and it is one of the most institutionalized sources of donations for human services organizations.

However, United Way organizations have faced decreasing capacity to raise funds, threats to their primary purpose, and internal tensions. Large-scale layoffs at major corporations, the primary source of workplace solicitations, make it difficult for United Way to maintain donation levels, especially since most do not have the capacity (at least in larger cities) to systematically solicit potential donor segments that are growing rapidly, for example, small or medium-sized corporations, independent contractors, or retirees. Growing absentee ownership threatens corporate loyalties to the United Way and local communities with implications for donations to and leadership in the system. In addition, corporations increasingly use philanthropic activities to serve marketing and other strategic interests. United Way's traditional community allocation system does not serve those interests as effectively as more targeted donations with corporate name tags.

Corporate employees are also now demanding the right to designate which nonprofits receive their support. The pressure toward donor designation means that although the United Way may still be collecting large amounts of funds, smaller proportions will be allocated to local member agencies. This undermines the claim to "community planning" that United Way has traditionally used as a major justification for its workplace monopoly. It also introduces explicit competition among member agencies.

Partly because of scarce resources, there are increasing tensions in the system. Some relate to the allocation of funds; others are more explicitly political in nature. The latter include competition among adjacent United Ways, conflict related to affirmative action policies (gender, religion, sexual orientation), and tension between targeting funding to performance in particular services and general support (Grønbjerg et al. 1996).

The same factors that threaten the workplace success of United Way campaigns also limit direct corporate donations to human services nonprofits. Growing international competition and corporate takeovers encourage corporations to link philanthropic activities to marketing, promotions, or public relations. Frequently, that means seeking out prestigious and well-known nonprofits, such as major arts and cultural organizations or institutions of higher education, that bring corporate visibility, enhance the quality of life for corporate elites (arts and culture), or serve direct corporate interests (higher education).

Nationally, corporate donations doubled on a per capita basis (in constant dollars) between 1977 and the early 1980s (Grønbjerg 1993, 76–77) but since then have stabilized at around $8–9 billion (AAFRC 2002). Corporate support for health and human services has remained level throughout the period, reflecting a relative shift in corporate support away from these service areas during the earlier period. Total corporate contributions to all nonprofit fields, including United Way support, amounted to $9 billion in 2001.

Foundations (excluding corporate foundations) made grant payments of almost $26 billion in 2001 (ibid.), although this does not include all grants made by the 64,000 private foundations registered with the IRS in 1998 (Weitzman et al. 2002, Table 5.1). Total foundation giving has more than tripled in constant dollars since 1971 (AAFRC 2002). Estimates from the Foundation Center in 2002 suggest that human services received about 14 percent of noncorporate foundation grants, with foundation support for education taking a 25 percent share and health 21 percent.

Private foundations are closely tied to corporations. Many have founders whose wealth derived from business activities, they typically have corporate or business representatives as members of their boards, and foundation assets and earnings frequently stem from corporate earnings. The rapid run-up in stock prices in recent years has significantly expanded the assets of many foundations. Because foundations must pay out at least 5 percent of their assets each year (averaged over three years), foundation grant amounts have increased correspondingly. By the same token, the more recent decline in stock values has depressed the level of foundation grantmaking.

More relevant for the present analysis is how philanthropic institutions position themselves with regard to the human services field. An in-depth study of such institutions for the Chicago area (Grønbjerg and Martell 2000) shows that philanthropic funding for human services is highly fragmented. Although a substantial proportion of grantmaking foundations or giving programs provide support for human service–related activities, funders vary greatly in the relative importance they accord human services and in how much their volume of grants fluctuate over time. They differ also in how they focus their efforts, structure their grantmaking, modify priorities and grant structures, and select agencies to fund.

The findings suggest that philanthropic funders may not share a common set of values, norms, or perceptions. Only a handful of philanthropic funders appear to be intimately aware of how other funders operate or to actively coordinate their activities with those of their peers (Grønbjerg and Jones 1997). In addition, vaguely articulated funding objectives and reluctance to evaluate grant performances point to an ambiguous core technology and the absence of a well-developed knowledge base. Many funders find it difficult to sort among proposals and agencies, narrow funding foci, limit eligibility, focus on known and trusted agencies, or monitor agencies on an ongoing basis.

Instead, philanthropic funders rely extensively on personal networks, rather than institutional norms or rational assessment of the effectiveness of grants, in making grant decisions. Indeed, many are vague, at times deliberately so, about their objectives and funding criteria. Agencies that are not already part of the funding stream face significant transaction costs in obtaining sufficiently accurate and timely information to increase their chances of success. The low turnover rates among funded agencies that characterize many funders lend direct support to the argument that it is difficult for new agencies to break into a funder's pool of supported agencies. The procedures by which philanthropic funders make decisions about activities to support are closely intertwined with the relationships they have with funded agencies.

The portrait of philanthropic funders that emerges suggests we should not expect coherent and coordinated responses by philanthropic funders to major developments in the human services field. Indeed, some philanthropic funders see themselves as the last domino to fall—public policy affects agencies and agency needs affect them. Many are captured by their own particular perceptions and priorities and uncertain about their capacity to go much beyond funding agencies they know and trust. In small communities, there may be few philanthropic funders; they may fund virtually all relevant agencies, but they may not have sufficient resources to do this adequately. In larger communities, the cast of philanthropic funders and potential grant recipient organizations is sufficiently large to create major problems of finding effective matches and addressing community needs comprehensively. The necessary institutional framework does not appear to be in place.

Kirsten A. Grønbjerg

References and further reading

American Association of Fundraising Counsel (AAFRC) Trust for Philanthropy. 2002. *Giving USA 2002: The Annual Report on Philanthropy for the Year 2001, 47th Annual Issue.* Indianapolis: AAFRC Trust for Philanthropy.

Avery, R. B. 1994. "The Pending Intergenerational Transfer." *Philanthropy* 8, no. 1 (Winter).

Bickers, Kenneth N. 1999. "Second Order Devolution and the Coalitional Responses of Nonprofit Organizations." Paper presented at the ARNOVA Conference, Washington, DC, November 4–6.

Bielefeld, Wolfgang, and John J. Corbin. 1996. "The Institutionalization of Nonprofit Human Service

Delivery: The Role of Political Culture." *Administration and Society* 28: 362–389.

Brown, Dorothy M., and Elizabeth McKeown. 1997. *The Poor Belong to Us: Catholic Charities and American Welfare.* Cambridge: Harvard University Press.

Crimmins, James C., and Mary Kiel. 1990. "Enterprise in the Nonprofit Sector." In *The Nonprofit Organization: Essential Readings,* edited by David L. Gies, Steven J. Ott, and Jay M. Sharfitze, 315–327. Pacific Grove, CA: Brooks/Cole.

Foundation Center. 2002. "Foundation Giving Trends: Highlights," http://www.fdncenter.org (cited June 5).

Frumkin, Peter, and Alice Andre-Clark. 2000. "When Missions, Markets, and Politics Collide: Values and Strategy in the Nonprofit Human Services." *Nonprofit and Voluntary Sector Quarterly* 29, no. 1 (Supplement): 141–164.

Grønbjerg, Kirsten A. 1993. *Understanding Nonprofit Funding: Managing Revenues in Social Service and Community Development Organizations.* San Francisco: Jossey-Bass.

———. 2001. "The U.S. Nonprofit Human Service Sector: A Creeping Revolution." *Nonprofit and Voluntary Sector Quarterly* 30, no. 2 (June): 276–297.

Grønbjerg, Kirsten A., Lori Harmon, Aida Olkkonen, and Asif Raza. 1996. "The United Way System at the Crossroads: Community Planning and Allocation." *Nonprofit and Voluntary Sector Quarterly* 25, no. 4 (December): 428–452.

Grønbjerg, Kirsten A., and Edwina Jones. 1997. "Philanthropic Human Service Funders in a Changing Environment." Paper presented at the ARNOVA Conference, Indianapolis, IN, December 3–6.

Grønbjerg, Kirsten A., and Laura Martell, with Laurie Paarlberg. 2000. "Philanthropic Funding of Human Services: Solving Ambiguity through the Two-Stage Competitive Process." *Nonprofit and Voluntary Sector Quarterly* 29, no. 1 (Supplement): 9–40.

Grønbjerg, Kirsten A., and Stephen Rathgeb Smith. 1999. "Nonprofit Organizations and Public Policies in the Delivery of Human Services." In *Philanthropy and the Nonprofit Sector in a Changing America,* edited by Charles Clotfelter and Thomas Ehrlich, 139–172. Bloomington: Indiana University Press.

Hacsi, Timothy A. 1997. *Second Home: Orphan Asylums and Poor Families in America.* Cambridge: Harvard University Press.

Hall, Peter. 1987. "A Historical Overview of the Private Nonprofit Sector." In *The Nonprofit Sector: A Research Handbook,* edited by Walter Powell, 3–26. New Haven, CT: Yale University Press.

Hodgkinson, Virginia A., and Murray S. Weitzman, with Eric A. Crutchfield, Aaron J. Heffron, and Arthur D. Kirsch. 1996. *Giving and Volunteering in the United States: Findings from a National Survey.* Washington, DC: Independent Sector.

Milward, H. Brinton, and Keith G. Provan. 2002. "Governing the Hollow State." *Journal of Public Administration Research and Theory* 10, no. 2 (April): 359–379.

Morton, Marian J. 1993. *And Sin No More: Social Policy and Unwed Mothers in Cleveland, 1855–1990.* Columbus: Ohio State University Press.

Nielsen, Waldemar A. 1979. *The Endangered Sector.* New York: Columbia University Press.

Paarlberg, Laurie, and Kirsten A. Grønbjerg. 1999. "Nonprofit Fee-for-Service Income." Report prepared for the Aspen Institute's Nonprofit Strategy Group.

Rooney, Patrick, Kathryn S. Steinberg, and Paul Schervish. 2001. "A Methodological Comparison of Giving Surveys: Indiana as a Test Case." *Nonprofit and Voluntary Sector Quarterly* 30, no. 3 (September): 551–568.

Rosentraub, Mark S. 1991. "Political Culture, Nonprofit Organizations and the Financing of Human Services." *Nonprofit and Voluntary Sector Quarterly* 20 (1): 95–111.

Salamon, Lester M. 1995. *Partners in Public Service: Government-Nonprofit Relations in the Modern Welfare State.* Baltimore: Johns Hopkins University Press.

———. 1999. *America's Nonprofit Sector: A Primer,* 2d ed. New York: Foundation Center.

Smith, Stephen Rathgeb. 2002. "Social Services." In *The State of the Nonprofit Sector,* edited by Lester M. Salamon. Washington, DC: Brookings Institution.

United Way of America. 2002. "2000–01 Campagin Results," http://national.unitedway.org/aboutuwa/publications/2000campaignresults/ (cited June 6).

Weitzman, Murray S., Nadine T. Jalandoni, Linda M. Lampkin, and Thomas H. Pollak. 2002. *The New Nonprofit Almanac and Desk Reference: The Essential Facts and Figures for Managers, Researchers, and Volunteers.* New York: Jossey-Bass.

Wolpert, Julian. 1989. "Key Indicators of Generosity in Communities." In *The Future of the Nonprofit Sector,* edited by Virginia A. Hodgkinson and Richard W. Lyman. San Francisco: Jossey-Bass.

Hull-House

See Addams, Jane